Reactive Design Patterns

ROLAND KUHN

WITH BRIAN HANAFEE
AND JAMIE ALLEN

FOREWORD BY JONAS BONÉR

MANNING
SHELTER ISLAND

For online information and ordering of this and other Manning books, please visit
www.manning.com. The publisher offers discounts on this book when ordered in quantity.
For more information, please contact

    Special Sales Department
    Manning Publications Co.
    20 Baldwin Road
    PO Box 761
    Shelter Island, NY 11964
    Email: orders@manning.com

Manning Publications Co.
20 Baldwin Road
PO Box 761
Shelter Island, NY 11964

Development editor:	Jennifer Stout
Technical development editor:	Brian Hanafee
Project editors:	Tiffany Taylor and Janet Vail
Line editor:	Ben Kovitz
Copyeditor:	Tiffany Taylor
Proofreader:	Katie Tennant
Technical proofreader:	Thomas Lockney
Typesetter:	Dottie Marsico
Cover designer:	Leslie Haimes

ISBN 9781617291807
Printed in the United States of America
1 2 3 4 5 6 70 8 9 10 – EBM – 22 21 20 19 18 17

To my children
   — Roland

brief contents

contents

foreword

I'm grateful that Roland has taken the time to write this foundational book, and I can't think of anyone more capable of pulling it off. Roland is an unusually clear and deep thinker; he coauthored the Reactive Manifesto, has been the technical lead for the Akka project for several years, has coauthored and taught the very popular Coursera course on Reactive programming and design, and is the best technical writer I have met.

Clearly, I'm very excited about this book. It outlines what Reactive architecture/design is all about, and does an excellent job explaining it from first principles in a practical context. Additionally, it is a catalog of patterns that explains the bigger picture, how to think about system design, and how it is all connected—much like what Martin Fowler's *Patterns of Enterprise Application Architecture* did 15 years ago.

During my professional life, I have seen the immense benefits of resilient, loosely coupled, message-driven systems firsthand, especially when compared with more-traditional approaches that propose to hide the nature of distributed systems. In 2013, I had the idea of formalizing the experiences and lessons learned: the Reactive Manifesto was born. It started out as a set of rough notes that I remember presenting to the company at one of Typesafe's (now Lightbend) internal technical meetups. Coincidentally, this meetup was collocated with the Scala Days New York conference, where Roland, Martin Odersky, and Erik Meijer shot their bad, and unintentionally quite funny, promotion video of their Coursera course on Reactive programming. The story around the Reactive principles resonated with the other engineers and was published in July of 2013. Since then, the Manifesto has been receiving a lot of great feedback from the community. It was rewritten and vastly improved by Roland, Martin Thompson, Dave Farley, and myself, leading up to version 2.0 published in September 2014.

By the end of 2016, it had been signed by more than 17,000 people. During this time, we have seen Reactive progress from a virtually unacknowledged technique used only by fringe projects within a select few corporations to a part of the overall platform strategy of numerous big players in many different fields, including middleware, financial services, retail, social media, betting/gaming, and so on.

The Reactive Manifesto defines "Reactive Systems" as a set of architectural design principles that are geared toward meeting the demands that systems face—today and tomorrow. These principles are most definitely not new; they can be traced back to the '70s and '80s and the seminal work by Jim Gray and Pat Helland on the Tandem System, as well as Joe Armstrong and Robert Virding on Erlang. However, these pioneers were ahead of their time, and it was not until the past five years that the technology industry was forced to rethink current best practices for enterprise system development and learned to apply the hard-won knowledge of the Reactive principles to today's world of multicore architectures, Cloud Computing, and the Internet of Things.

By now, the Reactive principles have had a big impact on the industry, and as with many successful ideas, they get overloaded and reinterpreted. This is not a bad thing; ideas need to evolve to stay relevant. However, this can also cause confusion and lead to dilution of the original intent. One example is the unfortunate emerging misconception that Reactive is nothing but programming in an asynchronous and nonblocking style using callbacks or stream-oriented combinators—techniques that are aptly classified as Reactive Programming. Concentrating on this aspect alone means missing out on many of the benefits of the Reactive principles. It is the contribution of this book to take a much larger perspective—a systems view—moving the focus from how individual components function in isolation to the design of collaborative, resilient, and elastic systems: Reactive systems.

This future classic belongs on the shelf of every professional programmer, right next to GoF[1] and *Domain-Driven Design.*[2] Enjoy the ride—I certainly did!

JONAS BONÉR
CTO AND FOUNDER OF LIGHTBEND
CREATOR OF AKKA

---

[1] *Design Patterns: Elements of Reusable Object-Oriented Software* by Gamma, Helm, Johnson, and Vlissides (Addison-Wesley, 1995).
[2] *Domain-Driven Design* by Eric Evans (Addison-Wesley, 2004).

preface

Even before I had officially joined the Akka team, Mike Stephens from Manning tried to convince me to write a book on Akka. I was tempted to say yes, but in the context of an impending change of jobs and countries, my wife brought me to my senses: such a project would be too much to handle. The idea of writing a book stuck in my head, though. Three years later—after the Reactive Manifesto had been published—Martin Odersky, Erik Meijer, and I taught the course Principles of Reactive Programming on the Coursera platform, reaching more than 120,000 students in two iterations. The idea for that course had been born at a Typesafe engineering meeting where I suggested to Martin that we should nurture the blossoming movement of Reactive programming by demonstrating how to use these tools effectively while avoiding the pitfalls—my own experience answering questions on the Akka mailing list had given me a good idea of the topics people commonly struggled with.

A video course is a wonderful way of reaching a large number of students, interacting with them on the discussion forums, and in general improving the lives of others. Unfortunately, the discussion of the subject is necessarily limited in its depth and breadth by the format: only so much can be shown in seven weekly lectures. Therefore, I still longed for formalizing and passing on my knowledge about Reactive systems by writing a book. It would have been straightforward to write about Akka, but I felt that if I wrote a book, its scope should be wider than that. I love working on Akka—it has literally changed the course of my life—but Akka is merely a tool for expressing distributed and highly reliable systems, and it is not the only tool needed in this regard.

Thus began the journey toward the work you are holding in your hands right now. It was a daunting task, and I knew that I would need help. Luckily, Jamie was just about to finish *Effective Akka*[3] and was immediately on board. Neither of us had the luxury of writing during daytime; consequently, the book started out slow and kept lagging behind the plan. Instead of having three chapters ready to enter the early access program during the first iteration of the course Principles of Reactive Programming, we could only announce it several months later. It is astonishing how much detail one finds missing when starting out from the viewpoint that the contents are basically already known and just need to be transferred into the computer. Over time, Jamie got even busier with his day job, until he had to stop contributing entirely. Later, Brian joined the project as Manning's technical development editor, and it soon became clear that he could not only make very good suggestions but also implement them. We made it official by signing him up as a coauthor, and then Brian helped me push the manuscript over the finish line.

This book contains not only advice on when and how to use the tools of Reactive programming, but also the reasoning behind the advice, so that you may adapt it to different requirements and new applications. I hope that it will inspire you to learn more and to explore the wonderful world of Reactive systems.

ROLAND KUHN

---

[3] *Effective Akka* by Jamie Allen (O'Reillly Media, 2013).

acknowledgments

ROLAND KUHN   My first thanks go to Jamie, without whom I would not have dared take on this project. But my deepest gratitude is to Jonas Bonér, who created Akka, entrusted Akka to my care for many years, and supported me on every step along the way. I am also deeply thankful to Viktor Klang for countless rigorous discussions about all topics of life (and distributed systems) but, more importantly, for teaching me how to lead by example and how important it is to not let the devil over the bridge. Jonas, Viktor, and Patrik Nordwall also deserve special thanks for covering my duties as Akka Tech Lead while I took a mini-sabbatical of three months to work intensely on this book. I greatly appreciate Brian and Jamie stepping up and shouldering part of the tremendous weight of such a project: it is gratifying and motivating to work alongside such trusted companions.

For helpful reviews of the early manuscript, I would like to thank Sean Walsh and Duncan DeVore, as well as Bert Bates, who helped shape the overall arrangement of how the patterns are presented. I also thank Endre Varga, who spent considerable effort developing the KVStore exercise for Principles of Reactive Programming that forms the basis for the state replication code samples used in chapter 13. Thanks also go to Pablo Medina for helping me with the CKite example code in section 13.2, and to Thomas Lockney, technical proofreader, who kept a sharp eye out for errors. The following peer reviewers gave generously of their time: Joel Kotarski, Valentine Sinitsyn, Mark Elston, Miguel Eduardo Gil Biraud, William E. Wheeler, Jonathan Freeman, Franco Bulgarelli, Bryan Gilbert, Carlos Curotto, Andy Hicks, William Chan, Jacek Sokulski, Dr. Christian Bridge-Harrington, Satadru Roy, Richard Jepps, Sorbo Bagchi, NenkoTabakov, Martin Anlauf, Kolja Dummann, Gordon Fische, Sebastien Boisver, and Henrik Løvborg. I am grateful to the Akka community for being such a welcoming and fertile place for developing our understanding of distributed systems.

I would like to thank the team at Manning who made this book possible, especially Mike Stephens for nagging until I gave in, Jenny Stout for urging me to make progress, and Candace Gillhoolley from marketing. I would like to distinguish Ben Kovitz as an extremely careful and thorough copy editor, and I thank Tiffany Taylor for finding even more redundant words to be removed from the final text, as well as Katie Tennant for identifying and fixing unclear passages.

Finally, in the name of all readers, I extend my utmost appreciation and love to my wife, Alex. You endured my countless hours of spiritual absence with great compassion.

JAMIE ALLEN   I wish to thank my wife, Yeon, and my three children, Sophie, Layla, and James. I am also grateful to Roland for allowing me to participate in this project, and to Brian for pushing the project over the finish line and contributing his expertise.

BRIAN HANAFEE   I thank my wife, Patty, for supporting me, always, and my daughters, Yvonne and Barbara, for helping me with Doctor Who history and sometimes pretending my jokes are funny. Thank you, Susan Conant and Bert Bates, for getting me started and teaching me how to edit and teach in book form. Finally, thank you, Roland and Jamie, for showing me Reactive principles and welcoming me into this project.

about this book

This book is intended to be a comprehensive guide to understanding and designing Reactive systems. Therefore, it includes not only an annotated version of the Reactive Manifesto, but also the reasoning that led to its inception. The main part of the book is a selection of design patterns that implement many facets of Reactive system design, with pointers toward deeper literature resources for further study. While the presented patterns form a cohesive whole, the list is not exhaustive—it cannot be—but the included background knowledge will enable the reader to identify, distill, and curate new patterns as the need arises.

Whom this book is for

This book was written for everyone who may want to implement Reactive systems:

- It covers the architecture of such systems as well as the philosophy behind it, giving architects an overview of the characteristics of Reactive applications and their components and discussing the applicability of the patterns.
- Practitioners will benefit from a detailed discussion of the scenario solved by each pattern, the steps to take in applying it—illustrated with complete source code—as well as a guide to transfer and adapt the pattern to different cases.
- Learners wishing to deepen their knowledge, for example, after viewing the course material of Principles of Reactive Programming, will be delighted to read about the thought processes behind the Reactive principles and to follow the literature references for further study.

This book does not require prior knowledge of Reactive systems; it builds upon familiarity with software development in general and refers to some experience with the difficulties arising from distributed systems. For some parts, a basic understanding of functional programming is helpful (in the sense of programming with immutable values and pure functions), but category theory does not feature in this book.

How to read this book

The contents of this book are arranged such that it lends itself well to being read as a story, cover to cover, developing from an introductory example and an overview of the Reactive Manifesto and the Reactive toolbox, continuing with the philosophy behind Reactive principles, and culminating in the description of patterns covering the different aspects of designing a Reactive system. This journey covers a lot of ground and the text contains references to additional background information. Reading it in one go will leave you with an intuition of the scope of the book and what information is found where, but it will typically only be the entry point for further study; you will return for the extraction of deeper insights while applying the acquired knowledge in projects of your own.

If you are already familiar with the challenges of Reactive systems, you may skip the first chapter, and you will likely skim chapter 3 on the tools of the trade because you have already worked with most of those. The impatient will be tempted to start reading the patterns in part 3, but it is recommended to take a look at part 2 first: the pattern descriptions frequently refer to the explanations and background knowledge of this more theoretical part that form the basis on which the patterns have been developed.

It is expected that you will return to the more philosophical chapters—especially chapters 8 and 9—after having gained more experience with the design and implementation of Reactive systems; don't worry if these discussions do not immediately become fully transparent upon first reading.

Conventions

Due to the overloading of the English term "future" for a programming concept that deviates significantly from the original meaning, all uses of the word referring to the programming concept appear capitalized as Future, even when not appearing in code font.

The situation is slightly different for the term "actor," which in plain English refers to a person on stage as well as a participant in an action or process. This term appears capitalized only when referring specifically to the Actor model, or when the name of the Actor trait appears in code font.

Source code for the examples

All source code for the examples used in this book are available for download on GitHub here: https://github.com/ReactiveDesignPatterns/CodeSamples/.

GitHub also offers facilities for raising issues with the samples or discussing them; please make use of them. You are also welcome to open pull requests with improvements; this way, all future readers will benefit from your thoughtfulness and experience.

Most of the samples are written in Java or Scala and use sbt for the build definition; please refer to www.scala-sbt.org/ for detailed documentation. A Java development kit supporting Java 8 will be required to build and run the samples.

Other online resources

An overview of the presented patterns as well as further material is available at www.reactivedesignpatterns.org/. In addition, purchase of *Reactive Design Patterns* includes free access to a private web forum run by Manning Publications where you can make comments about the book, ask technical questions, and receive help from the lead author and from other users. To access the forum and subscribe to it, point your web browser to www.manning.com/books/reactive-design-patterns. This page provides information on how to get on the forum once you are registered, what kind of help is available, and the rules of conduct on the forum.

Manning's commitment to our readers is to provide a venue where a meaningful dialog between individual readers and between readers and authors can take place. It is not a commitment to any specific amount of participation on the part of the authors, whose contribution to the AO forum remains voluntary (and unpaid). We suggest you try asking them some challenging questions lest their interest stray! The Author Online forum and the archives of previous discussions will be accessible from the publisher's website as long as the book is in print.

about the authors

Dr. Roland Kuhn studied physics at the Technische Universität München and obtained a doctorate with a dissertation on measurements of the gluon spin structure of the nucleon at a high-energy particle physics experiment at CERN (Geneva, Switzerland). This entailed usage and implementation of large computing clusters and fast data processing networks, which laid the foundation for his thorough understanding of distributed computing. Afterward, he worked for four years at the German space operations center, building control centers and ground infrastructure for military satellite missions, before joining the Akka team at Lightbend (then called Typesafe), which he led from November 2012 to March 2016. During this time he co-taught the course Principles of Reactive Programming on the Coursera platform together with Martin Odersky and Erik Meijer, a course that was visited by more than 120,000 students. Together with Jonas Bonér, he authored the first version of the Reactive Manifesto, published in June 2013. Currently, Roland is CTO of Actyx, a Munich-based company he cofounded, bringing the benefits of modern Reactive systems to small and midsize manufacturing enterprises across Europe.

Brian Hanafee received his BS in EECS from the University of California, Berkeley. He is a Principal Systems Architect at Wells Fargo Bank, where he designs internet banking and payment systems and is a consistent advocate for raising the technology bar. Previously he was with Oracle, working on new and emerging products and systems for interactive television and for text processing. He sent his first email from a moving vehicle in 1994. Prior to that, Brian was an Associate at Booz, Allen & Hamilton and at Advanced Decision Systems, where he applied AI techniques to military planning systems. He also wrote software for one of the first ejection-safe helmet-mounted display systems.

Jamie Allen is the Director of Engineering for the UCP project at Starbucks, an effort to redefine the digital experience for every customer across all of our operating models and locations. He is the author of *Effective Akka* (O'Reilly, 2013), and previously worked with Roland and Jonas at Typesafe/Lightbend for over four years. Jamie has been a Scala and actor developer since 2008, and has worked with numerous clients around the world to help them understand and adopt Reactive application approaches.

Part 1

Introduction

Have you ever wondered how high-profile web applications are implemented? Social networks and huge retail sites must have some secret ingredient that makes them work quickly and reliably, but what is it? In this book, you will learn about the design principles and patterns behind such systems that never fail and are capable of serving the needs of billions of people. Although the systems you build may not have such ambitious requirements, the primary qualities are common:

- You want your application to work reliably, even though parts (hardware or software) may fail.
- You want it to keep working when you have more users to support, and you want to be able to add or remove resources to adapt its capacity to changing demand (capacity planning is hard to get right without a crystal ball).

In chapter 1, we will sketch the development of an application that exhibits these qualities and more. We will illustrate the challenges you will encounter and present solutions based on a concrete example—a hypothetical implementation of the Gmail service—but we will do so in a technology-agnostic fashion.

This use case sets the stage for the detailed discussion of the Reactive Manifesto that follows in chapter 2. The manifesto is written in a concise, high-level form in order to concentrate on its essence: the combination of individually useful program characteristics into a cohesive whole that is larger than the sum of its parts. We will show this by breaking the high-level traits into smaller pieces and explaining how everything fits back together.

We will complete this part of the book in chapter 3 with a whirlwind tour through the tools of the trade: functional programming, Futures and Promises, Communicating Sequential Processes (CSP), Observers and Observables (Reactive Extensions), and the Actor model.

Why Reactive?

We start from the desire to build a system that is *responsive* to users. This means the system should respond to user input in a timely fashion under all circumstances. Because any single computer can fail at any time, we need to distribute such a system over multiple computers. Adding this fundamental requirement for distribution makes us recognize the need for new architecture patterns (or to rediscover old ones). In the past, we developed methods that allowed us to retain the illusion of single-threaded local processing while having it magically executed on multiple cores or network nodes, but the gap between that illusion and reality is becoming prohibitively large.[1] The solution is to make the distributed, concurrent nature of our applications explicit in the programming model, using it to our advantage.

This book will teach you how to write systems that stay responsive in the face of partial outages, program failure, changing loads, and even bugs in the code. You will see that this requires adjustments to the way you think about and design your applications. Here are the four tenets of the Reactive Manifesto,[2] which defines a common vocabulary and lays out the basic challenges that a modern computer system needs to meet:

- It must react to its users (*responsive*).
- It must react to failure and stay available (*resilient*).
- It must react to variable load conditions (*elastic*).
- It must react to inputs (*message-driven*).

---

[1] For example, Java EE services allow us to transparently call remote services that are wired in automatically, possibly even including distributed database transactions. The possibility of network failure or remote service overload, and so on, is completely hidden, abstracted away, and consequently out of reach for developers to meaningfully take into account.

[2] http://reactivemanifesto.org

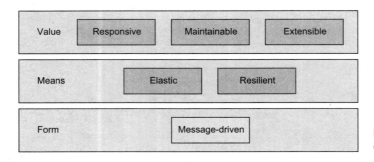

Figure 1.1   **The structure of Reactive values**

In addition, creating a system with these properties in mind will guide you toward better modularization, both of the runtime deployment and of the code itself. Therefore, we add two more attributes to the list of benefits: *maintainability* and *extensibility*. Another way to structure the attributes is shown in figure 1.1.

In the following chapters, you will learn about the reasoning of the Reactive Manifesto in detail, and you will get to know several tools of the trade and the philosophy behind their design, enabling you to effectively use these tools to implement reactive designs. The design patterns that emerge from these tools are presented in the third part of the book. To set the stage for diving into the manifesto, we will first explore the challenges of creating a Reactive application, using the example of a well-known email service: we will imagine a reimplementation of Gmail.

1.1   *The anatomy of a Reactive application*

The first task when starting such a project is to sketch an architecture for the deployment and draft the list of software artifacts that need to be developed. This may not be the final architecture, but you need to chart the problem space and explore potentially difficult aspects. We will start the Gmail example by enumerating the different high-level features of the application:

- The application must offer a view of the mailboxes to the user and display their contents.
- To this end, the system must store all emails and keep them available.
- It must allow the user to compose and send email.
- To make this more comfortable, the system should offer a list of contacts and allow the user to manage them.
- A good search function for locating emails is required.

The real Gmail application has more features, but this list will suffice for our purposes. Some of these features are more intertwined than the others: for example, displaying emails and composing them are both part of the user interface and share (or compete for) the same screen space, whereas the implementation of email storage is only distantly related to these two. The implementation of the search function will need to be closer to the storage than the front-end presentation.

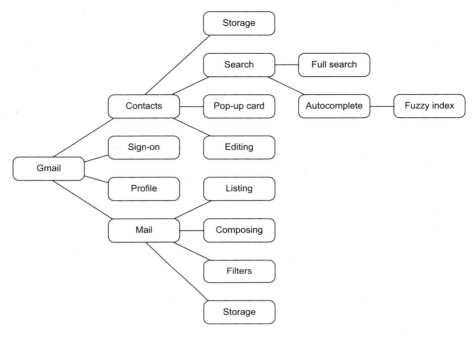

Figure 1.2   Partially decomposed module hierachy of the hypothetical Gmail implementation

These considerations guide the hierarchical decomposition of Gmail's overall functionality into smaller and smaller pieces. More precisely, you can apply the *Simple Component pattern* as described in chapter 12, making sure you clearly delimit and segregate the different responsibilities of the entire application. The *Error Kernel pattern* and the *Let-It-Crash pattern* complement this process, ensuring that the application's architecture is well suited to reliable failure handling—not only in case of machine or network outages, but also for rare failure conditions in the source code that are handled incorrectly (a.k.a. *bugs*).

The result of this process will be a hierarchy of components that need to be developed and deployed. An example is shown in figure 1.2. Each component may be complex in terms of its function, such as the implementation of search algorithms; or it may be complex in its deployment and orchestration, such as providing email storage for billions of users. But it will always be simple to describe in terms of its responsibility.

1.2   Coping with load

The resources necessary to store all those emails will be enormous: hundreds of millions of users with gigabytes of emails each will need exabytes[3] of storage capacity. This magnitude of persistent storage will need to be provided by many distributed

---

[3] One exabyte is 1 billion gigabytes (using decimal SI prefixes; using binary SI prefixes, one EB is roughly 1.07 billion GB).

machines. No single storage device offers so much space, and it would be unwise to store everything in one location. Distribution makes the dataset resilient against local perils like natural disasters; but, more important, it also allows the data to be accessed efficiently from a larger region. For a worldwide user base, the data should be globally distributed as well. It would be preferable to have the emails of a Japanese user stored in or close to Japan (assuming that is where the user logs in from most of the time).

This insight leads us to the *Sharding pattern* described in chapter 17: you can split up the overall dataset into many small pieces—or *shards*—that you then distribute. Because the number of shards is much smaller than the number of users, it is practical to make the location of each shard known throughout the system. In order to find a user's mailbox, you only need to identify the shard it belongs to. You can do that by equipping every user with an ID that expresses geographical affinity (for example, using the first few digits to denote the country of residence), which is then mathematically partitioned into the correct number of shards (for example, shard 0 contains IDs 0–999,999; shard 1 contains IDs 1,000,000–1,999,999; and so on).

The key here is that the dataset naturally consists of many independent pieces that can easily be separated from each other. Operations on one mailbox never affect another mailbox directly, so the shards also do not need to communicate among themselves. Each serves only one particular part of the solution.

Another area in which the Gmail application will need a lot of resources is in the display of folders and emails to the user. It would be impossible to provide this functionality in a centralized fashion, not only for reasons of latency (even at the speed of light, it takes noticeable time to send information around the globe) but also due to the sheer number of interactions that millions of users perform every second. Here, you will also split the work among many machines, starting with the users' computers: most of the graphical presentation is rendered within the browser, shifting the workload very close to where it is needed and in effect sharding it for each user.

The web browser will need to get the raw information from a server, ideally one that is close by to minimize network round-trip time. The task of connecting a user with their mailbox and routing requests and responses accordingly is one that can also easily be sharded. In this case, the browser's network address directly provides all needed characteristics, including an approximate geographic location.

One noteworthy aspect is that in all the aforementioned cases, resources can be added by making the shards smaller, distributing the load over more machines. The maximum number is given by the number of users or used network addresses, which will be more than enough to provide sufficient resources. This scheme will need adjustment only when serving a single user requires more computing power than a single machine can provide, at which point a user's dataset or computing problem needs to be broken down into smaller pieces.

This means that by splitting a system into distributable parts, you gain the ability to scale the service capacity, using a larger number of shards to serve more users. As long as the shards are independent from each other, the system is in theory infinitely scalable. In practice, the orchestration and operation of a worldwide deployment with millions of nodes requires substantial effort and must of course be worth it.

1.3 Coping with failures

Sharding datasets or computational resources solves the problem of providing sufficient resources for the nominal case, when everything is running smoothly and networks are operational. In order to cope with failures, you need the ability to keep running when things go wrong:

- A machine may fail temporarily (for example, due to overheating or kernel panic) or permanently (electrical or mechanical failure, fire, flood, and so on).
- Network components may fail, both within a computing center as well as outside on the internet—including the case that intercontinental overseas cables go down, resulting in a split of the internet into disconnected regions.
- Human operators or automated maintenance scripts may accidentally destroy parts of the data.

The only solution to this problem is to replicate the system—its data or functionality—in more than one location. The geographical placement of the replicas needs to match the scope of the system; a global email service should serve each customer from multiple countries, for example.

Replication is a more difficult and diverse topic than sharding because intuitively you mean to have the same data in multiple places—but keeping the replicas synchronized to match this expectation comes at a high cost. Should writing to the nearest location fail or be delayed if a more distant replica is momentarily unavailable? Should it be impossible to see the old data on a distant replica after the nearest one has already signaled completion of the operation? Or should such inconsistency just be unlikely or very short-lived? These questions will be answered differently between projects or even for different modules of one particular system. Therefore, you are presented with a spectrum of solutions that allows you to make trade-offs between operational complexity, performance, availability, and consistency.

We will discuss several approaches covering a wide range of characteristics in chapter 13. The basic choices are as follows:

- *Active–passive replication*—Replicas agree on which one of them can accept updates. Fail-over to a different replica requires consensus among the remaining ones when the active replica no longer responds.
- *Consensus-based multiple-master replication*—Each update is agreed on by sufficiently many replicas to achieve consistent behavior across all of them, at the cost of availability and latency.
- *Optimistic replication with conflict detection and resolution*—Multiple active replicas disseminate updates and roll back transactions during conflict or discard conflicting updates that were performed during a network partition.

- *Conflict-free replicated data types*—This approach prescribes merge strategies such that conflicts cannot arise by definition, at the cost of providing only eventual consistency and requiring special care when creating the data model.

In the Gmail example, several services should provide consistency to the user: if a user successfully moves an email to a different folder, they expect it to stay in that folder regardless of which client they use to access their mailboxes. The same goes for changes to a contact's telephone number or the user's profile. For these data, you could use active–passive replication to keep things simple by making the failure response actions coarse-grained—that is, on a per-replica scope. Or you could use optimistic replication under the assumption that a single user will not concurrently make conflicting changes to the same data item—but keep in mind that this is a fair assumption only for human users.

Consensus-based replication is needed within the system as an implementation detail of sharding by user ID, because the relocation of a shard must be recorded accurately and consistently for all clients. It would lead to user-visible distortions like an email disappearing and then reappearing if a client were to flip-flop between decommissioned and live replicas.

1.4   *Making the system responsive*

The previous two sections introduced reasons for distributing the system across several machines, computing centers, or possibly even continents, matching the scope and reliability requirements of the application. The foremost purpose of this exercise is to build an email service for end users, though, and for them the only metric that counts is whether the service does what they need when they need it. In other words, the application must respond quickly to any request a user makes.

The easiest way to achieve this is, of course, to write an application that runs locally and that has all emails stored on the local machine as well: going across the network to fetch an answer will always take longer and be less reliable than having the answer close by. There is, thus, a tension between the need to distribute and the need to stay responsive. All distribution must be justified, as in the Gmail example.

Where distribution is necessary, you encounter new challenges in the quest for responsiveness. The most annoying behavior of many distributed applications today is that their user interaction grinds to a halt when network connectivity is poor. Interestingly, it seems much simpler to deal with the complete absence of a connection than with a trickling flow of data. One pattern that is helpful in this context is the *Circuit Breaker pattern* discussed in detail in chapter 12. With this tool, you can monitor the availability and performance of a service that you are calling on for some function so that when the quality falls below a threshold (either too many failures or too long a response latency), the circuit breaker trips, forcing a switch to a mode where that service is not used. The unavailability of parts of the system needs to be considered from the beginning; the Circuit Breaker pattern addresses this concern.

Another threat to responsiveness arises when a service that the application depends on becomes momentarily overloaded. A backlog of requests will accumulate, and while these are processed, response latencies will be much longer than normal. This situation can be avoided by employing *flow control*, as described in chapter 16. In the Gmail example, there are several points at which circuit breakers and flow control are needed:

- Between the front end that runs on the users' devices and the web servers that provide access to back-end functionality
- Between the web servers and back-end services

The reason for the first point has already been mentioned: the desire to keep the user-visible part of the application responsive under all conditions, even if sometimes the only thing it can do is signal that the server is down and that the request will be completed at a later time. Depending on how much functionality can or should practically be duplicated in the front end for this *offline mode*, some areas of the user interface may need to be deactivated.

The reason for the second point is that the front end would otherwise need to have different circuit breakers for different kinds of requests to the web server, each circuit breaker corresponding to the specific subset of back-end services needed by one kind of request. Switching the entire application to offline mode when only a small part of the back-end services are unavailable would be an unhelpful over-response. Tracking this in the front end would couple its implementation to the precise structure of the back end, requiring the front-end code to be changed whenever the service composition of the back end was altered. The web-server layer should hide these details and provide its clients with responses as quickly as possible under all circumstances.

Take, for example, the back-end service that provides the information shown on the contact card that pops up when hovering the pointer over an email sender's name. This is a nonessential function, considering the overall function of Gmail, so the web server may return a temporary failure code for such requests while that back-end service is unavailable. The front end does not need to track this state; it can merely refrain from showing the pop-up card and retry the request when interaction with the user triggers it again.

This reasoning applies not only at the web server layer. In a large application that consists of hundreds or thousands of back-end services, it is imperative to confine the treatment of failure and unavailability in this fashion; otherwise, the system would be unreasonable in the sense that its behavior could no longer be understood by humans. Just as functionality is modularized, the treatment of failure conditions must be encapsulated in comprehensible scopes as well.

1.5   *Avoiding the ball of mud*

The Gmail application at this point consists of a front-end part that runs on the user's device, back-end services that provide storage and functionality, and web servers that act as entry points into the back end. The latter serve an important purpose beyond the responsiveness discussed in the previous section: they decouple the front end from the back end architecturally. Having this clearly defined ingress point for client requests makes it simpler to reason about the interplay between the part of the application that runs on the users' devices and the part that runs on servers in the cloud.

The back end so far consists of a multitude of services whose partitioning and relationships resulted from the application of the Simple Component pattern. By itself, this pattern does not provide the checks and balances that keep the architecture from devolving into a large mess where every service talks with almost every other service. Such a system would be hard to manage even with perfect individual failure handling, circuit breakers, and flow control; it certainly would not be possible for a human to understand it in its entirety and confidently make changes to it. This scenario has informally been called the *big ball of mud*.

With the problem lying in the unrestrained interaction between arbitrary back-end services, the solution is to focus on the communication paths within the entire application and to specifically design them. This is called *message flow* and is discussed in detail in chapter 15.

The service decomposition shown in figure 1.2 is too coarse-grained to serve as an example for a "ball of mud," but an illustration for the principle of message-flow design would be that the service that handles email composition probably should not talk directly to the contact pop-up service: if composing an email entails showing the contact card of someone mentioned in the email, then instead of making the back end responsible for that, the front end should ask for the pop-up, just as it does when the user hovers the mouse pointer over an email header. In this way, the number of possible message-flow paths is reduced by one, making the overall interaction model of back-end services a little simpler.

Another benefit of carefully considering message flow lies in facilitating testing and making it easier to ensure coverage of all interaction scenarios. With a comprehensive message-flow design, it is obvious which other services a component interacts with and what is expected from the component in terms of throughput and latency. This can be turned around and used as a canary in the coal mine: whenever it is difficult to assess which scenarios should be tested for a given component, that is a sign that the system is in danger of becoming a big ball of mud.

1.6   *Integrating nonreactive components*

The final important aspect of creating an application according to Reactive principles is that it will, in most cases, be necessary to integrate with existing systems or infrastructure that does not provide the needed characteristics. Examples are device drivers that lack encapsulation (for example, by terminating the entire process in case of failure), APIs that execute their effects synchronously and thereby block the caller from reacting to other inputs or timeouts in the meantime, systems with unbounded input queues that do not respect bounded response latency, and so on.

Most of these issues are dealt with using the *resource-management patterns* discussed in chapter 14. The basic principle is to retrofit the needed encapsulation and asynchronous boundaries by interacting with the resource within a dedicated Reactive component, using extra threads, processes, or machines as necessary. This allows these resources to be integrated seamlessly into the architecture.

When interfacing with a system that does not provide bounded response latency, it is necessary to retrofit the ability to signal momentary overload situations. This can to some degree be achieved by employing circuit breakers, but in addition you must consider what the response to overload should be. The *flow-control patterns* described in chapter 16 help in this case as well.

An example in the context of the Gmail application is a hypothetical integration with an external utility, such as a shared shopping list. Within the Gmail front end, the user can add items to the shopping list by extracting the needed information semiautomatically from emails. This function would be supported in the back end by a service that encapsulates the external utility's API. Assuming that the interaction with the shopping list requires the use of a native library that is prone to crash and bring down the process it is running in, it is desirable to dedicate a process to this task alone. This encapsulated form of the external API is then integrated via the operating system's interprocess communication (IPC) facilities, such as pipes, sockets, and shared memory.

Assuming further that the shopping list's implementation employs a practically unbounded input queue, you need to consider what should happen when latencies increase. For example, if it takes minutes for an item to show up on the shopping list, users will be confused and perhaps frustrated. A solution to this problem would be to monitor the shopping list and observe the latency from the Gmail back-end service that manages this interaction. When the currently measured latency exceeds the acceptable threshold, the service will either respond to requests with a rejection and a temporary failure code, or perform the operation and include a warning notice in the response. The front-end application can then notify the user of either outcome: in one case it suggests retrying later, and in the other it informs them about the delay.

1.7 Summary

In this chapter, we explored the Reactive landscape in the context of the principles laid out in the Reactive Manifesto and surveyed the main challenges facing you when building applications in this style. For a more detailed example of designing a Reactive application, please refer to appendix B. The next chapter takes a deep dive into the manifesto itself, providing a detailed discussion of the points that are condensed into a compressed form in appendix C.

A walk-through of
the Reactive Manifesto

This chapter introduces the manifesto in detail: where the original text is as short as possible and rather dense, we unfold it and discuss it in great depth. For more background information on the theory behind the manifesto, please refer to part 2 of the book.

2.1   Reacting to users

So far, this book has used the word *user* informally and mostly in the sense of humans who interact with a computer. You interact only with your web browser in order to read and write emails, but many computers are needed in the background to perform these tasks. Each of these computers offers a certain set of services, and the consumer or user of these services will in most cases be another computer that is acting on behalf of a human, either directly or indirectly.

The first layer of services is provided by the front-end server and consumed by the web browser. The browser makes requests and expects responses—predominantly using HTTP, but also via WebSockets. The resources that are requested can pertain to emails, contacts, chats, searching, and many more (plus the definition of the styles and layout of the website). One such request might be related to the images of people you correspond with: when you hover over an email address, a pop-up window appears that contains details about that person, including a photograph or an avatar image. In order to render that image, the web browser makes a request to the front-end server. Figure 2.1 shows how this might be implemented using a traditional servlets approach.

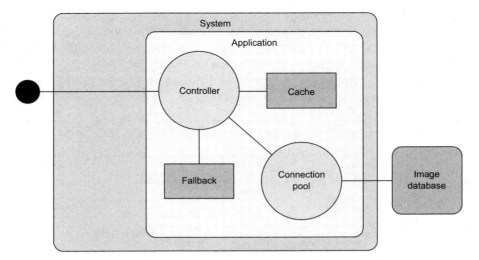

Figure 2.1 The front-end server for images first checks an in-memory cache, then attempts to retrieve the image from storage, and finally returns a fallback image if neither is successful.

The user action of hovering the mouse pointer over an email address sets in motion a flurry of requests via the web browser, the front-end server, and the internal image service down to the storage system, followed by their respective responses traveling in the opposite direction until the image is properly rendered on the screen. Along this chain are multiple relationships from user to service, and all of them need to meet the basic challenges outlined in the introduction; most important is the requirement to respond quickly to each request.

When designing the overall implementation of a feature like the image service, you need to think about services and their users' requirements not only on the outside but also on the inside. This is the first part of what it means to build reactive applications. Once the system has been decomposed in this way, you need to turn your focus to making these services as responsive as necessary to satisfy their users at all levels.

To understand why Reactive systems are better than the traditional alternatives, it is useful to examine a traditional implementation of an image service. Even though it has a cache, a connection pool, and even a fallback image for when things go wrong, it can fail badly when the system is stressed. Understanding how and why it fails requires looking beyond the single-thread illusion. Once you understand the failures, you will see that even within the confines of a traditional framework, you can improve the image service with a simplified version of the Managed Queue pattern that is covered in chapter 16.

2.1.1 Understanding the traditional approach

We will start with a naive implementation to retrieve an image from a database. The application has a controller that first checks a cache to see whether the image has been retrieved recently. If the controller finds the image in the cache, it returns the image right away. If not, it tries to retrieve the image from the database. If it finds the image there, the image is added to the cache and also returned to the original requester. If the image is not found, a static fallback image is returned, to avoid presenting the user with an error. This pattern should be familiar to you. This simplistic controller might contain code like the following.

Listing 2.1 Excerpt from a simple controller for an image service

```java
public interface Images {
  Image get(String Key);
  void add(String key, Image image);
}

public Images cache;          ⟵── Assumed thread-safe
public Images database;       ⟵─┐ Wraps a database
                                 │ connection pool
Image result = cache.get(key);
if (result != null) {
  return result;              ⟵── Image is found in the cache
} else {
  result = database.get(key);      Image is found in the
  if (result != null) {            database, added to the cache,
    cache.add(key, result);   ⟵─┘ and returned to the client
    return result;
  } else {
    return fallback;          ⟵─┐ Image is not retrieved
  }                              │ from the database
}
```

At the next level of detail, the application may be built on a framework that has some ability to handle concurrency, such as Java servlets. When a new request is received, the application framework assigns it to a request thread. That thread is then responsible for carrying the request through to a response. The more request threads are configured, the more simultaneous requests the system is expected to handle.

On a cache hit, the request thread can provide a response immediately. On a cache miss, the internal implementation of Images needs to obtain a connection from the pool. The database query itself may be performed on the request thread, or the connection pool may use a separate thread pool. Either way, the request thread is obliged to wait for the database query to complete or time out before it can fulfill the request.

When you are tuning the performance of a system such as this, one of the key parameters is the ratio of request threads to connection-pool entries. There is not much point in making the connection pool larger than the request-thread pool. If it is the same size and all the request threads are waiting on database queries, the system may find itself temporarily with little to do other than wait for the database to respond. That would be unfortunate if the next several requests could have been served from the cache; instead of being handled immediately, they will have to wait for an unrelated database query to complete so that a request thread will become available. On the other hand, setting the connection pool too small will make it a bottleneck; this risks the system being limited by request threads stuck waiting for a connection.

The best answer for a given load is somewhere between the extremes. The next section looks at finding a balance.

2.1.2 *Analyzing latency with a shared resource*

The simplistic implementation can be analyzed first by examining one extreme consisting of an infinite number of request threads sharing a fixed number of database connections. Assume each database query takes a consistent time W to complete, and for now ignore the cache. We will revisit the effect of the cache in section 2.3.1, when we introduce Amdahl's Law. You want to know how many database connections L will be used for a given load, which is represented as λ. A formula called *Little's Law* gives the answer:

$$L = \lambda \times W$$

Little's Law is valid for the long-term averages of the three quantities independent of the actual timing with which requests arrive or the order in which they are processed. If the database takes on average 30 ms to respond, and the system is receiving 500 requests per second, you can apply Little's Law:

$$L = 500 \text{ requests/second} \times 0.03 \text{ seconds/request}$$

$$L = 15$$

The average number of connections being used will be 15, so you will need at least that many connections to keep up with the load.

If there are requests waiting to be serviced, they must have some place to wait. Typically, they wait in a queue data structure somewhere. As each request is completed, the next request is taken from the queue for processing. Referring to figure 2.2, you may notice that there is no explicit queue. If this were coded using traditional synchronous Java servlets, the queue would consist of an internal collection of request threads waiting for their turn with the database connection. On average, there would be 15 such threads waiting. That is not good, because, whereas a queue is a lightweight data structure, the request threads in the queue are relatively expensive resources. Worse, 15 is just the average: the peaks are much higher. In reality, the thread pool will not be infinite. If there are too many requests, they will spill back into the TCP buffer and eventually back to the browser, resulting in unhelpful errors rather than the desired fallback image.

The first thing you might do is increase the number of entries in the database connection pool. As long as the database can continue to handle the resulting load, this will help the average case. The important thing to note is that you are still working with

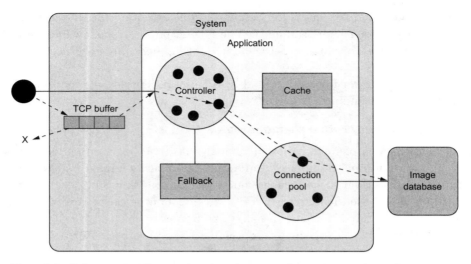

Figure 2.2   Using standard listener threads and a connection pool results in the listeners acting as queue entries, with overflow into the system TCP buffers.

average times. Real-world events can lead to failure modes that are far worse. For example, if the database stops responding at all for several minutes, 500 requests per second will overwhelm an otherwise sufficient thread pool. You need to protect the system.

2.1.3   *Limiting maximum latency with a queue*

The initial implementation blocked and waited for a database connection to become available; it returned `null` only if the requested image was not found in the database. A simple change will add some protection: if a database connection is not available, return `null` right away. This will free the request thread to return the fallback image rather than stalling and consuming a large amount of resources.

This approach couples two separate decisions into one: the number of database queries that can be accepted simultaneously is equal to the size of the connection pool. That may not be the result you want: it means the system will either return right away if no connection is available or return in 30 ms if one is available. Suppose you are willing to wait a bit longer in exchange for a much better rate of success. At this point, you can introduce an explicit queue, as shown in figure 2.3. Now, instead of returning right away if no connection is available, new requests are added to the queue. They are turned away only if the queue itself is full.

The addition provides much better control over system behavior. For example, a queue with a maximum length of only 3 entries will respond in no more than a total of 120 ms, including 90 ms progressing through the queue and another 30 ms for the database query. The size of the queue provides an upper bound that you can control. Depending on the rate of requests, the average response may be lower, perhaps less

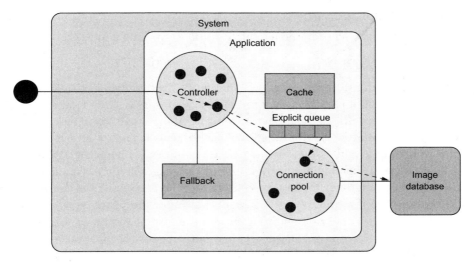

Figure 2.3 Adding an explicit queue to manage access to the database connection pool allows you to manage the maximum system latency separately from the listener thread pool size and the connection pool size.

than 100 ms. If the cache that was ignored in the analysis is now considered, the average drops still further. With a 50% cache-hit rate, the image server could offer an average response time of less than 50 ms.

Given what you know about how that 50 ms average is achieved, you also would know not to set a timeout less than 120 ms. If that time was not acceptable, the simpler solution would be to use a smaller queue. A developer who knows only that the average is less than 50 ms might assume it is a Gaussian distribution and be tempted to set a timeout value at perhaps 80 or 100 ms. Indeed, the assumptions that went into this analysis are vulnerable to the same error, because the assumption that the database provides a *consistent* 30 ms response time would be questionable in a real-world implementation. Real databases have caches of their own.

Setting a timeout has the effect of choosing a boundary at which the system will be considered to have failed. Either the system succeeded or it failed. When viewed from that perspective, the average response time is less important than the maximum response time. Because systems typically respond more slowly when under heavy load, a timeout based on the average will result in a higher percentage of failures under load and will also waste resources when they are needed most. Choosing timeouts will be revisited in section 2.4 and again in chapter 11. For now, the important realization is that the average response time often has little bearing on choosing the maximum limits.

2.2   *Exploiting parallelism*

The simplest case of a user–service relationship is invoking a method or function:

```
val result = f(42)
```

The user provides the argument "42" and hands over control of the CPU to the function f, which might calculate the 42nd Fibonacci number or the factorial of 42. Whatever the function does, you expect it to return some result value when it is finished. This means that invoking the function is the same as making a request, and the function returning a value is analogous to it replying with a response. What makes this example so simple is that most programming languages include syntax like this, which allows direct usage of the response under the assumption that the function does indeed reply. If that were not to happen, the rest of the program would not be executed, because it could not continue without the response. The underlying execution model is that the evaluation of the function occurs synchronously, on the same thread, and this ties the caller and the callee together so tightly that failures affect both in the same way.

Sequential execution of functions is well supported by all popular programming languages out of the box, as illustrated in figure 2.4 and shown in this example using Java syntax:

```
ReplyA a = computeA();
ReplyB b = computeB();
ReplyC c = computeC();
Result r = aggregate(a, b, c);
```

The sequential model is easy to understand. It was adequate for early computers that had only one processing core, but it necessitates waiting for all the results to be computed by the same resource while other resources remain idle.

2.2.1   *Reducing latency via parallelization*

In many cases, there is one possibility for latency reduction that immediately presents itself. If, for the completion of a request, several other services must be involved, then the overall result will be obtained more quickly if the other services can perform their

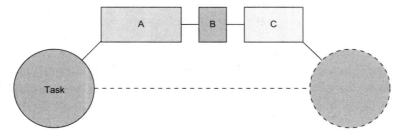

Figure 2.4   A task consisting of three subtasks that are executed sequentially: the total response latency is given by the sum of the three individual latencies.

functions in parallel, as shown in figure 2.5. This requires that no dependency exists such that, for example, task B needs the output of task A as one of its inputs, which frequently is the case. Take as an example the Gmail app in its entirety, which is composed of many different but independent parts. Or the contact information pop-up window for a given email address may contain textual information about that person as well as their image, and these can clearly be obtained in parallel.

When performing subtasks A, B, and C sequentially, as shown in figure 2.4, the overall latency depends on the sum of the three individual latencies. With parallel execution, overall latency equals the latency of whichever of the subtasks takes longest. In the implementation of a real social network, the number of subtasks can easily exceed 100, rendering sequential execution entirely impractical.

Parallel execution usually requires some extra thought and library support. For one thing, the service being called must not return the response directly from the method call that initiated the request, because in that case the caller would be unable to do anything while task A was running, including sending a request to perform task B in the meantime. The way to get around this restriction is to return a *Future* of the result instead of the value itself:

```
Future<ReplyA> a = taskA();
Future<ReplyB> b = taskB();
Future<ReplyC> c = taskC();
Result r = aggregate(a.get(), b.get(), c.get());
```

A Future is a placeholder for a value that may eventually become available; as soon as it does, the value can be accessed via the Future object. If the methods invoking subtasks A, B, and C are changed in this fashion, then the overall task just needs to call them to get back one Future each. Futures are discussed in greater detail in the next chapter.

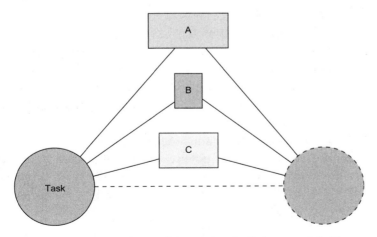

Figure 2.5   A task consisting of three subtasks that are executed in parallel: the total response latency is given by the maximum of the three individual latencies.

The previous code snippet uses a type called `Future` that is defined in the Java standard library (in the package `java.util.concurrent`). The only method it defines for accessing the value is the blocking `get()` method. *Blocking* here means the calling thread is suspended and cannot do anything else until the value has become available. We can picture the use of this kind of Future like so (written from the perspective of the thread handling the overall task):

> When my boss gives me the task to assemble the overview file of a certain client, I will dispatch three runners: one to the client archives to fetch the address, photograph, and contract status; one to the library to fetch all articles the client has written; and one to the post office to collect all new messages for this client. This is a vast improvement over having to perform these tasks myself, but now I need to wait idly at my desk until the runners return, so that I can collate everything they bring into an envelope and hand that back to my boss.

> It would be much nicer if I could leave a note telling the runners to place their findings in the envelope and telling the last one to come back to dispatch another runner to hand it to my boss without involving me. That way I could handle many more requests and would not feel useless most of the time.

2.2.2 *Improving parallelism with composable Futures*

What the developer should do is describe how the values should be composed to form the final result and let the system find the most efficient way to compute the values. This is possible with *composable Futures*, which are part of many programming languages and libraries, including newer versions of Java (`CompletableFuture` is introduced in JDK 8). Using this approach, the architecture turns completely from synchronous and blocking to asynchronous and nonblocking; the underlying machinery needs to become *task-oriented* in order to support this. The result is far more expressive than the relatively primitive precursor, the callback. The previous example transforms into the following, using Scala syntax:[1]

```
val fa: Future[ReplyA] = taskA()
val fb: Future[ReplyB] = taskB()
val fc: Future[ReplyC] = taskC()
val fr: Future[Result] = for (a <- fa; b <- fb; c <- fc)
                         yield aggregate(a, b, c)
```

Initiating a subtask as well as its completion are just events that are raised by one part of the program and reacted to in another part: for example, by registering an action to be taken with the value supplied by a completed Future. In this fashion, the latency of the method call for the overall task does not even include the latencies for subtasks A, B, and C, as shown in figure 2.6. The system is free to handle other requests while

---

[1] This would also be possible with the Java 8 `CompletionStage` using the `andThen` combinator, but due to the lack of for-comprehensions, the code would grow in size relative to the synchronous version. The Scala expression on the last line transforms to corresponding calls to `flatMap`, which are equivalent to `CompletionStage`'s `andThen`.

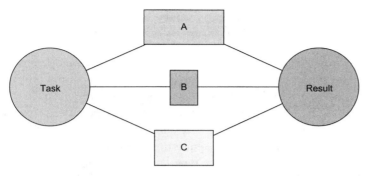

Figure 2.6 A task consisting of three subtasks that are executed as Futures: the total response latency is given by the maximum of the three individual latencies, and the initiating thread does not need to wait for the responses.

those are being processed, eventually reacting to their completion and sending the overall response back to the original user.

An added benefit is that additional events like task timeouts can be added without much hassle, because the entire infrastructure is already there. It is entirely reasonable to perform task A, couple the resulting Future with one that holds a TimeoutException after 100 ms, and use the combined result in the processing that follows. Then, either of the two events—completion of A or the timeout—triggers the actions that were attached to the completion of the combined Future.

> **THE NEED FOR ASYNCHRONOUS RESULT COMPOSITION** You may be wondering why this second part—asynchronous result composition—is necessary. Would it not be enough to reduce response latency by exploiting parallel execution? The context of this discussion is achieving bounded latency in a system of nested user–service relationships, where each layer is a user of the service beneath it. Because parallel execution of the subtasks A, B, and C depends on their initiating methods returning Futures instead of strict results, this must also apply to the overall task. That task is very likely part of a service that is consumed by a user at a higher level, and the same reasoning applies on that higher level as well. For this reason, it is imperative that parallel execution be paired with asynchronous and task-oriented result aggregation.

Composable Futures cannot be fully integrated into the image server example discussed earlier using the traditional servlet model. The reason is that the request thread encapsulates all the details necessary to return a response to the browser. There is no mechanism to make that information available to a future result. This is addressed in Servlet 3 with the introduction of AsyncContext.

2.2.3 *Paying for the serial illusion*

Traditionally, ways of modeling interactions between components—like sending to and receiving from the network—are expressed as blocking API calls:

```
final Socket socket = ...
socket.getOutputStream.write(requestMessageBytes);
final int bytesRead = socket.getInputStream().read(responseBuffer);
```

Each of these blocking calls interacts with the network equipment, generating messages and reacting to messages under the hood, but this fact is completely hidden in order to construct a synchronous façade on top of the underlying message-driven system. The thread executing these commands will suspend its execution if not enough space is available in the output buffer (for the first line) or if the response is not immediately available (on the second line). Consequently, this thread cannot do any other work in the meantime: every activity of this type that is ongoing in parallel needs its own thread, even if many of those are doing nothing but waiting for events to occur.

If the number of threads is not much larger than the number of CPU cores in the system, then this does not pose a problem. But given that these threads are mostly idle, you want to run many more of them. Assuming that it takes a few microseconds to prepare the requestMessageBytes and a few more microseconds to process the responseBuffer, whereas the time for traversing the network and processing the request on the other end is measured in milliseconds, it is clear that each thread spends more than 99% of its time in a waiting state.

In order to fully utilize the processing power of the available CPUs, this means running hundreds if not thousands of threads, even on commodity hardware. At this point, you should note that threads are managed by the operating system kernel for efficiency reasons.[2] Because the kernel can decide to switch out threads on a CPU core at any point in time (for example, when a hardware interrupt happens or the time slice for the current thread is used up), a lot of CPU state must be saved and later restored so that the running application does not notice that something else was using the CPU in the meantime. This is called a *context switch* and costs thousands of cycles[3] every time it occurs. The other drawback of using large numbers of threads is that the scheduler—the part of the kernel that decides which thread to run on which CPU core at any given time—will have a hard time finding out which threads are runnable and which are waiting and then selecting one such that each thread gets its fair share of the CPU.

The takeaway of the previous paragraph is that using synchronous, blocking APIs that hide the underlying message-driven structure wastes CPU resources. If messages were made explicit in the API such that instead of suspending a thread, you would just suspend the computation—freeing up the thread to do something else—then this overhead would be reduced substantially. The following example shows (remote) messaging between Akka Actors from Java 8:

---

[2] Multiplexing several logical user-level threads on a single OS thread is called a *many-to-one model* or *green threads*. Early JVM implementations used this model, but it was abandoned quickly (http://docs.oracle.com/cd/E19455-01/806-3461/6jck06gqh/index.html).

[3] Although CPUs have gotten faster, their larger internal state has negated the advances made in pure execution speed such that a context switch has taken roughly 1 µs without much improvement for two decades.

```
CompletionStage<Response> future =
    ask(actorRef, request, timeout)
        .thenApply(Response.class::cast);
future.thenAccept(response -> <process it>);
```

Sends a message to the actor reference, using a CompletionStage as the destination for the response

Maps the response to its expected type, failing upon mismatch

Registers further processing to be done once a response is received and mapped

Here, the sending of a request returns a handle to the possible future reply—a composable Future, as discussed in chapter 3—to which a callback is attached that runs when the response has been received. Both actions complete immediately, letting the thread do other things after having initiated the exchange.

2.3 The limits of parallel execution

Loose coupling between components—by design as well as at runtime—includes another benefit: more efficient execution. Although hardware used to increase capacity primarily by increasing the computing power of a single sequential execution core, physical limits[4] began impeding progress on this front around 2006. Modern processors now expand capacity by adding ever more cores, instead. In order to benefit from this kind of growth, you must distribute computation even within a single machine. When using a traditional approach with shared state concurrency based on mutual exclusion by way of locks, the cost of coordination between CPU cores becomes very significant.

2.3.1 Amdahl's Law

The example in section 2.1 includes an image cache. The most likely implementation would be a map shared among the request threads running on multiple cores in the same JVM. Coordinating access to a shared resource means executing those portions of the code that depend on the integrity of the map in some synchronized fashion. The map will not work properly if it is being changed at the same time it is being read. Operations on the map need to happen in a *serialized* fashion in some order that is globally agreed on by all parts of the application; this is also called *sequential consistency*. There is an obvious drawback to such an approach: portions that require synchronization cannot be executed in parallel. They run effectively single-threaded. Even if they execute on different threads, only one can be active at any given point in time. The effect this has on the possible reduction in runtime that is achievable by parallelization is captured by Amdahl's Law, shown in figure 2.7.

$$S(n) = \frac{T(1)}{T(N)} = \frac{1}{\alpha + \frac{1-\alpha}{N}} = \frac{N}{1 + \alpha(N-1)}$$

Figure 2.7   Amdahl's Law specifies the maximum increase in speed that can be achieved by adding additional threads.

---

[4] The finite speed of light as well as power dissipation make further increases in clock frequency impractical.

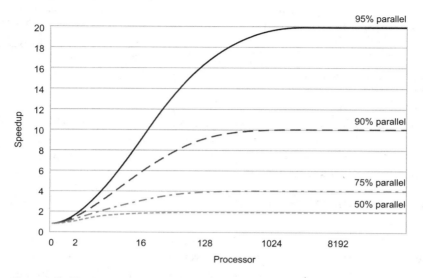

Figure 2.8 **The increase in speed of a program using multiple processors in parallel computing is limited by the sequential fraction of the program. For example, if 95% of the program can be parallelized, the theoretical maximum speedup using parallel computing will be 20 times, no matter how many processors are used.**

Here, N is the number of available threads, α is the fraction of the program that is serialized, and $T(N)$ is the time the algorithm needs when executed with N threads. This formula is plotted in figure 2.8 for different values of α across a range of available threads—they translate into the number of CPU cores on a real system. You will notice that even if only 5% of the program runs inside these synchronized sections, and the other 95% is parallelizable, the maximum achievable gain in execution time is a factor of 20; getting close to that theoretical limit would mean employing the ridiculous number of about 1,000 CPU cores.

2.3.2 Universal Scalability Law

Amdahl's Law also does not take into account the overhead incurred for coordinating and synchronizing the different execution threads. A more realistic formula is provided by the Universal Scalability Law,[5] shown in figure 2.9.

$$S(n) = \frac{N}{1 + \alpha(N-1) + \beta N(N-1)}$$

Figure 2.9 **The Universal Scalability Law provides the maximum increase in speed that can be achieved by adding additional threads, with an additional factor to account for coordination.**

---

5 N. J. Gunther, "A Simple Capacity Model of Massively Parallel Transaction Systems," 2003, www.perfdynamics .com/Papers/njgCMG93.pdf. See also "Neil J. Gunther: Universal Law of Computational Scalability," Wikipedia, https://en.wikipedia.org/wiki/Neil_J._Gunther#Universal_Law_of_Computational_Scalability.

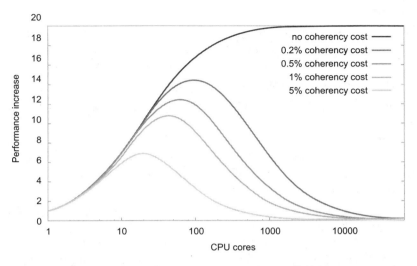

Figure 2.10 At some point, the increase in speed from adding more resources is eaten up by the cost of maintaining coherency within the system. The precise point depends on the parallel program fraction and the time spent on coherency.

The Universal Scalability Law adds another parameter describing the fraction of time spent ensuring that the data throughout the system is consistent. This factor is called the *coherency* of the system, and it combines all the delays associated with coordinating between threads to ensure consistent access to shared data structures. This new term dominates the picture when you have a large number of cores, taking away the throughput benefits and making it unattractive to add more resources beyond a certain point. This is illustrated in figure 2.10 for rather low assumptions on the coherency parameter; distributed systems will spend considerably more than a small percentage of their time on coordination.

The conclusion is that synchronization fundamentally limits the scalability of your application. The more you can do without synchronization, the better you can distribute your computation across CPU cores—or even network nodes. The optimum would be to share nothing—meaning no synchronization would be necessary—in which case scalability would be perfect. In figure 2.9, α and β would be zero, simplifying the entire equation to

$$S(n) = n$$

In plain words, this means that using n times as many computing resources, you achieve n times the performance. If you build your system on fully isolated compartments that are executed independently, then this will be the only theoretical limit, assuming you can split the task into at least n compartments. In practice, you need to exchange requests and responses, which requires some form of synchronization as well, but the cost of that is very low. On commodity hardware, it is possible to exchange several hundred million messages per second between CPU cores.

2.4   *Reacting to failure*

The previous sections concern designing a service implementation such that every request is met with a response within a given time. This is important because otherwise the user cannot determine whether the request has been received and processed. But even with flawless execution of this design, unexpected things will happen eventually:

- *Software will fail.* There will always be that exception you forgot to handle (or that was not documented by the library you are using); or you may get synchronization only a tiny bit wrong, causing a deadlock to occur; or the condition you formulated for breaking a loop may not cope with a weird edge case. You can always trust the users of your code to figure out ways to eventually find all these failure conditions and more.

- *Hardware will fail.* Everyone who has operated computing hardware knows that power supplies are notoriously unreliable; that hard disks tend to turn into expensive door stops, either during the initial burn-in phase or after a few years; and that dying fans lead to the silent death of all kinds of components by overheating them. In any case, your invaluable production server will, according to Murphy's Law, fail exactly when you most need it.

- *Humans will fail.* When you task maintenance personnel with replacing a failed hard disk in RAID5, a study[6] finds that there is a 10% chance that they will replace the wrong one, leading to the loss of all data. An anecdote from Roland's days as a network administrator is that cleaning personnel unplugged the power of the main server for the workgroup—both redundant cords at the same time—in order to connect the vacuum cleaner. None of these things should happen, but it is human nature that you will have a bad day from time to time.

- *Timeout is failure.* The reason for a timeout may not be related to the internal behavior of the system. For example, network congestion can delay messages between components of your system even when all the components are functioning normally. The source of delay may be some other system that shares the network. From the perspective of handling an individual request, it does not matter whether the cause is permanent or transient. The fact is that the one request has taken too long and therefore has failed.

The question therefore is not *if* a failure occurs but only *when* or *how often*. The user of a service does not care how an internal failure happened or what exactly went wrong, because the only response the user will get is that no normal response is received. Connections may time out or be rejected, or the response may consist of an opaque internal error code. In any case, the user will have to carry on without the response, which for humans probably means using a different service: if you try to book a flight

---

[6]   Aaron B. Brown (IBM Research), "Oops! Coping with Human Error," *ACM Queue* 2, no. 8 (Dec. 6, 2004), http://queue.acm.org/detail.cfm?id=1036497.

and the booking site stops responding, then you will take your business elsewhere and probably not come back anytime soon (or, in a different business, like online banking, users will overwhelm the support hotline).

A high-quality service is one that performs its function very reliably, preferably without any downtime at all. Because failure of computer systems is not an abstract possibility but is in fact certain, the question arises: how can you hope to construct a reliable service? The Reactive Manifesto chooses the term *resilience* instead of *reliability* precisely to capture this apparent contradiction.

> ### What does resilience mean?
> Merriam-Webster defines resilience as follows:
>
> - The ability of a substance or object to spring back into shape
> - The capacity to recover quickly from difficulties

The key notion here is to aim at fault tolerance instead of fault avoidance, because avoidance will not be fully successful. It is of course good to plan for as many failure scenarios as you can, to tailor programmatic responses such that normal operations can be resumed as quickly as possible—ideally without the user noticing anything. The same must also apply to those failure cases that were not foreseen and explicitly accommodated in the design, knowing that these will happen as well.

But resilience goes one step further than fault tolerance: a resilient system not only withstands a failure but also recovers its original shape and feature set. As an example, consider a satellite that is placed in orbit. In order to reduce the risk of losing the mission, every critical function is implemented at least twice, be it hardware or software. For the case that one component fails, there are procedures that switch to the backup component. Exercising such a fail-over keeps the satellite functioning, but from then on the affected component will not tolerate additional faults because there was only one backup. This means the satellite subsystems are fault tolerant but not resilient.

There is only one generic way to protect your system from failing as a whole when a part fails: *distribute* and *compartmentalize*. The former can informally be translated as "don't put all your eggs in one basket," and the latter adds "protect your baskets from one another." When it comes to handling a failure, it is important to *delegate*, so that the failed compartment itself is not responsible for its own recovery.

Distribution can take several forms. The one you probably think of first involves replicating an important database across several servers such that, in the event of a hardware failure, the data are safe because copies are readily available. If you are really concerned about those data, then you may go as far as placing the replicas in different buildings in order not to lose all of them in the case of fire—or to keep them independently operable when one of them suffers a complete power outage. For the really paranoid, those buildings would need to be supplied by different power grids, better yet in different countries or on separate continents.

2.4.1   *Compartmentalization and bulkheading*

The further apart the replicas are kept, the smaller the probability of a single fault affecting all of them. This applies to all kinds of failures, whether software, hardware, or human: reusing one computing resource, operations team, set of operational procedures, and so on creates a coupling by which multiple replicas can be affected synchronously or similarly. The idea behind this is to isolate the distributed parts or, to use a metaphor from ship building, to use *bulkheading*.

Figure 2.11 shows the schematic design of a large cargo ship whose hold is separated by bulkheads into many compartments. When the hull is breached for some reason, only those compartments that are directly affected will fill up with water; the others will remain properly sealed, keeping the ship afloat.

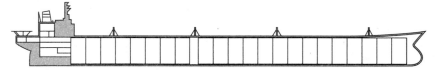

Figure 2.11   The term *bulkheading* comes from ship building and means the vessel is segmented into fully isolated compartments.

One of the first examples of this building principle was the *Titanic*, which featured 15 bulkheads between bow and stern and was therefore considered unsinkable.[7] That particular ship did in fact sink, so what went wrong? In order to not inconvenience passengers (in particular the higher classes) and to save money, the bulkheads extended only a few feet above the water line, and the compartments were not sealable at the top. When five compartments near the bow were breached during the collision with the iceberg, the bow dipped deeper into the water, allowing the water to flow over the top of the bulkheads into more and more compartments until the ship sank.

This example—although certainly one of the most terrible incidents in marine history—perfectly demonstrates that bulkheading can be done wrong in such a way that it becomes useless. If the compartments are not truly isolated from each other, failure can cascade among them to bring down the entire system. One example from distributed computing designs is managing fault tolerance at the level of entire application servers, where one failure can lead to the failure of other servers by overloading or stalling them.

Modern ships employ full compartmentalization where the bulkheads extend from keel to deck and can be sealed on all sides, including the top. This does not make the ships unsinkable, but in order to obtain a catastrophic outcome, the ship needs to be mismanaged severely and run with full speed against a rock.[8] That metaphor translates in full to computer systems.

---

[7] "There is no danger that *Titanic* will sink. The boat is unsinkable and nothing but inconvenience will be suffered by the passengers." —Phillip Franklin, White Star Line vice president, 1912.

[8] See, for example, the *Costa Concordia* disaster: https://en.wikipedia.org/wiki/Costa_Concordia_disaster.

2.4.2 *Using circuit breakers*

No amount of planning and optimization will guarantee that the services you implement or depend on abide by their latency bounds. We will talk more about the nature of the things that can go wrong when discussing resilience, but even without knowing the source of the failure, there are some useful techniques for dealing with services that violate their bounds.

When users are momentarily overwhelming a service, then its response latency will rise, and eventually it will start failing. Users will receive their responses with more delay, which in turn will increase their own latency until they get close to their own limits. In the image server example in section 2.1.2, you saw how adding an explicit queue protected the client by rejecting requests that would take more than the acceptable response time to service. This is useful when there is a short spike in demand for the service. If the image database were to fail completely for several minutes, the behavior would not be ideal. The queue would fill with a backlog of requests that, after a short time, would be useless to process. A first step would be to cull the old queue entries, but the queue would refill immediately with still more queries that would take too long to process.

In order to stop this effect from propagating across the entire chain of user–service relationships, users need to shield themselves from the overwhelmed service during such time periods. The way to do this is well known in electrical engineering: install a circuit breaker, as shown in figure 2.12.

The idea here is simple: when involving another service, monitor the time it takes for the response to come back. If the time is consistently greater than the allowed threshold this user has factored into its own latency budget for this particular service

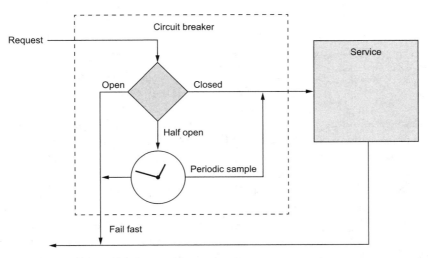

Figure 2.12   A circuit breaker in electrical engineering protects a circuit from being destroyed by a current that is too high. The software equivalent does the same thing for a service that would otherwise be overwhelmed by too many requests.

call, then the circuit breaker trips; from then on, requests will take a different route of processing that either fails fast or gives degraded service, just as in the case of overflowing the bounded queue in front of the service. The same should also happen if the service replies with failures repeatedly, because then it is not worth the effort to send requests.

This not only benefits the user by insulating it from the faulty service but also has the effect of reducing the load on the struggling service, giving it some time to recover and empty its queues. It would also be possible to monitor such occurrences and reinforce the resources for the overwhelmed service in response to the increased load.

When the service has had some time to recuperate, the circuit breaker should snap back into a half-closed state in which some requests are sent in order to test whether the service is back in shape. If not, then the circuit breaker can trip again immediately; otherwise, it closes automatically and resumes normal operations. The Circuit Breaker pattern is discussed in detail in chapter 12.

2.4.3 *Supervision*

In section 2.2, a simple function call returned a result synchronously:

```
val result = f(42)
```

In the context of a larger program, an invocation of f might be wrapped in an exception handler for reasonable error conditions, such as invalid input leading to a divide-by-zero error. Implementation details can result in exceptions that are not related to the input values. For example, a recursive implementation might lead to a stack overflow, or a distributed implementation might lead to networking errors. There is little the user of the service can do in those cases:

```
try {
  f(i)
} catch {                                                          Reasonable
  case ex: java.lang.ArithmeticException => Int.MaxValue  <—┘      response
  case ex: java.lang.StackOverflowError => ???
  case ex: java.net.ConnectException => ???               | Now what?
}
```

Responses—including validation errors—are communicated back to the user of a service, whereas failures must be handled by the one who operates the service. The term that describes this relationship in a computer system is *supervision*. The supervisor is responsible for keeping the service alive and running.

Figure 2.13 depicts these two different flows of information. The service internally handles everything it knows how to handle; it performs validation and processes requests, but any exceptions it cannot handle are escalated to the supervisor. While the service is in a broken state, it cannot process incoming requests. Imagine, for example, a service that depends on a working database connection. When the connection breaks, the database driver will throw an exception. If you tried to handle this

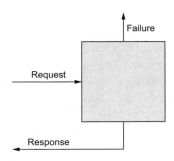

Figure 2.13 Supervision means that normal requests and responses (including negative ones such as validation errors) flow separately from failures: while the former are exchanged between the user and the service, the latter travel from the service to its supervisor.

case directly within the service by attempting to establish a new connection, then that logic would be mixed with all the normal business logic of this service. But, worse, this service would need to think about the big picture as well. How many reconnection attempts make sense? How long should it wait between attempts?

Handing those decisions off to a dedicated supervisor allows the separation of concerns—business logic versus specialized fault handling—and factoring them out into an external entity also enables the implementation of an overarching strategy for several supervised services. The supervisor could, for example, monitor how frequently failures occur on the primary database back-end system and fail over to a secondary database replica when appropriate. In order to do that, the supervisor must have the power to start, stop, and restart the services it supervises: it is responsible for their lifecycle.

The first system that directly supported this concept was Erlang/OTP, implementing the Actor model (discussed in chapter 3). Patterns related to supervision are described in chapter 12.

2.5 *Losing strong consistency*

One of the most famous theoretical results on distributed systems is Eric Brewer's CAP theorem,[9] which states that any networked shared-data system can have at most two of three desirable properties:

- Consistency (C) equivalent to having a single up-to-date copy of the data
- High availability (A) of that data (for updates)
- Tolerance to network partitions (P)

This means that during a network partition, at least one of consistency and availability must be sacrificed. If modifications continue during a partition, then inconsistencies can occur. The only way to avoid that would be to not accept modifications and thereby be unavailable.

As an example, consider two users editing a shared text document using a service like Google Docs. Hopefully, the document is stored in at least two different locations

---

[9] S. Gilbert and N. Lynch, "Brewer's Conjecture and the Feasibility of Consistent, Available, Partition-Tolerant Web Services," *ACM SIGACT News* 33, no. 2 (2002), 51-59, http://dl.acm.org/citation.cfm?id=564601.

in order to survive a hardware failure of one of them, and both users randomly connect to some replica to make their changes. Normally, the changes will propagate between them, and each user will see the other's edits; but if the network link between the replicas breaks down while everything else keeps working, both users will continue editing and see their own changes but not the changes made by the other. If both replace the same word with different improvements, then the result will be that the document is in an inconsistent state that needs to be repaired when the network link starts working again. The alternative would be to detect the network failure and forbid further changes until it is working again—leading to two unhappy users who not only will be unable to make conflicting changes but also will also be prevented from working on completely unrelated parts of the document.

Traditional data stores are relational databases that provide a very high level of consistency guarantees, and customers of database vendors are accustomed to that mode of operation—not least because a lot of effort and research has gone into making databases efficient in spite of having to provide ACID[10] transaction semantics. For this reason, distributed systems have so far concentrated critical components in a way that provides strong consistency.

In the example of two users editing a shared document, a corresponding strongly consistent solution would mean that every change—every keypress—would need to be confirmed by the central server before being displayed locally, because otherwise one user's screen could show a state that was inconsistent with what the other user saw. This obviously does not work, because it would be irritating to have such high latency while typing text—we are used to characters appearing instantly. This solution would also be costly to scale up to millions of users, considering the high-availability setups with log replication and the license fees for the big iron database.

Compelling as this use case may be, Reactive systems present a challenging architecture change: the principles of resilience, scalability, and responsiveness need to be applied to all parts of the system in order to obtain the desired benefits, eliminating the strong transactional guarantees on which traditional systems were built. Eventually, this change will have to occur, though—if not for the benefits outlined in the previous sections, then for physical reasons. The notion of ACID transactions aims at defining a global order of transactions such that no observer can detect inconsistencies. Taking a step back from the abstractions of programming into the physical world, Einstein's theory of relativity has the astonishing property that some events cannot be ordered with respect to each other: if even a ray of light cannot travel from the location of the first event to the location of the second before that event happens, then the observed order of the two events depends on how fast an observer moves relative to those locations.

Although we do not yet need to worry about computers traveling near the speed of light with respect to each other, we do need to worry about the speed of light between

---

[10] Atomicity, consistency, isolation, durability.

even computers that are stationary. Events that cannot be connected by a ray of light as just described cannot have a causal order between them. Limiting the interactions between systems to proceed, at most, at the speed of light would be a solution to avoid ambiguities, but this is becoming a painful restriction already in today's processor designs: agreeing on the current clock tick on both ends of a silicon chip is one of the limiting factors when trying to increase the clock frequency.

2.5.1 *ACID 2.0*

Systems with an inherently distributed design are built on a different set of principles. One such set is called BASE:

- Basically available
- Soft state (state needs to be actively maintained instead of persisting by default)
- Eventually consistent

The last point means that modifications to the data need time to travel between distributed replicas, and during this time it is possible for external observers to see data that are inconsistent. The qualification "eventually" means the time window during which inconsistency can be observed after a change is bounded; when the system does not receive modifications any longer and enters a quiescent state, it will eventually become fully consistent again.

In the example of editing a shared document, this means although you see your own changes immediately, you might see the other's changes with some delay; and if conflicting changes are made, then the intermediate states seen by both users may be different. But once the incoming streams of changes end, both views will eventually settle into the same state for both users.

In a note[11] written 12 years after the CAP conjecture, Eric Brewer remarks thus:

> This [see above] expression of CAP served its purpose, which was to open the minds of designers to a wider range of systems and tradeoffs; indeed, in the past decade, a vast range of new systems has emerged, as well as much debate on the relative merits of consistency and availability. The "2 of 3" formulation was always misleading because it tended to oversimplify the tensions among properties. Now such nuances matter. CAP prohibits only a tiny part of the design space: perfect availability and consistency in the presence of partitions, which are rare.

In the argument involving Einstein's theory of relativity, the time window during which events cannot be ordered is very short—the speed of light is rather fast for everyday observations. In the same spirit, the inconsistency observed in eventually consistent systems is also short-lived; the delay between changes being made by one user and being visible to others is on the order of tens or maybe hundreds of milliseconds, which is good enough for collaborative document editing.

---

[11] Eric Brewer, "CAP Twelve Years Later: How the 'Rules' Have Changed," InfoQ, May 30, 2012, https://www .infoq.com/articles/cap-twelve-years-later-how-the-rules-have-changed.

BASE has served as an important step in evolving our understanding of which properties are useful and which are unattainable, but as a definitive term it is too imprecise. Another proposal brought forward by Pat Helland at React Conf 2014 is ACID 2.0:

- Associative
- Commutative
- Idempotent
- Distributed

The last point just completes the familiar acronym, but the first three describe underlying mathematical principles that allow operations to be performed in a form that is eventually consistent by definition: if every action is represented such that it can be applied in batches (associative) and in any order (commutative) and such that applying it multiple times is not harmful (idempotent), then the end result does not depend on which replica accepts the change and in which order the updates are disseminated across the network—even resending is fine if reception is not yet acknowledged.

Other authors, such as Peter Bailis and Martin Kleppmann, are pushing the envelope of how far we can extend consistency guarantees without running into the forbidden spot of the CAP theorem: with the help of tracking the causality relationship between different updates, it seems possible to get very close to ACID semantics while minimizing the sacrifice in terms of availability. It will be interesting to see where this field of research will be in 10 years.

2.5.2 Accepting updates

Only during a network partition is it problematic to accept modifications on both disconnected sides, although even for this case solutions are emerging in the form of conflict-free replicated data types (CRDTs). These have the property of merging cleanly when the partition ends, regardless of the modifications that were done on either side.

Google Docs employs a similar technique called *operational transformation*.[12] In the scenario in which replicas of a document get out of sync due to a network partition, local changes are still accepted and stored as operations. When the network connection is back in working condition, the different chains of operations are merged by bringing them into a linearized sequence. This is done by rebasing one chain on top of the other so that instead of operating on the last synchronized state, the one chain is transformed to operate on the state that results from applying the other chain before it. This resolves conflicting changes in a deterministic way, leading to a consistent document for both users after the partition has healed.

Data types with these nice properties come with certain restrictions in terms of which operations they can support. There will naturally be problems that cannot be

---

[12] David Wang, Alex Mah, and Soren Lassen, "Google Wave Operational Transformation," July 2010, http://mng.bz/Bry5.

stated using them, in which case you have no choice but to concentrate these data in one location only and forgo distribution. But our intuition is that necessity will drive the reduction of these issues by researching alternative models for the respective problem domain, forming a compromise between the need to provide responsive services that are always available and the business-level desire for strong consistency. One example from the real world is automated teller machines (ATMs): bank accounts are the traditional example of strong transactional reasoning, but the mechanical implementation of dispensing cash to account owners has been eventually consistent for a long time.

When you go to an ATM to withdraw cash, you would be annoyed with your bank if the ATM did not work, especially if you needed the money to buy that anniversary present for your spouse. Network problems do occur frequently, and if the ATM rejected customers during such periods, that would lead to lots of unhappy customers—we know that bad stories spread a lot easier than stories that say "It just worked as it was supposed to." The solution is to still offer service to the customer even if certain features like overdraft protection cannot work at the time. You might, for example, get less cash than you wanted while the machine cannot verify that your account has sufficient funds, but you would still get some bills instead of a dire "Out of Service" error. For the bank, this means your account may be overdrawn, but chances are that most people who want to withdraw money have enough to cover the transaction. And if the account has turned into a mini loan, there are established means to fix that: society provides a judicial system to enforce those parts of the contract that the machine could not, and in addition the bank charges fees and earns interest as long as the account holder owes it money.

This example highlights that computer systems do not have to solve all the issues around a business process in all cases, especially when the cost of doing so would be prohibitive. It can also be seen as a system that falls back to an approximate solution until its nominal functionality can be restored.

2.6   *The need for Reactive design patterns*

Many of the discussed solutions and most of the underlying problems are not new. Decoupling the design of different components of a program has been the goal of computer science research since its inception, and it has been part of the common literature since the famous 1994 *Design Patterns* book.[13] As computers became more and more ubiquitous in our daily lives, programming moved accordingly into the focus of society and changed from an art practiced by academics and later by young "fanatics" in their basements to a widely applied craft. The growth in sheer size of computer systems deployed over the past two decades led to the formalization of designs building on top of the established best practices and widening the scope of what we consider

---

[13] Erich Gamma et al., *Design Patterns: Elements of Reusable Object-Oriented Software*, Addison-Wesley Professional (1994).

charted territory. In 2003, *Enterprise Integration Patterns*[14] covered message passing between networked components, defining communication and message-handling patterns—for example, implemented by the Apache Camel project. The next step was called *service-oriented architecture* (SOA).

While reading this chapter, you will have recognized elements of earlier stages, such as the focus on message passing and services. The question naturally arises, what does this book add that has not already been described sufficiently elsewhere? Especially interesting is a comparison to the definition of SOA in Arnon Rotem-Gal-Oz's *SOA Patterns* (Manning, 2012):

> DEFINITION: Service-oriented architecture (SOA) is an architectural style for building systems based on interactions of loosely coupled, coarse-grained, and autonomous components called services. Each service exposes processes and behavior through contracts, which are composed of messages at discoverable addresses called endpoints. A service's behavior is governed by policies that are external to the service itself. The contracts and messages are used by external components called service consumers.

This definition focuses on the high-level architecture of an application, which is made explicit by demanding that the service structure be coarse-grained. The reason for this is that SOA approaches the topic from the perspective of business requirements and abstract software design, which without doubt is very useful. But as we have argued, technical reasons push the coarseness of services down to finer levels and demand that abstractions like synchronous blocking network communication be replaced by explicitly modeling the message-driven nature of the underlying system.

2.6.1 *Managing complexity*

Lifting the level of abstraction has proven to be the most effective measure for increasing the productivity of programmers. Exposing more of the underlying details seems like a step backward on this count, because abstraction is usually meant to hide complications from view. This consideration neglects the fact that there are two kinds of complexity:

- *Essential complexity* is the kind that is inherent in the problem domain.
- *Incidental complexity* is the kind that is introduced solely by the solution.

Coming back to the example of using a traditional database with transactions as the backing store for a shared document editor, the ACID solution tries to hide the essential complexity present in the domain of networked computer systems, introducing incidental complexity by requiring the developer to try to work around the performance and scalability issues that arise.

---

[14] Gregor Hohpe and Bobby Woolf, *Enterprise Integration Patterns: Designing, Building, and Deploying Messaging Solutions*, Addison-Wesley Professional (2003).

A proper solution exposes all the essential complexity of the problem domain, making it accessible to be tackled as is appropriate for the concrete use case, and avoids burdening the user with incidental complexity that results from a mismatch between the chosen abstraction and the underlying mechanics.

This means that as your understanding of the problem domain evolves—for example, recognizing the need for distribution of computation at much finer granularity than before—you need to keep reevaluating the existing abstractions in view of whether they capture the essential complexity and how much incidental complexity they add. The result will be an adaptation of solutions, sometimes representing a shift in which properties you want to abstract over and which you want to expose. Reactive service design is one such shift, which makes some patterns like synchronous, strongly consistent service coupling obsolete. The corresponding loss in level of abstraction is countered by defining new abstractions and patterns for solutions, akin to restacking the building blocks on top of a realigned foundation.

The new foundation is message orientation, and in order to compose large-scale applications on top of it, you need suitable tools to work with. The patterns discussed in the third part of this book are a combination of well-worn, comfortable instruments like the Circuit Breaker pattern as well as emerging patterns learned from wider usage of the Actor model. But a pattern consists of more than a description of a prototypical solution; more important, it is characterized by the problem it tries to solve. The main contribution of this book is therefore to discuss Reactive design patterns in light of the four tenets of the Reactive Manifesto.

2.6.2 *Bringing programming models closer to the real world*

Our final remark on the consequences of Reactive programming takes up the strands that shone through in several places already. You have seen that the desire to create self-contained pieces of software that deliver service to their users reliably and quickly led to a design that builds on encapsulated, independently executed units of computation. The compartments between the bulkheads form private spaces for services that communicate only using messages in a high-level messaging language.

These design constraints are familiar from the physical world and from our society: humans also collaborate on larger tasks, perform individual tasks autonomously, communicate via high-level language, and so on. This allows us to visualize abstract software concepts using well-known, customary images. We can tackle the architecture of an application by asking, "How would you do it given a group of people?" Software development is an extremely young discipline compared to the organization of labor between humans over the past millennia, and by using the knowledge we have built up, we have an easier time breaking down systems in ways that are compatible with the nature of distributed, autonomous implementation.

Of course, we should stay away from abuses of anthropomorphism: we are slowly eliminating terminology like "master/slave" in recognition that not everybody takes the technical context into account when interpreting them.[15] But even responsible use offers plentiful opportunities for spicing up possibly dull work a little: for example, by calling a component responsible for writing logs to disk a `Scribe`. Implementing that class will have the feel of creating a little robot that will do certain things you tell it to and with which you can play a bit—others call that activity *writing tests* and make a sour face while saying so. With Reactive programming, you can turn this around and realize: it's fun!

2.7   Summary

This chapter laid the foundation for the rest of the book, introducing the tenets of the Reactive Manifesto:

- Responsive
- Resilient
- Elastic
- Message-driven

We have shown how the need to stay responsive in the face of component failure defines resilience, and likewise how the desire to withstand surges in the incoming load elucidates the meaning of scalability. Throughout this discussion, you have seen the common theme of message orientation as an enabler for meeting the other three challenges.

In the next chapter, we will introduce the tools of the trade: event loops, Futures and Promises, Reactive Extensions, and the Actor model. All these make use of the functional programming paradigm, which we will look at first.

---

[15] Although terminology offers many interesting side notes: for example, a *client* is someone who obeys (from the Latin *cluere*), whereas *server* derives from *slave* (from the Latin *servus*)—so a client–server relationship is somewhat strange when interpreted literally.

An example of naming that can easily prompt out-of-context interpretation is a hypothetical method name like `harvest_dead_children()`. In the interest of reducing nontechnical arguments about code, it is best to avoid such terms.

Tools of the trade

The previous chapter explained *why* you need to be Reactive. Now we will turn our attention to the question of *how* you can achieve this goal. In this chapter, you will learn:

- The earliest Reactive approaches
- Important functional programming techniques
- Strengths and weaknesses of the existing Reactive tools and libraries

3.1 Early Reactive solutions

Over the past 30 years, people have designed many tools and paradigms to help build Reactive applications. One of the oldest and most notable is the Erlang programming language (www.erlang.org), created by Joe Armstrong and his team at Ericsson in the mid-1980s. Erlang was the first language that brought Actors, described later in this chapter, into mainstream popularity.

Armstrong and his team faced a daunting challenge: to build a language that would support the creation of distributed applications that are nearly impervious to failure. Over time, Erlang evolved in the Ericsson laboratory, culminating with its use in the late 1990s to build the AXD 301 telephone switch, which reportedly achieved "nine nines" of uptime—availability 99.9999999% of the time. Consider exactly what that means. For a single application running on a single machine, that would be roughly 3 seconds of downtime in 100 years!

```
100 years
    * 365 days/year
    * 24 hours/day
    * 60 minutes/day
    * 60 seconds/minute
        = 3,153,600,000 seconds
```

```
3,153,600,000 seconds
   * 0.000000001 expected downtime
      = 3.1536 seconds of downtime in 100 years
```

Of course, such long-lasting, near-perfect uptime is purely theoretical; modern computers haven't even been around 100 years. The study upon which this claim was based was performed by British Telecom in 2002–2003 and involved 14 nodes and a calculation based on 5 node-years of study.[1] Such approximations of downtime depend as much on the hardware as on the application itself, because unreliable computers put an upper limit on the availability of even the most resilient software. But such theoretical uptime illustrates the extraordinary fault tolerance possible in a Reactive application. Amazingly, no other language or platform has made claims comparable to Erlang's.

Erlang employs a dynamic type system and ubiquitous pattern matching to capture the dynamic nature of Actor systems, and it copies message data for every message it passes between Actors. The data has to be copied as shown in figure 3.1 because there is no shared heap space between two Actor processes in the BEAM VM, the virtual machine on which Erlang runs. Data sent between Actors must be copied into the receiving Actor process's heap prior to sending the message, to guarantee isolation of Actors and to prevent concurrent access to the data.

Although these features provide additional safety, ensuring that any Erlang Actor can receive any message and no data can be shared, they lower the application's potential throughput. On the other hand, garbage collection can be performed independently for all process heaps[2] and thus completes more quickly and with predictable latency.

All this copying would not be necessary if the Actors all shared the same heap. Then, two Actors could share a pointer to the same message. For this to work, though, one critical condition must be met: the data cannot be allowed to change. Functional programming addresses this challenge.

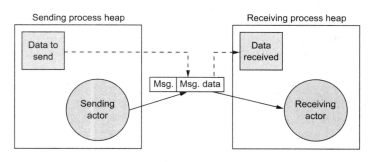

Figure 3.1 In Erlang, data in a sending Actor's heap is transferred via a message to the heap of a receiving Actor.

---

[1] Mats Cronqvist, "The Nine Nines," 2012, www.erlang-factory.com/upload/presentations/243/ErlangFactory SFBay2010-MatsCronqvist.pdf.

[2] One exception are binary strings longer than 64 bytes, which are stored in a separate heap and managed by reference counting.

3.2   *Functional programming*

The concepts of functional programming have been around for a very long time, but only recently have they gained favor in mainstream programming languages. Why did functional programming disappear from the mainstream for so long, and why is its popularity surging now?

The period between 1995 and 2008 was essentially the Dark Ages of functional programming, as languages such as C, C++, and Java grew in usage, and the imperative, object-oriented programming style became the most popular way to write applications and solve problems. The advent of multiple cores opened up new opportunities for parallelization, but imperative programming constructs with side effects can be difficult to reason about in such an environment. Imagine a C or C++ developer who already has the burden of managing their own memory usage in a single-threaded application. In a multicore world, they must now manage memory across multiple threads while also trying to figure out who can access shared mutable memory at what time. This makes a job that was hard to do and verify in the first place into something that is daunting for even the most senior C/C++ developers.

This has led to a veritable Renaissance in functional programming. Many languages now include constructs from functional programming, because these better support reasoning about problems in concurrent and parallelized applications. Code written in a functional style makes it easier for developers to reason about what the application is doing at any given point in time.

The core concepts of functional programming have been around for many years: they were first defined in the lambda calculus by Alonzo Church in the 1930s.[3] The essence of functional programming is the insight that programs can be written in terms of pure mathematical functions: that is, functions that return the same value every time they are passed the same inputs and that cause no side effects. Writing code in functional programming is analogous to composing functions in mathematics. With tools for functional programming now at our disposal, it is truly a wonderful time to be a programmer again, because we can solve problems with languages that support the functional, the side-effecting, or both paradigms simultaneously.

Next, we will examine some core concepts of functional programming that go beyond pure function composition: immutability, referential transparency, side effects, and functions as first-class citizens.

3.2.1   *Immutability*

A variable is said to have *mutable state* when it can refer to different values at different times. In an otherwise purely functional program, mutable state is called *impure* and is considered dangerous. Mutability is represented by any variable or field that is not stable or final and can be changed or updated while the application is running; some

---

[3]   Alonzo Church, "The Calculi of Lambda-Conversion," *Annals of Mathematical Studies* 6, Princeton University Press (1941).

examples are shown in listing 3.1. When you use a final, immutable variable, you can reason more easily about what value it will have at a given time because you know that nothing can possibly change it after it is defined. This applies to data structures as well as to simple variables: any action performed on an immutable data structure results in the creation of a new data structure, which holds the result of the change. The original data structure remains unchanged. Therefore, any other part of the program that continues to use the original data structure does not see the change.

By using immutability throughout an application, you can limit the places where mutation is possible to a very small section of code. So, the possibility of *contention*, where multiple threads attempt to access the same resource at the same time and some are forced to wait their turn, is limited in scope to a small region. Contention is one of the biggest drains on performance in code that runs on multiple CPU cores; it should be avoided where possible.

The astute reader will notice the tension between funneling all changes through a single point and trying to avoid contention. The key to solving this apparent paradox is that having all code that performs mutation within a small scope makes contention easier to manage. With full oversight of the problem, you can tune the behavior: for example, by dividing a complex state representation into several mutable variables that can usually be updated independently—hence, without contention.

Listing 3.1   Unsafe, mutable message class, which may hide unexpected behavior

```
import java.util.Date;

public class Unsafe {
    private Date timestamp;                        ← Fields should be final
    private final StringBuffer message;              so the compiler can
                                                     enforce immutability.

    public Unsafe(Date timestamp, StringBuffer message) {   ← Mutable because the
        this.timestamp = timestamp;                            content of the buffer
        this.message = message;                                is not stable
    }

    public synchronized Date getTimestamp() {
        return timestamp;
    }

    public synchronized void setTimestamp(Date timestamp) {   ←
        this.timestamp = timestamp;
    }

    public StringBuffer getMessage() {
        return message;
    }
}
```

Mutable because the content of the buffer is not stable → `public StringBuffer getMessage() {`

Mutable because the timestamp can be changed via the setter. Synchronizing both the getter and setter adds thread safety but does nothing to relieve contention between threads accessing the object.

It is better to enforce immutability using the compiler rather than convention. This implies passing values to the constructor rather than calling setters, and using language features such as final in Java and val in Scala. Sometimes that is not possible, such as when an API requires an object to be created before all of its member values are known. In those situations, you may have to resort to initialization flags to prevent values from being set more than once or after the object is already in use.

Immutable data structures like the one shown in listing 3.2 ensure that the values returned by an object do not change. It does little good to ensure that the variable holding a Date is not reassigned if its content can be changed. The problem is not thread safety. The problem is that mutable state makes it far more difficult to reason about what the code is doing. There are several alternatives:

- The first choice is to use an intrinsically immutable data structure. Some languages provide extensive libraries of immutable collection implementations, or you might incorporate a third-party library.
- You can write a wrapper class to block access to the mutating methods. Ensure that no references remain to the backing mutable data structure once it is initialized. They can inadvertently defeat the purpose of the wrapper.
- *Copy-on-read semantics* creates and returns a complete copy of the data structure every time it is read from the object. This ensures that readers do not have access to the original object, but it can be expensive. As with immutable wrappers, you must ensure that no outside references remain to the still-writable data structure within the object.
- *Copy-on-write semantics* creates and returns a complete copy of the data structure whenever it is modified and ensures that users of the object cannot modify it through references they received from accessor methods. This prevents callers from changing the object's underlying, mutable data structure, and it leaves previously acquired reader references unchanged.
- The data structure can block use of the mutators once the data structure is initialized. This typically requires adding a flag to mark the data structure as read-only after it has been initialized.

Listing 3.2 Immutable message class that behaves predictably and is easier to reason about

```java
import java.util.Date;

public class Immutable {
    private final Date timestamp;
    private final String message;

    public Immutable(final Date timestamp, final String message) {
        this.timestamp = new Date(timestamp.getTime());
        this.message = message;
    }

    public Date getTimestamp() {
        return new Date(timestamp.getTime());
    }

    public String getMessage() {
        return message;
    }
}}
```

All fields are final and contain stable data structures.

It is good practice to declare the parameters final, too.

Ensures that the timestamp cannot be changed by other code

Getters but no setters

Java does not make everything immutable by default, but liberal use of the `final` keyword is helpful. In Scala, case classes provide immutability by default as well as additional, very convenient features such as correct equality and hash-code functions:

```
import java.util.Date

case class Message(timestamp: Date, message: String)
```

> **Even with case classes, you must take care that the fields hold immutable data structures—using the Date's setters will break this.**

3.2.2   *Referential transparency*

An expression is said to be *referentially transparent* if replacing it with a single value (a constant) has no impact on the execution of the program.[4] So, evaluating a referentially transparent expression—that is, performing an operation on some data—has no impact on that data, and no side effects can occur. For example, the act of adding, removing, or updating a value in an immutable list results in a new list being created with the changed values; any part of the program still observing the original list sees no change.

Consider Java's `java.lang.StringBuffer` class. If you call the `reverse` method on a `StringBuffer`, you will get a reference to a `StringBuffer` with the values reversed. But the original `StringBuffer` reference refers to the same instance and therefore now also has changed its value:

```
final StringBuffer original = new StringBuffer("foo");
final StringBuffer reversed = myStringBuffer.reverse();
System.out.println(String.format(
    "original '%s', new value '%s'",
    original,
    reversed));              ◁──  Result: original 'oof', new value 'oof'
```

This is an example of *referential opacity:* the value of the expression `myStringBuffer.reverse()` changes when it is evaluated. It cannot be replaced by its result without altering the way the program executes. The `java.lang.StringBuilder` class has the same problem.

Note, however, that a function call can be referentially transparent even if the function modifies internal state, as long as the function call can be replaced with its result without affecting the program's output. For example, if an operation is likely to be performed multiple times, internally caching the result the first time can speed up execution without violating referential transparency. An example of this approach is shown in the next listing.

---

[4] http://en.wikipedia.org/wiki/Referential_transparency_(computer_science)

Listing 3.3 Referential transparency: allowing substitution of precomputed values

```
public class Rooter {
    private final double value;              Mutable field for caching
    private Double root = null;      <──┐    a computed value

    public Rooter(double value) {
        this.value = value;
    }

    public double getValue() {
        return value;
    }

    public double getRoot() {
        if (root == null) {
            root = Math.sqrt(value);
        }                                     Mutability is never
        return root;                 <──┐     observable outside.
    }
}
```

3.2.3 Side effects

Side effects are actions that break the referential transparency of later method calls by changing their environment such that the same inputs now lead to different results. Examples are modifying some system property, writing log output to the console, and sending data over a network. *Pure* functions have no side effects. Some functional programming languages such as Haskell enforce rules about where side effects can exist and when they can take place—a great help when reasoning about the correctness of code.

Side effects matter because they limit how an object can be used. Consider the following class.

Listing 3.4 Limiting usability with side effects

```
import java.io.Serializable;

public class SideEffecting implements Serializable, Cloneable {

    private int count;

    public SideEffecting(int start) {
        this.count = start;
    }

    public int next() {
        this.count += Math.incrementExact(this.count);
        return this.count;
    }
}
```

Every call to next() will return a different value. Consequently, the result of something like the example in listing 3.5 can give you a very unpleasant experience:

```
final int next = se.next();
if (logger.isDebugEnabled()) {
    logger.debug("Next is " ++ se.next());    ◁─┐ Probably meant to
}                                                  reference the variable!
return next;
```

Even worse, something like new SideEffecting(Integer.MAX_VALUE - 2) will cause the side effect after a few calls to become an ArithmeticException.

Sometimes side effects are more subtle. Suppose the object needs to be passed remotely. If it is immutable and without side effects, it can be serialized and reconstituted on the remote system, which then will have its own identical and unchanging copy. If there are side effects, the two copies will diverge from each other. This is especially problematic when the original system was not envisioned to have distributed operations. You may blithely assume that updates are being applied to the one and only instance of an object, without realizing the trouble that will cause when scalability requirements lead to copies of the object being kept on multiple servers.

3.2.4 *Functions as first-class citizens*

In a language where functions are first-class citizens, a function is a value just like an Integer or a String and can be passed as an argument to another function or method. The idea of doing so is to make code more composable: a function that takes a function as an argument can compose the calculation performed by its argument with calculations of its own, as illustrated by the call to .map in the following snippet:

```
final List<Integer> numbers = Arrays.asList(1, 2, 3);
final List<Integer> numbersPlusOne =
    numbers.stream()                      ┌ Passes a function that
        .map(number -> number + 1)    ◁─┘ increments its argument by 1
        .collect(Collectors.toList());
```

Many languages that are otherwise not supportive of functional programming have functions as first-class citizens, including JavaScript and Java 8. In the previous example, the function passed as an argument is a *lambda expression*. It has no name and exists only within the context of its call site. Languages that support functions as first-class citizens also allow you to assign this function to a named variable as a *function value* and then refer to it from wherever you see fit. In Python, you could do this like so:

```
>>> def addOne(x):
...     return x + 1
...
>>> myFunction = addOne
>>> myFunction(3)
4
```

3.3 *Responsiveness to users*

Beyond functional programming, to build Reactive applications you also need to use tools that give you responsiveness. This is not responsive web design,[5] as it is known in the user-experience world, where a front end is said to be "responsive" if it resizes itself appropriately for the user's viewing device. Responsiveness in Reactive applications means being able to quickly respond to user requests in the face of failure that can occur anywhere inside or outside the application. The performance trade-offs of Reactive applications are defined by the axiom that you can choose any two of the following three characteristics:

- High throughput
- Low latency, but also smooth and not jittery
- Small footprint

These will all be defined further along in this section.

3.3.1 *Prioritizing the three performance characteristics*

When you make architecture choices for a Reactive application, you are in essence giving priority to two of those three characteristics and choosing to sacrifice the remaining characteristic where necessary. This is not a law or theorem, but more of a guiding principle that is likely to be true in most cases. To get a very fast application with smooth, low latency, you typically have to give it more resources (footprint). An example of this is a high-performance messaging library written in Java, known as the *Disruptor* (http://lmax-exchange.github.io/disruptor). To get its tremendous throughput and smooth latency, the Disruptor has to preallocate all the memory it will ever use for its internal ring buffer, in order to prevent allocations at runtime that could lead to stop-the-world garbage collections and compaction pauses in the Java virtual machine. The Disruptor gains throughput by pinning itself to a specific execution core, thereby avoiding the cost of context switches[6] between threads being swapped in and out on that core. This is another aspect of application footprint: there is now one fewer execution core available for use by other threads on that computer.

The Storm framework (https://github.com/nathanmarz/storm), created by Nathan Marz and released in 2011 to much acclaim, provides capabilities for distributed processing of streaming data. Storm was created at Marz's startup, BackType, which was purchased by Twitter and became the basis for its real-time analytics applications. But the implementation was not particularly fast, because it was built using Clojure and pure functional programming constructs. When Marz released version 0.7 in 2012, he used the Disruptor to increase throughput by as much as three times, at the cost of footprint. This trade-off matters to those who choose to deploy an application that uses Storm, particularly in the cloud, where one core on the VM must be

---

[5] http://en.wikipedia.org/wiki/Responsive_web_design
[6] http://en.wikipedia.org/wiki/Context_switch

devoted solely to the Disruptor to maintain its speed. Note that the number of cores available to an application in a virtual environment is not an absolute value. As Doug Lea,[7] the author of many concurrency libraries on the JVM, such as the ForkJoinPool and CompletableFuture, has said, "Ask your hypervisor how much memory you have, or how many cores you have. It'll lie. Every time. It's designed to lie. You paid them money so it would lie."[8] Developers have to take these variables into account when considering footprint in a cloud deployment.

Some platforms have constraints that limit their ability to make these trade-offs. For example, a mobile application typically cannot give up footprint to increase throughput and make latency smoother, because a mobile platform typically has very limited resources. Imagine the cost of pinning a core on a mobile phone, both in terms of reduced resource availability for other applications and the phone's operating system. A mobile phone has limited memory as well as constraints on power usage: you don't want to drain the battery so quickly that no one would want to use your application. So, mobile applications typically attempt to minimize footprint while increasing throughput at the expense of latency, because users are more willing to accept latency on a mobile platform. Anyone who has used an application from a phone has experienced slowness due to network issues or packet loss.

3.4 *Existing support for Reactive design*

Now that we have reviewed the basic concepts needed to understand and evaluate tools and language constructs for implementing Reactive design, it is time to look at the leading examples. Many languages have innovated in the area of dividing work and making it asynchronous.

For each concept or implementation described in this section, we will provide an evaluation of how well it meets the tenets of the Reactive Manifesto. Note that although all are asynchronous and nonblocking in and of themselves, it is still up to you to ensure that the code you write remains asynchronous and nonblocking as well, in order to remain Reactive.

3.4.1 *Green threads*

Some languages do not include built-in constructs for running multiple threads within the same operating system process. In these cases, it is still possible to implement asynchronous behavior via *green threads:* threads scheduled by the user process rather than the operating system.[9]

Green threads can be very efficient but are restricted to a single physical machine. It is impossible, without the aid of delimited portable continuations,[10] to share the

---

[7] http://en.wikipedia.org/wiki/Doug_Lea

[8] Doug Lea, "Engineering Concurrent Library Components" (talk, Emerging Technologies Conference, 2013), http://chariotsolutions.com/screencast/phillyete-screencast-7-doug-lea-engineering-concurrent-library-components.

[9] http://en.wikipedia.org/wiki/Green_threads

[10] http://en.wikipedia.org/wiki/Delimited_continuation

processing of a thread across multiple physical machines. Delimited portable continuations allow you to mark points in logic where the execution stack can be wrapped up and exported either locally or to another machine. These continuations can then be treated as functions. This is a powerful idea, implemented in a Scheme library called Termite (https://code.google.com/p/termite). But green threads and continuations do not provide for resilience, because there is currently no way to supervise their execution; they are therefore lacking with respect to fault tolerance.

Waldo et al. note[11] that it is not a good idea to try to make logic that executes in a distributed context appear to be local. This postulate applies to green threads as well. If we take "local" to mean local to the thread, and "distributed/remote" to mean on another thread and thus asynchronous, you would not want "distributed/remote" to appear "local" because this would obscure the difference between synchronous and asynchronous operations. It would be hard to tell which operations can block the program's progress and which cannot!

REACTIVE EVALUATION OF GREEN THREADS

Green threads are asynchronous and nonblocking, but they do not support message passing. They do not scale up to use multiple cores on a machine by themselves, although if the runtime supports it, it is possible to have more than one in a process, or multiple processes can be run. They do not scale outward across nodes in a network. They also do not provide any mechanisms for fault tolerance, so it is up to developers who use them to write their own constructs to handle any failure that may occur.

3.4.2 *Event loops*

When a language or platform does not support multiple threads in one process, you can still get asynchronous behavior by making green threads that share an event loop. This loop provides a mechanism for sharing a single execution thread among several logical threads at the same time. The idea is that although only a single thread can execute at a given moment, the application should not block on any operation and should instead make each thread yield until such time as the external work it needs, such as calling a data store, is completed. At that time, the application can invoke a callback to perform a predefined behavior. This is very powerful: Node.js (http://nodejs.org), for example, uses a single-threaded JavaScript runtime to perform considerably more work because it doesn't have to wait for every operation to complete before handling other work.

Event loops are most typically implemented with callbacks. This would be okay if only a single callback could be referenced at a time, but as an application's functionality grows, this typically is not the case. The terms *callback hell* and *pyramid of doom* have been coined to represent the interwoven spaghetti code that often results from popular tools like Node.js. Furthermore, event loops based on a single-threaded process are viable

---

[11] Jim Waldo, Geoff Wyant, Ann Wollrath, Sam Kendall: "A Note on Distributed Computing," Sun Microsystems Laboratories, 1994, http://citeseerx.ist.psu.edu/viewdoc/summary?doi=10.1.1.41.7628.

only for uses that are I/O-bound or when the use case is specific to handling input and output. Trying to use an event loop for CPU-bound operations will defeat the advantage of this approach.

Here is a simple example of a Node.js application. Note that running this server and using Google's Chrome browser to send requests to the address 127.0.0.1:8888 may result in a doubling of the counter value on each request. Chrome has a known issue with sending an additional request for favicon.ico with every request:[12]

```
var http = require('http');                       Sets up the server, with a
var counter = 0;                                  callback function applied to
                                                  respond to each request
http.createServer(function (req, res) {      ◄─┘
  counter += 1;
  res.writeHead(200, {'Content-Type': 'text/plain'});      Informs the user
  res.end('Response: ' + counter + ' via callback\n');     where the server
}).listen(8888, '127.0.0.1');                                is reachable

console.log('Server up on 127.0.0.1:8888, send requests!');    ◄─
```

REACTIVE EVALUATION OF EVENT LOOPS

The suitability of an event loop for a Reactive application depends on the implementation. As deployed via Node.js in JavaScript, event loops are similar to green threads in that they are asynchronous and nonblocking but do not support message passing. They do not scale up to use multiple cores on a machine by themselves, although if the runtime supports it, it is possible to have more than one in a process, or multiple processes can be run. They do not scale outward across nodes in a network. They also do not provide any mechanisms for fault tolerance, so it is up to developers to write their own constructs to handle any failure that may occur.

But there are alternative implementations, such as Vert.x (http://vertx.io), which runs on the JVM and has a feel similar to Node.js but supports multiple languages. Vert.x is a compelling solution because it provides a distributed approach to the event-loop model, using a distributed event bus to push messages between nodes. In a JVM deployment, it does not need to use green threads because it can use a pool of threads for multiple purposes. In this respect, Vert.x is asynchronous and nonblocking and does support message passing. It also scales up to use multiple cores, as well as scales out to use multiple nodes in a network. Vert.x does not have a supervision strategy for fault tolerance, but it is an excellent alternative to an event loop, particularly because it supports JavaScript just as Node.js does.

3.4.3 *Communicating Sequential Processes*

Communicating Sequential Processes (CSP) is a mathematical abstraction of multiple processes, or threads in a single process, that communicate via message passing.[13] You

---

[12] Chrome issue report: https://code.google.com/p/chromium/issues/detail?id=39402.

[13] C.A.R. Hoare, "Communicating Sequential Processes," *Communications of the ACM* 21, no. 8 (1978): 666–677.

can define work to be performed concurrently in separate processes or threads, which then pass messages between them to share information.

What makes CSP unique is that the two processes or threads do not have to know anything about one another, so they are nicely decoupled from the standpoint of sender and receiver but still coupled with respect to the value being passed. Rather than assuming that messages accumulate in queues until read, CSP uses *rendezvous messaging*: for a message to be passed, the sender and receiver must reach a point where the sender is ready to send and the receiver is ready to receive. Consequently, receipt of a message always synchronizes both processes. This is fundamentally different from Actors, which will be discussed in section 3.4.6. This also limits the two processes or threads in how distributed they can be, depending on how CSP is implemented. For example, CSP on the JVM as implemented by Clojure's core.async library cannot be distributed across multiple JVM instances, even on the same machine. Neither can Go's channels, also known as *goroutines*.

Because CSP is defined formally and mathematically, it is theoretically *provable* whether a deadlock can or cannot occur inside of it, via a method called *process analysis*. Being able to statically verify the correctness of concurrency logic is a powerful idea. Note, however, that neither Clojure's core.async nor Go's channels have this capability; but if it is practical to implement, it would be very useful.

Because no process or thread in a CSP-based application has to know about another, there is a form of location transparency: to write the code for one process or thread, you do not need to know about any other process or thread with which it will communicate. But the most popular implementations of CSP to date do not support communication between different nodes on a network, so they cannot support true location transparency. They also have difficulties with fault tolerance, because failure between two processes or threads cannot be managed easily. Instead, the logic in each process or thread must have the ability to manage any failure that could occur when communicating with the other side. Another potential downside is that nontrivial use of CSP can be difficult to reason about, because every process/thread can potentially interact with every other process/thread at each step.

Here is a simple example of two communicating processes in Go. Interestingly, a Go function can create a channel and put values onto it as well as consume them, in effect stashing values off to the side for use later. In this example, one function produces messages and puts them onto the channel, and a second function consumes them:

```
package main

import (
    "fmt"
    "time"
)

func main() {
    iterations := 10
    myChannel := make(chan int)
```

Imports required language libraries

Creates a communication channel for integer values

```
        go producer(myChannel, iterations)          Starts asynchronous execution
        go consumer(myChannel, iterations)          of producer and consumer

        time.Sleep(500 * time.Millisecond)
}

func producer(myChannel chan int, iterations int) {
    for i := 1; i <= iterations; i++ {
        fmt.Println("Sending: ", i)
        myChannel <- i                    <--- Sends a message to the channel
    }
}

func consumer(myChannel chan int, iterations int) {
    for i := 1; i <= iterations; i++ {
        recVal := <-myChannel             <--- Receives a message from the channel
        fmt.Println("Received: ", recVal)
    }
}
```

REACTIVE EVALUATION OF CSP

CSP is asynchronous and nonblocking and supports message passing in rendezvous fashion. It scales up to use multiple cores on a machine, but none of the current implementations scale outward across nodes. CSP does not provide any mechanisms for fault tolerance, so it is up to developers to write their own constructs to handle any failure that may occur.

3.4.4   *Futures and promises*

A Future is a read-only handle to a value or failure that may become available at some point in time; a Promise is the corresponding write-once handle that allows the value to be provided. Note that these definitions are not universally established; the terminology chosen here is that used in C++, Java, and Scala.[14] A function that returns its result asynchronously constructs a Promise, sets the asynchronous processing in motion, installs a completion callback that will eventually fulfill the Promise, and returns the Future associated with the Promise to the caller. The caller can then attach code to the Future, such as callbacks or transformations, to be executed when the Future's value is provided. Normally, a function that returns a Future does not expose the underlying Promise to its caller.

All Future implementations provide a mechanism to turn a code block—for example, a lambda expression—into a Future such that the code is dispatched to run on a different thread, and its return value fulfills the Future's Promise when it becomes available. Futures therefore provide a simple way to make code asynchronous and implement parallelism. Futures return either the result of their successful evaluation or a representation of whatever error may have occurred during evaluation.

---

[14] See https://en.wikipedia.org/wiki/Futures_and_promises for an overview.

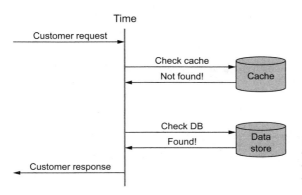

Figure 3.2 Sequential lookup: first, check the cache; then, if the data are not found, retrieve them from the database.

We turn now to an elegant example of Futures in practice: retrieval of data from multiple sources, where you prefer to access sources in parallel (simultaneously) rather than sequentially. Imagine a service that needs to return customer information that may be stored in a database somewhere far away but may also be cached in a store that is closer for performance reasons. To retrieve the data, the program should check the cache first to see whether it has the data needed to avoid an expensive database lookup. If there is a cache miss—if the information is not found—the program must look it up in the database.

In a sequential lookup shown in figure 3.2, the calling thread tries to retrieve the data from the cache first. If the cache lookup fails, it then makes a call to the database and returns its response—at the cost of two lookups that took place one after the other. In a parallel lookup shown in figure 3.3, the calling thread sends requests to the cache and the database simultaneously. If the cache responds with a found customer record first, the response is sent back to the client immediately. When the database responds later with the same record, it is ignored. But if the cache lookup fails, the calling thread doesn't have to make a subsequent database call, because that has already been done. When the database responds, the response is sent to the client right away, theoretically sooner than if the client had made sequential calls.

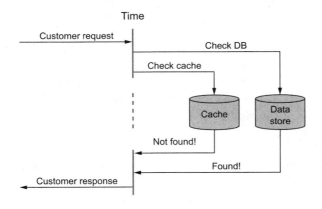

Figure 3.3 Parallel lookup: send requests to the cache and the database simultaneously; the result is the first value returned.

The code for parallel lookup may look similar to the following listing, written in Java 8 to exploit its nonblocking `CompletableFuture` class.

> **Listing 3.5   Retrieving the result from the faster source**

```
public class ParallelRetrievalExample {
    final CacheRetriever cacheRetriever;
    final DBRetriever dbRetriever;

    ParallelRetrievalExample(CacheRetriever cacheRetriever,
                             DBRetriever dbRetriever) {
        this.cacheRetriever = cacheRetriever;
        this.dbRetriever = dbRetriever;
    }

    public Object retrieveCustomer(final long id) {
        final CompletableFuture<Object> cacheFuture =
            CompletableFuture.supplyAsync(() -> {
                    return cacheRetriever.getCustomer(id);
                });
        final CompletableFuture<Object> dbFuture =
            CompletableFuture.supplyAsync(() -> {
                    return dbRetriever.getCustomer(id);
                });

        return CompletableFuture.anyOf(
            cacheFuture, dbFuture);
    }
}
```

Performing these two operations sequentially would be expensive, and there is rarely an opportunity to cache data beforehand without knowing what a client will ask for next. Futures provide a handy way to perform both operations in parallel. Using Futures, you can easily create two tasks to search the cache and the database virtually simultaneously, letting whichever task completes first provide the response to the client.

Concurrent lookup thus marshals more resources (footprint) to reduce time from request to response (latency). But concurrent lookups fail when neither the cache lookup nor the database lookup returns soon enough to meet the nonfunctional requirements of the client. So, to be Reactive, any Future implementation must have a timeout mechanism to enable the service to communicate to a client that an operation is taking too long, and that the client will either need to make another attempt to request the data or communicate upstream that there is a failure taking place within the system. Without timeouts, the application cannot be responsive to a user about what is happening and allow the user to decide what to do about it.

Futures are not nonblocking by definition and can vary by implementation. For example, Java prior to version 8 had a Future implementation, but there was no way to get the value out of the Future without blocking in some fashion. You could write a loop that calls the `isDone()` method on one or more Future instances to see if they were completed, or you could call the `get()` method, which would block until the Future failed or completed successfully. Check that the Future implementation in the version of the language you are using is nonblocking; if it is not, consider alternatives without this shortcoming.

Similar to event loops, Futures can be implemented with callbacks, allowing you to predefine logic to be applied upon the completion of the Future. But, as with Node.js, callbacks can quickly turn ugly when more than one is applied at a time. Some languages that support functional programming allow you to map over a Future: this defines behavior that occurs only when the Future successfully completes, but not if it fails. By means of higher-order functions[15] such as map, these languages frequently give you the ability to compose behavior that depends on successful completion of many Futures into simple, elegant logic using syntactic sugar such as a for- or list-comprehension.[16] This is particularly useful when staging results from multiple Futures into a single result, as in the next example.

Listing 3.6 Aggregating a single result from two futures in Scala

```
def getProductInventoryByPostalCode(
        productSku: Long,
        postalCode: String):
        Future[(Long, Map[Long, Long])] = {                    The thread pool on
                                                               which the Futures
                                                               will be executed
    implicit val ec = ExecutionContext.fromExecutor(new ForkJoinPool())   ⟵

    val localInventoryFuture = Future {              ⟵    Creates both Futures
      inventoryService.currentInventoryInWarehouse(        up front to start the
        productSku, postalCode)                            queries in parallel
    }
    val overallInventoryFutureByWarehouse = Future {
      inventoryService.currentInventoryOverallByWarehouse(
        productSku)
    }
                                                     A for-comprehension in Scala:
                                                     equivalent to nested function
    for {                                            calls to flatMap and map
      local <- localInventoryFuture              ⟵
      overall <- overallInventoryFutureByWarehouse
    } yield (local, overall)              ⟵── Returns the combined result
}
```

Multiple Futures can "race" to fulfill a single Promise, where the first Future to complete supplies the Promise's value. Because a Promise's value can be written only once, you can be sure the Future that gets its value *from* that Promise will not change its value even if other asynchronous tasks, completing later, try to rewrite it. Listing 3.6 demonstrates this technique with the .anyOf method of CompletableFuture: it returns whichever Future finishes first. Notice that this Future's value is not defined by a code block within retrieveCustomer: a Promise can be fulfilled with a value provided by any event—even synchronously, if it is already available.

---

[15] http://en.wikipedia.org/wiki/Higher-order_function
[16] http://en.wikipedia.org/wiki/List_comprehension

Some languages provide higher-level tools built on Futures and Promises, such as first-class continuations and Dataflow. The beauty of these constructs is that they let you write code that appears synchronous but is actually compiled into Futures. This is possible because order can be maintained: each block of code can only be executed after all code that it depends on has been evaluated. Despite the asynchronous nature of Dataflow code, the logic is still deterministic (as long as it is free of side effects, as explained in section 3.2.3). So, each time it is executed, it will behave the same way. If an application were to enter a deadlock state in Dataflow code one time, it would have to do so every time, because the evaluation order is always the same. An example of this is the async-await construct in C# and Scala:

```
val resultFuture = async {                                    Starts asynchronous retrieval
  val localInventoryFuture = async {          ←
    inventoryService.currentInventoryInWarehouse(productSku, postalCode)
  }
  val overallInventoryFutureByWarehouse = async {
    inventoryService.currentInventoryOverallByWarehouse(productSku)
  }
  (await(localInventoryFuture), await(overallInventoryFutureByWarehouse))  ←
}
```

Starts another asynchronous retrieval

Suspends until both retrievals are done and then provides a combined result

This code snippet shows an alternative way to implement the same functionality as the for-comprehension syntax near the end of listing 3.6.

There is an emerging concept of a *safe* Future, where methods that can be executed concurrently are annotated or marked in some way, merely giving the runtime the option to optimize them for parallelization where no data is shared. This is a compelling idea, but it is still subject to errors, such as when someone accidentally exposes data to other methods in a method marked as safe. Also, it provides no oversight for failure. Futures in general are a very narrow abstraction: they allow you to define a single operation that will take place off-thread one time and needs to be treated as a single unit of work. They do not handle resilience particularly well: you have to use Future implementations that communicate what went wrong when failure occurs on their execution thread.

REACTIVE EVALUATION OF FUTURES AND PROMISES

Futures and Promises are asynchronous and nonblocking, but they do not support message passing. They do scale up to use multiple cores on one machine. Current implementations do not scale outward across nodes in a network. They do provide mechanisms for fault tolerance when a single Future fails, and some implementations aggregate failure across multiple Futures such that if one fails, all fail.

3.4.5   *Reactive Extensions*

Reactive Extensions (Rx, https://rx.codeplex.com) is a library that originated in the .NET world; it was originally devised and built by Erik Meijer and his team at Microsoft, and it was ported to the JVM in a library called RxJava (http://github.com/ReactiveX /RxJava).[17] Recently this type of API has also seen widespread uptake among Java-Script frameworks like React.js and Cycle.js. It combines two control-flow patterns: Iterable and Observer.[18] Both patterns involve somehow handling a potentially unknown number of items or events. With an Iterable, you write a loop to get each item individually and perform work on it—synchronously and always in control of when the work is to occur. With an Observer, you register a callback to be invoked each time a certain asynchronous event occurs.

The combined construct in Rx is called an Observable. With an Observable, you write a looping construct that reacts to events that occur elsewhere. This is similar to *streaming* semantics, where data are endlessly iterated over as they arrive for processing. The library includes extensions for composing functions using standard operators such as filter and accumulate, and even operators for performing time-sensitive functions based on when events occur. Whereas Futures asynchronously return a single value, Observables are abstractions over streams of data that can be handled in groups. Observables can also tell a consumer when they are finished, much like an Iterator.

The design goal of Rx is not to cover all angles of a Reactive system with one abstraction. It focuses only on passing data in a Reactive fashion through the internal processing steps of a single component in a Reactive system. So, its failure-handling model is restricted to propagating errors downstream (in the same direction as the flow of data) and sending cancellation requests upstream, leaving the treatment of failures to external components. RxJava contains the necessary utilities for back pressure propagation across asynchronous boundaries.[19] This enables it to distribute processing across multiple threads, achieving vertical scalability by utilizing several CPU cores. Failure handling and load management must be delegated to systems like Netflix's Hystrix.

Observables are defined in relation to a source of some kind: a collection, a network socket, and so on. A subscriber provides the handler functions that tell what to do when a chunk of data is ready to be processed or when an error occurs. An RxJava Observable to handle streams could look like this:

```
import rx.Observable;

public class RxJavaExample {
    public void observe(String[] strings) {
        Observable.from(strings).subscribe((s) -> {
            System.out.println("Received " + s);
```

---

[17] See also ReactiveX (http://reactivex.io).

[18] http://en.wikipedia.org/wiki/Observer_pattern

[19] As defined by the Reactive Streams specification: see http://reactive-streams.org.

```
        });
    }
}
```

A driver that produces the events consumed by that Observable might look like this:

```
package org.reactivedesignpatterns.chapter3.rxjava;

public class RxJavaExampleDriver {
    final RxJavaExample rxJavaExample = new RxJavaExample();

    public static void main(String[] args) {
        String[] strings = { "a", "b", "c" };
        rxJavaExample.observe(strings);
    }
}
```

REACTIVE EVALUATION OF REACTIVE EXTENSIONS

Rx provides facilities to process streams of data in an asynchronous and nonblocking fashion. The current implementations scale up to use multiple cores on a machine but not outward across nodes in a network. Rx does not provide a mechanism for delegating failure handling, but it does include provisions to reliably tear down a failed stream-processing pipeline via dedicated termination signals. RxJava in particular is a useful building block for implementing components of a Reactive system.

3.4.6   *The Actor model*

The Actor model, first introduced by Carl Hewitt in 1973, is a model of concurrent computation in which all communication occurs between entities called *Actors*, via message passing on the sending side and mailbox queues on the receiving side.[20] The Erlang programming language, one of the earliest to support Reactive application development, uses Actors as its primary architectural construct. With the success of the Akka toolkit on the JVM, Actors have had a surge in popularity of late.

INHERENTLY ASYNCHRONOUS

The definition of Reactive states that interactions should be message-driven, asynchronous, and nonblocking. Actors meet all three of these criteria. Therefore, you do not have to do anything extra to make program logic asynchronous besides creating multiple Actors and passing messages between them. You need only avoid using blocking primitives for synchronization or communication within Actors, because these would negate the benefits of the Actor model.

FAULT TOLERANCE VIA SUPERVISION

Most implementations of Actors support organization into supervisor hierarchies to manage failure at varying levels of importance. When an exception occurs inside an Actor, that Actor instance may be resumed, restarted, or stopped, even though the

---

[20] Carl Hewitt, Peter Bishop, and Richard Steiger, "A Universal Modular ACTOR Formalism for Artificial Intelligence," *Proceedings of the 3rd International Joint Conference on Artificial Intelligence* (1973).

failure occurred on a different asynchronous thread. Erlang's Open Telecom Platform (OTP, https://github.com/erlang/otp) defines a pattern for building supervision hierarchies for Actors, allowing a parent Actor to manage failure for all children below it, possibly elevating some failures to an appropriate "grandparent" Actor.

This approach makes failure handling part of the application's domain, just like classes that represent application-specific data. When designing an Actor application, you should take the time to think of all the ways the application could fail at all levels of the supervisor hierarchy, and what each level should do about each kind of failure. You should also consider how to handle failures that you cannot foresee, and allow the application to respond to those as well. Even though you cannot anticipate the precise cause of every failure, you can always safely assume that the component that failed is now in an invalid state and needs to be discarded. This principle, called *let it crash*, enables people to design thoughtful responses to failure scenarios beyond those they can think of in advance. Without a supervision hierarchy, this kind of resilience would not be feasible; at best you would have failure-handling code strewn about the logic of the application. All of the aforementioned fault-tolerance patterns are described in detail in chapter 12.

LOCATION TRANSPARENCY

Erlang and Akka provide proxies through which all Actor interactions must take place: a PID in Erlang and an ActorRef in Akka. So, an individual Actor does not need to know the physical location of the Actor to which it is sending a message—a feature called *location transparency*, treated at length in chapter 5. This makes message-sending code more declarative, because all the physical "how-to" details of how the message is actually sent are dealt with behind the scenes. Location transparency enables you to add even such sophisticated features as starting a new Actor and rerouting all messages to it if a receiving Actor goes down mid-conversation, without anyone needing to alter the message-sending code.

A drawback of the Actor model is that producers and consumers of messages are coupled to one another: the sender of a message must have a reference to the Actor instance that it wants to send to. This reference is just as necessary as a recipient address on a letter, without which the mail service would not know where to deliver it. An Actor reference is much like a postal address in that it only tells where to transport messages, not what the recipient looks like or what state they are in. A benefit of this approach is that each Actor is somewhat decoupled from failures occurring in another, because Actors have no access to each other except through these references. A supervising Actor responsible for handling failures is also protected by this isolating layer of message passing.

NO CONCURRENCY WITHIN ONE ACTOR

Because each Actor contains only a single thread of execution within itself, and no thread can call into an Actor directly, there is no concurrency within an Actor instance unless you intentionally introduce it by other means. Therefore, Actors can encapsulate mutable state and not worry about requiring locks to limit simultaneous access to variables.

This greatly simplifies the logic inside Actors, but it does come at some cost. Actors can be implemented in two ways: as heavyweight, thread-based Actors, each with a dedicated thread assigned to it; or as lightweight, event-driven Actors that share a thread pool and therefore consume less memory. Regardless of the implementation, some concept of *fairness* has to be introduced, where you define how many messages an Actor will handle before yielding the CPU. This must be done to prevent *starvation*: no one Actor should use a thread and/or CPU core so long that other Actors cannot do their own work. Even if a thread-based Actor is not sharing its thread with other Actors, it is most likely sharing execution cores at the hardware level.

DIFFERENCES BETWEEN ERLANG AND AKKA

Given the two prevalent Actor libraries in existence, Erlang and Akka, how do you choose which is more appropriate for a given application? This boils down to the application's requirements and the platforms on which implementations of Erlang and Akka are available.

In the case of Erlang, the BEAM VM allows each Actor to be implemented as a distinct and isolated process. This is a fundamental reason for the remarkable fault tolerance of Erlang applications.

Erlang Actors use a pattern called *Selective Receive*, where an Actor receives a message and determines whether it is able to handle that message at that time. If the Actor cannot handle the message right then, it puts the message aside for the time being and proceeds to the next message. This continues until the Actor receives a message that its current receive block can handle, at which time it processes that message and then attempts to retry all messages that were put aside. This is, in effect, a memory leak, because if those messages are never handled, they continue to be set aside and reviewed after every successfully handled message. Fortunately, because the processes in the BEAM VM are isolated, a single Actor's process can fail for exceeding its available memory without bringing down the entire virtual machine.

On the JVM, there is no such luxury. An exact port of Erlang and OTP on the JVM with Selective Receive would be a memory leak that would eventually, given enough time, take down the entire JVM with an `OutOfMemoryError`, because all Actors share the same heap. For this reason, Akka Actors have the ability to *stash* messages on demand, not automatically. They also provide programmatic means to unstash and replay those messages at leisure.

Listing 3.7 shows an example of an Akka Actor application with fault tolerance built in. A parent Actor supervises two child Actors, which send a counter value back and forth to each other, incrementing it each time. When a child receives a value exceeding 1,000, it throws a `CounterTooLargeException`, causing the supervising parent to restart the children, thus resetting their counters.

Listing 3.7 An Actor example in Akka

```scala
package org.reactivedesignpatterns.chapter3.actor

import akka.actor.{Actor, ActorLogging, Props, ActorSystem, OneForOneStrategy}
import akka.actor.SupervisorStrategy.Restart
import akka.event.LoggingReceive

case object Start
case class CounterMessage(counterValue: Int)
case class CounterTooLargeException(
  message: String) extends Exception(message)

class SupervisorActor extends Actor with ActorLogging {
  override val supervisorStrategy = OneForOneStrategy() {
    case _: CounterTooLargeException => Restart
  }

  val actor2 = context.actorOf(
                 Props[SecondActor], "second-actor")
  val actor1 = context.actorOf(
                 Props(new FirstActor(actor2)),
                 "first-actor")

  def receive = {
    case Start => actor1 ! Start
  }
}

class AbstractCounterActor extends Actor with ActorLogging {
  var counterValue = 0

  def receive = {
    case _ =>
  }

  def counterReceive: Receive = LoggingReceive {
    case CounterMessage(i) if i <= 1000 =>
      counterValue = i
      log.info(s"Counter value: $counterValue")
      sender ! CounterMessage(counterValue + 1)
    case CounterMessage(i) =>
      throw new CounterTooLargeException(
        "Exceeded max value of counter!")
  }

  override def postRestart(reason: Throwable) = {
    context.parent ! Start
  }
}

class FirstActor(secondActor: ActorRef) extends
  AbstractCounterActor {
  override def receive = LoggingReceive {
    case Start =>
      context.become(counterReceive)
      log.info("Starting counter passing.")
      secondActor ! CounterMessage(counterValue + 1)
  }
}
```

```
class SecondActor() extends AbstractCounterActor {
  override def receive = counterReceive
}

object Example extends App {
  val system = ActorSystem("counter-supervision-example")
  val supervisor = system.actorOf(Props[SupervisorActor])
  supervisor ! Start
}
```

COMBINING ACTORS WITH OTHER CONSTRUCTS

The location transparency and supervision features of Actors make them a suitable choice to build the distributed foundation of a Reactive application. But within the context of a larger application, local orchestration often does not require the location transparency, supervision, and resiliency of the complete Actor system. In those cases, you will typically combine Actors with more lightweight Reactive constructs such as Futures or Observables, depending on the API offered by libraries or other parts of the system. Those choices sacrifice the full Actor characteristics in exchange for lower memory cost and invocation overhead.

In those cases, is it important to remember the differences. Actors are explicit about their message passing. Spawning and composing Futures from within an Actor may lure you into accessing or modifying the Actor's state from within a Future's execution context. That breaks the single-threaded model and leads to concurrency bugs that can be difficult to detect. Even when the state is carefully kept separate, you will need to think about which thread pool executes the Futures' callbacks or the Observables' combinators.

REACTIVE EVALUATION OF ACTORS

Actors are asynchronous and nonblocking, and support message passing. They scale up to use multiple cores on one machine, and they scale outward across nodes in both the Erlang and Akka implementations. They provide supervision mechanisms, as well, in support of fault tolerance. They meet all the requirements for building Reactive applications. This does not mean Actors should be used for every purpose when building an application, but they can easily be used as a backbone, providing architectural support to services that use other Reactive technologies.

3.4.7   *Summary*

We have now reviewed the essential concepts and constructs required to build Reactive applications, providing fault tolerance and scalability to help you be responsive to your users. In the following chapters, we will delve into the Reactive philosophy and discuss how these and other concepts relate to it. At this point, you should have a clear understanding of the following:

- The costs of building an application that is not Reactive
- What functional programming is and how it relates to Reactive applications

- The trade-offs involved in choosing between high throughput, low/smooth latency, and small footprint
- Pros and cons of all application toolkits that support the Reactive model
- How the Actor model simultaneously addresses both fault tolerance and scalability

Part 2

The philosophy in a nutshell

Part 1 took a comprehensive look at what it means for a system to be Reactive. You saw how the requirement to always react to user input entails resilience and scalability in order to retain responsiveness even during failures and varying load conditions. Throughout our exploration of these desirable properties, you encountered the need for the underlying implementation to be message-driven.

Part 2 complements the description of the four Reactive traits: it presents a set of building blocks from which a Reactive architecture can be constructed. Where part 1 described what we want to achieve and why, this part focuses on how to do it. The guiding principles developed here, together with the tools of the trade introduced in chapter 3, form the foundation on which the patterns in part 3 are built.

We decided to present the material in a contiguous, cohesive fashion so that it can serve as a compact reference when you are gauging the design of your own patterns that you develop as you build Reactive applications. As a 360-degree view of a fully reactive architecture, this part covers a lot of ground. You may want to read chapter 4 and then skim the rest of this part, returning to it after you have studied the corresponding patterns in part 3 of this book.

In this part, you will learn about the following:

- Enabling encapsulation and isolation with explicit asynchronous message passing
- Improving compositionality and adding horizontal scalability with location transparency

- Structuring your system in hierarchical modules following *divide et regna*[1]
- How this hierarchy allows principled failure handling
- Achieving sufficiently consistent program semantics in a distributed system
- Avoiding nondeterminism where possible and adding it where necessary
- Guiding application design based on the topology of its message flows

---

[1] Latin: literal translation is "divide and reign;" commonly translated "divide and conquer."

Message passing 4

The fundamental notion on which message passing is built is that of an event: the fact that a certain condition has occurred (the *event*) is bundled together with contextual information—like who did what when and where—and is signaled by the *producer* as a *message*. Interested parties are informed by the producer using a common transport mechanism and *consume* the message.

In this chapter, we will discuss in detail the main aspects of message passing:

- The difference between focusing on messages or events
- Whether to do it synchronously or asynchronously
- How messages can be transmitted without overwhelming the recipient and with varying degrees of reliability

You will also see how message passing enables vertical scalability. Finally, we will discuss the correspondence between events and messages—or how to model one in terms of the other.

4.1 Messages

In the real world, when you mail a letter to someone, you do not expect the contents of the letter to change after it is sent. You expect the letter that arrives to be the same as the one that was sent, and after it arrives you do not expect it to change into a different letter. This is true regardless of whether the letter is sent around the world and takes days or weeks to arrive, or is sent across town, or even is handed to the recipient in person. Immutability is important.

In the first part of chapter 3, we touched on Erlang and an early implementation of the Actor model. In that model, Actors communicate by sending *messages* to each other. Those messages are between processes, but that doesn't always have to be the case. Messages may be sent to other computers, to other processes in the same computer, or even within the same process. You have to ensure that a message can be serialized for transmission, unless you know for sure that it will never leave the current process. Ideally, you should never make that assumption. Message passing often provides an excellent boundary to scale an application horizontally by moving the receiver to a different process.

You can conceive of a simple method call as consisting of two messages: a message containing all the input parameters and a return message containing the result. This may seem a bit extreme, but languages going back more than three decades to Smalltalk-80 have demonstrated that it is a useful approach.[2] If there is no return message, the language may refer to it as a procedure or perhaps say that the method returns a void value.

4.2   *Vertical scalability*

Imagine a busy post office in Manhattan back when computers and machines were not yet capable of sorting letters. Multiple clerks might sort letters in parallel, speeding up the process as shown in figure 4.1. The same idea applies to Reactive applications wherever the order of requests is not crucial (see chapter 14 for specifics).

Figure 4.1   Two clerks sorting mail in parallel at a post office

---

[2] https://en.wikipedia.org/wiki/Smalltalk#Messages

Imagine a piece of code that performs an expensive calculation (prime factorization, graph search, XML transformation, or the like). If this code is accessible only by synchronous method calls, the onus is on the caller to provide for parallel execution in order to benefit from multiple CPUs—say, by using Futures to dispatch the method calls onto a thread pool. One problem with this is that only the implementer of the called code knows if it can be run in parallel without concurrency issues. A typical problem occurs when the calculation stores and reuses auxiliary data structures within its enclosing class or object without proper internal synchronization.

Message passing solves this problem by decoupling sender and receiver. The implementation of the calculation can distribute incoming messages across several execution units without the sender needing to know.

The beauty of this approach is that the semantics of message passing do not depend on how a receiver will process a message. Scaling a computation vertically on dozens of processor cores can be realized transparently, hidden from the calling code as an implementation detail or a configuration option.

4.3 Event-based vs. message-based

There are two models for connecting data consumers with data producers: *event-based* and *message-based*. Event-based systems provide a way to attach responses to specific events. The system then becomes responsible for executing the correct response to an event whenever that event occurs. Event-based systems are typically organized around an event loop. Whenever something happens, the corresponding event is appended to a queue. The event loop continually pulls events from this queue and executes the callbacks that have been attached to them. Each callback is typically a small, anonymous procedure that responds to a specific event such as a mouse click. It may generate new events, which are then also appended to the queue and processed when their turn comes. This model is employed by single-threaded runtimes like Node.js and by the GUI toolkits for most graphical operating systems.

In contrast, message-based systems provide a way to send messages to specific recipients. The anonymous callback is replaced by an active recipient that consumes messages received from potentially anonymous producers. Whereas in an event-based system, event producers are addressable so that callbacks can be registered with them, in a message-based system the consumers are addressable so they can be given responsibility for processing certain messages. Neither the message producer nor the messaging system need concern itself with the correct response to a message; the current configuration of consumers determines that. For example, when some part of a system produces a log event, it does not worry about whether log events are being consumed by the network, a database, or the file system, or whether log files are rotated every 6 or 24 hours. The logger, which receives the log event, is responsible for doing the right thing with it.

Making the consumer responsible for processing its own incoming messages has several advantages:

- It allows processing to proceed sequentially for individual consumers, enabling stateful processing without the need for synchronization. This translates well at the machine level because consumers will aggregate incoming events and process them in one go, a strategy for which current hardware is highly optimized.
- Sequential processing enables the response to an event to depend on the current state of the consumer. So, previous events can have an influence on the consumer's behavior. A callback-based scheme, in contrast, requires the consumer to decide what its response will be when it subscribes to the event, not when the event occurs.
- Consumers can choose to drop events or short-circuit processing during system overload. More generally, explicit queueing allows the consumer to control the flow of messages. We will explain more about flow control in section 4.5.
- Last but not least, it matches how humans work in that we also process requests from our coworkers sequentially.

The last point may be surprising to you, but we find familiar mental images helpful for visualizing how a component behaves. Take a moment to imagine an old-fashioned post office, as shown in figure 4.2, where the clerk sorts letters from an incoming pile into different boxes for delivery. The clerk picks up an envelope, inspects the address label, and makes a decision. After throwing the letter into the right box, the clerk turns back to the pile of unsorted mail and either picks up the next letter or notices that the time is already past noon and takes a lunch break. With this picture in mind, you already have an intuitive understanding of a message router. Now you only need to dump that into code. This task is a lot easier than it would have been before this little mental exercise.

The similarity between message passing and human interaction goes beyond sequential processes. Instead of directly reading (and writing) each others' thoughts, we exchange messages: we talk, we write notes, we observe facial expressions, and so on. We express the same principle in software design by forming encapsulated objects that interact by passing messages. These objects are not the ones you know from languages like Java, C#, or C++, because communication in those languages is synchronous and the receiver has no say in whether or when to handle the request. In the anthropomorphic view, that corresponds to your boss calling you on the telephone and insisting that you find out the answer to a question on the spot. We all know that this kind of call should be the exception rather than the rule, lest no work get done. We prefer to answer, "Yes, I will get back to you when I have the result"; or, even better, the boss should send an email instead of making a disruptive telephone call, especially if finding the answer may take some time. The "I will get back to you" approach corresponds to a method that returns a Future. Sending email is equivalent to explicit message passing.

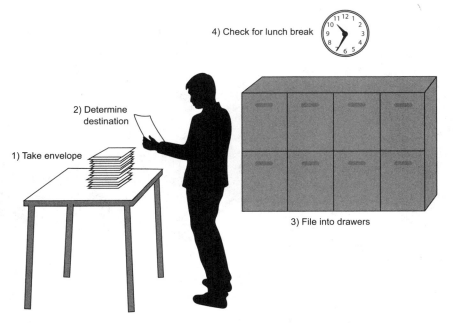

Figure 4.2 A clerk in the back room of a post office sorts mail from an incoming pile into addressee boxes.

Now that we have established that message passing is a useful abstraction, we need to address two fundamental problems that arise while handling messages, whether in a postal service or in a computer:

- Sometimes we must be able to guarantee the delivery of a certain very important letter.
- If messages are sent faster than they can be delivered, they will pile up somewhere, and eventually either the system will collapse or mail will be lost.

We will look at the issue of delivery guarantees later in this chapter. Next, we will take a peek at how Reactive systems control the flow of messages to ensure that requests can be handled in a timely fashion and without overwhelming the receiver.

4.4   *Synchronous vs. asynchronous*

The communication from producer to consumer can be realized in two ways:

- In *synchronous* communication, both parties need to be ready to communicate at the same time.
- In *asynchronous* communication, the sender can send whether the recipient is ready or not.

Figure 4.3 illustrates synchronous message passing at a post office. A customer, Jill, has run out of postage stamps, so she needs to ask the clerk, James, for assistance. Luckily,

Figure 4.3   **A message that a customer is seeking assistance is passed to the clerk using a bell.**

there is no queue in front of the counter, but James is nowhere to be seen. He is somewhere in the back, stowing away a parcel that he just accepted from the previous customer. While James works, Jill is stuck at the counter waiting for him. She cannot go to work or shop for groceries or do whatever else she wants to do next. If she waits too long, she will give up on mailing the letter for now and try again later, perhaps at a different post office.

In real life, we deal gracefully with situations where a receiver is unavailable for too long. In programming, the corresponding timeouts and their proper handling are often considered only as an afterthought.

In contrast, asynchronous message passing means that Jill posts the letter by placing it in the mailbox. She can then immediately be on her way to her next task or appointment. The clerk will empty the mailbox some time later and sort the letters into their correct outboxes. This is much better for everyone involved: Jill does not need to wait for the clerk to have time for her, and the clerk gets to do things in batches, which is a much more efficient use of his time. Hence, we prefer this mode of operation whenever we have a choice.

When there are multiple recipients, the superiority of asynchronous message passing is even clearer. It would be very inefficient to wait until all the recipients of a message are ready to communicate at the same time, or even to pass the message synchronously to one recipient at a time. In the human metaphor, the former would mean the producer would have to arrange a full team meeting and notify everybody at the same time; the latter would mean walking around, patiently waiting at each recipient's desk until they're available. It would be far preferable to send an asynchronous message instead—a letter in the old days, probably an email today. So, for convenience, when we say *message passing* we will always mean *asynchronous communication between a producer and any number of consumers using messages.*

A personal anecdote

The Actor toolkit Akka was built to express message passing from the very beginning; this is what the Actor model is all about. But before version 2.0, this principle was not pervasive throughout Akka. It was only present at the surface, in the user-level API. Under the covers, we used locks for synchronization and called synchronously into the supervisor's strategy when a supervised Actor failed. Consequently, remote supervision was not possible with this architecture. In fact, everything concerning remote Actor interactions was a little quirky and difficult to implement. Users began to notice that the creation of an Actor was executed synchronously on the initiator's thread, leading to a recommendation to refrain from performing time-consuming tasks in an Actor's constructor and send an initialization message instead.

When the list of these and similar issues grew too long, we sat down and redesigned the entire internal architecture of Akka to be based purely on asynchronous message passing. Every feature that was not expressible under this rule was removed, and the inner workings were made fully nonblocking. As a result, all the pieces of the puzzle clicked into place: with the removal of tight coupling between the individual moving parts, we were able to implement supervision, location transparency, and extreme scalability at an affordable engineering price. The only downside is that certain parts—for example, propagating failure up a supervisor hierarchy—do not tolerate message loss, which now requires more effort to implement for remote communication.

To put this another way, asynchronous message passing means the recipient will eventually learn about a new incoming message and then consume it as soon as appropriate. There are two ways in which the recipient can be informed: it can register a callback describing what should happen in case of a certain event, or it can receive the message in a mailbox (also called a *queue*) and decide on a case-by-case basis what to do with it.

4.5   *Flow control*

Flow control is the process of adjusting the transmission rate of a stream of messages to ensure that the receiver is not overwhelmed. Whenever this process informs the sender that it must slow down, the sender is said to experience *back pressure.*

Direct method invocations, such as are common in languages from the C family, by their nature include a specific kind of flow control: the sender of a request is blocked by the receiver until processing is finished. When multiple senders compete for a receiver's resources, processing is commonly serialized through some form of synchronization like locks or semaphores, which additionally blocks each sender until previous senders' messages have been serviced. This implicit back pressure may sound convenient at first, but as systems grow and nonfunctional requirements become more important, it turns into an impediment. Instead of implementing the business logic, you find yourself debugging performance bottlenecks.

Message passing gives you a wider range of options for flow control because it includes the notion of queueing. For example, as discussed in chapter 2, if you use a bounded queue, you have options for how to respond when the queue is full: you can drop the newest message, the oldest message, or all the messages, according to what best suits the requirements. A case where you might drop all messages would be a real-time system aimed at displaying the latest data. You might include a small buffer to smooth out processing or latency jitter, but moving new messages through the queue quickly is more important than processing backlogged messages. Because the consuming process reads from the message queue, it can make whatever decision is appropriate when it finds itself backlogged.

Another option is that you can sort incoming messages into multiple queues based on priorities and dequeue them according to specific bandwidth allocations. You can also generate an immediate negative reply to a sender when dropping messages, if desired. We will discuss these and other possibilities in chapter 15.

Two basic flow-control schemes are depicted in figure 4.4: the left clerk tries to deliver sacks full of letters to the right clerk, who sorts them at a table. In *negative acknowledgment (NACK)*, the right clerk rejects a new delivery when the table is full. In *positive acknowledgment (ACK)*, the left clerk waits to be informed by the right clerk that the right clerk has run out of letters to sort. There are many variations on this scheme, some of which are presented in chapter 15. The subject lends itself well to human metaphors like the one given here; feel free to let your mind roam and discover some of them in everyday life.

In essence, message passing unbundles the implied flow control from common object-oriented programming languages and allows customized solutions. This choice does not come without a cost, of course: at the least, you need to think about which flow-control semantics you want, and, hence, you must choose the granularity at which to apply message passing and below which direct method calls and object-oriented composition are preferable. To illustrate, imagine a service-oriented architecture with asynchronous interfaces. The services themselves might be implemented in traditional synchronous style and communicate among each other via message passing. When refactoring one of the service implementations, you might find it appropriate to apply more fine-grained flow control within it, thus lowering the granularity level. This choice can be made differently depending on the service's requirements as well as how the responsible development team likes to work.

With a basic understanding of how to avoid overloading a message-delivery system, we can now turn our attention to the issue of how to ensure delivery of certain important messages.

Flow control with negative acknowledgement

Flow control with positive acknowledgement

Figure 4.4 Two basic flow-control schemes

4.6   *Delivery guarantees*

Despite every postal clerk's best efforts, sometimes a letter gets lost. The probability may be low, but still it happens—several times per year. What happens then? The letter might have contained birthday wishes, in which case it will hopefully be discovered by the sender and receiver when they meet for the next time. Or it might have been an invoice, in which case it will not be paid, and a reminder will be sent. The important theme to note here is that humans normally follow up on interactions, allowing the detection of message loss. In some cases, there are unpleasant consequences when a message is lost, but life goes on and we do not stop our entire society because one letter was not delivered. In this section, we will show you how Reactive applications work the same way, but we will start at the opposite end: with synchronous systems.

When we write down a method call, we can be pretty certain that it will be executed when the program reaches the corresponding line; we are not used to losses between lines. But strictly speaking, we need to take into account the possibility that the process will terminate or the machine will die; or it could overflow the call stack or otherwise raise a fatal signal. As you saw earlier, it is not difficult to think of a method call as a message sent to an object, and with this formulation we could say that even in a synchronous system, we have to address the possibility that a message— a method invocation—can get lost. We could thus take the extreme standpoint that there can never be an unbreakable guarantee that a request will be processed or result in a response.

Very few people, however, would deem such a stance constructive, because we reasonably accept limitations and exceptions to rules. We apply common sense and call those who don't pedantic. For example, human interaction usually proceeds under the implicit assumption that neither party dies. Instead of dwelling on the rare cases, we concern ourselves more with managing our inherent unreliability, making sure communications were received, and reminding colleagues of important work items or deadlines. But when transforming a process into a computer program, we expect it to be completely reliable: to perform its function without fail. It is our nature to loathe the hassle of countering irregularities, and we turn to machines to be rid of it. The sad fact is that the machines we build may be faster and more reliable, but they are not perfect, and we must therefore continue to worry about unforeseen failures.

Everyday life again provides a good model to borrow from. Whenever one person requests a service from another, they have to deal with the possibility that there will be no reply. The other person may be busy, or the request or reply may get lost along the way—for example, if a letter (or email) is lost. In these cases, the person who made the request needs to try again until they get a response or the request becomes irrelevant, as illustrated in figure 4.5. Analogous activity in the realm of computer programming is obvious: a message sent from one object to another may be lost, or the receiving object may be unable to handle the request because something it depends on is currently unavailable—the disk may be full or a database may be down—and so the sending object will need to either retry until the request is successful or give up.

Figure 4.5   The Retry pattern in daily life

With synchronous method calls, there is usually no way to recover from a "lost message." If a procedure doesn't return, usually it is because of something catastrophic like abnormal program continuation; there is no way for the caller to try to recover and continue. Message passing makes it feasible to persist the request and retry it whenever the failure condition is corrected. Even if an entire computing center goes down because of a power outage, a program can continue after the power comes back on as long as the needed messages were held in nonvolatile storage. As with flow control, you need to choose an appropriate granularity at which to apply message passing, based on each application's requirements.

With this in mind, it becomes natural to design an application based on reduced message-delivery guarantees. Building in this knowledge from the beginning makes the resulting application resilient against message loss, no matter whether it is caused by network interruption, a back-end service outage, excessive load, or even programming errors.

Implementing a runtime environment with very strong delivery guarantees is expensive in that extra mechanisms need to be built in—for example, resending network messages until receipt is confirmed—and these mechanisms degrade performance and scalability even when no failures occur. The cost rises dramatically in a distributed system, mostly because confirmations require network round trips having latencies orders of magnitude larger than on a local system (for example, between two cores on a single CPU). Providing weaker delivery guarantees allows you to implement the common cases much more simply and quickly, and pay the price for stronger guarantees only where truly needed. Note the correspondence with how the postal service charges for normal and registered mail.

The principal choices for delivery guarantees are as follows:

- *At-most-once delivery*—Each request is sent once and never retried. If it is lost or the recipient fails to process it, there is no attempt to recover. Therefore, the desired function may be invoked once or not at all. This is the most basic delivery guarantee. It has the lowest implementation overhead, because neither sender nor receiver is required to maintain information on the state of their communication.

- *At-least-once delivery*—Trying to guarantee that a request is processed requires two additions to at-most-once semantics. First, the recipient must acknowledge receipt or execution (depending on the requirements) by sending a confirmation message. Second, the sender must retain the request in order to resend it if the sender doesn't receive the confirmation. Because a resend can be the result of a lost confirmation, the recipient may receive the message more than once. Given enough time and the assumption that communication will eventually succeed, the message will be received at least once.

- *Exactly once delivery*—If a request must be processed but must not be processed twice, then, in addition to at-least-once semantics, the recipient must deduplicate messages: that is, they must keep track of which requests have already been processed. This is the most costly scheme because it requires both sender and receiver to track communication state. If, in addition, requests must be processed in the order they were sent, then throughput may be further limited by the need to complete confirmation round trips for each request before proceeding with the next—unless flow-control requirements are compatible with buffering on the receiver side.

Implementations of the Actor model usually provide at-most-once delivery out of the box and allow the other two layers to be added on top for communication paths that require them. Interestingly, local method calls also provide at-most-once delivery, albeit with a tiny probability for nondelivery.

Consideration of flow-control and message-delivery guarantees is important because message passing makes limitations of communication explicit and clearly exposes inconvenient corner cases. In the next section, we will focus on the natural match between messages and real-world events and how this promotes a simple consistency across layers in an application.

4.7   *Events as messages*

In hard real-time systems, the foremost concern is keeping the maximal response time to external events within strict limits—that is, to enforce a tight temporal coupling between each event and its response. At the other end of the spectrum, a high-volume storage system for archiving log messages needs high throughput much more than it needs short latency: how long it takes to store a log message matters little as long as the message eventually gets stored. Requirements for responding to events may vary enormously, but interactions with computers always boil down to this: raising events and responding to them.

Messages naturally represent events, and message passing naturally represents event-driven interactions. An event propagating through a system can also be seen as a message being forwarded along a chain of processing units. Representing events as messages enables the trade-off between latency and throughput to be adjusted on a case-by-case basis or even dynamically. This is useful in cases where response times usually need to be short, but the system also needs to degrade gracefully when the input load increases.

The reception and processing of network packets illustrates varying latency requirements within one sequence of interactions, as shown in figure 4.6. First, the network interface controller (NIC) informs the CPU of the availability of data using a synchronous interrupt, which needs to be handled as quickly as possible. The operating system kernel takes the data from the NIC and determines the right process and socket to transfer them to. From this point on, the latency requirements are more relaxed, because the data are safe and sound in the machine's memory—although of course you would still like the user-space process responsible for replying to the incoming request to be informed as quickly as possible. The availability of data on the socket is then signaled—say, by waking up a selector—and the application requests the data from the kernel.

Notice a fundamental pattern here: within one computer, data received over the wire propagate as a series of events upward through successively higher software layers. Each successfully received packet eventually reaches the user-level program in a representation that bears the same information (possibly combined with other packets for efficiency). At the lowest level, interactions between computers take the form of messages in which a physical representation of data propagates from one computer to another; reception of each message is signaled as an event. It is therefore natural to model network I/O at *all* layers as a stream of events, reified as a stream of messages. We picked this example because we recently reimplemented the network I/O layer in Akka in this fashion,

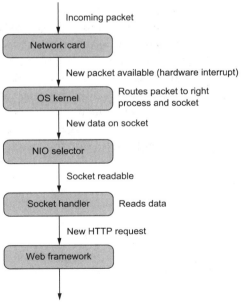

Figure 4.6 Steps of a web request from packet reception to calling the web framework

but opportunities for exploiting the correspondence between messages sent at different levels are ubiquitous. All the lowest-level inputs to a computer are event-based (keyboard and mouse, camera and audio frames, and so on) and can be conveniently passed around as messages. In this way, message passing is the most natural form of communication between independent objects of any kind.

4.8 Synchronous message passing

Explicit message passing often provides a convenient way for isolated parts of an application to communicate, or helps delineate source code components, even when there is no need for asynchronous communication. But if asynchrony is not needed, using asynchronous message passing to decouple components introduces an unnecessary cost: the administrative runtime overhead of dispatching tasks for asynchronous execution as well as extra scheduling latency. In this case, synchronous message passing is usually a wiser choice.

We mention this because synchronous message propagation is often useful for stream processing. For example, fusing a series of transformations together keeps the transformed data local to one CPU core and thereby makes better use of its associated caches. Synchronous messaging thus serves a different purpose than decoupling parts of a Reactive application, and our derivation of the necessity of asynchrony in section 4.4 does not apply.

4.9 Summary

In this chapter, we have discussed in detail the motivation for message passing, especially in contrast to synchronous communication. We have illuminated the difference between addressable event sources in event-driven systems and addressable message recipients in message-driven systems. We have examined the greater variety of forms of flow control that message passing affords, and you have learned about the different levels of message-delivery guarantees.

We briefly touched on the correspondence between events and messages, and you have seen how message passing enables vertical scalability. In the following chapter, we will show how location transparency complements this by enabling horizontal scalability.

Location transparency

The previous chapter introduced message passing as a way to decouple collaborating objects. Making communication asynchronous and nonblocking instead of calling synchronous methods enables the receiver to perform its work in a different execution context, such as a different thread. But why stop at interactions within one computer? Message passing works the same way in both local and remote interactions. There is no fundamental difference between scheduling a task to run later on the local machine and sending a network packet to a different host to trigger execution there. In this chapter, we will explore the possibilities offered by this perspective as well as the consequences it has for quantitative aspects of performance such as latency, throughput, and probability of message loss.

5.1   What is location transparency?

You may recall the example shown in figure 5.1 from section 1.1, where we discussed the tenets of the Reactive Manifesto using a hypothetical simplified view of the Gmail application. If you were to start designing this system, you would split it into services with various presumed dependencies between them; you would begin mapping out the interfaces that support interservice communication; and you would probably spend a thought or two on how the entire application will be deployed on the available hardware (or what hardware is needed). You would then implement the design by writing each of the services and codifying the drafted dependencies and communication patterns—for example, using an asynchronous HTTP client to talk with another service's REST API or using a message broker.

Message passing in this example is clearly marked out within the program code, using different syntax than for local interactions. Consequently the calling object needs to be aware of the location of the receiving object, or at least it needs to know that the receiver does not support normal method calls.

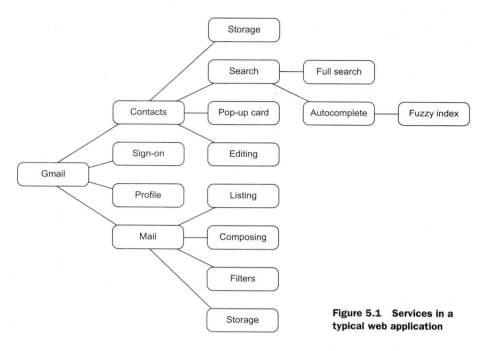

Figure 5.1   Services in a typical web application

Location transparency is the property that source code for sending a message looks the same regardless of where the recipient will process it. Application components interact with each other in a uniform fashion defined by explicit message passing. An object that allows a message to be sent then becomes just a handle pointing to its designated recipient. This handle is mobile and can be passed around freely among network nodes.

5.2   *The fallacy of transparent remoting*

Since the advent of ubiquitous computer networks, several attempts have been made to unify the programming model for local and remote method invocations through *transparent remoting*: making remote invocations appear the same as local ones. CORBA, Java RMI, and DCOM were all introduced with this promise, and all of them failed. The reason they failed lies in a mismatch between implied and actual guarantees or execution semantics, as Waldo et al. have noted.[1]

The most obvious problem is partial failure. When calling a method, you expect either a result or an exception, but if the method call is routed through a network to a different computer, there are more things that can go wrong. The method may not be called at all because the invocation could not be transmitted. Or, if the method is invoked, the result may be lost. In both cases, there is no outcome to report. This is

---

[1]   Jim Waldo, Geoff Wyant, Ann Wollrath, and Sam Kendall, "A Note on Distributed Computing," Sun Microsystems Laboratories, 1994, http://citeseerx.ist.psu.edu/viewdoc/summary?doi=10.1.1.41.7628.

typically resolved by raising a timeout exception in the caller's thread. This requires that the calling code deal with the uncertainty of whether the desired function was invoked.

Other problems arise from the performance expectations associated with a method call. Traversing the network incurs an increase in latency of at least the time of one round trip: the invocation needs to be sent to the recipient, and the result needs to travel back to the sender. This is several orders of magnitude longer than the overhead involved in executing a method locally. A local method call takes about a nanosecond on current hardware; a remote call takes tens to hundreds of microseconds in a local network and up to hundreds of milliseconds in a globally distributed system. You need to take this latency into account in order to ensure that an algorithm's implementation fulfills its nonfunctional requirements. If an innocent-looking method call takes a million times longer than you would naïvely expect, the consequences can be devastating.

In addition to increased latency, remote invocations also suffer from much lower throughput than their local counterparts. Passing huge in-memory datasets as arguments to a local method may be slow due to the need to bring the relevant data into CPU caches, but that is still much faster than serializing the data and sending them over the network. The difference in throughput can easily exceed a factor of 1,000.

Therefore, giving remote interactions the same semantics as local ones is not desirable in theory, nor has it been successful in practice. Waldo et al. argue that the inverse—changing local semantics to match the constraints of remote communication—would be too invasive and so should also not be done. They recommend clearly delineating local and remote computing and choosing different representations in the source code.

5.3 *Explicit message passing to the rescue*

You have seen that message passing models the semantics of remote communication naturally: there is no preconceived expectation that messages will be transmitted instantaneously or processed immediately. Replies are also messages, and messages may be lost. Two components communicating with messages can thus be located on the same machine or on different network hosts without changing any characteristic quality of their interaction. The components' inner workings may comprise any number of objects collaborating by synchronous local method calls, as long as message passing is explicitly different, as explained above.

Location transparency does not aim to make remote interactions look like local ones. Its goal, rather, is to unify the expression of message passing under a common abstraction for both local and remote interaction. A concrete example of this is the Actor model from chapter 3, where all communication between Actors is mediated through stable placeholders—called *ActorRefs* in Akka or *process IDs* and *registered names* in Erlang—whose only purpose is to offer a generic message-passing facility:

```
actorRef ! message
```

This code snippet[2] sends the message given on the right to the Actor represented by the reference on the left. Note that this operation does not call a method on the Actor itself. Instead, the Actor reference is a façade that transfers the message—across the network if necessary—to wherever the Actor is located. There, it is appended to the Actor's incoming message queue for later processing.

This is the crucial point where location transparency and transparent remoting differ. With location transparency, message passing is always explicit. Every instance of message passing is *potentially* remote, yet the sender need not concern itself with whether the Actor is local or remote, nor with the mechanics of sending the message, nor with whether the message will be transmitted in nanoseconds or microseconds. The sender also does not stop to wait for a response. It is satisfied when the message has been passed to the Actor reference.

Contrast this with transparent remoting, where a local proxy object is created and the desired method is called directly on it, hiding the fact that message passing happens underneath. Additional concrete problems arise with transparent remoting in defining the semantics of methods that do not return a value: for example, should the current thread block until the remote object has processed the call, or should it return to its caller immediately?

By treating all message passing as potentially remote, you gain the freedom to relocate components without having to change their code. You can write software once and deploy it on different hardware setups by just changing where the parts are instantiated. Akka, for example, allows remote deployment of Actors to be specified in the configuration file. The operations team can therefore in principle determine the hardware layout without regard for which partitioning the engineering team foresaw. Of course, this depends on the assumption that all message passing was considered potentially remote during implementation. It would be prudent for the development and operations teams to consult with each other in order to have a common understanding of the deployment scenarios.

5.4   *Optimization of local message passing*

Local message passing can thus become merely an optimization of remote message passing. Without changing the source code, local messages could be passed by reference, obviating the need to serialize and deserialize them, greatly reducing latency and increasing throughput. Erlang, however, by default maintains full correspondence between local and remote and does not apply this optimization: it serializes and deserializes all message sends, including purely local ones. This further decouples different components from each other at the cost of performance.

The advantages of message passing as discussed so far—loose coupling, horizontal scalability, and flow control—can of course be desirable for a purely local program. In

---

[2] Readers unfamiliar with Scala may find the syntax `actorRef ! message` strange. The `!` is the name of a method defined on the trait `ActorRef`. Scala allows a call to a method with a single parameter to be simplified by eliminating the `.` and the parentheses, so the code snippet is equivalent to `actorRef.!(message)`.

this scenario, it does not make sense to go to great lengths to minimize the serialized size of transmitted messages. Therefore, location transparency is a feature that you can use to great effect on a higher level of abstraction while choosing not to apply it within subprograms. It is possible to apply it at the service level in a service-oriented architecture and lower the granularity into the implementation of a service if its deployment likely will not fit on a single machine. We will discuss this notion further in the following chapters.

5.5   *Message loss*

A message passed remotely is subject to many more ways of being lost than one passed locally: network hardware may be faulty or overloaded, leading to packet loss, and so on. Hence, remote message passing brings a higher probability of message loss. TCP mitigates certain kinds of network errors, but it is not a panacea. For example, when connections are dropped by active network components, TCP is powerless.

In addition, both locally *and* remotely, a sender may fail to receive a reply for reasons other than message loss. Sometimes processing fails in unforeseen ways, resulting in no reply being sent. You might be tempted to just write catch-all error handlers to send back failure messages, but this still does not ensure a reply. If, say, the system runs out of memory or the receiving object does not get scheduled on a CPU for a long time, the catch-all will not be executed. Even if it is executed, it cannot tell whether the original operation succeeded or failed. The error that triggered it might be something trivial, such as a logger failing after the relevant operation succeeded.

When a message is lost or not processed, the only information the sender gets is that no confirmation came back. It may be that the sender is not interested in a confirmation because the operation was not that important (debug logging, for example, does not require confirmation), or the sender may need to react to the reception or absence of the confirmation.

To illustrate the second case, we return to the example of the Gmail application. When you hover your pointer over the sender of an email, a small contact card pops up, showing that person's connection to you in Google's social network, a picture, possibly alternative email addresses, and so on. To display this window, the web browser sends a request to the Gmail front-end servers, which then dispatch requests to the different internal services that look up and return the desired information, as shown in figure 5.2 (this and the following figures use a slightly relaxed form of the diagram syntax defined in appendix A: every arrow is assumed to be a message dispatch, with the sequence defined by the adjacent numbers as usual). The front-end service stores contextual information about where to send the result. The front end adds replies from the internal services to this context as they come in, and when the information is complete, it sends the aggregated reply back to the original requester. But what if one of the expected replies never arrives?

Absence of a message can be expressed by triggering a timeout of the kind "Send me this reminder in 100 milliseconds." The next step depends on which message is received first. If the desired reply arrives before the timeout, processing continues

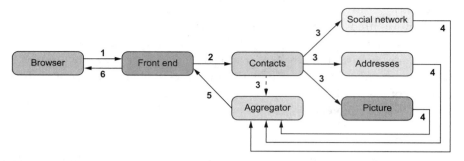

Figure 5.2   Request-and-reply chain when retrieving contact information

normally, and the timeout can be canceled if the system supports that. On the other hand, if the timeout arrives before any suitable reply, then the recovery path needs to be executed, possibly resending the original message, falling back to a backup system or default value, or aborting the original request. This is depicted in figure 5.3.

There are different possible responses, depending on which reply is missing. As long as the social network's status can be retrieved, it makes sense to send a partially successful reply, perhaps missing the part that would normally contain alternate email addresses. But the request will have to be answered with an overall failure if the social network is unavailable. Patterns like this are described in section 15.5.

As we discussed in section 2.1.3 under the topic of bounded latency, timeouts have the disadvantage that they need to be set long enough to allow for slow responses, in order not to trigger too often. When a back-end service stops responding, it makes sense to fail requests early and only send out a message every few seconds to check whether the service has come back up. This is called the *Circuit Breaker* pattern and is discussed in chapter 12.

It may seem superfluous to use these patterns even for local message passing; you may think that a good local optimization would be to assume successful delivery of all messages. As you have just seen, though, processing faults can contribute to the same failure symptoms. So, a happy result of writing your application under the assumption of remote communication—and by applying location transparency—is that you make

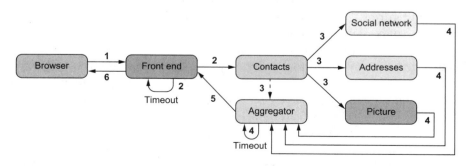

Figure 5.3   Request-and-reply chain with timeout

it more resilient at the same time. As with message passing, the benefits result from being explicit about failure-recovery mechanisms instead of relying on implicit and incomplete hidden guarantees.

5.6   *Horizontal scalability*

You have seen that message passing decouples caller and callee, turning them into sender and receiver. This enables vertical scalability because the receiver is now free to use different processing resources than those of the sender, a feat made possible by not executing both on the same call stack. Location transparency adds *horizontal scalability* to message passing: you can improve performance by adding more computers to the network.

Location-transparent message passing enables the receiver to be placed anywhere on a reachable computer network without the sender needing to know where. For example, in Akka, an ActorRef could refer to a single Actor on the local node, but it could also dispatch the messages sent through it to a set of Actors spread out over a compute grid. The method to send messages is the same in both cases.

In the example of the Gmail application, consider the translation service: normally you see email as the author sent it, but if the application determines that the language is foreign to you, it offers you a link to have the text translated. The translation service, which performs this expensive transformation, can be run on as many computers as needed to fulfill its throughput requirements. On a system with location transparency, as depicted in figure 5.4, people can add and remove translation servers as needed, without altering the front-end code that invokes the service. You can test the translation service on your notebook with a local installation; the staging test-bed can (and should) contain several remote nodes to test this deployment scenario; and, in production, the operations team is free to scale the hardware up and down as much as they need to react to load spikes.

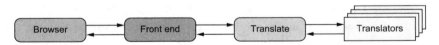

Figure 5.4   Scaling out to multiple translation services

5.7   *Location transparency makes testing simpler*

The previous point deserves separate discussion from a different perspective. Horizontal scalability not only enables you to expand a service outward to run on more computers but also allows you to run the entire system on a single computer when desirable. This is useful during functional testing and local exploration during development, and continuous integration testing becomes much simpler if the service under test can be wired to local communication partners or even stubs of them. You have probably written similar code that connects to an ephemeral local database for the purpose of testing—using, for example, classical dependency injection by configuring the database's URI.

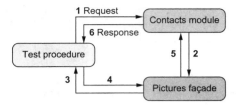

Figure 5.5   Stubbing out a service means intercepting the requests made by the module under test and injecting replies to verify the response.

Depending on the concrete implementation, stubbing out a service can be done without involving mocking frameworks or writing a lot of boilerplate code. For example, Akka comes with a TestKit, which contains a generic TestProbe for mocking an ActorRef. Because there is only one method to simulate—sending a message—this is all you need to replace a back-end service with a stub that replies with success or failure according to the test plan.

In our Gmail example, the front-end services talk to several other services in order to perform their function. In order to test them in isolation, you can replace, for example, the storage back end for people's contact images with one that knows about a certain John Doe and can be configured not to reply or to reply with a failure when required. Such a test setup is diagrammed in figure 5.5. This aspect of testing is discussed in depth in chapter 11.

5.8   Dynamic composition

In a service-oriented architecture, wiring is usually done using a dependency-injection framework that provides the exact location of each dependency. A location typically is a combination of a protocol, an address (for example, host name and port), and some protocol-specific details such as a path name. Dependency resolution first determines the location for a resource and then creates a proxy object to represent it in the context into which it is injected. This process is performed during start-up, and the wiring usually stays the same throughout the lifecycle of the application or service.

Sending a message is typically mediated through some kind of handle, such as a database connection handle. Location-transparent handles can themselves be sent through the network and used by their recipients, because in the end such handles are nothing but addresses or descriptors of the objects they refer to. Location-transparent handles are therefore similar to the proxy objects created by dependency-injection frameworks, except that a location-transparent handle can be used on any node in the network, not just the machine it was created on. This enables another form of dependency injection: one service can include references to other services in a request or reply so that the receiver uses them as dynamic wiring.

In the example Gmail application, this technique can be used by the authentication service. When a request comes in, the front end dispatches the query to this service to authenticate the requester and retrieve authorization information. In addition to verifying the user's access token, the authentication service can inject references to other services into the request before handing it on to the contacts service, as shown

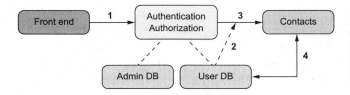

Figure 5.6 Dynamic dependency injection allows the `authentication` module to give the `contacts` module access to either the user or admin database.

in figure 5.6. In this example, authorization to access either the admin or the user database is passed along in the form of a service reference that the `contacts` module will use while processing the user request. This same scheme could also be used to offer different storage back ends or translation services with different capabilities for different subscription levels. The overall service mix available to a user can be customized in this way without having to introduce all parts everywhere or having to carry authorization information around throughout the entire system.

This concept is not new in the context of Actor systems, where the capability to access a certain service is modeled by the possession of a reference to the Actor providing it. Handing out this capability means passing that reference to another Actor, which can then use the service on its own; we say that an *introduction* has been made between the two Actors.

Another use for this technique is to fall back to secondary services when the primary ones are unavailable—rewiring dependencies at runtime as sketched in figure 5.7. This is useful not only on the server side: Imagine a client of a blog-management service that runs on a mobile device. The user interface needs to communicate with the back end to retrieve the data to display and to persist changes the user wants to make. When no connection is available, the UI can instead talk to local stubs of the various services, serving cached data or queueing actions for later transmission where appropriate. Location transparency enables the UI code to be written without regard for this difference in any way.[3] All the fallback logic can be confined to a single service that connects the UI to either the real or a fake back end.

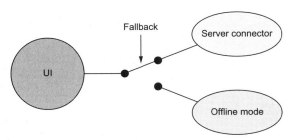

Figure 5.7 In a web client, the UI can switch between online and offline modes by using different service references.

---

[3] In the interest of keeping the user apprised of all important status information, it will typically be advisable to indicate offline operation whenever this mode has an influence on the semantics or performance of operations. Offline status should be indicated clearly and unambiguously, but also unobtrusively—unlike, say, a modal dialog.

5.9   *Summary*

In this chapter, you have seen how explicit message passing enables you to view local messages as a special case of fully distributed remote messaging—in contrast to transparent remoting, which aims to make remote interactions look like local ones. We discussed how differences in latency, throughput, and message-loss probability affect your ability to treat local and remote interactions in a unified way.

You have also seen the benefits of location-transparent messaging: it extends the vertical scalability afforded by message passing to scalability along the horizontal axis; it eases testing of software components; and it allows software components to be composed dynamically. In the next chapter, we will look more deeply into what a component is and how you can break a larger task into independent, smaller ones.

Divide and conquer 6

The previous chapter presumed that programs typically consist of multiple parts that are segregated in some way. Different areas of functionality may be developed by separate teams, modules are accessed via interfaces and packaged such that they can be replaced, and so on. Over the past few decades, much effort has been spent on syntax and semantics for defining modules in programming languages and on libraries and the infrastructure needed to deploy them. The important question is, how do we go about dividing up a problem in order to successfully solve it?

Rewinding the clock more than 2,000 years, we find one of the earliest practitioners of the governance maxim *divide et regna*: Julius Caesar. The idea is simple: when faced with a number of enemies, create discord and divide them. This will allow you to vanquish them one by one, even though they would easily have defeated you if they had stood united. This strategy was used by the Roman Empire both internally and externally: the key was to purposefully treat different opponents differently, handing out favors and punishment asymmetrically. And this treatment was probably applied recursively, with senators and prefects learning from Caesar's success.[1]

We do not have the problem of leading a huge empire, nor is fomenting discord one of our methods, but we can still learn from this old Latin saying. We can break a large programming problem down into a manageable handful of subproblems, and then do the same to the subproblems. Thus, we can gradually narrow the scope of what we are working on, drilling progressively deeper into the details of how to implement each particular piece.

---

[1] The authors have no direct evidence for this, but it sounds implausible to propose the opposite.

6.1   *Hierarchical problem decomposition*

Imagine that you are building the Gmail application from scratch. You begin with the diffuse intuition that the task is an entangled mess of ad hoc requirements. One way to proceed would be to start from experience or with educated guesses about which technology components will play a role and postulate certain modules based on them: you will need modules for authentication and authorization, for rendering and notifications, and for monitoring and analytics, as well as appropriate storage for all these. You explore and perhaps build proofs of concept, improving your understanding and letting the modules—and their siblings whose necessity you discover—gradually take shape. Bite by bite, you take apart the big task, assigning requirements and features to each module. Many small things end up in `utils` or `misc` packages. Ultimately, you end up with hundreds of components that hopefully will work together peacefully to allow users to read their email.

Although possibly not far from the reality of many projects, this approach is not ideal. Breaking down a problem into a lot of smaller problems incurs the overhead of making the individual solutions coexist in the final product. This turns the initial, frighteningly complex problem into an army of smaller problems that may overwhelm you.

6.1.1   *Defining the hierarchy*

Staying with the example of building Gmail, you might split the responsibilities at the top layer into sign-on, profile, contacts, and mail. Within the contacts module, you must maintain the list of contacts for every user, providing facilities for addition, removal, and editing. You also need query facilities: for example, to support autocompletion while the user is typing recipient addresses in an email (low latency but possibly out of date) and for refined searches (higher latency but fully up to date and complete). The low-latency search function needs to cache an optimized view of the contacts data, which will need to be refreshed from the master list when it changes. The cache and the refreshing service could be separate modules that communicate with one another.

The important difference between this design and the initial one is that you not only break the overall task down into manageable units—you will probably arrive at the same granularity in the end—but also define a hierarchy among the modules. At the bottom of the hierarchy are the nitty-gritty implementation details. Moving up the hierarchy, the components become more and more abstract, approaching the logical high-level functionality that you aim to implement. The relation between a module and its direct descendants is tighter than just a dependency: the low-latency search function, for example, clearly depends on the cache and the refreshing service, but it also provides the scope within which these two modules work—it defines the boundaries of the problem space they solve.

This allows you to focus on a specific problem and solve it well, without trying to generalize prematurely, a practice that is often futile or even destructive. Of course, generalization will eventually happen—most likely at the lower levels of the hierarchy—but it will be a natural process of recognizing that the same (or a very similar) problem has already been solved, and therefore you can reuse the previous solution. Intuitively, you already have experience with this kind of generalization. It is common to reuse low-level libraries, such as collections frameworks. The concept of a list, map, or set is useful across any number of applications. At the next level up, some reuse remains likely. A low-level cache with a refreshing service might be reused in many places. Continuing up the hierarchy, there might be reuse of an interface to an LDAP server to acquire contact information, but it would be more limited. The higher in the hierarchy a module is situated, the more likely it is to be specific to a concrete use case. It is unlikely that the `mail` module in Gmail will be reused as is in a different application. If you need `mail` in another context, you are probably better off copying and adapting. Most of the descendant modules will probably be reusable, because they provide more narrowly scoped parts of the solution.

To recapitulate: we can break the task of "building Gmail" into a set of high-level features, such as `mail` and `contacts`, defining a module for each one. These modules collaborate to provide the Gmail function, and that is also their only purpose. The `contacts` module provides a clearly scoped part of the functionality, which is split up across lower-level modules such as autocomplete, which again collaborate to provide the overall `contacts` function. This hierarchy is depicted in figure 6.1.

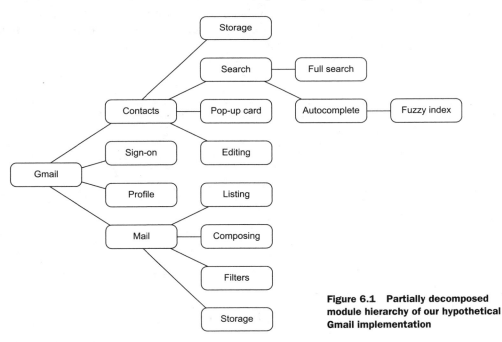

Figure 6.1 Partially decomposed module hierarchy of our hypothetical Gmail implementation

6.2   *Dependencies vs. descendant modules*

In the hierarchical decomposition process, we glossed over one aspect that deserves elaboration: because the mail component in the Gmail example must work with contact information, does its module hierarchy contain that functionality? So far, we have only talked about the piecewise narrowing of problem scope. If that is all you do, parts of the `contacts` functionality will appear in several places: the module that displays lists of emails will need access to contact details; the module for composing an email will need access to at least the low-latency contact search; and the same goes for the filter-rule editor.

It does not make sense to replicate the same functionality in multiple places. We would like to solve each problem only once, in source code as well as in deployment and operations. Notice that none of the modules we mentioned *owns* the `contacts` functionality. It is not a core concern of any of them. *Ownership* is an important notion when it comes to decomposition. In this case, the question is, who owns which part of the problem space? There should be only one module that is responsible for any given functionality, possibly with multiple concrete implementations; all other modules that need to access that functionality have a *dependency* on the module that owns it.

We hinted at this distinction earlier when we said that the relationship between a module and its descendants is tighter than just a dependency. Descendant modules cater to a bounded subset of the problem space owned by their parent, each owning its smaller piece in turn. Functionality that lies outside this bound is incorporated by reference, and some other module is responsible for providing it, as illustrated in figure 6.2.

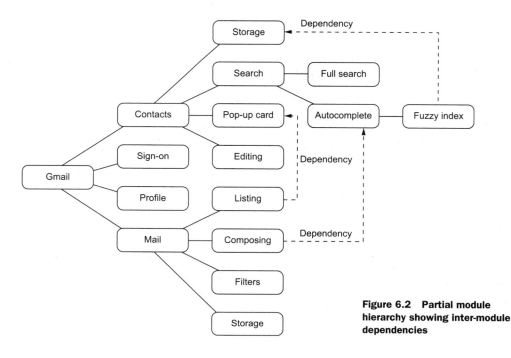

Figure 6.2   **Partial module hierarchy showing inter-module dependencies**

6.2.1 *Avoiding the matrix*

The organization of the development team can be at cross-purposes with establishing a good hierarchical decomposition of the software. A common way to organize people is by skill. Put all the front-end JavaScript experts into one group, the server developers in another, and the structured-database developers in a third, have yet another group focus on bulk storage, and so on. Conway's Law—"Any organization that designs a system will inevitably produce a design whose structure is a copy of the organization's communication structure"[2]—tells us that the result in the Gmail example would be a front-end module, an application module, and a database module. Within each module, each team would likely define its own submodules for contacts, sign-on, profile, and mail, as shown in figure 6.3.

This is not the same as having a `contacts` module with submodules for the front end, application, and database. The difference is that in the skill-oriented decomposition, there are small, horizontal dependencies between the modules at each level rather than just at the top level of the hierarchy. These dependencies are especially pernicious because they do not usually appear to be a major problem while the first

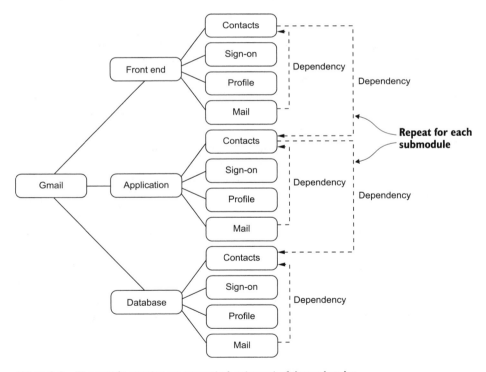

Figure 6.3 The matrix creates an unwanted extra set of dependencies.

---

[2] Paraphrase of Melvin Conway, "How Do Committees Invent?" *Datamation* (April 1968), www.melconway.com /Home/pdf/committees.pdf.

version is being built. Early in the lifecycle of a piece of software, nearly every submodule typically needs to be changed in every release; so whether a given module is deployed as part of the latest whole application release or as part of the latest contacts release makes no difference. Later, horizontal dependencies become problematic. They force a release focused on a single technology, such as upgrading the database version, to affect every module at the same level in the hierarchy. At the same time, every major feature release affects every module along a vertical axis.

6.3 *Building your own big corporation*

A metaphor that often works well for picturing and speaking about hierarchical problem decomposition is that of a big corporation. At the top, management defines the overall goal and direction (CEO, Chief Architect, and so on). Then there are departments that handle different, very high-level aspects of the goal. Each department is structured into various subgroups of different granularity, until at the bottom we reach the small teams that carry out very specific, narrowly scoped tasks. The ideas behind this structure are similar to the responsibility-oriented problem decomposition described previously: without proper segregation of the responsibilities of the departments, their members would constantly step on each other's toes while doing their work.

As you work through this hierarchy, think ahead to something that will be considered more in the next chapter: handling failures. If an individual in the hierarchy fails to do their job, the next person up in the hierarchy must handle it. Responsibility flows toward the person in charge, not in lazy circles among coworkers!

If you think now, "Well, that all sounds nice in theory, but my own experience has been that this is exactly how corporations do *not* work," the good news is that when applying these techniques to a programming problem, you get to choose the structure and define the relationships between the parts of the hierarchy you create—you get the chance to create your own BigCorp and do it right![3] You get the chance to not repeat the management mistakes of the past. "Matrix management" schemes were popular from the late 1970s to the early 1980s, and they did not work well. The title of an article published in the aftermath of the fad provides some insight: *Matrix Management: Not a Structure, a Frame of Mind.*[4]

A hierarchical decomposition of responsibilities is shown in figure 6.4, on the example of our venerable Gmail application. Naming the modules according to the role they play within the overall organization of the application helps establish a common vocabulary among the teams and stakeholders involved in development.

---

[3] You will probably discover that things are not as easy as you think they should be, which is equally instructive.

[4] Christopher A. Bartlett and Sumantra Ghoshal, "Matrix Management: Not a Structure, a Frame of Mind," *Harvard Business Review* (July-August 1990).

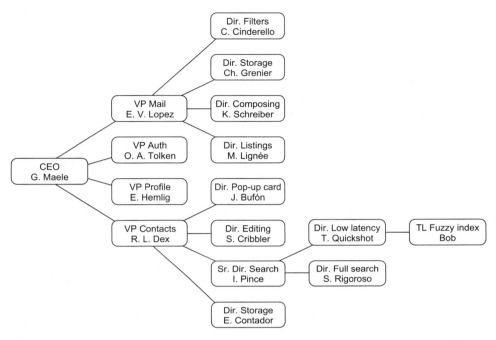

Figure 6.4   The BigCorp view of our hypothetical Gmail application (all names are purely fictional, and any similarities to real persons are entirely unintentional).

6.4   *Advantages of specification and testing*

The process of breaking down a complex task as sketched in the previous sections is iterative, both in the sense of working your way from the root to the leaves of the hierarchy as well as gradually refining your ability to anticipate the decision process. If you find that a component is difficult to specify, meaning its function requires a complex description or is too vague, then you need to step back and possibly retrace your steps to correct a mistake that was made earlier. The guiding principle is that the responsibilities of every module should be clear. A simple measure of that clarity is how concise the complete specification of each module is.

A distinct scope and small rule set also make it easier to verify a module's implementation: meaningful tests can only be written for properties that are definitive and clearly described. In this sense, the acronym TDD should be taken to mean *testability-driven design* instead of its usual expansion, *test-driven development*. Not only should the focus on testing indirectly lead to better design, but problem decomposition according to *divide et regna* should focus directly on producing modules that are easy to test.

In addition to helping with the design process, recursive division of responsibility helps concentrate communication between different parts of the application into pieces that can be replaced as a whole for the purpose of testing. When testing (parts of) the mail component of the hypothetical Gmail service, the internal structure of the `contacts` module will not be of interest, so it can be stubbed out as a whole. When testing `contacts`, you can apply the same technique to its submodules by stubbing out both the low-latency and the refined-search modules. The hierarchical structure enables tests to focus only on specific levels of granularity or abstraction, replacing siblings, descendants, and ancestors in the hierarchy with test stubs.

This is different from hardwiring a special database handle into the application for test, staging, or production mode: the database handle itself is only an implementation detail of whatever module uses the database for storage—for example, call it `UserModule`. You only need to select a database server from your test bed when testing `UserModule`; for all other testing, you create an implementation of `UserModule` that does not use a database at all and contains hardcoded test data instead. This allows everyone who does not develop `UserModule` itself to write and execute tests on their personal computer without having to install the complete test bed.

6.5   *Horizontal and vertical scalability*

What have you achieved so far? If you apply what you've seen in this chapter, you obtain modules with clearly segregated responsibilities and simple, well-specified interaction protocols. These protocols lend themselves to communication via pure message passing, regardless of whether the collaborating modules are executed within the same (virtual) machine or on different network hosts. The ability to test in isolation is at the same time a testament to the distributability of the components.

The Gmail example encapsulates the low-latency search module in a way that makes it possible to run any number of replicas of it, and so you are free to scale it up or down to handle whatever load users generate. When more instances are needed, they can be deployed to the available computing infrastructure and start populating their special-purpose caches. When ready, they will be called upon to service autocomplete requests from users. This works by having a request router set up as part of the overall low-latency search service. Whenever a new instance comes up, it registers itself with this router. Because all requests are independent of each other, it does not matter which instance performs the job as long as the result is returned within the allotted time.

In this example, depicted in figure 6.5, the size of the deployment directly translates into the end users' observed latency. Having one instance of the search module running for each user will reduce latency to the minimum possible, given the network's transfer times and the search algorithm. Reducing the number of instances will eventually lead to congestion, resulting in added latency due to search requests queuing up on the router or on the worker instances. This will in turn reduce the frequency of search requests generated per user (assuming that the client-side code refrains from sending a new request while the old one has not yet answered or timed out).

Thus, you can choose deployment size so that the search latency is as good as it needs to be, but no better.[5] This is important because running one instance per user is

---

[5] Remember that search latency needs to be formulated in terms of, for example, the 99th percentile, not the average, as explained in chapter 2.

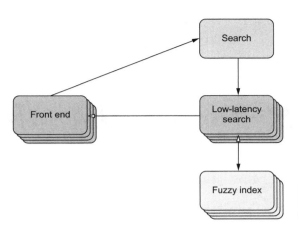

Figure 6.5 Scalable deployment of the low-latency search service is monitored and scaled up/down by the search supervisor.

obviously ridiculously wasteful. Reducing the number of instances as much as you can is in your best business interest.

6.6   *Summary*

By taking inspiration from ancient Roman emperors, we have derived a method of splitting an enormous task into a handful of smaller ones and repeating this process with each subtask until we are left with the components that collaboratively make up our entire application. Focusing on responsibility boundaries allows us to distinguish between who uses a component versus who owns it. We illustrated this procedure with the example of how a big corporation is structured.

On this journey, you have seen that such a hierarchical component structure benefits the specification and hence the testing of components. We also noted that components with segregated responsibilities naturally form units for scaling application deployment vertically as well as horizontally. We will study another benefit of this structure in the next chapter when we talk about failure handling.

Principled failure handling 7

You have seen that resilience requires distributing and compartmentalizing systems. Distribution is the only way to avoid being knocked out by a single failure, be that hardware, software, or human; and compartmentalization isolates the distributed units from each other such that the failure of one of them does not spread to the others. The conclusion was that in order to restore proper function after a failure, you need to delegate the responsibility of reacting to this event to a *supervisor*.

The importance of ownership appeared already within the decomposition of a system according to *divide et regna*, expressed as the difference between a descendant module and a dependency. Descendants own a piece of the parent's functionality, but foreign functions are incorporated only by reference. The resulting hierarchy gives the supervision structure for the modules.

7.1   *Ownership means commitment*

In the previous chapter, you saw an analogy between a system hierarchy and a corporate organization. Imagine yourself for the moment to be a customer in a store belonging to one of these organizations. If you are talking to a sales clerk about buying a shirt and that person tells you that they do not like their job and wanders off midconversation, it is not your responsibility to resolve the situation. It is the responsibility of the store manager to handle it. This seems obvious and perhaps even humorous, but consider the situation with software. It is not at all uncommon for software to tell callers about internal problems it is having, by throwing exceptions.

This does not make much sense.

The caller is rarely in a position to do something useful about the failure. If the failing module has been properly encapsulated, the caller must be completely insulated from the implementation details, but those implementation details are often exposed in the exception. For example, suppose a simple lookup function is implemented using a database query. The caller might implement some handling for a SQLException to cover the more common database failures. Now, suppose the database-based lookup function is replaced by a microservice making HTTP calls: depending on how the exceptions were declared, the complete system may or may not compile. It has certainly broken backward compatibility with existing callers. The system may appear to work as long as the new implementation is running correctly, but whatever was put in place to handle database exceptions most likely is completely unprepared to handle network exceptions due to HTTP failures.[1]

It is worth remembering that validation errors are part of the normal operation protocol between modules, but failures are those cases in which the normal protocol cannot be executed any longer and the supervision channel is needed. Validation goes to the *user* of a service, whereas failure is handled by the *owner* of the service. The sales clerk asking what size and style of shirt you want is validation. The sales clerk who wanders off midconversation is a failure condition.

If a certain piece of the problem is owned by a module, that means this module needs to solve that part and provide the corresponding functionality. No other module will do so in its stead. Dependent modules will rely on this fact and will not operate correctly or to their full feature set when the module that is supposed to offer these functions is not operational. In other words, ownership of a part of the problem implies a commitment to provide the solution, because the rest of the application will depend on this.

Every function of an application is implemented by a module that owns it; and, according to the hierarchical decomposition performed in the previous chapter, this module has a chain of ancestors reaching all the way up to the top level. That one corresponds to the high-level overall mission statement for the full system design as well as its top-most implementation module, which is typically an application bundle or a deployment configuration manager for large distributed applications.

This ancestor chain is necessary because we know that failures will happen, and by *failures* we mean incidents where a module cannot perform its function any longer (for example, because the hardware it was running on stopped working). In the example of the Gmail contacts service, the low-latency search module can be deployed on several network nodes, and if one of them fails, then the capacity of the system will be reduced unintentionally. The search service is the next owner in the ancestor chain, the *supervisor*. It is responsible for monitoring the health of its descendant modules and initiating the start of new ones in case of failure. Only when that does not work— for whatever reason—does it signal this problem to its own supervisor. This process is illustrated in figure 7.1.

The rationale for this setup is that other parts of the application will depend on the search service and all the services it offers for public consumption; therefore, this

---

[1] The FreeBSD fortune command may sometimes respond with "Steinbach's Guideline for Systems Programming: Never test for an error condition you don't know how to handle." This turns out to be better advice than it might seem at first glance.

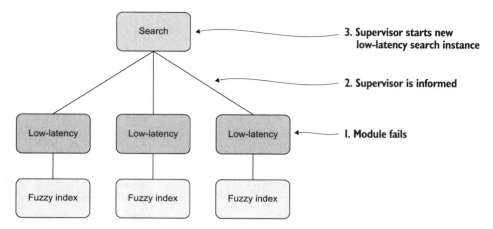

Figure 7.1 A failure is detected and handled within the search part of the contacts module's hierarchy. The search supervisor creates a new instance of the low-latency search that has previously failed—for whatever reason.

module needs to ensure that its submodules function properly at all times. Responsibility is delegated downward in the hierarchy to rest close to the point where each function is implemented. The unpredictable nature of failure makes it necessary to delegate failure-handling upward when lower-level modules cannot cope with a given situation. This works exactly as in an idealized (properly working) corporate structure, assuming that failure is treated as an expected fact of life and not swept under the carpet, and is in contrast to the traditional method of throwing exceptions back to the calling module. Even on small systems, expecting the caller to handle faults creates problems with system cohesion. This is greatly compounded when the system is distributed and location of the failing module may not be known to the caller.

7.2   *Ownership implies lifecycle control*

The scheme of failure handling developed in the previous section implies that a module will need to create all submodules that it owns. The reason is that the ability to re-create them in case of a failure depends on more than just the spiritual ownership of the problem space: the supervisor must literally own the lifecycle of its submodules. That is its responsibility. Imagine some other module creating the low-latency search module and then handing it out to contacts as a dependency, by reference. The contacts module would have to ask that other module to create a new low-latency search when it needed one, because that other module might not realize that the old instance had failed. Replacing a failed instance includes clearing out all associated state, such as removing it from routing tables and in general dropping all references to it so the runtime can then reclaim the memory and other resources that the failed module occupied.

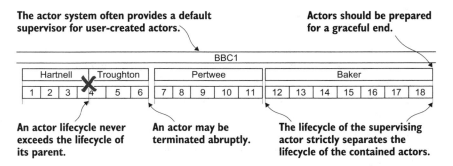

Figure 7.2   The lifecycle of each actor is bounded by the lifecycle of its supervisor. The supervisor is therefore responsible for creating supervised actors and for terminating them if necessary.

This has an interesting consequence in that the lifecycle of descendant modules is strictly bounded by its supervisor's lifecycle: the supervisor creates it, and without a supervisor it cannot continue to exist. Figure 7.2 illustrates this bounding. An actor system, BBC1, is required to have an actor available to fulfill a particular role. As with our sales clerk previously, actors do not last forever in the role. When Hartnell leaves, he is replaced successively by Troughton, Pertwee, and Baker. In each case, the actor may have spawned further actors to accomplish additional tasks. When the actor is terminated, its spawned actors are terminated as well. There is no mechanism to hand off actors from one supervisor to the next. Attempting to do so would require a level of coordination that would impose severe design limitations on the actor system in the best of circumstances. In addition, there would be risks even if the hand-off were successful, because the reason the parent actor is being shut down is that something is irreparably wrong. It would not be safe to assume that all child actors are healthy and that the problem is limited to the parent.

Dependencies are not restricted in this fashion. In traditional dependency injection, it is customary to create the dependencies first such that they are available when dependent modules are started up. Similarly, they are terminated only after all dependents have stopped using them. That can create dependencies that are untenable. If the customer depends on the sales clerk, the sales clerk cannot be replaced until the customer activity is complete. That is convenient in theory but could put the system in an unstable state if the sales clerk fails in the midst of a customer interaction. With dynamic composition, as described in chapter 5 on location transparency, this coupling becomes optional. Dependencies can come and go at arbitrary points in time, changing the wiring between modules at runtime.

Considering the lifecycle relationship between modules therefore also helps in developing and validating the hierarchical decomposition of an application. Ownership implies a lifecycle bound, whereas inclusion by reference allows independent lifecycles. The latter requires location transparency in order to enable references to dependencies to be acquired dynamically.

7.3   *Resilience on all levels*

The way you deal with failure is inherently hierarchical; this is true in our society as well as in programming. The most common way to express failure in a computer program is to raise an exception, which is then propagated up the call stack by the runtime and delivered to the innermost enclosing exception handler that declares itself responsible. The same principle is expressed in pure functional programming by the return type of a called function in that it models either a successful result or an error condition (or a list thereof, especially for functions that validate input to the program). In both cases, the responsibility of handling failure is delegated upward; but in contrast to the Reactive approach described in this chapter, these techniques conflate the usage hierarchy with supervision—the user of a service gets to handle its failures as well.

The principled approach to handling failure described in this chapter adds one more facet to the module hierarchy: every module is a unit of resilience. This is enabled by the encapsulation afforded by message passing and by the flexibility inherent in location transparency. A module can fail and be restored to proper function without its dependents needing to take action. The supervisor will handle this for everyone else's benefit.

This is true at all levels of the application hierarchy, although obviously the amount of work to be done during a restart depends on the fraction of the application that has failed. Therefore, it is important to isolate failure as early as possible, keeping the units small and the cost of recovery low, which will be discussed in detail as the Error Kernel pattern in section 12.2. Even in those cases where more drastic action is needed, the restart of the complete `contacts` service of the example Gmail application will leave most of the `mail` functionality intact (searching, viewing, and sorting mail does not depend critically on it; only convenience may suffer). Consequently, resilience can be achieved at all levels of granularity, and a Reactive design will naturally lend itself well to this goal.

7.4   *Summary*

In this chapter, we used the hierarchical component structure to determine a principled way of handling failure. The parent component is responsible for the functionality of its descendants, so it is logical to delegate the handling of such failures that cannot be dealt with locally to that same parent. This pattern allows the construction of software that is robust even in unforeseen cases, and it is the cornerstone for implementing resilience.

The next chapter investigates another aspect of building distributed components: consistency comes at a price. Once again, we will split the problem into a hierarchy of independent components.

Delimited consistency

One possible definition of a *distributed system* is a system whose parts can fail independently.[1] Reactive design is distributed by its very nature: you want to model components that are isolated from each other and interact only via location-transparent message passing in order to create a resilient supervisor hierarchy. This means the resulting application layout will suffer the consequences of being distributed. In a stateless system, the consequences relate primarily to failure handling, and recovery is handled as described in the previous chapter. When the system has state, it is not so simple. Even when each part of the system works perfectly, time is a factor. As you learned in chapter 2, a consequence of being distributed is that *strong* consistency cannot be guaranteed. In this chapter, you will learn about *delimited* consistency, which is the next-best alternative.

This can be illustrated by the example of the `mail` functionality of our example Gmail application. Because the number of users is expected to be huge, you will have to split the storage of all mail across many different computers located in multiple data centers distributed across the world. Assuming that a person's folders can be split across multiple computers, the act of moving an email from one folder to another may imply that it moves between computers. It will be either copied first to the destination and then deleted at the origin, or placed in transient storage, deleted at the origin, and then copied to the destination.

In either case, the overall count of emails for that person should stay constant throughout the process; but if you count the emails by asking the computers involved in their storage, you may see the email "in flight" and count it either twice

---

[1] A more humorous one by Leslie Lamport is as follows: "A distributed system is one in which the failure of a computer you didn't even know existed can render your own computer unusable." (Email message, May 28, 1987, http://research.microsoft.com/en-us/um/people/lamport/pubs/distributed-system.txt.)

or not at all. Ensuring that the count is consistent would entail excluding the act of counting while the transfer was in progress. The cost of strong consistency is therefore that otherwise independent components of the distributed system need to coordinate their actions by way of additional communication, which means taking more time and using more network bandwidth. This observation is not specific to the Gmail example but holds true in general for the problem of having multiple distributed parties agree on something. This is also called *distributed consensus.*

8.1 Encapsulated modules to the rescue

Fortunately, these consequences are not as severe as they may seem at first. Pat Helland,[2] a pioneer and long-time contributor to the research on strong consistency, argues that once a system's scale grows to a critical size, it can no longer be strongly consistent. The cost of coordinating a single global order of all changes that occur within it would be forbiddingly high, and adding more (distributed) resources at that point will only diminish the system's capacity instead of increasing it. Instead, we will be constructing systems from small building blocks—*entities*[3]—that are internally consistent but interact in an eventually consistent fashion.

The dataset contained within such an entity can be treated in a fully consistent fashion, applying changes such that they occur—or at least appear to occur—in one specific order. This is possible because each entity lives within a *distinct scope of serializability,* which means the entity itself is not distributed and the datasets of different entities cannot overlap. The behavior of such a system is strongly consistent—*transactional*—only for operations that do not span multiple entities.

Helland goes on to postulate that we will develop platforms that manage the complexity of distributing and interacting with these independent entities, allowing the expression of business logic in a fashion that does not need to concern itself with the deployment details as long as it obeys the transaction bounds. The entities he talks about are very similar to the encapsulated modules developed in this book so far. The difference is mainly that he focuses on managing the data stored within a system, whereas we have concerned ourselves foremost with decomposing the functionality offered by a complex application. In the end, both are the same: as viewed by a user, the only thing that matters is that the obtained responses reflect the correct state of the service at the time of the request, where *state* is nothing more than the dataset the service maintains internally. A system that supports Reactive application design is therefore a natural substrate for fulfilling Pat Helland's prediction.

---

[2] See his paper "Life Beyond Distributed Transactions," CIDR (2007), http://www.ics.uci.edu/~cs223/papers/cidr07p15.pdf.

[3] In the context of domain-driven design, these would be called *aggregate roots*; the different uses of the word *entity* are owed to its intrinsic generality.

8.2 Grouping data and behavior according to transaction boundaries

The example problem of storing a person's email folders in a distributed fashion can be solved by applying the strategy outlined in the previous section. If you want to ensure that emails can be moved without leading to inconsistent counts, then each person's complete email dataset must be managed by one entity. The example application decomposition would have a module for this purpose and would instantiate it once for every person using the system. This does not mean all mail would be literally stored within that instance. It only means all access to a person's email content would be via this dedicated instance.

In effect, this acts like a locking mechanism that serializes access, with the obvious restriction that an individual person's email cannot be scaled out to multiple managers in order to support higher transaction rates. This is fine, because a human is many orders of magnitude slower than a computer when it comes to processing email, so you will not run into performance problems by limiting scalability in this direction. What is more important is that this enables you to distribute the management of all users' mailboxes across any number of machines, because each instance is independent of all others. The consequence is that it is not possible to move emails between different people's accounts while maintaining the overall email count, but that is not a supported feature anyway.

To formalize what we just discussed, the trick is to slice the behavior and accompanying dataset in such a way that each slice offers the desired features in isolation and no transactions are necessary that span multiple slices. This technique is applied and discussed in great detail in the literature on domain-driven design (DDD).[4]

8.3 Modeling workflows across transactional boundaries

The way in which the dataset is sliced accommodates performing a certain set of operations in a strongly consistent manner but precludes this quality of behavior for all other conceivable operations. In most cases, there will be operations that are desirable but not supported. Slicing the data in another way is not an option, because that would break more important use cases. In this situation, the design must fall back to an eventually consistent way of performing those other operations, meaning that although it keeps the atomicity of the transaction, it abandons complete consistency and isolation.

To illustrate this, consider the case of moving an email from Alice's mailbox to that of another person named Bob, possibly stored in a data center on another continent. Although this operation cannot occur such that both the source and destination mailboxes execute this operation at the same time, it can ensure that the email eventually will be present only in Bob's mailbox. You can facilitate this by creating an instance of

---

[4] See, for example, Eric Evans, *Domain-Driven Design*, Addison-Wesley (2003); or Vaughn Vernon, *Implementing Domain-Driven Design*, Addison-Wesley (2013).

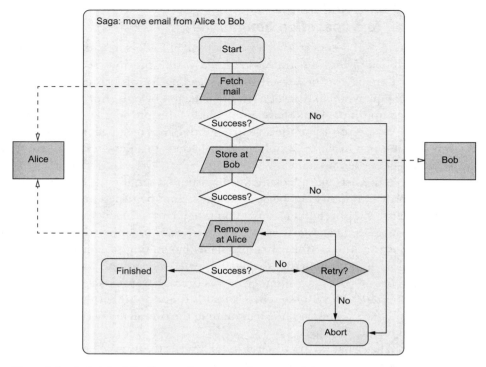

Figure 8.1   A sketch of the Saga pattern for moving an email from Alice's account to Bob's account, not including the cases for handling timeouts when communicating with the two accounts

a module that represents the transfer procedure. This module will communicate with the mailbox instances for Alice and Bob to remove the email from one and store it in the other. This so-called *Saga* pattern is known in the transactional database world as a mitigation strategy for long-running transactions. It is shown in figure 8.1 and discussed in detail in chapter 14.

Just as the mailbox modules will persist their state to survive failures, the Saga module also can be persistent. This ensures that even if the transfer is interrupted by a service outage, it will eventually complete when the mailboxes for Alice and Bob are back online.

8.4   *Unit of failure = unit of consistency*

Coming back to the initial definition of a distributed system at the beginning of this chapter, distributed entities are characterized by their ability to fail independently. Therefore, the main concern of grouping data according to transactional boundaries is to ensure that everything that must be consistent is not distributed. A consistent unit must not fail partially; if one part of it fails, then the entire unit must fail.

In the example of the transfer of an email between Alice's and Bob's mailboxes, the Saga that performs this task is one such unit. If one part of it fails, then the whole transfer must fail; otherwise, the email could be duplicated or vanish completely. This does not preclude the different subtasks being performed by submodules of the Saga, but it requires that if one of the submodules fails, the Saga must fail as a whole.

Pat Helland's entities and our units of consistency therefore match up with the modules of the supervisor hierarchy developed earlier in this chapter. This is another helpful property that can guide and validate the hierarchical decomposition of a system.

8.5 *Segregating responsibilities*

We have postulated that the process of breaking a problem into smaller pieces repeats iteratively until the remaining parts are bite-sized and can be efficiently specified, implemented, and tested. But what exactly is the right size? The criteria so far are as follows:

- A module does one job and does it well.
- The scope of a module is bounded by the responsibility of its parent.
- Module boundaries define the possible granularity of horizontal scaling by replication.
- Modules encapsulate failure, and their hierarchy defines supervision.
- The lifecycle of a module is bounded by that of its parent.
- Module boundaries coincide with transaction boundaries.

You have seen along the way that these criteria go hand in hand and are interrelated; abiding by one of them is likely to satisfy the others as well. You have a choice as to how big to make your modules. During the process of implementing and testing them—or, with experience, even during the design process—you may find that you did not choose wisely.

In the case of a too-fine-grained split, you will notice the need to use messaging patterns like Saga excessively often, or have difficulty achieving the consistency guarantees you require. The cure is relatively simple. The act of combining the responsibilities of two modules means you compose their implementations, which is unlikely to lead to new conflicts because the modules previously were completely independent and isolated from each other.

If the split is too coarse, you will suffer from complicated interplay of different concerns within a module. Supervision strategies will be difficult to identify or will inhibit necessary scalability. This defect is not as simple to repair, because separating out different parts of the behavior entails introducing new transaction boundaries between them. If the different parts become descendant modules, this may not have grave consequences because the parent module can still act as the entry point that serializes operations. If the issue that prompted the split was insufficient scalability, then this will not work because the implied synchronization cost by way of going through a single funnel was precisely the problem.

Segregating the responsibilities of such an object will necessarily require that some operations be relegated to eventually consistent behavior. One possibility that often applies is to separate the mutating operations (the *commands*) from the read operations (the *queries*). Greg Young coined the term *Command and Query Responsibility Segregation* (CQRS) describing this split, which allows the write side of a dataset to be scaled and optimized independently from its read side. The write side will be the only place where modifications to the data are permitted, allowing the read side to act as a proxy that only passively caches the information that can be queried.

Changes are propagated between modules by way of events, which are immutable facts that describe state changes that have already occurred. In contrast, the commands that are accepted at the write side merely express the intent that a change shall happen.

> **COMPARING CQRS TO A DATABASE VIEW**   Relational databases have the concept of a *view*, which is similar to the query side of CQRS. The difference lies in when the query is executed. Database implementations typically force the administrator to decide ahead of time. A traditional, pure implementation always defers execution until the data is requested, which can cause a significant performance impact on reads. In response to that, some implementations allow the result of the query to be stored physically in a *snapshot*. This typically moves the cost of updating the query result to the time the data is written, so the write operations are delayed until all the snapshots are also updated. CQRS sacrifices consistency guarantees in exchange for more flexibility about when the updates appear in the query results.

In the Gmail example, you might implement the module that generates the overview of all folders and their unread email counts such that it accesses the stored folder data whenever it is asked for a summary to be displayed in the user's browser. The storage module will have to perform several functions:

- Ingest new email as it arrives from the filtering module
- List all emails in a folder
- Offer access to the raw data and metadata for individual emails

The state of an email—for example, whether it has been read or not—will reside naturally with the message itself, in the raw email object storage. One initial design may be to store the folders to which it belongs together with each message; consequently you obtain one fully consistent dataset for each user into which all emails are stored. This dataset is then queried in order to get the overview of read and unread message counts per folder. The corresponding query must traverse the metadata of all stored emails and tally them according to folder name and status.

Doing that is costly, because the most frequent operation—checking for new email—will need to touch all the metadata, including old emails that were read long ago. An additional downside is that ingesting new email will suffer from this merely observer function, because both kinds of activities typically will be executed by the

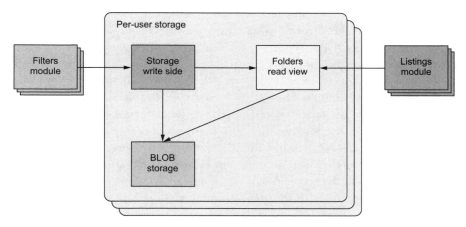

Figure 8.2 Per-user storage segregated into command and query responsibilities. New emails are written to the storage, informing the read view about changes to the metadata. Summary queries can be answered by the read view, whereas raw email contents are retrieved directly from shared binary storage.

storage module one after the other in order to avoid internal concurrency and thereby nondeterminism.

This design can be improved by separating the responsibilities for updating and querying the email storage, as shown in figure 8.2. Changes to the storage contents—such as the arrival of new email, adding and removing folder membership from messages, and removing the "unread" flag—are performed by the write side, which persists these changes into the binary object storage. Additionally, the write side informs the read view about relevant metadata changes so that this view can keep itself up to date about the read and unread email counts in each folder. This allows overview queries to be answered efficiently without having to traverse the metadata storage. In case of a failure, the read view can always be regenerated by performing this traversal once. The view itself does not need to be persistent.

8.6 *Persisting isolated scopes of consistency*

The topic of achieving persistence in systems designed for scalability is discussed in detail in chapter 17, but the application design described in this chapter has implications for the storage layer that deserve further elaboration. In a traditional database-centric application, all data are held in a globally consistent fashion in a transactional data store. This is necessary because all parts of the application have access to the entire dataset, and transactions can span various parts of it. Effort is required to define and tune the transactions at the application level as well as to make the engine efficient at executing these complex tasks at the database level.

With encapsulated modules that each fully own their datasets, these constraints are solved during the design phase. You would need one database per module instance, and each database would support modifications only from a single client. Almost all the complexity of a traditional database would go unused with such a use case because there would be no transactions to schedule or conflicts to resolve.

Coming back to CQRS, we note that there is logically only one flow of data from the active instances to the storage engine: The application module sends information about its state changes in order to persist them. The only information it needs from the storage is confirmation of successful execution of this task, upon which the module can acknowledge reception of the data to its clients and continue processing its tasks. This reduces the storage engine's requirements to just act as an append-only log of the changes—*events*—that the application modules generate. This scheme is called *event sourcing* because the persisted events are the source of truth from which application state can be recovered as needed.

An implementation with this focus is much simpler and more efficient than using a transactional database, because it does not need to support mutual exclusion of concurrent updates or any form of altering persisted data. In addition, streaming consecutive writes is the operation for which all current storage technologies achieve the highest possible throughput. Logging a stream of events for each module has the additional advantage that these streams contain useful information that can be consumed by other modules: for example, updating a dedicated read view onto the data or providing monitoring and alerting functionality, as discussed in chapter 17.

8.7   *Summary*

In this chapter, you saw that strong consistency is not achievable across a distributed system. It is limited to smaller scopes and to units that fail as a whole. This has led to adding a new facet of the component structure: the recommendation that you consider the business domain of the application in order to determine bounded contexts that are fully decoupled from each other. The terminology here is taken from domain-driven design.

The driving force behind this search for a replacement for traditional transactionality and serializability stems from the nondeterminism that is inherent in distributed systems. The next chapter places this finding into the larger context of the full range from logic programming and deterministic dataflow to full-on nondeterminism experienced with threads and locks.

Nondeterminism by need

9

This chapter is the most abstract part of this book, and it is not required for initial understanding of the later chapters. You are welcome to skip ahead to chapter 10, as long as you promise to come back here at a later time.

In chapter 3, we introduced functional programming as one of the tools of the Reactive trade. The second part of this book has up to this point been concerned with splitting a problem into encapsulated modules that interact only via asynchronous message passing, an act that is fundamentally impure: sending a message to an external object implies that the state change of that other object cannot be modeled within the sender. It is necessarily a side effect. That is not incidental; it is the sole reason to compartmentalize.[1]

It seems at first sight that the design we have chosen is fundamentally at odds with one of the core paradigms that we advertise. But this contradiction is not real, as you will see now, during a journey that could be titled "The Gradual Expulsion from Paradise."

9.1 *Logic programming and declarative data flow*

Ideally, we would want to specify input data and the characteristics of the solution, and the programming language would do the rest for us. An example is to specify that, given a list of values, we demand in return a list that contains the same elements, but in ascending order; for this, we would say that the nth element should always be greater than the $(n-1)$th element. The interpreter for our program would then figure out a sorting algorithm and apply it to any input we supplied to

---

[1] Tracking the sending of a message as an effect can of course be done, but the gain is small. It would have to be done in close proximity to the place it originates, and the modules in our hierarchical decomposition are intended to be small.

the resulting program—but it would first tell us that the input list could not contain duplicate elements. Having such a programming language would free us from the concerns of how the inputs were combined and processed; the computer would automatically figure out the correct algorithm and perform it. This process would be fully deterministic as far as the formulated desired characteristics were concerned.

Research in this direction led to the discipline of *logic programming* and the creation of programming languages like Prolog and Datalog in the 1980s. Although not quite as advanced as the aforementioned ideal—which does sound too good to be true in the sense of "do what I mean"—these languages allow us to state the rules of a domain and ask the compiler to prove additional theorems that then correspond to the solution for a given problem. Logic programming so far has not had significant influence on mainstream software development, foremost due to its disadvantages with respect to runtime performance in comparison with imperative languages that are much farther removed from paradise.

A step toward the mainstream takes us to pure functional programming, expressing programs and algorithms with functions and immutable values, where a function is an example of such a value. This way of programming is close to mathematics in that functions describe transformations that can be composed with other functions without having to specify the input values up front—a program can first calculate which sequence of functions to apply and then feed the inputs to them. Compared with logic programming, we trade decent runtime performance for the duty of figuring out the correct algorithms ourselves. Instead of generating the algorithm for us, the compiler can at best verify that the algorithm we provided has the desired properties. This verification requires the use of a type system that is powerful enough to encode the characteristics we want. In this camp, we find a large number of languages to choose from, including Haskell, Coq, Agda, and, recently, Idris. Many of the code samples in this book are written in the Scala language, which can express pure functional programs but incorporates support for mutability and object orientation as well.

Programming in a pure functional style means the evaluation of every expression always yields the same result when given the same inputs. There are no side effects. This enables the compiler to schedule evaluation on an as-needed basis instead of doing it strictly in the order given in the source code, including the possibility of parallel execution. The necessary precondition for this is that all values are immutable—nothing can change after it has been created. This has the very beneficial consequence that values can be freely shared among concurrently executing threads without any need for synchronization.

A close cousin of the functional paradigm is dataflow programming. The difference is that the former focuses on functions and their composition, whereas the latter concentrates on the movement of data through a network (more precisely, a directed acyclic graph) of connected computations. Every node of this network is a single-assignment variable that is calculated once all inputs of its defining expressions have been determined. Therefore, the result of injecting data into the processing network is always fully deterministic, even though all computations within it conceptually run in parallel. Dataflow programming is, for example, part of the Oz language,[2] but it can also be embedded in a language like Scala using composable Futures, as shown in chapter 3.

9.2 Functional reactive programming

A hybrid between the application of (pure) functions and the description of a processing network is *functional reactive programming* (FRP), which focuses on the propagation and transformation of change: for example, from measurements that arrive from a sensor to a GUI element on the human operator's screen. In its pure form, FRP is close to dataflow programming in that it determines the changes to all input signals of a given transformation before evaluating it. This restricts implementations to run effectively single-threaded in order to avoid the problem of *glitches*, which refers to the phenomenon that the output of an element fluctuates during the propagation of an update throughout the network.

Recently, the term FRP has also been used for implementations that are not glitch-free, such as Rx.NET, RxJava, and various JavaScript frameworks like React, Knockout, Backbone, and so on. These concentrate on the efficient propagation of events and convenient wiring of the processing network, compromising on mathematical purity. As an example, consider the following functions:

```
f(x) = x + 1
g(x) = x - 1
h(x) = f(x) - g(x)
```

In mathematical terms, `h(x)` would always be exactly 2, because we can substitute the definitions of the other two functions into its body and witness that the only variable input cancels out. Written in the aforementioned frameworks, the result would be 2 most of the time, but the values 1 and 3 would also be emitted from time to time (unless you took care to manually synchronize the two update streams for `f` and `g`).

This deviation from fully deterministic behavior is not random coincidence, and it is also not due to defects in these frameworks. It is a consequence of allowing the concurrent execution of effectful code, meaning code that manipulates the state of the universe surrounding the program. Both aspects—concurrency and effects—are essential to achieve good performance on today's hardware, making nondeterminism a necessary evil. Another angle on this is presented in languages like Bloom[3] that employ the CALM[4] correspondence to identify those parts of a program that require explicit coordination, expressing the rest as so-called *disorderly programming*.

---

[2] See http://mozart.github.io/mozart-v1/doc-1.4.0/tutorial/node8.html for more details on dataflow concurrency.

[3] See www.bloom-lang.net/features for an overview.

[4] Consistency and logical monotonicity. For a formal treatment, see Ameloot et al., "Relational Transducers for Declarative Networking," *Journal of the ACM* 60, no. 2 (2010), http://arxiv.org/pdf/1012.2858v1.pdf.

Glitch-free applications can be written using frameworks that are not glitch-free. The only problematic operations are those that merge streams of updates that come from a common source and should therefore show a certain correlation. Processing networks that do not contain such operations will not suffer from nondeterminism.

9.3   *Sharing nothing simplifies concurrency*

When concurrency as well as stateful behavior are required, there is no escape from nondeterminism. This is obvious when considering the distributed execution of components that communicate via asynchronous message passing: the order in which messages from Alice and Bob reach Charlie is undefined unless Alice and Bob expend considerable effort to synchronize their communication.[5] The answer to Bob's question, "Have you heard from Alice yet?" would thus vary unpredictably among different executions of this scenario.

In the same way that distribution entails concurrency, the opposite is also true. Concurrency means two threads of execution can make progress at the same time, independent of each other. In a non-ideal world, this means both threads can also fail independently, making them distributed by definition.

Therefore, whenever a system comprises concurrent or distributed components, there will be nondeterminism in the interaction between these components. Nondeterminism has a significant cost in terms of the ability to reason about the behavior of the program, and consequently we spend considerable effort on ensuring that all possible outcomes have been accounted for. In order to keep this overhead limited to what is required, we want to bound the nondeterminism we allow in a program to that which is caused by the distributed nature of its components, meaning that we only consider the unpredictability in the messaging sequence between encapsulated modules and forbid any direct coupling between them.

In this sense, the term *shared-nothing concurrency* means the internal mutable state of each module is safely stowed away inside it and not shared directly with other modules. An example of what is forbidden is sending a reference to a mutable object (for example, a Java array) from one module to another while also keeping a reference. If both modules subsequently modify the object from within their transaction boundary, their logic will be confused by the additional coupling that has nothing to do with message passing.

The strategies to deal with nondeterminism can be classified into two groups:

- We can reject those orderings of events that are problematic, introducing explicit synchronization to reduce the effect of nondeterminism to a level at which it no longer changes the program's characteristics.

---

[5] For example, Alice could wait until Bob has heard back from Charlie—and told her so—before sending her message.

- Alternatively, we can restrict the program to use of operations that are commutative, which means the order in which they are executed has no influence on the final result of the distributed computation.[6]

The former involves a runtime cost for coordination, whereas the latter involves a development cost for restricting the exchanged dataset to be expressible efficiently in a conflict-free representation.

9.4 *Shared-state concurrency*

The final step of the journey away from paradise brings us into the world of threads and locks and atomic CPU instructions, and it can be argued whether this corresponds to the necessary evil (that is, the here and now) or places us directly in Hell. The background for this scenario is that current computers are based on the Von Neumann architecture, with the extension that multiple independent execution units share the same memory. The way data are transferred between CPU cores is therefore by reading to and writing from this shared memory instead of sending messages directly, with the consequence that all cores need to carefully coordinate their accesses.

Programming with threads and synchronization primitives maps directly to this architecture,[7] and it is your duty to embed the correct level of coordination in your program because the CPU would otherwise operate in its fastest possible and most reckless mode. The resulting code contains a tightly interwoven web of business logic and low-level synchronization, because memory accesses are so ubiquitous.

The problem with this code is that synchronization protocols do not compose well: if Alice knows how to conduct a conversation with Bob without getting confused, and Bob knows how to converse with Charlie, that does not mean the same way of talking with each other will allow a shared group conversation among all three of them. We also know from social experience that getting a larger group of people to agree on something is disproportionately more difficult than achieving agreement between just two persons.

9.5 *So, what should we do?*

Along the journey from paradise toward the netherworld, we have gradually lost the ability to predict the behavior of our programs. Toward the end, it became nearly impossible to validate a design by reasoning about the way it is built up from simpler parts because the interplay between the building blocks entangles their internal behavior. This leads to the necessity of performing extensive testing and hopefully exhaustive verification scenarios for programs that are constructed directly upon threads and locks.

---

[6] These are called *conflict-free replicated data types* (CRDT). See Shapiro et al., INRIA (2011), http://citeseerx.ist .psu.edu/viewdoc/download?doi=10.1.1.231.4257&rep=rep1&type=pdf.

[7] We are glossing over the fact that threads are an illusion provided by the operating system to allow more concurrent executions than the number of available CPU cores.

Threads and low-level synchronization primitives are important tools for situations where performance requirements or the nature of the problem (such as writing a low-level device driver) force us to exercise precise control over how the CPU instructions are carried out. This situation is one that most programmers will rarely find themselves in. We can in almost all cases rely on someone else to have solved that level of the problem for us. An example is the implementation of an Actor framework that uses low-level features to provide users with a higher level of abstraction.

Retracing our steps, we see that going from shared-state concurrency to shared-nothing concurrency eliminates an entire class of problems from the application domain. We no longer need to concern ourselves with the way CPUs synchronize their actions, because we write encapsulated components that only send immutable messages that can be shared without issues. Freed from this concern, we can concentrate on the essence of distributed programming for solving our business problems, and this is where we want to be in case distribution is necessary.

The next step backward removes the need for concurrency and distribution, enabling the resulting program to shed all nondeterminism and greatly enhance the power of reasoning about the composition of a larger application from simple pieces. This is desirable because it eliminates yet another class of defects from the application domain. We no longer need to worry about having to manually ensure that things run in the correct sequence. With FRP or dataflow, we reason only about how data are transformed, not how the machine executes this transformation. Pure functional programming allows us to compose the application of calculations much in the same way we would write them down mathematically—time no longer plays a role.[8]

Absent an efficient and proven implementation of logic programming, this last step brought us to the place we want to be: a fully deterministic, reasonable programming model. The tools to program in this way are widely available, so we should use them wherever we can.

The dividing line between concurrent nondeterminism and reasonable determinism is established by the need for distribution. A distributed system can never be fully deterministic because of the possibility of partial failure. Employing a distributed solution must always be weighed against the associated cost; and apart from the distributed parts of a program, we should always strive to stay as close to functional and declarative programming with immutable values as is feasible.

In chapters 4–8, we have detailed the reasons why and when distribution is necessary and useful; the desire to stay nondistributed as long as possible does not change this reasoning. The contribution of this chapter is to present a weight on the opposite side of resilience, scalability, and responsibility segregation. You will have to place

---

[8] Roland's favorite analogy is cooking: "I know in principle how to cook all parts of a meal, and in practice I can also do it one part at a time (for example, concentrating on the meat until it is finished), but as soon as I try to do several things at once, I start making mistakes. It would be nice if time could be eliminated from this process, because that would allow me to do one thing after the other without the hassle of switching my focus repeatedly. This is much like the difference between explicit concurrency and declarative programming."

both on the scales and balance them well for each design you develop. For further reading on this topic, we recommend the literature detailing the design of the Oz language, in particular Peter van Roy's paper "Convergence in Language Design."[9]

9.6 *Summary*

This chapter has taken you all the way from pure, deterministic programming approaches via shared-nothing concurrency to threads and locks. You have seen that all these tools have a place in your tool belt and that you should be careful to stay as close to the initially mentioned paradigms as you can. Only employ nondeterministic mechanisms where needed, whether for scalability or resilience. In the next chapter, we will complete part 2 of this book by coming back to where we set out from in chapter 1: considering how messages flow through applications.

---

[9] Peter van Roy, "Convergence in Language Design: A Case of Lightning Striking Four Times in the Same Place," *Proceedings of the 8th International Conference on Functional and Logic Programming* (2006): 2–12, https://mozart.github.io/publications.

Message flow

10

Now that you have established a hierarchy of encapsulated modules that represent an application, you need to orchestrate them and realize the solution. The key point developed throughout the previous chapters is that modules communicate only asynchronously by passing messages. They do not directly share mutable state. You have seen many advantages of this approach along the way, enabling scalability and resilience, especially in concert with location transparency. The alternative, shared-state concurrency, is hard to get right.

There is one further advantage: basing a distributed design exclusively on messages allows you to model and visualize the business processes within your application as message flows. This helps avoid limitations to scalability or resilience early in the planning process.

10.1 Pushing data forward

The fastest way for a message to travel from Alice via Bob to Charlie is if every station along the path sends the message onward as soon as the station receives it. The only delays in this process are due to the transmission of the message between the stations and the processing of the message within each station.

As obvious as this statement is, it is instructive to consider the overhead added by other schemes. Alice could, for example, place the message in shared storage and tell Bob about it. Bob would then retrieve the message from storage, possibly writing it back with some added information, and then tell Charlie about it, who would also look at the shared storage. In addition to the two message sends, you would have to perform three or four interactions with a shared storage facility. Sharing mutable data between distributed entities is not the path to happiness.

Alice also might be concerned about whether Bob currently has time to deal with the message, and might ask him for permission to send it. Bob would reply

120

when ready, Alice would send the message, and then the same procedure would be repeated between Bob and Charlie. Each of the two initial message sends would be accompanied by two more messages that conveyed readiness: first, that of the sender to send more; and then, that of the recipient to receive it.

Patterns like these are well established for purposes of persistence (such as durable message queues) or flow control (as we will discuss in depth in chapter 16), and they have their uses; but when it comes to designing the flow of messages through a Reactive application, it is important to keep the paths short and the messages flowing in one direction as much as possible, always toward the logical destination of the data. You will frequently need to communicate successful reception back to the sender, but that data stream can be kept lean by employing batching to send cumulative acknowledgments.

The previous examples were simplistic, but the same principle applies more broadly. Coming back to the Gmail implementation, incoming emails that are sent to the system's users need to be transmitted from the SMTP module of the `mail` part of the application into the per-user storage. On their way, they need to pass through the module that applies user-defined filters to sort each email into the folder it belongs to.

As soon as emails are in per-user storage, they are visible to the user in folder listings and so on; but in order to support a search function across the entire dataset owned by a user, there needs to be an index that is kept up to date at all times. This index could periodically sync up with the current state of the mailbox storage and incorporate new emails, but that would be as inefficient as Bob periodically asking Alice whether there has been a new message since the last one. Keeping the data flowing forward means, in this case, that a copy of the email will be sent to the indexing service after the email has been classified by the `filter` module, which updates the index in real time. The full process is illustrated in figure 10.1.

In this fashion, the number of messages that are exchanged is kept to a minimum, and data are treated while they are "hot," which signifies both their relevance to the user as well as their being in active memory in the computers involved. The alternative of polling every few minutes would be to ask the storage service for an overview of its data and thereby force it to keep the data in memory or read the data back in after a resource shortage or outage.

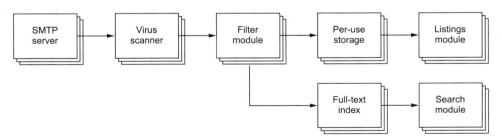

Figure 10.1 Data flows forward from the source (the SMTP server module) toward the destination, feeding to the indexing service in parallel to storing the raw data.

10.2   *Modeling the processes of your domain*

Programming with messages exchanged between autonomous modules also lends itself well to the use of *ubiquitous language* as practiced in domain-driven design. Customers of the software development process, who can be users or product owners, will be most comfortable describing what they want in terms that they understand. This can be exploited for mutual benefit by turning the common language of the problem domain into modules and messages of the application architecture, giving concrete and rigorous definitions. The resulting model will be comprehensible for customers and developers alike, and it will serve as a fixed point for communicating about the emerging product during the development process.

We hinted at the reason behind this utility in section 2.6.2: anthropomorphic metaphors help humans visualize and choreograph processes. It is an act we enjoy, and this creates a fertile ground for finding ways of moving abstract business requirements into the realm of intuitive treatment. This is the reason we talk about Alice, Bob, and Charlie instead of nodes A, B, and C; in the latter case, we would struggle to try to keep our reasoning technical, whereas in the former case we can freely apply the wealth of social experience we have accumulated. It is not surprising that we find good analogies for distributed computing in our society: we are the prototypical distributed system!

Intuition is widely applicable in this process: when two facts need to be combined to perform a certain task, then you know there must be one person who knows both and combines them. This corresponds to the delimited consistency rule. Hierarchical treatment of failure is based on how our society works, and message passing expresses exactly how we communicate. You should use these helpers wherever you can.

10.3   *Identifying resilience limitations*

When laying out message flows within an application according to the business processes you want to model, you will see explicitly who needs to communicate with whom, or which module will need to exchange messages with what other module. You have also created the hierarchical decomposition of the overall problem and thus obtained the supervision hierarchy, and this will tell you which message flows are more or less likely to be interrupted by failure.

When sending to a module that is far down in the hierarchy and performing work that is intrinsically risky, such as using an external resource, you must foresee communication procedures for reestablishing the message flow after the supervisor has restarted the module. As shown in figure 10.2, in some cases it can be better to send messages via the supervisor from the start so the clients that are the senders of the messages need not reacquire a reference to the freshly started target module so often. They still will need to have recovery procedures in place to implement proper compartmentalization and isolation, but invoking those less frequently will further reduce the effect of a failure.

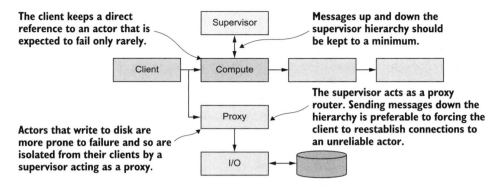

Figure 10.2   Messages may be sent directly to an actor or to a supervisor acting as a router if the actor itself performs risky operations such as I/O.

Messages may be sent directly to an actor or to a supervisor acting as a router if the actor itself performs risky operations such as I/O.

For this reason, you will see some message flows that are directed from a module to its descendant; but in most cases the supervisor is only involved as a proxy, and the real client is not part of the same supervision subtree. In general, most message flows are horizontal, and supervision is performed on the vertical axis, coming back to the notion that usually the *user* and the *owner* of a service are not the same.

10.4   *Estimating rates and deployment scale*

Focusing on message flows and sketching them out across the application layout allows you to make some educated guesses or apply input rates from previous experience or measurement. As messages flow through the system and are copied, merged, split up, and disseminated, you can trace the associated rate information to obtain an impression of the load the application modules will experience.

When the first prototypes of the most critical modules are ready for testing, you can begin evaluating their performance and use Little's formula to estimate the necessary deployment size, as detailed in section 2.1.2. You can validate your assumption as to which modules need to be scaled out for performance reasons and where you can consolidate pieces that were split up erroneously.

The ability to perform these predictions and assessments stems from the fact that you have defined messages as concrete units of work that can be counted, buffered, spread out, and so on. You benefit from being explicit about message passing in the design. If you were to hide the distributed nature of the program behind synchronous RPC, this planning tool would be lost, and you would be more concerned about trying to anticipate the size of the thread pools needed in your processes. That is more difficult to do because it requires understanding both the domain *and* the characteristics of the system where the application will be deployed, which may vary over the life of the system and across the different development, test, and production systems.

10.5   *Planning for flow control*

Closely related to the estimation process is that you need to foresee bulkheads between different parts of your application. When input message rates exceed the limits you planned for, or when the dynamic scaling of the application is not fast enough to cope with a sudden spike in traffic, you must have measures in place to contain the overflow and protect the other parts of the system.

With a clear picture of how increased message rates are propagated within the application, you can determine at which points requests will be rejected (presumably close to the entrance of the application) and where you need to store messages on disk so that they are processed after the spike has passed or more capacity has been provisioned. These mechanisms will need to be activated at runtime when their time comes, and this process should be fully automatic. Human responses are typically too slow, especially on Sunday morning at 3:00 a.m. You need to propagate the congestion information upstream to enable the sender of a message stream to act on it and refrain from overwhelming the recipient. Patterns for implementing this are discussed in chapter 15; of particular interest are Reactive Streams (www.reactive-streams.org) as a generic mechanism for mediating back pressure in a distributed setting.

10.6   *Summary*

In this and the previous chapters in part 2 of the book, we have discussed the driving principles behind a Reactive application design. The central concept is to decompose the overall business problem in a hierarchical fashion according to *divide et regna* into fully encapsulated modules that communicate only by asynchronous, nonblocking, location-transparent message passing. The modularization process is guided and validated by the following rules:

- A modules does one job and does it well.
- The responsibility of a module is bounded by the responsibility of its parent.
- Module boundaries define the possible granularity of horizontal scaling by replication.
- Modules encapsulate failure, and their hierarchy defines supervision.
- The lifecycle of a module is bounded by that of its parent.
- Module boundaries coincide with transaction boundaries.

We illuminated different paradigms ranging from logic programming to shared-state concurrency and concluded that you should prefer a functional, declarative style within these modules and consider the cost of distribution and concurrency when choosing the granularity of your modules. You saw the advantages of explicitly modeling message flows within the system for the purposes of keeping communication paths and latencies short, modeling business processes using ubiquitous language, estimating rates and identifying resilience limitations, and planning how to perform flow control.

Part 3

Patterns

We have spent a fair amount of time so far discussing the *what* and *why* of being Reactive. Now it is time to focus on the *how*. In part 3, we will present patterns of development that will help you implement Reactive applications. We will begin by discussing how to test to ensure that your application is Reactive so you can build forward with confidence that you are meeting the Reactive contract, from the smallest components to an entire cross–data center deployment. Then we will delve into specific patterns for building Reactive systems across all dimensions of Reactive concepts.

In this part, you will learn about the following:

- Testing Reactive systems, with a specific emphasis on asynchronous testing
- Layering internal and external fault tolerance into your application
- Managing the resources used by your Reactive application
- Managing the flow of messages and data within and between your applications
- Managing state and persist data in Reactive systems

We will present the individual patterns by first introducing their essence in one short paragraph (for easy reference when you revisit them), followed by information about where the pattern emerged, and then details of an example where the pattern is applied to a concrete problem. Each pattern is then summarized with the concerns it addresses, its quintessential features, and its scope of applicability.

Part 2 discussed the building blocks on which a Reactive system can be built. It may be worthwhile to frequently recall that background while reading forward—in our experience, it is usually the second approach to a topic that brings the "eureka!" moments.

Testing reactive applications

Now that we have covered the philosophy, we need to discuss how to verify that the Reactive applications you build are elastic, resilient, and responsive. Testing is covered first because of the importance of proving Reactive capabilities. Just as test-driven design (TDD) allows you to ensure that you are writing logic that meets your requirements from the outset, you must focus on putting into place the infrastructure required to verify elasticity, resilience, and responsiveness.

What we will not cover is how to test your business logic—countless good resources are available on that topic. We will assume that you have picked a methodology and matching tools for verifying the local and synchronous parts of your application and will focus instead on the aspect of distribution that is inherent to Reactive systems.

11.1 How to test

Testing applications is the foremost effort developers can undertake to ensure that code is written to meet all its requirements without defects. Here, a truly Reactive application has several dimensions beyond merely fulfilling the specifications for the logic to be implemented, guided by the principles of responsiveness, elasticity, and resilience. In this book, where patterns are outlined to enable Reactive applications, testing is integral to each pattern described so that you can verify that your application is Reactive. In this chapter, we lay the foundations for this by covering common techniques and principles.

Before delving into patterns of testing, we must define a vocabulary. For anyone who has worked for a mature development organization, testing as a means to reduce risk is ingrained. Consulting firms are also well known for having stringent testing methodologies, in order to reduce the risk of a lawsuit from clients who have expectations about the level of quality for software being delivered. Every test plan is reviewed and approved by each level of the project leadership, from team leads through architects and project management, with the ultimate responsibility residing with the partner or organizational stakeholder to ensure that accountability exists for any improper behavior that may occur. As a result, many levels of functional tests have been identified and codified into standards for successful delivery.

ERRORS VS. FAILURES In this chapter—in particular, when we touch on resilience—it will be helpful to recall the distinction between *errors* and *failures*, as defined by the glossary[1] of the Reactive Manifesto:

> *A failure is an unexpected event within a service that prevents it from continuing to function normally. A failure will generally prevent responses to the current, and possibly all following, client requests. This is in contrast with an error, which is an expected and coded-for condition—for example an error discovered during input validation—that will be communicated to the client as part of the normal processing of the message. Failures are unexpected and will require intervention before the system can resume at the same level of operation. This does not mean that failures are always fatal, rather that some capacity of the system will be reduced following a failure. Errors are an expected part of normal operations, are dealt with immediately and the system will continue to operate at the same capacity following an error.*

NOTE Examples of failures are hardware malfunctions, processes terminating due to fatal resource exhaustion, and program defects that result in corrupted internal state.

11.1.1 Unit tests

Unit tests are the best known of all the kinds of tests: an independent unit of source code, such as a class or function, is tested rigorously to ensure that every line and condition in the logic meets the specification outlined by the design or product owner. Depending on how the code is structured, this can be easy or difficult—monolithic functions or methods inside such a source unit can be difficult to test due to all the varying conditions that can exist in these units.

It is best to structure code into individual, atomic units of work that perform only one action. When this is done, writing unit tests for these units is simple—what are the expected inputs that should successfully result in a value against which assertions can be made, and what are the expected inputs that should not succeed and result in an exception or error?

Because unit tests focus on whether the right response is delivered for a given set of inputs, this level of testing typically does not involve testing for Reactive properties.

---

[1] www.reactivemanifesto.org/glossary#Failure

11.1.2 Component tests

Component tests are also generally familiar to anyone who writes tests: they test a service's application programming interface (API). Inputs are passed to each public interface exposed by the API, and, for several variations of correct input data, it is verified that the service returns a valid response.

Error conditions are tested by passing invalid data into each API and checking that the appropriate validation error is returned from the service. Validation errors should be an important design consideration for any public API, in order to convey an explicit error for any input that is deemed invalid for the service to handle appropriately.

Concurrency should also be explored at this level, where a service that should be able to handle multiple requests simultaneously returns the correct value for each client. This can be difficult to test for systems that are synchronous in nature, because concurrency in this case can involve locking schemes; it can be difficult for the person writing the test to create a setup to prove that multiple requests are being handled at the same time.

At this level, you also start testing the responsiveness of a service, to see whether it can reliably keep its service-level agreement (SLA) under nominal conditions. And, for a component that acts as a supervisor for another, you will also encounter aspects of resilience: does the supervisor react correctly to unexpected failures in its subordinates?

11.1.3 String tests

Now we diverge from the ordinary practices of testing, where you need to verify that requests into one service or microservice that depends on other such services or microservices can return the appropriate values. It is important to avoid getting bogged down in the low-level details of functionality that has already been tested at the unit- and component-test levels.

At this level, you also begin to consider failure scenarios in addition to the nominal and error cases: how should a service react to the inability of its dependencies to perform their functions? In addition, it is important to verify that SLAs are kept when dependent services take longer to respond than usual, both when they meet and when they do not meet their respective SLAs.

11.1.4 Integration tests

Typically, systems you build do not exist in a vacuum; prior to this level of testing, dependencies on external components are stubbed out or mocked so that you do not require access to these systems to prove that everything else in the system meets your requirements. But when you reach the level of integration testing, you should ensure that such interactions are proven to work and handle nominal as well as erroneous input as expected.

At this level, you also test for resilience by injecting failures: for example, by shutting off services to see how their communication partners and supervisors react. You also need to verify that SLAs are kept under nominal as well as failure scenarios and under varying degrees of external load.

11.1.5 *User-acceptance tests*

This final level of testing is not always explicitly executed. Most notable exceptions include situations where the consequences of failing to meet the requirements are severe (for example, space missions, high-volume financial processing, and military applications). The purpose is to prove that the overall implementation meets the project goals set by the client paying for the system to be built. But such testing can be applicable for organizations who treat the product owner as a client and the delivery team as the consulting firm. User-acceptance testing is the level at which the check-writer defines proofs that the system meets their needs, in isolation from those tests implemented by the consulting firm. This provides independent validation that the application, with all its various components and services, fulfills the ultimate goal of the project.

This level of testing may sound unnecessary for projects where an external contractor or firm has been hired to build the implementation, but we argue otherwise. One of the great benefits of test tooling such as behavior-driven development (BDD)[2] is to provide a domain-specific-language (DSL)[3] for testing that even nontechnical team members can read or even implement. Using tools like well-known implementations and variants of Cucumber (https://cucumber.io)—such as Cuke4Duke (https://github.com/cucumber/cuke4duke), Specs2 (http://etorreborre.github.io/specs2), and ScalaTest (www.scalatest.org)—provides business-process leaders on teams with the capability to write and verify tests.

11.1.6 *Black-box vs. white-box tests*

When testing a component, you must decide whether the test will have access to the component's internal details. Such details include being able to send commands that are not part of the public interface or to query the internal state that is normally encapsulated and hidden. Testing without access to these is called *black-box testing* because the component is viewed as a box that hides its inner workings in darkness. The opposite is termed *white-box testing* because all details are laid bare, like in a laboratory clean room where all internals can be inspected.

A Reactive system is defined by its responses to external stimulus, which means testing for the Reactive properties of your applications or components will primarily be black-box testing, even if you prefer to use white-box testing within the unit tests for the business logic itself. As an example, you might have a minute specification that is very precise about how the incoming data are to be processed, and the algorithm is implemented such that intermediate results can be inspected along the way. The unit tests for this part of the application will be tightly coupled to the implementation itself; and for any change made to the internals, there is a good chance that some test cases will be invalidated.

---

[2] http://en.wikipedia.org/wiki/Behavior-driven_development
[3] http://en.wikipedia.org/wiki/Domain-specific_language

This piece of code will form the heart of your application, but it is not the only part: data need to be ingested for processing, the algorithm must be executed, and results need to be emitted, and all these aspects require communication and are governed by Reactive principles. You will hence write other tests that verify that the core algorithm is executed when appropriate and with the right inputs and that the output arrives at the desired place after the allotted time in order to keep the SLA for the service you are implementing. All these aspects do not depend on the internal details of the core algorithm; they operate without regard to its inner workings. This has the added benefit that the higher-level tests for responsiveness, elasticity, and resilience will have a higher probability of staying relevant and correct while the core code is being refactored, bugs are fixed, or new features are added.

11.2 Test environment

An important consideration for writing tests is that they must be executed on hardware that is at least somewhat representative of that on which it will ultimately be deployed, particularly for systems where latency and throughput must be validated (to be discussed in section 11.7). This may provide some insight into how well a component or an algorithm may perform, particularly if the task is CPU-intensive, relative to another implementation tested on the same platform.

Many popular benchmarks in the development community are run on laptops: machines with limited resources with respect to number of cores, size of caches and memory, disk subsystems that do not perform data replication, and operating systems that do not match intended production deployments. A laptop is typically constructed with different design goals than a server-class machine, leading to different performance characteristics where some activities may be performed faster and others slower than on the final hardware. Although the laptop may have capabilities that exceed a specific server-class machine (for example, a solid-state drive as opposed to a hard disk for storage) and that make it perform better in certain situations, it likely will not represent the performance to be expected when the application reaches production. Basing decisions on the results of tests executed in such an environment may lead to poor decisions being made about how to improve the performance of an application.

It is an expensive proposition to ask all companies, particularly those with limited financial resources such as startups, to consider mirroring their production environment for testing purposes. But the cost of not doing so can be enormous if an organization makes a poor choice based on meaningless findings derived from a development environment.

Note that deployment in the cloud can make testing more difficult as well. Hypervisors do not necessarily report accurately about the resources they make available in a multitenancy environment, particularly with respect to the number of cores available to applications at any given time. This can make for highly dynamic and unpredictable performance in production. Imagine trying to size thread pools in a very specific way for smaller instances in the cloud where you are not expecting access to more than four virtual CPUs, but there is no guarantee you will receive that at any given moment. If you must verify specific performance via throughput and/or latency, dedicated hardware is a considerably better option.

11.3 Testing asynchronously

The most prominent difficulty that arises when testing Reactive systems is that the pervasive use of asynchronous message passing requires a different way of formulating test cases. Consider testing a translation function that can turn Swedish text into English.

Listing 11.1 Testing a purely synchronous translation function

```
val input = "Hur mår du?"
val output = "How are you?"
translate(input) should be(output)
```

This example uses ScalaTest syntax. The first two lines define the expected input and output strings, and the third line invokes the translation function with the input and asserts that this should result in the expected output. The underlying assumption is that the `translate()` function computes its value synchronously and that it is done when the function call returns.

A translation service that can be replicated and scaled out will not have the possibility of directly returning the value: it must be able to asynchronously send the input string to the processing resources. This could be modeled by returning a Future[4] for the result string that will eventually hold the desired value:

```
val input = "Hur mår du?"
val output = "How are you?"
val future = translate(input)
// what now?
```

The only thing you can assert at this point is that the function does indeed return a Future, but probably there will not yet be a value available within it, so you cannot continue with the test procedure.

Another presentation of the translation service might use Actor messaging, which means the request is sent as a one-way message and the reply is expected to be sent as another one-way message at a later point in time. In order to receive this reply, there needs to be a suitable recipient:

```
val input = "Hur mår du?"
val output = "How are you?"
val probe = TestProbe()                          ◁———— An Akka utility
translationService ! Translate(input, probe.ref)
// when can we continue?
```

---

[4] Recall that a Future is a handle to a value that may be delivered asynchronously at a later time. The code that supplies the value will fulfill the corresponding Promise with it, enabling code that holds a reference to the Future to react to the value using callbacks or transformations. Flip back to chapter 2 to refresh yourself on the details if necessary.

`TestProbe` is an object that contains a message queue to which messages can be sent via the corresponding `ActorRef`. You use it as the return address in the message to the translation service Actor. Eventually the service will reply, and the message with the expected output string should arrive within the probe; but again, you cannot proceed with the test procedure at this point because you do not know when exactly that will be the case.

11.3.1 *Providing blocking message receivers*

> **NOTE** The methods used to implement the solutions that follow typically are not recommended for regular use because of their thread-blocking nature, but bear with us: even for testing, we will present nicely nonblocking solutions later. Using classical test frameworks can require you to fall back to what is discussed here, and it is educational to consider the progression presented in this section.

One solution to the dilemma is to suspend the test procedure until the translation service has performed its work and then inspect the received value. In case of the Future, you can poll its status in a loop:

```
while (!future.isCompleted) Thread.sleep(50)
```

This will check every 50 ms whether the Future has received its value or was completed with an error, not letting the test continue before one or the other occurs. The syntax used is that of `scala.concurrent.Future`; in other implementations, the name of the status query method could be `isDone()` (`java.util.concurrent.Future`), `isPending()` (JavaScript Q), or `inspect()` (JavaScript when), to name a few examples. In a real test procedure, the number of loop iterations must be bounded:

```
var i = 20
while (!future.isCompleted && i > 0) {
  i -= 1
  Thread.sleep(50)
}
if (i == 0) fail("translation was not received in time")
```

This will wait only for up to roughly 1 second and fail the test if the Future is not completed within that time window. Otherwise, message loss or a programming error could lead to the Future never receiving a value; then the test procedure would hang and never yield a result.

Most Future implementations include methods that support awaiting a result synchronously. A selection is shown in table 11.1.

Table 11.1   Methods for synchronously awaiting a Future result

Language	Synchronous implementation
Java	`future.get(1, TimeUnit.SECONDS);`
Scala	`Await.result(future, 1.second)`
C++	`std::chrono::milliseconds span(1000);` `future.wait_for(span);`

These methods can be used in tests to retain the same test procedure as for the verification of the synchronous translation service.

Listing 11.2   Awaiting the result blocks synchronously on the translation

```
val input = "Hur mår du?"
val output = "How are you?"
val result = Await.result(translate(input), 1.second)
result should be(output)
```

With this formulation, you can take an existing test suite for the translation service and mechanically replace all invocations that used to return a strict value so that they synchronously await the value using the returned `Future`. Because the test procedure is typically executed on its own dedicated thread, this should not interfere with the implementation of the service on its own.

It must be stressed that this technique is likely to fail if applied outside of testing and in production code. The reason is that the caller of the translation service will then no longer be an isolated external test procedure; it will most likely be another service that may use the same asynchronous execution resources. If enough calls are made concurrently in this thread-blocking fashion, then all threads of the underlying pool will be consumed, idly waiting for responses, and the desired computation will not be executed because no thread will be available to pick it up. Timeouts or deadlock will ensue.

Coming back to the test procedures, we still have one open question: how does this work for the case of one-way messaging as in the Actor example? You used a `TestProbe` as the return address for the reply. Such a probe is equivalent to an Actor without processing capabilities of its own, which provides utilities for synchronously awaiting messages. The test procedure would in this case look like the following.

Listing 11.3   Expecting replies with a `TestProbe`

```
val input = "Hur mår du?"
val output = "How are you?"
val probe = TestProbe()
translationService ! Translate(input, probe.ref)
probe.expectMsg(1.second, output)
```

The expectMsg() method will wait up to 1 second for a new message to arrive and, if that happens, compare it to the expected object—the output string, in this case. If nothing or the wrong message is received, then the test procedure will fail with an assertion error.

11.3.2 *The crux of choosing timeouts*

Most synchronous test procedures verify that a certain sequence of actions results in a given sequence of results: set up the translation service, invoke it, and compare the returned value to the expected one. This means the aspect of time does not play a role in these tests: the test result will not depend on whether running the test is a matter of milliseconds or takes a few hours. The basic assumption is that all processing occurs in the context of the test procedure, literally beneath its frame of control. Therefore, it is enough to react to returned values or thrown exceptions. There will always be a result—infinite loops will be noticed eventually by the human observer.

In an asynchronous system, this assumption no longer holds: it is possible that the execution of the module under test occurs far removed from the test procedure, and replies may not only arrive late, they can also be lost. The latter can be due to programming errors (not sending a reply message, not fulfilling a Promise in some edge case, and so on), or it can be due to failures like message loss on the network or resource exhaustion—if an asynchronous task cannot be enqueued to be run, then its result will never be computed.

For this reason, it is unwise to wait indefinitely for replies during test procedures, because you do not want the entire test run to grind to a halt halfway through just because of one lost message. You need to place an upper bound on waiting times, fail tests that violate it, and move on.

This upper bound should be long enough to allow natural fluctuations in execution times without leading to sporadic test failures; such flakiness would waste resources during development in order to investigate each test failure as to whether it was legitimate or bad luck. Typical sources of bad luck include garbage-collection pauses, network hiccups, and temporary system overload, and all of these can cause a message send that normally takes microseconds to be delayed by up to several seconds.

On the other hand, the upper bound needs to be as low as possible, because it defines the time it takes to give up and move on. You do not want to wait for a verification run to take several hours when one hour would suffice.

SCALING TIMEOUTS FOR DIFFERENT TEST ENVIRONMENTS

Choosing the right timeouts is therefore a compromise between worst-case test execution time and false positive error probability. On current notebook computers, it is realistic to expect asynchronous scheduling to occur on the scale of tens of milliseconds. Normally, it happens much faster; but if you are, for example, executing a large test suite with thousands of tests on the JVM, you need to take into account that the garbage collector will occasionally run for a few milliseconds, and you do not want that to lead to test failures because it is expected behavior for a development system.

If you develop a test suite this way and then let it be run on a continuous integration server in the cloud, you will discover that it fails miserably. The server will likely share the underlying hardware with other servers through virtualization, and it may also perform several test runs simultaneously. These and other effects of not having exclusive access to hardware resources lead to greater variations in the execution timing and thereby force you to relax your expectations as to when processing should occur and replies should be received.

Toward this end, many asynchronous testing tools as well as the test suites themselves contain provisions to adapt the given timeouts to different runtime environments. In its simplest form, this means scaling by a constant factor or adding a constant amount to account for the expected variance.

NOTE   Adapting timeouts to different runtime environments is realized in the ScalaTest framework by mixing in the trait `ScaledTimeSpans` and overriding the method `spanScaleFactor()`. Another example is the Akka test suite, which allows the external configuration of a scaling factor that is applied to durations used in `TestProbe.expectMsg()` and friends (the configuration key is `akka.test.timefactor`).

TESTING SERVICE TIMINGS

Another issue can arise with testing asynchronous services: due to the inherent freedom of when to reply to a request, we can imagine services that reply only after a certain time has passed or that trigger the periodic execution of some action. All such use cases can be modeled as external services that arrange for messages to be sent at the right times so that other services can depend on them for their scheduling needs.

The difference between testing the timing behavior of a service versus using timeouts for verifying its correctness is illustrated in figure 11.1. If you want to assert that

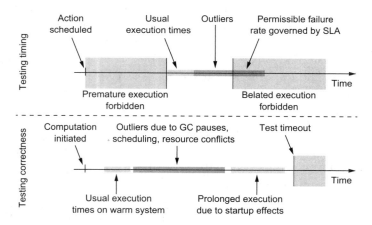

Figure 11.1 Testing a system for correctness and testing it for its timing properties are significantly different activities.

the correct answer is received, you choose a timeout that bounds the maximal waiting time such that normally the test succeeds even if the execution is delayed much longer than would be expected during production use. Testing a service for its timing shifts the aspect of time from a largely ignored bystander role into the center of focus: you now need to put more stringent limits on what to accept as valid behavior, and you may need to establish lower bounds as well.

How do you implement a test suite for a scheduler? As an example, the following listing formulates a test case for a scheduler service that is implemented as an Actor, using again a `TestProbe` as the communication partner that is controlled by the test procedure.

> **Listing 11.4   Using a `TestProbe` to receive the response from the scheduler**

```
val probe = TestProbe()

val start = Timestamp.now
scheduler ! Schedule(probe.ref, "tick", 1.second)
probe.expectMsg(2.seconds, "tick")              ⟵── Checks that it arrives

val stop = Timestamp.now

val duration = stop - start
assert(duration > 950.millis, "tick came in early")
assert(duration < 1050.millis, "tick came in late")
```

Here, verification proceeds in two steps. First, you verify that the scheduled message does indeed arrive, using a relaxed time constraint with reasoning similar to that of the timing-agnostic tests discussed in the previous section. Second, you note the time that elapsed between sending the request and receiving the scheduled message and assert that this time interval matches the requested schedule.

The second part is subject to all the timing variations due to external influences earlier, which poses a problem. You cannot evade the issues by relaxing the verification constraints this time, because that would defeat the purpose of the test. This leaves only one way forward: you need to run these timing-sensitive tests in an environment that does not suffer from additional variances. Instead of including them with all the other test suites that you run on the continuous integration servers, you may choose to execute them only on reliable and fast developer machines, which work much better in this regard.

But this is also problematic in that a scheduler that passes these local tests under ideal circumstances may fail to meet its requirements when deployed in production. Therefore, such services need to be tested in an environment that closely matches the intended production environment, in terms of both the hardware platforms used and the kind of processes running simultaneously and their resource configurations. It makes a difference if the timing-sensitive service commands independent resources or shares a thread pool with other computation.

TESTING SERVICE-LEVEL AGREEMENTS

In chapter 1, we discussed the importance of establishing reliable upper bounds for service response times in order to conclude whether the service is currently working. In other words, each service needs to abide by its SLA in addition to performing the correct function. The test procedures you have seen so far only concentrate on verifying that a given sequence of actions produces the right sequence of results, where in certain cases the result timing may be constrained as well. To verify the SLA, it is necessary to test aspects like the 95th percentile of the request latency: for example, asserting that it must be less than 1 ms. These tests are inherently statistical in nature, necessitating additions to your set of testing tools.

Formulating test cases concerned with latency percentiles for a given request type means you need to perform such requests repeatedly and keep track of the time elapsing between each matching request–response pair. The simplest way to do this is to sequentially perform one request after the other, as shown in the following example, which tests 200 samples and discards the slowest 5%.

Listing 11.5   Determining 95th percentile latency

```
val probe = TestProbe()
val echo = echoService("keepSLA")          ←── Obtains a service ActorRef
val N = 200
val timings = for (i <- 1 to N) yield {                Generates strings
  val string = s"test$i"              ←──               test1, test2, ... testN
  val start = Timestamp.now
  echo ! Request(string, probe.ref)
  probe.expectMsg(100.millis, s"test run $i", Response(string))   ←──
  val stop = Timestamp.now                              Includes a hint about
  stop - start                                          which step failed, in
}                                                       case of a timeout
val sorted = timings.sorted
val ninetyfifthPercentile = sorted.dropRight(N * 5 / 100).last ←── Discards the
                                                                   top 5%
ninetyfifthPercentile should be < 1.millisecond
```

Returns the elapsed time for this run

This test procedure takes note of the response latency for each request in a normal collection, which is sorted in order to extract the 95th percentile (by dropping the highest 5% and then looking at the largest element). This shows that no histogramming package or statistics software is necessary to perform this kind of test, so there is no excuse for skimping on their use. To learn more about the performance characteristics and dynamic behavior of the software you write, though, it is recommended that you visualize the distribution of request latencies; this can be done for regular test runs or in dedicated experiments, and statistics tools will help in this regard.

In the previous listing, requests are fired one by one, so the service will not experience any load during this procedure. The obtained latency values will therefore reflect the performance under ideal conditions; it is likely that under nominal production conditions, the timings will be worse. In order to simulate a higher incoming

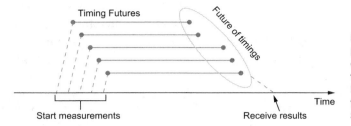

Figure 11.2 The test procedure initiates multiple calls to the service under test, which may be executed in parallel; aggregates the timings; and verifies that the SLA is met.

request rate—corresponding to multiple simultaneous uses of the same service instance—you need to parallelize the test procedure, as shown in figure 11.2. The easiest way to do this is to use Futures.

Listing 11.6 Generating the test samples in parallel with the Ask pattern

```
val echo = echoService("keepSLAfuture")
val N = 10000
val timingFutures = for (i <- 1 to N) yield {
  val string = s"test$i"
  val start = Timestamp.now
  (echo ? (Request(string, _))) collect {          ◁── Using the Ask pattern
    case Response(`string`) => Timestamp.now - start
  }
}
val futureOfTimings = Future.sequence(timingFutures)
val timings = Await.result(futureOfTimings, 5.seconds)
val sorted = timings.sorted
val ninetyfifthPercentile = sorted.dropRight(N * 5 / 100).last  ◁──┐ Discards the
                                                                   │ top 5%
ninetyfifthPercentile should be < 100.milliseconds
```

This time, you use the ? operator to turn the one-way Actor message send into a request–response operation: this method internally creates an `ActorRef` that is coupled to a Promise and uses the passed-in function to construct the message to be sent. Scala's function-literal syntax makes this convenient using the underscore shorthand—you can mark the "hole" into which the `ActorRef` will be placed. The first message sent to this `ActorRef` will fulfill the Promise, and the corresponding Future is returned from the ? method (pronounced "ask").

You then transform this Future using the .collect combinator: if it is the expected response, you replace that with the elapsed time. It is essential to remember that Future combinators execute when the Future is completed, in the future. Hence, taking a timestamp in the collect transformation serves as the second look to the watch, whereas the result of the first look was obtained from the test procedure's context and stored in the start timestamp that you then later reference from the Future transformation.

The for-comprehension returns a sequence of all Futures, which you can turn into a single Future holding a sequence of time measurements by using the `Future` `.sequence()` operation. Synchronously awaiting the value for this combined Future lets you then continue in the same fashion as for the sequentially requesting test procedure.

If you execute this parallel test, you will notice that the timings for the service are markedly changed for the worse. This is because you very rapidly fire a burst of requests that pile up in the `EchoService`'s request queue and then are processed one after the other. On my machine, I had to increase the threshold for the 95th percentile to 100 ms; otherwise, I experienced spurious test failures.

Just as the fully sequential version exercised an unrealistic scenario, the fully parallel one tests a rather special case as well. A more realistic test would be to limit the number of outstanding requests to a given number at all times: for example, keeping 500 in flight. Formulating this with Futures will be tedious and complex;[5] in this case, it is preferable to call on another message-passing component for help. The following example uses an Actor to control the test sequence.

> **Listing 11.7 Using a custom Actor to bound the number of parallel test samples**

```
val echo = echoService("keepSLAparallel")
val probe = TestProbe()
val N = 10000
val maxParallelism = 500
val controller = system.actorOf(Props[ParallelSLATester],
                                "keepSLAparallelController")
controller ! TestSLA(echo, N, maxParallelism, probe.ref)
val result = probe.expectMsgType[SLAResponse]
val sorted = result.timings.sorted
val ninetyfifthPercentile = sorted.dropRight(N * 5 / 100).last   ⟵  Discards the
                                                                     top 5%
ninetyfifthPercentile should be < 2.milliseconds
```

You can find the code for the Actor in the accompanying source code archives. The idea is to send the first `maxParallelism` requests when starting the test and then send one more for each received response until all requests have been sent. For each request that is sent, a timestamp is stored together with the unique request string; when the corresponding response is received, the current time is used to calculate this request's response latency. When all responses have been received, a list of all latencies is sent back to the test procedure in an `SLAResponse` message. From there on, the calculation of the 95th percentile proceeds as usual.

REFINING PARALLEL MEASUREMENTS Looking at the code in the source archive, you will notice listing 11.7 is slightly simplified: instead of directing the responses to the `ParallelSLATester`, a dedicated Actor is used, which timestamps the responses before sending them on to the `ParallelSLATester`.

---

[5] Assuming that the responses can arrive in a different order than the order in which you sent the corresponding requests. This assumption is necessary to make for a service that can be scaled by replication.

The reason is that otherwise the timings might be distorted, because the `ParallelSLATester` might still be busy sending requests when a response arrives, leading to an artificially prolonged time measurement.

Another interesting aspect is the thread pool configuration. You are welcome to play with the `parallelism-max` setting to find out when the results are stable across multiple test runs and when they become optimal; for a discussion, see the comments in the source code archives.

11.3.3 Asserting the absence of a message

All verification you have done so far concerned messages that were expected to arrive, but it is equally important to verify that certain messages are not sent. When components interact with protocols that are not purely request–response pairs, this need arises frequently:

- After cancelling a repeating scheduled task
- After unsubscribing from a publish–subscribe topic
- After having received a dataset that was transferred via multiple messages

Depending on whether the messaging infrastructure maintains the ordering for messages traveling from sender to recipient, you can either expect the incoming message stream to cease immediately after having confirmation that the other side will stop, or allow for some additional time during which stragglers may still arrive. The absence of a message can only be asserted by letting a certain amount of time elapse and verifying that indeed nothing is received during this time.

Listing 11.8   Verifying that no additional messages are received

```
val probe = TestProbe()
scheduler ! ScheduleRepeatedly(probe.ref, 1.second, "tick")
val token = expectMsgType[SchedulerToken]
probe.expectMsg(1500.millis, "tick")
scheduler ! CancelSchedule(token, probe.ref)
probe.expectMsg(100.millis, ScheduleCanceled)
probe.expectNoMsg(2.seconds)          Now you don't expect
                                      any more ticks.
```

Looking at the expected message timings and summing them up, this procedure should take a bit more than 3 seconds: 1 for the first tick to arrive, some milliseconds for the communication with the scheduler service, and 2 more seconds during which you do nothing. Verifications like this increase the time needed to run the entire test suite, usually even more than most tests that spend their time more actively. It is therefore desirable to reduce occurrences of this pattern as much as possible.

One way to achieve this is to rely on message-ordering guarantees where available. Imagine a service implementing data ingestion and parsing: you send it a request that points it to an accessible location—a file or a web resource—and you get back a series of data records followed by an end-of-file (EOF) marker. Each instance of this service processes requests in a purely sequential fashion, finishing one response series before picking up the next work item. This makes the service easier to write, and scaling it out will be trivial by running multiple instances in parallel; the only externally visible effect is that requests need to contain a correlation ID, because multiple series can be in flight at the same time. The following test procedure demonstrates the interface.

Listing 11.9   Matching responses to requests with a correlation ID

```
val probe = TestProbe()
ingestService ! Retrieve(url, "myID", probe.ref)          Includes a correlation
                                                          ID in the message
val replies = probe.receiveWhile(1.second) {
    case r @ Record("myID", _) => r          Matches only responses with
  }                                          the correct correlation ID
probe.expectMsg(0.seconds, EOF)
                                             EOF is not handled and
                                             will terminate the loop
```

Instead of following this with an `expectNoMsg()` call to verify that nothing arrives after the EOF message, you might append a second query. During testing, you can ensure that only one instance is active for this service, which means as soon as you receive the elements of the second response series, you can be sure the first one is properly terminated.

11.3.4 *Providing synchronous execution engines*

The role of timeouts in tests that are not timing-sensitive is only to bound the waiting time for a response that is expected. If you could arrange for the service under test to be executed synchronously instead of asynchronously, then this waiting time would be zero: if the response is not ready when the method returns, then it also will not become available at a later time, because no asynchronous processing facilities are there to enable this.

Such configurability of the execution mechanism is not always available: synchronous execution can be successful only if the computation does not require intrinsic parallelism. It works best for processes that are deterministic, as discussed in chapter 9. If a computation is composed from Futures in a fully nonblocking fashion, then this criterion is satisfied. Depending on the platform that is used, there may be several ways to remove asynchrony during tests. Some implementations, like Scala's Future, are built on the notion of an `ExecutionContext` that describes how the execution is realized for all tasks involved in the processing and chaining of Futures. In this case, the only preparation necessary is to allow the service to be configured with an `Execution-Context` from the outside, either when it is constructed or for each single request. Then the test procedure can pass a context that implements a synchronous event loop. Revisiting the translation service, this might look like the following.

```
val input = "Hur mår du?"
val output = "How are you?"
val ec = SynchronousEventLoop
val future = translate(input, ec)
future.value.get should be(Success(output))
```

For implementations that do not allow the execution mechanism to be configured in this fashion, you can achieve the same effect by making the result container configurable. Instead of fixing the return type of the translate method to be a Future, you can abstract over this aspect and allow any composable container to be passed in.[6] Future composition uses methods like map/flatMap/filter (Scala Future), then (JavaScript), and thenAccept (Java CompletionStage). The only source code change needed is to configure the service to use a specific factory for creating Futures so that you can inject one that performs computations synchronously.

When it comes to other message-based components, chances are not as good that you can find a way to make an asynchronous implementation synchronous during tests. One example is the Akka implementation of the Actor model, which allows the execution of each Actor to be configured by way of selecting a suitable dispatcher. For test purposes, there exists a CallingThreadDispatcher that processes each message directly within the context that uses the tell operator. If all Actors that contribute to the function of a given service are using only this dispatcher, then sending a request will synchronously execute the entire processing chain such that possible replies are already delivered when the tell operator invocation returns. You can use this as follows.

```
val translationService = system.actorOf(
        Props[TranslationServiceActor].withDispatcher(       Uses a calling
        "akka.test.calling-thread-dispatcher"))         <──┘ thread dispatcher
val input = "Hur mår du?"
val output = "How are you?"
val probe = TestProbe()
translationService ! Translate(input, probe.ref)
probe.expectMsg(0.seconds, output)         <─── Asserts immediately
```

The important change is that the Props describing the translation service Actor are configured with a dispatcher setting instead of leaving the decision to the Actor-System. This needs to be done for each Actor that participates in this test case, meaning

---

[6] In other words, you abstract over the particular kind of monad that is used to sequence and compose the computation, allowing the test procedure to substitute the Future monad for the identity monad. In dynamically typed languages, it is sufficient to create the monad's unit() and bind() functions, whereas in statically typed languages extra care needs to be taken to express the higher-kinded type signature of the resulting translate() method.

if the translation service creates more Actors internally, it must be set up to propagate the dispatcher configuration setting to these (and they to their child Actors, and so on; see the source code archives for details). Note that this also requires several other assumptions:

- The translation service cannot use the system's scheduler, because that would invoke the Actors asynchronously, potentially leading to the output not being transmitted to the probe when you expect it to be.
- The same holds for interactions with remote systems, because those are by nature asynchronous.
- Failures and restarts would in this case also lead to asynchronous behavior, because the translation service's supervisor is the system guardian that cannot be configured to run on the `CallingThreadDispatcher`.
- None of the Actors involved are allowed to perform blocking operations that might depend on other Actors running on the `CallingThreadDispatcher`, because that would lead to deadlocks.

The list of assumptions could be continued with minor ones, but it should be clear that the nature of the Actor model is at odds with synchronous communication: it relies on asynchrony and unbounded concurrency. For simple tests—especially those that verify a single Actor—it can be beneficial to go this route, whereas higher-level integration tests involving the interplay of multiple Actors usually require asynchronous execution.

So far, we have discussed two widely used messaging abstractions, Futures and Actors, and each of them provides the necessary facilities to do synchronous testing if needed. Due to the ubiquity of this form of verification, you will likely continue to see this support in all widespread asynchronous messaging abstractions, although there are already environments that are heavily biased against synchronous waiting—for example, event-based systems like JavaScript—and that will drive the transition toward fully asynchronous testing. We will embark on this spiritual journey in the following sections.

11.3.5 *Asynchronous assertions*

The first step toward asynchronous testing is the ability to formulate an assertion that will hold at a future point in time. In a sense, you have seen a special case of this already in the form of `TestProbe.expectMsg()`. This method asserts that within a time interval from now on, a message will be received that has the given characteristics. A generalization of this mechanism is to allow arbitrary assertions to be used. ScalaTest offers this through its `eventually` construct. Using this, you can rewrite the translation service test case as follows.

Listing 11.12 Moving the timeout parameters to an external configuration

```
val input = "Hur mår du?"
val output = "How are you?"
val future = translate(input)
eventually {
  future.value.get should be(Success(output))
}
```

This uses an implicitly supplied `PatienceConfiguration` that describes the time parameters of how frequently and for how long the enclosed verification is attempted before test failure is signaled. With this helper, the test procedure remains fully synchronous, but you obtain more freedom in expressing the conditions under which it will proceed.

11.3.6 *Fully asynchronous tests*

We have found ways to express test cases for Reactive systems within the framework of traditional synchronous verification procedures, and most systems to date are tested in this fashion. But it feels wrong to apply a different set of tools and principles in the production and verification code bases: there is an impedance mismatch between these two that should be avoidable.

The first step toward fixing this was taken when you devised an Actor to verify the response latency characteristics of `EchoService`. `ParallelSLATester` is a fully Reactive component that you developed to test a characteristic of another Reactive component. The only incongruous piece in that test was the synchronous procedure used to start the test and await the result. What you would like to write instead is the following.

Listing 11.13 Handling responses asynchronously to create fully Reactive tests

```
val echo = echoService()
val N = 10000
val maxParallelism = 500
val controller = system.actorOf(Props[ParallelSLATester],
                                "keepSLAparallelController")
val future = controller ? TestSLA(echo, N, maxParallelism, _)
for (SLAResponse(timings, outstanding) <- future) yield {

  val sorted = result.timings.sorted
  val ninetyfifthPercentile = sorted.dropRight(N * 5 / 100).last   <─┐ Discards the
                                                                     │ top 5%
  ninetyfifthPercentile should be < 2.milliseconds
}
```

Here, you initiate the test by sending the `TestSLA` command to the Actor, using the Ask pattern to get back a Future for the later reply. You then transform that Future to perform the calculation and verification of the latency profile, resulting in a Future that will either be successful or fail, depending on the outcome of the assertion in the next-to-last line. In traditional testing frameworks, this Future will not be inspected, making this approach futile. An asynchronous testing framework, on the other hand, will react to the completion of this Future in order to determine whether the test was successful.

Combining such a test framework with the `async/await` extension available for .Net languages or Scala makes it straightforward and easily readable to write fully asynchronous test cases. The running example of the translation service would look like this.

> **Listing 11.14 Using `async` and `await` to improve readability of asynchronous tests**

```
async {
  val input = "Hur mår du?"
  val output = "How are you?"
  await(translate(input).withTimeout(5.seconds)) should be(output)
}
```

This has exactly the same structure as the initial synchronous version in listing 11.1, marking out the asynchronous piece with `await()` and wrapping the entire case in an `async{}` block. The advantage over the intermediate version that used the blocking `Await.result()` construct in listing 11.2 is that the testing framework can execute many such test cases concurrently, reducing the overall time needed for running the entire test suite. This also means you can relax the timing constraints, because a missing reply will not bind as many resources as in the synchronous case. The Future for the next step of the test procedure will not be set in motion; the 5 seconds in this example will also not tick so heavily on the wall clock, because other test cases can make progress while this one is waiting.

As mentioned earlier, JavaScript is an environment that is heavily biased toward asynchronous processing; blocking test procedures as are common in other languages are not feasible in this model. As an example, you can implement the translation service test using Mocha and Chai assertions for Promises.

> **Listing 11.15 Testing the translation service in JavaScript**

```
describe('Translator', function() {
  describe('#translate()', function() {
    it('should yield the correct result', function() {
      return tr.translate('Hur mår du?')
            .should.eventually.equal('How are you?');
    })
  })
});
```

The Mocha test runner executes several test cases in parallel, each returning a Promise as in this case. The timeouts after which tests are assumed to be failed if they did not report back can be configured at each level (globally, per test suite, or per test case).

TESTING SERVICE-LEVEL AGREEMENTS

With test cases being written in an asynchronous fashion, you can revisit the latency percentile verification from another angle. The framework could allow the user to describe the desired response characteristics in addition to the test code and then automatically verify those by running the code multiple times in parallel. Doing so sequentially would be prohibitively expensive in many cases—you would not voluntarily have tested 10,000 iterations of the `EchoService` in the sequential version in listing 11.5—and, as discussed, it also would not be a realistic measurement. Going back to the SLA test of the echo service in listing 11.7, the test framework would replace the custom `ParallelSLATester` Actor that was used to communicate with the service under test.

Listing 11.16 Using a request–response factory to generate test traffic

```
async {
  val echo = echoService()
  val gauge = new LatencyTestSupport(system)
  val latenciesFuture =
    gauge.measure(count = 10000, maxParallelism = 500) { i =>
      val message = s"test$i"
      SingleResult((echo ? (Request(message, _))), Response(message))
    }
  val latencies = await(latenciesFuture, 20.seconds)
  latencies.failureCount should be(0)
  latencies.quantile(0.99) should be < 10.milliseconds
}
```

This is possible because the interaction between the test and the service is of a specific kind: you are performing a load test for a request–response protocol. In this case, you only need a factory for request–response pairs that you can use to generate the traffic as needed, and the shape of the traffic is controlled by the parameters to the `measure()` method. The asynchronous result of this measurement is an object that contains the actual collections of results and errors that the 10,000 individual tests produced. These data can then easily be analyzed in order to assert that the latency profile fulfills the service-level requirements.

11.3.7 Asserting the absence of asynchronous errors

The last consideration when testing asynchronous components is that not all interactions with them will occur with the test procedure. Imagine a protocol adapter that is mediating between two components that have not been developed together and therefore do not understand the same message formats. In the running example with the translation service, you may at first have a version of the API that is based on text string serialization (version 1).

Listing 11.17   Simple translation API

```
case class TranslateV1(query: String, replyTo: ActorRef)
```

The languages to be used for input and output are encoded within the query string, and the reply that is sent to the `replyTo` address will be just a `String`. This works for a proof of concept, but later you may want to replace the protocol with a more strictly typed, intuitive version (version 2).

Listing 11.18   Adding stricter types to the translation API

```
case class TranslateV2(phrase: String,
                       inputLanguage: String,
                       outputLanguage: String,
                       replyTo: ActorRef)

sealed trait TranslationResponseV2
case class TranslationV2(inputPhrase: String,
                         outputPhrase: String,
                         inputLanguage: Language,
                         outputLanguage: Language)
case class TranslationErrorV2(inputPhrase: String,
                              inputLanguage: Language,
                              outputLanguage: Language,
                              errorMessage: String)
```

This redesign allows more advanced features like automatic detection of the input language to be implemented. Unfortunately, other teams have progressed with implementing a translator using the version 1 protocol already. Let us assume that the decision is made to bridge between this and new clients by adding an adapter that accepts requests made with version 2 of the protocol and serves the replies that are provided by a translation service speaking the version 1 protocol in the background.

For this adapter, you will typically write integration tests, making sure that given a functioning version 1 back end, the adapter correctly implements version 2 of the protocol. To save maintenance effort, you will also write dedicated tests that concentrate on the transformation of requests and replies; this will save time when debugging failures, because you can more easily associate them with either the adapter or the back-end service. A test procedure could look like this.

Listing 11.19   Testing the translation version adapter

```
val v1 = TestProbe()
val v2 = system.actorOf(TranslationService.propsV2(v1.ref))
val client = TestProbe()                                          Initiates a
                                                                  request to
v2 ! TranslateV2("Hur mår du?", "sv", "en", client.ref)    ◁───   the adapter

val req1 = v1.expectMsgType[TranslateV1]        ◁──   Verifies that the adapter asks
req1.query should be("sv:en:Hur mår du?")             the V1 service back end

req1.replyTo ! "How are you?"        ◁───   Initiates a reply
```

```
client.expectMsg(TranslationV2("Hur mår du?",
"How are you?", "sv", "en"))
v2 ! TranslateV2("Hur är läget?", "sv", "en", client.ref)
val req2 = v1.expectMsgType[TranslateV1]
req2.query should be("sv:en:Hur är läget?")
req2.replyTo ! "error:cannot parse input 'Hur är läget?'"
client.expectMsg(TranslationErrorV2("Hur är läget?", "sv", "en",
  "cannot parse input 'Hur är läget?'"))
v1.expectNoMsg(3.seconds)
```

Verifies that the adapter transforms it correctly

Repeats for translation errors

Implicitly verifies that no other communication happened

Here the test procedure drives both the client side and the back-end side, stubbing each of them out as a TestProbe. The only active component that is executed normally is the protocol adapter. This allows you to not only formulate assertions about how the client-side protocol is implemented, but also control the internal interactions. One such assertion is shown in the last line, where you require the adapter to not make gratuitous requests to the service it is wrapping. Another benefit is that you can inspect the queries that are sent—see both occurrences of the TranslateV1 type—and fail early and with a clear error message if those are incorrect. In an integration test, you would see only overall failures in this case.

This approach works well for such a one-to-one adapter, but it can become tedious or brittle for components that converse more intensely or more diversely with different back ends. There is a middle ground between integration testing and fully controlled interactions: you can stub out the back-end services such that they are still executed autonomously, but in addition to their normal function, they keep the test procedure apprised of unexpected behavior of the component under test. To keep things simple, we will demonstrate this on the translation service adapter again.

Listing 11.20 Mocking error behavior

```
case object ExpectNominal
case object ExpectError
case class Unexpected(msg: Any)

class MockV1(reporter: ActorRef) extends Actor {
  def receive = initial

  override def unhandled(msg: Any) = {
    reporter ! Unexpected(msg)
  }

  val initial: Receive = {
    case ExpectNominal => context.become(expectingNominal)
    case ExpectError   => context.become(expectingError)
  }

  val expectingNominal: Receive = {
    case TranslateV1("sv:en:Hur mår du?", replyTo) =>
```

```
        replyTo ! "How are you?"
        context.become(initial)
    }

    val expectingError: Receive = {
      case TranslateV1(other, replyTo) =>
        replyTo ! s"error:cannot parse input '$other'"
        context.become(initial)
    }
}
```

This mock of the version 1 back end will provide the expected responses during a test, but it will do so only at the appropriate points in time: the test procedure has to explicitly unlock each of the steps by sending either an ExpectNominal or an Expect-Error message. Using this, the test procedure changes to the following.

Listing 11.21   Testing for correct error handling

```
val asyncErrors = TestProbe()
val v1 = system.actorOf(mockV1props(asyncErrors.ref))
val v2 = system.actorOf(propsV2(v1))
val client = TestProbe()                                    Initiates a request
                                                            to the adapter
v1 ! ExpectNominal
v2 ! TranslateV2("Hur mår du?", "sv", "en", client.ref)  ◁────┘
                                                            Certifies that
client.expectMsg(TranslationV2("Hur mår du?", "How are you?",   the adapter
  "sv", "en"))                                                transforms it
                                                          ◁───┘ correctly
asyncErrors.expectNoMsg(0.seconds)        ◁── Nonblocking check for async errors

v1 ! ExpectError
v2 ! TranslateV2("Hur är läget?", "sv", "en", client.ref)
client.expectMsg(TranslationErrorV2("Hur är läget?", "sv", "en",
  "cannot parse input 'sv:en:Hur är läget?'"))

asyncErrors.expectNoMsg(1.second)          ◁── Final check for async errors
```

Verifies translation errors (annotation pointing to `v1 ! ExpectError`)

The test procedure in this case still drives both the client side and the back end, but the latter is more autonomous and allows the test to be written more concisely. The first verification of the absence of asynchronous errors is performed such that it does not introduce additional latency; its purpose is only to aid in debugging test failures in case an asynchronous error from the nominal test step does not subsequently lead to directly visible test failures but instead only bubbles up in the last line of the test.

11.4   *Testing nondeterministic systems*

The previous section introduced the difficulties that arise from the asynchronous nature of Reactive systems. This had several interesting consequences even though the process that you were testing was fully deterministic: given a certain stimulus, the component will eventually respond with the correct answer—the translation of a given phrase should always yield the same result. In chapter 8, we discussed that in distributed systems, determinism cannot always be achieved: the main reasons are unreliable means of communication and inherent concurrency. Because distribution is integral to Reactive system design, you nevertheless need to be able to test components that exhibit genuine nondeterminism. Such tests are harder to express because the order of execution is not specified as a sequential progression of logic, and for a single test procedure, different outcomes or state transitions are possible and permissible.

11.4.1 *The trouble with execution schedules*

Anyone who has written tests that are based on a particular event occurring within a specified time has likely seen spurious failures, where a test succeeds most of the time but fails on occasion. What if the execution is correct but the timings are different because of varying insertion orders into queues, or different values being returned based on what was requested in what order?

It is imperative that application developers define all the correct behaviors that can occur based on varying execution schedules. This can be difficult, because it implies that the variance is finite and knowable; and the larger a system is, and with greater numbers of interactions, the more difficult this can be with respect to precision. An example of a tool that supports this kind of functionality is Apache JMeter (http://jmeter.apache.org), where you can use logical controllers to fire requests in varying orders and timings to see whether the responses received match expectations for system behavior. Logical controllers have other useful features as well, including request modification, request repeating, and more. By executing tests with tools such as JMeter, you can root out more logical inconsistencies in your Reactive application than if you always rely on tests being executed in one order and one timing.

11.4.2 *Testing distributed components*

With distributed systems, which Reactive applications are by definition, some more difficult problems must be considered. Foremost is the idea that a distributed interaction can succeed in one dimension while failing in another. For example, imagine a distributed system where data must be updated across four nodes, but suppose something goes awry on one of the servers and it never responds with a successful update response before a timeout occurs. These are known as *partial failures*,[7] where latency can increase and throughput can fall because interactions between the many services that make up the application are unable to complete all tasks (see figure 11.3).

What is particularly tricky about these kinds of failure is that it is unlikely that you can consider all the ways in which a Reactive application may fail partially and derive appropriate behavior for each case. Instead, you should consider what the application should do when something occurs that you did not expect. We discuss this in much more detail in chapter 12.

---

[7] http://en.wikipedia.org/wiki/Fault_tolerance

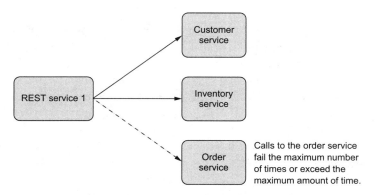

Figure 11.3   Illustration of a partial failure occurring when an interaction relies on three services and one interaction cannot be completed successfully

11.4.3 *Mocking Actors*

In order to show that a test passes or fails based on external interactions, a popular testing methodology is to mock or stub an external dependency. That means when a class to be tested is constructed, the external services on which it depends are passed into the constructor of the class so they are available at the time they are to be used. But mocking and stubbing a dependence class are two different approaches, each with its own tradeoffs.

MOCKS

Mocks are the concept of using an external library or framework to represent a fake instance of a class so that you can make assertions about whether a valid response can be properly handled. For example, imagine a class to be tested that would attempt to persist the data from the class into a database. For unit tests, you would not want to test that interaction to the database, only that the class gives the appropriate result based on whether the attempt to perform that interaction was successful.

To create such tests, many mocking frameworks have sprung up in the past decade that allow you to create a "mock" instance of the class, where calls to the mocking framework instance can be preconfigured to return a specific value for that test. Examples of such frameworks on the Java platform include EasyMock, JMock, Mockito, and ScalaMock. For each test, a mock instance is created and set up with the expected result to a particular interface; and when the call is made, that value is returned and permits you to make assertions that such behavior led to an appropriate result.

STUBS

Many developers consider the idea of using mocking frameworks to be an antipattern, where mocks do not represent an appropriate response mechanism for testing how such interactions take place. These developers instead prefer to use *stubs*, or test-only implementations of the interface that provide positive or negative responses for each interface based on the kind of response expected. This is considered less brittle at the time refactoring to an interface takes place, because the response from the stubbed method call is better defined.

There is a further consideration with respect to stubs: many developers complain that creating stubs for an interface is painful because it means they have to provide implementations of each public interface even when they are not used for a particular test, because the implementation of the interface specific to the test still requires each method in the interface to have defined behavior, even if that behavior is to do nothing. But developers such as Robert Martin have argued that using mocking frameworks is a "smell test" for APIs that have begun to exceed the single responsibility principle:[8] if the interface is painful to implement as a test stub because so many interfaces have to be implemented, then the class interface is trying to do too much and is exceeding the best practice rules for how each class should be defined with respect to the number of things it can do.

These kinds of arguments are best left to development teams to define, because it is easy to find edge cases that exceed such rules of thumb. As an extreme example, if you have an interface with 100 public interfaces, you will have to provide an implementation of all of them in order to construct a stub for a single test, and this is difficult to do. It is even more difficult to maintain as the API changes during development. If your interfaces are small and represent atomic, granular responsibilities, writing stubs is much simpler and allows for more expressive interpretations of how those dependencies can respond based on certain inputs, particularly when the interactions between the calling class under test and the dependency become more complex.

REVERSE ONION TESTING PATTERN

A key concept for building effective tests for all applications is to create tests for the entire application from the inside and work outward. This kind of testing is called the *Reverse Onion* pattern, where the approach is likened to peeling the layers of an onion inversely: putting them back from the center out. This blends directly into the strategy of testing that was discussed in the beginning of the chapter. In taking this approach, the most minute expressions and functions are tested first, moving outward to services in isolation and then to the interactions themselves.

11.4.4 *Distributed components*

Contextual handlers such as Akka TestKit's `TestProbe` are extremely handy for writing Reverse Onion tests. Constructs like these allow you to differentiate between the responses for each request. Each test must have the ability to provide implementations, whether by mocks or stubs, of the Actors/classes on which they depend, so that you can enforce and verify the behavior you expect based on their responses. Once

---

[8] http://en.wikipedia.org/wiki/Single_responsibility_principle

you have built tests with these characteristics, you can effectively test partial failure from the responses you get based on each failed interaction with each of those dependencies for an Actor/class. If you are making a call to three services and you want to test the behavior of the class when two of the three succeed and the third fails, you can do so by stubbing out behavior where the two successful stubs return expected values and the third returns an error (or never returns at all).

11.5   *Testing elasticity*

For many developers, the concept of testing load or volume is well known. But for Reactive applications, the focus changes from that traditional approach to being able to verify that your application deployment is elastic within the confines of your available infrastructure. Just like everything else in application development, your system needs bounds in time and space, and the space limitation should be the maximum number of nodes you can spin up before you begin applying back pressure. In some cases, you may be running on top of a platform as a service (PaaS) where you "spill over" into public infrastructure like AWS or Rackspace images. But for many companies, that is not an option.

To test and verify elasticity, you first have to know the bounds of throughput per node and the amount of infrastructure you will be deploying to. This should ideally come from the nonfunctional requirements of your application from the outset of the project; but if you have a clear idea of what your existing application's throughput profile looks like, you can start from there.

Assuming each node can handle 1,000 requests per second, and you have 10 nodes on which you can deploy, you want to test that traffic below a certain threshold only results in the minimum number of servers running that you specify. Tools such as Marathon with Mesos are run through Docker instances that you can query to see whether nodes are up or down, and Marathon has a REST API through which you can make other assertions about the status of the cluster. To provide load to the system, several useful free utilities do the job exceptionally well, such as Bees With Machine Guns (https://github .com/newsapps/beeswithmachineguns) and Gatling (http://gatling.io).

11.6   *Testing resilience*

Application resilience is a term that needs to be deconstructed. Failure can occur at many levels, and each of them needs to be tested to ensure that an application can be Reactive to virtually anything that can happen. The Reactive Manifesto states that "Resilience is achieved by replication, containment, isolation, and delegation." This means you need to be able to break down the varying ways that an application can fail, from the micro to the macro level, and test that it can withstand all the things that can go wrong. In every case, a request must be handled and responded to regardless of what happened after it was received.

11.6.1 Application resilience

First are the application concerns, where you must focus on behaviors specific to how the application was coded. These are the areas with which most developers are already familiar and usually involve testing that an exception was received or what the application did as a result of injecting some data or functionality that should fail. In a Reactive application, you should expect that exceptions or failures (as described in section 2.4.3) are not seen by the sender of a message, but communicated through other messages that elevate the failure to being domain events.

This is an important point. Failure has traditionally been regarded as separate from the domain of the application and is typically handled as a tactical issue that must be prevented or communicated outside the realm of the domain for which the application was built. By making failure messages first-class citizens of the application domain, you have the ability to handle failure in a much more strategic fashion. You can create two domains about the application—a domain of success and a domain of failure—and treat each appropriately with staged failure handling.

As an example, imagine an error retrieving valid data from an external source such as a database, where the call to retrieve the data succeeded but the data returned was not valid. This can be handled at one level of the application specific to that request, and either whatever valid data was retrieved is returned to the message sender, or a message connoting that the data was invalid is returned. But if the connection to the external source is lost, that is a broader domain event than the individual request for the data and should be handled by a higher-level component, such as whomever provided the connection that was used in the first place, so that it can begin the process of reestablishing the connection that was lost.

Application resilience comes in two forms: external and internal. *External resilience* is handled through validation, where data passed into the application is checked to ensure that it meets the requirement of the API; if not, a notification is passed back to the sender (for example, a telephone country code that does not exist in a database of known numbers against which it is checked). *Internal resilience* includes those errors that occur within the application's handling of that request once it has been validated.

EXECUTION RESILIENCE

As discussed in previous chapters, the most important aspect of execution resilience is supervision of the thread or process where failure can occur. Without it, there is no way for you to discern what happened to a thread or process that failed, and you may not have any way of knowing that a failure occurred at all. Once supervision is in place, you have the capability to handle failure, but you may not necessarily have the ability to test that you are doing the right thing as a result.

To get around this issue, developers sometimes expose internal state for the supervised functionality just so they can effectively test whether that state was unharmed or somehow affected by the supervisor's management of it. For example, an Actor that is resumed would see no change in its internal state, but an Actor that was restarted would see its internal state return to the initial values it should have after construction. But this has a couple of problems:

- How do you test an Actor that should be stopped based on a specific kind of failure?
- Is it a good idea to expose state that otherwise would not be exposed just for verification purposes? (This would represent a white-box test, by the way.)

To overcome these problems, a couple of patterns can be implemented that give you the ability to determine what failure has occurred or interact with a child Actor that has test-specific supervision implemented. These are patterns that sound similar but have different semantics.

It can be difficult to avoid implementing non-test-specific details in your tests. For example, if a test class attempts to create an Actor directly from the `ActorSystem` as a child Actor to the user guardian, you will not have control over how the supervision of errors that occur inside that Actor are handled. This may also be different than the expected behavior that is planned for the application and will lead to invalid unit test behavior. Instead, a `StepParent` can be a test-only supervisor that creates an instance of the Actor to be tested and delivers it back to the test client, which can then interact with the instance in any way it likes. The `StepParent` merely exists to provide supervision external to the test class so that the test class is not the parent. Assuming you have a basic Actor that you would like to test and that can throw an `Exception`, it can look as simple as the following.

Listing 11.22   Basic Actor to test

```
class MyActor extends Actor {
  def receive = {
    case _ => throw new NullPointerException
  }
}
```

With that basic implementation, you can now create a `StepParent` strictly for the purpose of testing that will create an instance of that Actor from its own context, thus removing the test class from trying to fulfill that responsibility.

Listing 11.23   Providing a test context for the Actor under test

```
class StepParent extends Actor {
  override val supervisorStrategy = OneForOneStrategy() {
    case thr => Restart
  }
  def receive = {
    case p: Props =>
      sender ! context.actorOf(p, "child")
  }
}
```

Now you can create a test that uses `StepParent` to create an Actor to be tested and begin to test whatever behavior you want without having the supervision semantics in the test.

Listing 11.24 Testing the Actor in the context of `StepParent`

```
class StepParentSpec extends WordSpec
with Matchers with BeforeAndAfterAll {
  implicit val system = ActorSystem()

  "An actor that throws an exception" must {
    "Be created by a supervisor" in {
      val testProbe = TestProbe()
        val parent = system.actorOf(Props[StepParent], "stepParent")
        parent.tell(Props[MyActor], testProbe.ref)
        val child = testProbe.expectMsgType[ActorRef]
        … // Test whatever we want in the actor
    }
  }

  override def afterAll(): Unit = {
    system.shutdown()
  }
}
```

A `FailureParent` looks similar, except that it also reports any failures it receives back to the testing class. Assuming that you are going to test the same `MyActor`, a `Failure-Parent` will receive whomever it is supposed to report the failures back to as a constructor argument and, on receipt of a failure, report it to that entity before performing whatever supervision work it intends to do.

Listing 11.25 Reporting failures back to a designated Actor

```
class FailureParent(failures: ActorRef) extends Actor {
  val props = Props[MyFailureParentActor]
  val child = context.actorOf(props, "child")

  override val supervisorStrategy = OneForOneStrategy() {
    case f => failures ! f; Stop
  }
  def receive = {
    case msg => child forward msg
  }
}
```

Now, you can create a test that uses `FailureParent` to create the Actor to be tested and begin to test whatever behavior you want without having the supervision semantics in the test.

Listing 11.26 Removing supervision from the test

```
case object TestFailureParentMessage

class FailureParentSpec extends WordSpec
    with Matchers with BeforeAndAfterAll {
  implicit val system = ActorSystem()

  "Using a FailureParent" must {
    "Result in failures being collected and returned" in {
        val failures = TestProbe()
        val failureParent = system.actorOf(
        val props = Props(new FailureParent(failures.ref))
        val failureParent = system.actorOf(props)
        failureParent ! TestFailureParentMessage
        failures.expectMsgType[NullPointerException]
    }
  }

  override def afterAll(): Unit = {
    system.shutdown()
  }
}
```

API RESILIENCE

The previous examples of using `StepParent` and `FailureParent` are also a form of API resilience, where the messages being sent between Actors are the API. In this way, you can think of Actors as being atomic examples of microservices. When requests are made of the service via its API, any data passed in must be validated to ensure that it meets the contract of what the service expects. Once proven to be valid, the service can perform the work required to fulfill the request.

When building your own APIs, consider the impact of passing in a mechanism for failure so that you can verify through tests that the behavior of the service is correct. These can be called *domain-specific failure injectors*.[9] This can be done either by providing a constructor dependency that will simulate or produce the failure, or by passing it as part of the individual request. It may be entirely useful to create a class whose sole purpose is to randomize various kinds of failure so that they are tested at different times or in different execution orders to prove more thoroughly that the failure is appropriately handled. The Akka team has done this with their `FailureInjector-TransportAdapter` class for internal testing.

11.6.2 *Infrastructure resilience*

Proving that your application is resilient is a great first step, but it is not enough. Applications depend on the infrastructure on which they run, and they have no control over failures that can take place outside of themselves. Therefore, it is also important that anyone who is serious about implementing a Reactive application also build

---

[9] http://en.wikipedia.org/wiki/Fault_injection

or use a framework to help them test the application's ability to cope with infrastructure failures that happen around it.

Some may use the term *partition* and mean only from the network perspective, but that is not necessarily true. Partitions happen any time a system has increased latency in response to any reason, including stop-the-world garbage collection, database latency, infinite looping, and so on.

NETWORK RESILIENCE (LAN AND WAN)

One of the most notorious kinds of infrastructure failures is a *network partition,*[10] where a network is incapable of routing between two or more subnetworks for various reasons. Networks can, and do, fail. Routers can go down just like any other computer, and occasionally paths provided by routing tables that are periodically revised and optimized cannot be resolved. It is best to assume that this will happen to your application and have a protocol for application management in the face of such an event.

CLUSTER RESILIENCE

In the case of a network partition, it is entirely plausible that two or more nodes in a clustered application will not be able to reach each other, and each will assume leadership of a new subcluster that cannot be rejoined or merged. This is called the *split-brain problem.*[11] The optimistic approach is to allow the two or more subclusters to continue as normal, but if there is any state to be shared between them, this can be difficult to maintain as far as updates that occur in each being resolved to the correct final answer if and when they rejoin. The pessimistic approach is to assume that all is lost, shut down both subclusters, and attempt to restart the application entirely, so that consistency is maintained.

Some cluster-management tools attempt to take a middling approach, where any subcluster with a majority of nodes (greater than 50% of known nodes) will automatically attempt to become the leader of a cluster that stays in operation. Any subcluster with less than 50% of known nodes will then automatically shut down. In theory, this sounds reasonable, but cluster splits can be unreasonable occurrences. It is entirely likely that such a split in the cluster will result in multiple subclusters with less than 50% of known nodes in all of them, and that they will all shut down as a result. The operations teams that manage distributed systems in production have to be always on guard for such events and, again, have a protocol in place for handling them.

NODE AND MACHINE RESILIENCE

Nodes, or instances, are processes running on a machine that represent one instance of an application currently able to perform work. If there is only one node in the entire application, it is not a distributed application and represents a *single point of failure*(SPOF). If there is more than one node, possibly running on the same physical machine or across several of them, it is a distributed application. If all nodes are running on just one machine, this represents another SPOF, because any failure to the

---

[10] http://en.wikipedia.org/wiki/Network_partition
[11] http://en.wikipedia.org/wiki/Split-brain_(computing)

machine will take down the entire application. To make an application provably Reactive, you must be able to test that the removal of any node or machine at runtime does not affect your ability to withstand your application's expected traffic.

DATA-CENTER RESILIENCE

Similar to the other infrastructural concepts, deploying an application to a single data center is an SPOF and not a Reactive approach. Instead, deployment to multiple data centers is a requirement to ensure that any major outage in one leaves your application with the capacity to handle all requests in others.

Testing resilience in production

Netflix has created a suite of tools to help it test the robustness of its applications while running in production, called the Simian Army.[a] Netflix has had major outages happen in production and prefers to continue testing its application's resiliency at the node and machine level even in production. This gives the company tremendous confidence that it can continue to service its customers even in the face of significant failures.

To test node resilience, Netflix uses Chaos Monkey, which randomly disables production instances when executed. Note that this tool is only executed with operations engineers in attendance who closely monitor for any outages that could occur as a result of the outages the tool induces. As a result of success with this tool, Netflix created a legion of other such tools to check for latency, security credential expiration, unused resources, and more.

To check resilience of an entire AWS availability zone, which is an isolation barrier within a deployment region, Netflix uses the Chaos Gorilla. This simulates a failure of an entire availability zone and checks whether the application is able to transition work to instances in other availability zones without downtime. To test data center resilience, Netflix uses the Chaos Kong tool, because the company currently uses multiple AWS regions for the United States alone.

Whether or not you use existing tools, such as those from Netflix, or build your own, it is critical that you test your application's resilience in the face of myriad infrastructure failures to ensure that your users continue to get the responses they expect. Focus on applying these tools for any application that is critical to the success of your business.

---

a. http://techblog.netflix.com/2011/07/netflix-simian-army.html

---

11.7 *Testing responsiveness*

When testing elasticity and resilience, the focus is primarily on the number of requests your application can handle at any given time and with any given conditions. But responsiveness is mostly about latency, or the time it takes to handle each request. As discussed in previous chapters, one of the biggest mistakes developers make is tracking latency by a metric defined qualitatively, typically by average. But average is a terrible way of tracking latency, because it does not accurately reflect the variance in latency that your application is likely to experience.

Instead, a latency target profile must be created for the application in order for the designers to understand how to assemble the system. For varying throughputs, the expectation must be defined from the outset of what latency is acceptable at specific percentiles. Such a profile might look like the example given in table 11.2.

Table 11.2 Example of expected latency percentiles in relation to external load

Request/s	99%	99.9%	99.99%	99.999%
1,000	10 ms	10 ms	20 ms	50 ms
5,000	20 ms	20 ms	50 ms	100 ms
20,000	50 ms	50 ms	100 ms	250 ms

What is critical about this profile is that it clearly shows the expectation of how well the application should be able to respond to increased load without failing. You need to create tests that will verify that the response time is mapped appropriately against each percentile for each level of throughput, and this must be part of the continuous integration process to ensure that commits do not impact latency too negatively. There are free tools, such as HdrHistogram (https://github.com/HdrHistogram/HdrHistogram), which can help with the collection of this data and display it in a meaningful way.

11.8 Summary

Testing to prove the ability to respond to varying loads, events, and failures is a critical component to building a Reactive application. Allow the tests to guide the design by making choices based on the results you see. At this point, you should have a clear understanding of the following:

- Testing must begin at the outset of the project and continue throughout every phase of its lifecycle.
- Testing must be functional and nonfunctional to prove that an application is Reactive.
- You must write tests from the inside of the application outward to cover all interactions and verify correctness.
- Elasticity is tested externally, whereas resilience is tested in both infrastructure and internal components of the application.

Fault tolerance and recovery patterns

12

In this chapter, you will learn how to incorporate the possibility of failure into the design of your application. We will demonstrate the patterns on the concrete use case of building a resilient computation engine that allows batch job submissions and their execution on elastically provisioned hardware resources. We will build on what you learned in chapters 6 and 7, so you may want to revisit them.

We will start by considering a single component and its failure and recovery strategies and then build up more-complex systems by means of hierarchical composition as well as client–server relationships. In particular, we will discuss the following patterns:

- The Simple Component pattern (a.k.a. the single responsibility principle)
- The Error Kernel pattern
- The Let-It-Crash pattern
- The Circuit Breaker pattern

12.1 The Simple Component pattern

A component shall do only one thing, but do it in full.

This pattern applies wherever a system performs multiple functions or the functions it performs are so complex that they need to be broken into different components. An example is a text editor that includes spell checking: these are two separate functions (editing can be done without spell checking, and spelling can also be checked on the finished text and does not require editing capabilities), but on the other hand, neither of these functions is trivial.

The Simple Component pattern derives from the *single responsibility principle* that was formulated by Tom DeMarco in his 1979 book *Structured Analysis and System Specification* (Prentice Hall). In its abstract form, it demands to "maximize cohesion and minimize coupling." Applied to object-oriented software design, it is usually stated as follows: "A class should have only one reason to change."[1]

From the discussion of *divide et regna* in chapter 6, you know that in order to break a large problem into a set of smaller ones, you can find help and orientation by looking at the responsibilities the resulting components will have. Applying the process of responsibility division recursively allows you to reach any desired granularity and results in a component hierarchy that you can then implement.

12.1.1 The problem setting

As an example, consider a service that offers computing capacity in a batch-like fashion: a user submits a job to be processed, stating the job's resource requirements and including an executable description of the data sources and the computation that is to be performed. The service has to watch over the resources it manages, implement quotas for the resource consumption of its clients, and schedule jobs in a fair fashion. It also has to persistently queue the jobs that it accepts such that clients can rely on their eventual execution.

The task: Your mission is to sketch the components that make up the full batch service, noting for each one its exact responsibility. Start from the top level, and work your way down until you reach components that are concrete and small enough that you could task teams with implementing them.

12.1.2 Applying the pattern

One separation you can immediately conclude is that the service implementation will be made up of two parts: one that does the coordination and that the clients communicate with, and another that is responsible for execution of the jobs; this is shown in figure 12.1. In

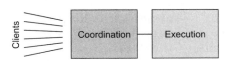

Figure 12.1 Initial component separation

order to make the entire service elastic, the coordinating part will tap into an external pool of resources and dynamically spin up or down executor instances. You can see that coordination will be a complex task, and therefore you want to break it up further.

Following the flow of a single job request through this system, you start with the job-submission interface that is offered to clients. This part of the system needs to present a network endpoint that clients can contact; it needs to implement a network protocol for this purpose; and it will interact with the rest of the system on behalf of the clients. You could break up responsibility along even finer lines, but for now let us consider this aspect of representing clients within the client as one responsibility; the client interface will thus be the second dedicated component.

---

[1] Robert Martin, "Principles of OOD," May 11, 2005, http://mng.bz/tJIk.

Once a job has been accepted and the client has been informed by way of an acknowledgment message, the system must ensure that eventually the job will be executed. This can only be achieved by storing the incoming jobs on some persistent medium, and you might be tempted to place this storage within the client interface component. But you can already anticipate that other parts of the system will have to access these jobs—for example, to start their execution. Thus, in addition to representing the clients, this component would assume responsibility for making job descriptions accessible to the rest of the system, which is in violation of the single responsibility principle.

Another temptation might be to share the responsibility for the handling of job descriptions between the interested parties—at least the client interface and the job executor, as you may surmise—but that would also greatly complicate each of these components, because they would have to coordinate their actions, running counter to the Simple Component pattern's goal. It is much simpler to keep one responsibility within one component and avoid the communication and coordination overhead that comes with distributing it across multiple components. In addition to these runtime concerns, you also need to consider the implementation: sharing the responsibility means one component needs to know about the inner workings of the other, and their development needs to be tightly coordinated as well. Those are the reasons behind the second part of *do only one thing, but do it in full.*

This leads you to identify the storage of job descriptions as another segregated responsibility of the system and thereby as the third dedicated component. A valid interjection at this point is that the client interface component may well benefit from persisting incoming jobs within its own responsibility. This would allow shorter response times for job-submission acknowledgment and also make the client interface component independent from the storage component in case of temporary unavailability. But such a persistent queue would only have the purpose of eventually delivering accepted jobs to the storage component, which then would take responsibility for them. Therefore, these notions are not in conflict with each other, and you may implement both if system requirements demand it.

Taking stock, you have now identified client interface, storage, and execution as three dedicated components with non-overlapping responsibilities. What remains to be done is to figure out which jobs to run in what order: this part is called *job scheduling.* The current state of the system's decomposition is shown in figure 12.2; now you will apply this pattern recursively until the problem is broken into simple components.

Probably the most complex task in the entire service is to figure out the execution schedule for the accepted jobs, in particular when prioritization or fairness is to be implemented between different clients that share a common pool of resources—the corresponding allocation of computing shares is usually a matter of intense discussion between competing parties.[2] The scheduling algorithm will need to have access to job descriptions in order to extract scheduling requirements (maximum running time,

---

[2] The authors have some experience with such allocation between different groups of scientists competing for data analysis resources in order to extract the insights they need for academic publications.

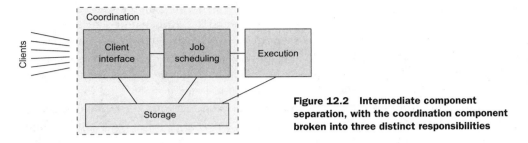

Figure 12.2　Intermediate component separation, with the coordination component broken into three distinct responsibilities

possible expiry deadline, which kind of resources are needed, and so on), so this is another client of the storage component.

It takes a lot of effort—both for the implementation and at runtime—to plan the execution order of those jobs that are accepted for execution, and this task is independent of deciding which jobs to accept. Therefore, it will be beneficial to separate the responsibility of job validation into its own component. This also has the advantage of removing rejected tasks before they become a burden for the scheduling algorithm. The responsibility for job scheduling now comprises two subcomponents, yet should be represented consistently to the rest of the system as a single component: for example, executors need to be able to retrieve the next job to run at any given time, independent of whether a scheduling run is in progress. For this reason, you place the external interactions in a Job Scheduling component whose validation and planning responsibilities are delegated to subcomponents. The resulting split of responsibilities for the entire system is shown in figure 12.3.

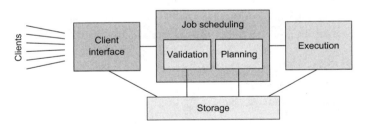

Figure 12.3　The resulting component separation

12.1.3　*The pattern, revisited*

The goal of the Simple Component pattern is to implement the single responsibility principle. You did that by considering the responsibilities of the overall system at the highest level—client interface, storage, scheduling, and execution—and separating these into dedicated components, keeping an eye on their anticipated communication needs. You then dove into the scheduling component and repeated the process, finding that there are sizable, non-overlapping subresponsibilities that you split out into their own subcomponents. This left the overall scheduling responsibility in a parent component, because you anticipate coordination tasks that will be needed independently of the subcomponents' functions.

By this process, you arrived at segregated components that can be treated independently during the further development of the system. Each of these has one clearly defined purpose, and each core responsibility of the system lies with exactly one component. Although the overall system and the internals of any component may be complex, the single responsibility principle yields the simplest division of components to further define—it frees you from always having to consider the entire picture when working on smaller pieces. This is its quintessential feature: it addresses the concern of system complexity. Additionally, following the Simple Component pattern simplifies the treatment of failures, a capability you will exploit in the following two patterns.

12.1.4 *Applicability*

Simple Component is the most basic pattern to follow, and it is universally applicable. Its application may lead you to a finer-grained division of responsibility or to the realization that you are dealing with only a single component—the important part is that afterward you know *why* you chose your system structure as you did. It helps with all later phases of design and implementation if you document and remember this, because when questions come up later about where to place certain functionality in detail, you can let yourself be guided by the simple question, "What is its purpose?" The answer will directly point you toward one of the responsibilities you identified, or it will send you back to the drawing board if you forgot to consider it.

It is important to remember that this pattern is meant to be applied in a recursive fashion, making sure that none of the identified responsibilities remain too complex or high-level. One word of warning, though: once you start dividing up components hierarchically, it is easy to get carried away and go too far—the goal is simple components that have a real responsibility, not trivial components without a valid reason to exist.

12.2 *The Error Kernel pattern*

In a supervision hierarchy, keep important application state or functionality near the root while delegating risky operations towards the leaves.

This pattern builds on the Simple Component pattern and is applicable wherever components with different failure probability and reliability requirements are combined into a larger system or application—some functions of the system must never go down, whereas others are necessarily exposed to failure. Applying the Simple Component pattern will frequently leave you in this position, so it pays to familiarize yourself well with the Error Kernel pattern.

This pattern has been established in Erlang programs for decades[3] and was one of the main inspirations for Jonas Bonér to implement an Actor framework—Akka—on the JVM. The name *Akka* was originally conceived as a palindrome of *Actor Kernel*, referring to this core design pattern.

---

[3] The legendary reliability of the Ericsson AXD301 is attributed in part to this design pattern. Its success popularized both the pattern and the Erlang language and runtime that were used in its implementation.

12.2.1 *The problem setting*

From the discussion of hierarchical failure handling in chapter 7, you know that each component of a Reactive system is supervised by another component that is responsible for its lifecycle management. This implies that if the supervisor component fails, all of its subordinates will be affected by the subsequent restart, resetting everything to a known good state and potentially losing intermediate updates. If the recovery of important pieces of state data is expensive, then such a failure will lead to extensive service downtimes, a condition that Reactive systems aim to minimize.

The task: Consider each of the six components identified in the previous example as a failure domain, and ask yourself which component should be responsible for reacting to its failures as well as which components will be directly affected by them. Summarize your findings by drawing the supervision hierarchy for the resulting system architecture.

12.2.2 *Applying the pattern*

Because recovering from a component's failure implies the loss and subsequent re-creation of its state, you will look for opportunities to separate likely points of failure from the places where important and expensive data are kept. The same applies to pieces that provide services that will be highly available: these should not be obstructed by frequent failure or long recovery times. In the example, you can identify the following disparate responsibilities:

- Communication with clients (accepting jobs and delivering their results)
- Persistent storage of job descriptions and their status
- Overall job-scheduling responsibility
- Validation of jobs against quotas or authorization requirements
- Job-schedule planning
- Job execution

Each of these responsibilities benefits from being decoupled from the rest. For example, communication with clients should not be obstructed by a failure of the job-scheduling logic, just as client-induced failures should not affect the currently running jobs. The same reasoning applies to the other pieces analogously. This is another reason, in addition to the single responsibility principle, for considering them as dedicated components, as shown again in figure 12.4.

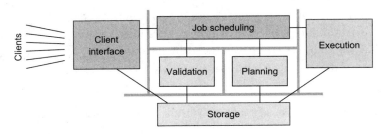

Figure 12.4   The six components drawn as separate failure domains

The next step is to consider the failure domains in the system and ask yourself how each of them should recover and how costly that process will be. Toward this end, you can follow the path by which a job travels through the system.

Jobs enter the service through the communication component, which speaks an appropriate protocol with the clients, maintaining protocol state and validating inputs. The state that is kept is short-lived, tied to the communication sessions that are currently open with clients. When this component fails, affected clients will have to reestablish a session and possibly send commands or queries again, but your component does not need to take responsibility for these activities. In this sense, it is effectively stateless—the state that it does keep is ephemeral and local. Recovery of such components is trivially accomplished by terminating the old and starting the new runtime instance.

Once a job has been received from a client, it will need to be persisted, a responsibility that you placed with the storage component. This component will have to allow all other components to query the list of jobs, selecting them by current status or client account and holding all necessary meta-information. Apart from caches for more efficient operation, this component does not hold any runtime state: its function is only to operate a persistent storage medium, and therefore it can easily be restarted in case of failure. This assumes that the responsibility for providing persistence will be split out into a subcomponent—which today is a likely approach—that you would have to consider as well. If the contents of the persistent storage become corrupted, then it is a business decision whether to implement (partial) automatic resolution of these cases or leave it to the operations personnel; automatic recovery would presumably interfere with normal operation of the storage medium and would therefore fall into the storage component's responsibility.

The next stop of a job's journey through the batch service is the scheduling component. At the top level, this component is responsible for applying quotas and resource request validation as well as providing the executor component with a queue of jobs to pick up. The latter is crucial for the operation of the overall batch service: without it, the executors would be idle and the system would fail to perform its core function. For this reason, you place this function at the top of the scheduling component's priorities and correspondingly at the root of its subcomponent hierarchy, as shown in figure 12.5.

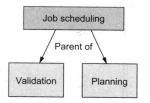

Figure 12.5   Job-scheduling subcomponent hierarchy

While applying the Simple Component pattern, you identified two subresponsibilities of the scheduling component. The first is to validate jobs against policy rules like per-client quotas[4] or general compatibility with the currently available resource set—it would not do to accept a

---

[4] For example, you may want to limit the maximal number of jobs queued by one client—both in order to protect the scheduling algorithm and to enforce administrative limits.

job that needs 20 executor units when only 15 can be provisioned. Those jobs that pass validation form the input to the second subcomponent that performs job-schedule planning for all currently outstanding and accepted jobs. Both of these responsibilities are task-based: they are started periodically and then either complete successfully or fail. Failure modes include hardware failures as well as not terminating within a reasonable time frame. In order to compartmentalize possible failures, these tasks should not directly modify the persistent state of jobs or the planned schedule but instead report back to their parent component, which then takes action, be that notifying clients (via the client interface component) of jobs that failed their submission criteria or updating the internal queue of jobs to be picked next.

Although restarting the subcomponents proved to be trivial, restarting the parent scheduling component is more complex—it will need to initiate one successful schedule planning run before it can reliably resume performing its duties. Therefore, you keep the important data and the vital functionality at the root and delegate the potentially risky tasks to the leaves. Here again, note that the Error Kernel pattern confirms and reinforces the results of the Simple Component pattern: you will frequently find that the boundaries of responsibilities and failure domains coincide and that their hierarchies match as well.

Once a job has reached the head of the scheduler's priority queue, it will be picked up for execution as soon as computing resources become available. You have so far considered execution to be an atomic component, but upon considering possible execution failures, you come to the conclusion that you will have to divide its function: the executor needs to keep track of which job is currently running where, and it will also have to monitor the health and progress of all worker nodes. The worker nodes are those components that on receiving a job description will interpret the contained information, contact data sources, and run the analysis code that was specified by the client. Clearly, the failure of each worker will be contained to that node and not spread to other workers or the overall executor, which implies that the execution manager supervises all worker nodes, as shown in figure 12.6.

If the system is elastic, the executor will also use the external resource-provision mechanism to create new worker nodes or shut down unused ones. The execution manager is also in the position of deciding whether to enlarge or shrink the worker pool, because it naturally monitors the job throughput and can easily be informed about the current job-queue depth—another approach would be to let the scheduler decide the desired pool size. In any case, the executor holds the responsibility of starting, restarting, or stopping worker nodes because it is the only component that knows when it is safe or required to do so.

Analogous to the client interface component, the same reasoning infers that communication with the external resource-provision mechanism should be isolated from the other activities of the execution manager. A communication

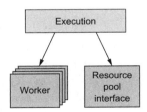

Figure 12.6 Execution subcomponent hierarchy

failure in that regard should not keep jobs from being assigned to already-running executor instances or job-completion notifications from being processed.

The execution of the job is the main purpose of the entire service, but the journey of a job through the components is not yet complete. After the assigned worker node has informed the manager about the completion status, this result needs to be sent back to the storage component in order to be persisted. If the job's nature was such that it must not be run twice, then the fact that the execution was about to start must also have been persisted in this fashion; in this case, a restart of the execution manager will need to include a check of which jobs were already started but not yet completed prior to the crash, and corresponding failure results will have to be generated. In addition to persisting the final job status, the client will need to be informed about the job's result, which completes the entire process.

Now that you have illuminated the functions and relationships of the different components, you recognize that you have omitted one in the earlier list of responsibilities: the service itself needs to be orchestrated, composed from its parts, supervised, and coordinated. You need one top-level component that creates the others and arranges for jobs and other messages to be passed between them. In essence, it is this component's function to oversee the message flow and thereby the business process of the service. This component will be top-level because of its integrating function, which is needed at all times, even though it may be completely stateless by itself. The complete resulting hierarchy is shown in figure 12.7.

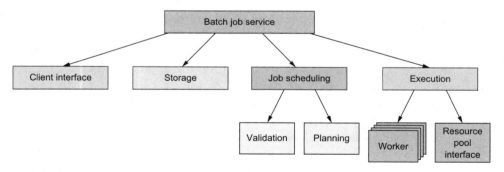

Figure 12.7   The hierarchical decomposition of the batch job service

12.2.3 *The pattern, revisited*

The essence of the previous example can be summarized in the following strategy: after applying the Simple Component pattern, pull important state or functionality toward the top of the component hierarchy, and push activities that carry a higher risk for failure downward towards the leaves. It is expected that responsibility boundaries coincide with failure domains and that narrower subresponsibilities will naturally fall toward the leaves of the hierarchy. This process may lead you to introduce new supervising components that tie together the functionality of components that are otherwise siblings in the hierarchy, or it may guide you toward a more fine-grained component structure in order to simplify failure handling or decouple and isolate critical functions to keep them out of harm's way. The quintessential function of the Error Kernel pattern is to integrate the operational constraints of the system into its responsibility-based problem decomposition.

12.2.4 Applicability

The Error Kernel pattern is applicable if any of the following are true:

- Your system consists of components that have different reliability requirements.
- You expect components to have significantly different failure probabilities and failure severities.
- The system has important functionality that it must provide as reliably as possible while also having components that are exposed to failure.
- Important information that is kept in one part of the system is expensive to re-create, whereas other parts are expected to fail frequently.

The Error Kernel pattern is not applicable if the following are true:

- No hierarchical supervision scheme is used.
- The system already uses the Simple Component pattern, so it does not have multiple failure probabilities.
- All components are either stateless or tolerant to data loss.

We will discuss the second kind of scenarios in more depth in the next chapter when we present the Active–Active Replication pattern.

12.3 The Let-It-Crash pattern

Prefer a full component restart to internal failure handling.

In chapter 7, we discussed *principled failure handling*, noting that the internal recovery mechanisms of each component are limited because they are not sufficiently separated from the failing parts—everything within a component can be affected by a failure. This is especially true for hardware failures that take down the component as a whole, but it is also true for corrupted state that is the result of some programming error only observable in rare circumstances. For this reason, it is necessary to delegate failure handling to a supervisor instead of attempting to solve it within the component.

This principle is also called *crash-only software*.[5] the idea is that transient but rare failures are often costly to diagnose and fix, making it preferable to recover a working system by rebooting parts of it. This hierarchical restart-based failure handling makes

---

[5] Both of the following articles are by George Candea and Armando Fox: "Recursive Restartability: Turning the Reboot Sledgehammer into a Scalpel," USENIX HotOS VIII, 2001, http://dslab.epfl.ch/pubs/recursive_restartability.pdf; and "Crash-Only Software," USENIX HotOS IX, 2003, https://www.usenix.org/legacy/events/hotos03/tech/full_papers/candea/candea.pdf.

it possible to greatly simplify the failure model and at the same time leads to a more robust system that even has a chance to survive failures that were entirely unforeseen.

12.3.1 *The problem setting*

We will demonstrate this design philosophy using the example of the worker nodes that perform the bulk of the work in the batch service whose component hierarchy was developed in the previous two patterns. Each of these is presumably deployed on its own hardware—virtualized or not—that it does not share with other components; ideally, there is no common failure mode between different worker nodes other than a computing center outage.

The problem you are trying to solve is that the workers' code may contain programming errors that rarely manifest—but when they do, they will impede the ability to process batch jobs. Examples of this kind are very slow resource leaks that can go undetected for a long time but will eventually kill the machine; such a leak could result from open files, retained memory, background threads, and so on, and it may not occur every time but could be caused by a rare coincidence of circumstances. Another example is a security vulnerability that allows the executed batch job to intentionally corrupt the state of the worker node in order to subvert its function and perform unauthorized actions within the service's private network—such subversion often is not completely invisible and leads to spurious failures that should not be papered over.

The task: Your mission is to consider the components you have identified for the batch service and describe how a crash and restart would affect each of them and which implementation constraints arise from the let-it-crash philosophy.

12.3.2 *Applying the pattern*

The Let-It-Crash pattern by itself is simple: whenever a component—for example, a worker node—is detected to be faulty, no attempt is made to repair the damage. Instead of doctoring its internal state, you restart it completely, releasing all of its resources and starting it up again from scratch. If you obtained the worker nodes by asking an infrastructure service to provision them, you can go back to the most basic state imaginable: you decommission the old worker node and provision an entirely new one. This way, no corruption or accumulated failure condition can have survived in the fresh instance, because you begin from a known good state again.

Applying this approach to the client interface nodes means all currently active client connections will be severed for the failed node, leading to connection-abort errors in the clients. Upon detecting such an abort condition, the client should try to reconnect, which is your first conclusion. The second follows immediately when considering that the new connection should not be routed to the failed node; this usually means changing the load balancer configuration to remove the failed node. Then, a new node needs to be brought online and added to the load balancer to restore the same processing capacity as before. With these measures, you can confidently crash and restart a client interface node at any given point in time. You do not need to consider the internal communication, because no other components depend on this one: the client interface has only dependencies, no dependents. The consequence of this is that new client requests that a fresh node receives will refer to the storage or scheduling components as the sources of truth—the client interface can be "stateless."[6]

For the storage component, a node failure means the stored data are invalid or lost—the consequence of either possibility is that the data cannot be relied on any longer, so these states are fundamentally equivalent. Because the purpose of the component is to store data permanently, you will have to distribute storage components as per the discussion in section 2.4. We will cover data replication in the next chapter; for now, it suffices to assume that there will be other storage nodes that hold copies of the data. After stopping the failed node, you will therefore need to start a new one that synchronizes itself with the other replicas, taking on the share of responsibility that the failed node had. If the new node uses the previous node's permanent storage device, then recovery can be speeded up by synchronizing only those updates that occurred after the failure. It should be noted that failure is not the same as shutting down and starting up again: the storage devices will keep the data across the shutdown, and the system will start up normally afterward—this can even be done in many cases of infrastructure outages (such as network or power failures).

In the case of the scheduling component, a crash and restart means repopulating the internal state from persistent job storage and resuming operations. This is trivial for an aborted planning run or a failure during job validation, and it can also be handled easily for the top-level scheduling component: you used the Error Kernel pattern to keep this piece of software simple so you could assume that a restart cycle takes a sufficiently short time to be deemed an acceptable downtime, unless specific requirements force you to use replication here as well.

The execution component works similarly in that the worker nodes can crash and be restarted as discussed, where the supervisor makes sure the affected batch job is started again on another available node (or on the newly provisioned one). For the resource pool interface, you can tolerate a short downtime while it is restarted, because its services are rarely needed; and when they are needed, reaction times will be of the order of many seconds or even minutes.

12.3.3   *The pattern, revisited*

We have looked at each of the components in the system's supervision hierarchy and considered the consequences of a failure and subsequent restart. In some cases, you encounter implementation constraints like having to update the request-routing infrastructure so that the failed node is no longer considered and the replacement is taken into account once it is ready. In other cases, you approach the formulation of SLAs by saying that a short downtime may be acceptable: in a real system, you would

---

[6]   This word has become so widely (mis)used that it does not stand on its own any longer. The authors' view is that a truly stateless service that does not contain any mutable internal state does not exist (it would not be a component with a purpose to exist), and a more meaningful interpretation is to equate statelessness with the absence of persistent mutable state.

quantify this both in the failure frequency (for example, by way of the mean time between failures [MTBF][7]) and the extent of the outage (also called the mean time to repair [MTTR][8]).

This pattern can also be turned around so that components are "crashed" intentionally on a regular basis instead of waiting for failures to occur—this could be termed the *Pacemaker pattern*. Deliberately inducing failures has been standard operating procedure for a long time in high-availability scenarios, to verify that failover mechanisms are effective and perform according to specification. The concept has been popularized in recent years by the Chaos Monkey employed by Netflix[9] to establish and maintain the resilience of the company's infrastructure. The chaotic nature of this approach manifests in that single nodes are killed at random without prior selection or human consideration. The idea is that in this way, failure modes are exercised that could potentially be missed in human enumeration of all possible cases. On a higher level, entire data centers and geographic regions are taken offline in a more prepared manner to verify global resource reallocation—this is done on the live production system because no simulation environment could practically emulate the load and client dynamics of such a large-scale application.

Another way to look at this is to consider the definition of availability: it is the fraction of time during which the system is not in a failure state and thus able to process requests, which in mathematical terms is (MTBF − MTTR) / MTBF. This can be increased either by making MTBF larger—which corresponds to less frequent but possibly extensive failures—or by making MTTR smaller. In the latter case, the maximum consecutive downtime period is smaller and the system operates more smoothly, which is the goal of the Let-It-Crash pattern.

12.3.4 *Implementation considerations*

Although this pattern is deeply ingrained in Reactive application design already, it is nevertheless documented here to take note of its important consequences on the design of components and their interaction:

- Each component must tolerate a crash and restart at any point in time, just as a power outage can happen without warning. This means all persistent state must be managed such that the service can resume processing requests with all necessary information and ideally without having to worry about state corruption.

- Each component must be strongly encapsulated so that failures are fully contained and cannot spread. The practical realization depends on the failure model for the hierarchy level under consideration; the options range from

---

[7] https://en.wikipedia.org/wiki/Mean_time_between_failures
[8] https://en.wikipedia.org/wiki/Mean_time_to_repair
[9] At the time of writing, the largest streaming video provider in the United States. Chaos Monkey is part of the Simian Army project that is available as open source software at https://github.com/Netflix/SimianArmy. The approach is described in detail at http://techblog.netflix.com/2012/07/chaos-monkey-released-into-wild.html.

shared-memory message passing over separate OS processes to separate hardware in possibly different geographic regions.

- All interactions between components must tolerate that peers can crash. This means ubiquitous use of timeouts and circuit breakers (described later in this chapter).

- All resources a component uses must be automatically reclaimable by performing a restart. In an Actor system, this means resources are freed by each Actor on termination or that they are leased from their parent; for an OS process, it means the kernel will release all open file handles, network sockets, and so on when the process exits; for a virtual machine, it means the infrastructure resource manager will release all allocated memory (also persistent filesystems) and CPU resources, to be reused by a different virtual machine image.

- All requests sent to a component must be as self-describing as is practical so that processing can resume with as little recovery cost as possible after a restart.

12.3.5 Corollary: the Heartbeat pattern

The Let-It-Crash pattern describes how failures are dealt with. The other side of this coin is that failures must first be detected before they can be acted on. In particularly catastrophic cases like hardware failures, the supervising component can only detect that something is wrong by observing the absence of expected behavior. This obviously requires that some behavior can be expected, which means supervisor and subordinate must communicate with each other on a regular basis. In cases where there would not otherwise be a reason for such interchange, the supervisor needs to send dummy requests whose sole purpose is to see whether the subordinate is still working properly. Due to their regular and vital nature, these are called *heartbeats*. The resulting pattern's diagram is shown in figure 12.8.

One caveat of using dedicated heartbeat messages is that the subordinate may have failed in a way that allows heartbeats to be processed, but nothing else will be answered properly. In order to guard against such unforeseen failures, health monitoring should be implemented by monitoring the service quality (failure rate, response latency, and so on) during normal operation where appropriate—sending such statistics to the supervisor on a regular basis can be used as a heartbeat signal at the same time if it is done by the subordinate (as opposed to being done by the infrastructure: for example, by monitoring the state of circuit breakers, as discussed in section 12.4).

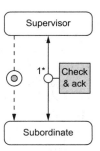

Figure 12.8 The supervisor starts the subordinate, and then it performs periodic health checks by exchanging messages with the subordinate until no satisfactory answer is returned.

12.3.6 Corollary: the Proactive Failure Signal pattern

Applying the Heartbeat pattern to all failure modes results in a high level of robustness, but there are classes of failures where patiently waiting for the heartbeat of the suspected component takes longer than necessary: the component can diagnose some failures itself. A prominent example is that all exceptions that are thrown from an Actor implementation are treated as failures—exceptions that are handled inside the Actor usually pertain to error conditions resulting from the use of libraries that use exceptions for this purpose. All uncaught exceptions can be sent by the infrastructure (the Actor library) to

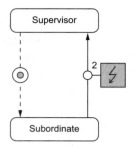

Figure 12.9 The supervisor starts the subordinate and reacts to its failure signals as they occur.

the supervisor in a message signaling the failure so that the supervisor can act on them immediately. Wherever this is possible, it should be viewed as an optimization of the supervisor's response time. The messaging pattern between supervisor and subordinate is depicted in figure 12.9 using the conventions established in appendix A.

Depending on the failure model, it can also be adequate to rely entirely on such measures. This is equivalent to saying that, for example, an Actor is assumed to not have failed until it has sent a failure signal. Monitoring the health of every single Actor in a system is typically forbiddingly expensive, and relying on these failure signals achieves sufficient robustness at the lower levels of the component hierarchy.

It is not uncommon to combine this pattern and the Heartbeat pattern to cover all bases. Where the infrastructure supports lifecycle monitoring—for example, see the DeathWatch[10] feature of Akka Actors—there is an additional way in which the supervisor can learn of the subordinate's troubles: if the subordinate has stopped itself while the supervisor still expected it to do something (or if the component is not expected to ever stop while the application is running), then the resulting termination notification can be taken as a failure signal as well. The full communication diagram for such a relationship is shown in figure 12.10.

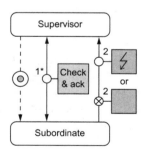

Figure 12.10 The supervisor first starts the subordinate, and then it performs periodic health checks by exchanging messages with it (step 1) until either no answer is returned or a failure signal is received (step 2).

It is important to note that these patterns are not specific to Akka or the Actor model; we use these implementations only to give concrete examples of their implementation. An application based on RxJava would, for

---

[10] See http://doc.akka.io/docs/akka/2.4.1/general/supervision.html#What_Lifecycle_Monitoring_Means and http://doc.akka.io/docs/akka/2.4.1/scala/actors.html#Lifecycle_Monitoring_aka_DeathWatch.

example, use the Hystrix library for health monitoring, allowing components to be restarted as needed. Another example is that the deployment of components as microservices on Amazon EC2 could use the AWS API to learn of some nodes' termination and react in the same fashion as just described for the DeathWatch feature.

12.4 *The Circuit Breaker pattern*

Protect services by breaking the connection to their users during prolonged failure conditions.

In previous sections, we discussed how to segregate a system into a hierarchy of components and subcomponents for the purpose of isolating responsibilities and encapsulating failure domains. This pattern describes how to safely connect different parts of the system so that failures do not spread uncontrollably across them. Its origin lies in electrical engineering: in order to protect electrical circuits from each other and introduce decoupled failure domains, a technique was established of breaking the connection when the transmitted power exceeds a given threshold.

Translated to a Reactive application, this means the flow of requests from one component to the next may be broken up deliberately when the recipient is overloaded or otherwise failing. Doing so serves two purposes: first, the recipient gets some breathing room to recover from possible load-induced failures; and second, the sender decides that requests will fail instead of wasting time with waiting for negative replies.

Although circuit breakers have been used in electrical engineering since the 1920s, the use of this principle has been popularized in software design only recently: for example, by Michael Nygard's book *Release It!* (Pragmatic Programmers, 2007).

12.4.1 *The problem setting*

The batch job execution facility designed in the previous three sections will serve you yet again. We already hinted at one situation that would do well to include a circuit breaker: when the service is offered to external clients who submit jobs at their own rate and schedule, and jobs are not naturally bounded by the capacity of the batch system.

To visualize what this means, we will consider a single client that contacts the batch service to submit a single job. The client will get multiple status updates as the submitted job progresses through the system:

- Upon having received and persisted the job description
- Upon having accepted the job for execution, or upon rejecting it due to policy violations
- Upon starting execution
- Upon finishing execution

The first of these steps is very important: it assures the client that there will be further updates about this job because it has been admitted into the system and will at least be examined. Providing this guarantee is costly—it involves storing the job description in nonvolatile and replicated memory—and therefore a client could easily generate more jobs per second than the system can safely ingest. In this case, the client interface would overload the storage subsystem: this would have a ripple effect for the job-scheduling and execution components, which would experience degraded performance when accessing job descriptions for their purposes. The system might still work in this state, but its performance characteristics would be quite different from normal operation; it would be in "overload mode."

The task: Your mission is to sketch the use of circuit breakers between the client interface component and the storage component to both ensure that clients cannot willfully overload the storage and ensure that the client interface gives timely responses even when the storage component is unreachable or has failed.

12.4.2 *Applying the pattern*

When implementing the client interface module, you will have to write one piece of code that sends requests to the storage subsystem. If you make sure all such requests take this single route, you will have an easy time reacting to the problematic scenarios outlined earlier. You need to keep track of the response latency for all requests that are made. When you observe that this latency rises consistently above the agreed limit, then you can switch into "emergency mode": instead of trying new requests, you will answer all subsequent ones immediately with negative replies. You will fabricate the negative replies on behalf of the storage subsystem, because it cannot do even that within the allowed time window under the current conditions.

In addition, you should monitor the failure rate of replies that come back from the storage subsystem. It does not make much sense to keep sending more storage requests when all of them will be answered negatively anyway; instead of wasting network bandwidth, you should again switch into emergency mode, fabricating the negative replies. An example implementation of this scheme in Akka would look like the following listing.

Listing 12.1 Using a circuit breaker to give a failed component time to recover

Makes an asynchronous request
to the storage subsystem

```
private object StorageFailed extends RuntimeException
private def sendToStorage(job: Job): Future[StorageStatus] = {
  val f: Future[StorageStatus] = . . .

  f.map {
    case StorageStatus.Failed => throw StorageFailed
    case other                => other
  }
}

private val breaker = CircuitBreaker(
    system.scheduler,
    5,
    300.millis,
    30.seconds,
  )
```

Maps storage failures
to Future failures to
alert the breaker

⟵ Used for scheduling timeouts
⟵ Number of failures in a row
⟵ Timeout for each service call
⟵ Time before trying to close after tripping

```
def persist(job: Job): Future[StorageStatus] =
  breaker
    .withCircuitBreaker(sendToStorage(job))
    .recover {
      case StorageFailed                => StorageStatus.Failed
      case _: TimeoutException          => StorageStatus.Unknown
      case _: CircuitBreakerOpenException => StorageStatus.Failed
    }
```

The other piece of client interface code will call the `persist` method and get back a Future representing the storage subsystem's reply, but the remote service invocation will be performed only if the circuit breaker is in the *closed* state. Negative replies (of type `StorageStatus.Failed`) and timeouts will be counted by the breaker: if it sees five failures in a row, it will transition into the *open* state in which it immediately provides a response consisting of a `CircuitBreakerOpenException`. After 30 seconds, exactly one request will be let through to the storage subsystem, and if that comes back successfully and in time, the breaker will flip back into the *closed* state.

What you have done so far is illustrated in figure 12.11: the client interface will reply to external clients within its allotted time, but in case of a storage-subsystem overload or failure, these replies will be fabricated and negative for all clients. Although this approach protects the system from attacks, it is not the best you can do. Just as in electrical engineering, you need to

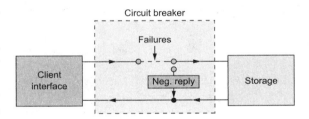

Figure 12.11 A circuit breaker between the client interface and the storage subsystem

break circuits at more than one level—what you have built so far is the main circuit breaker for the entire apartment building, but you are lacking the power-distribution boards that limit the damage each individual tenant can do.

There is one difference between these per-client circuit breakers and the main one: they do not react primarily to trouble downstream, but rather enforce a maximum current that can flow through them. In computer systems, this is called *rate limiting*. Instead of tracking the call latencies, you must remember the times of previous requests and reject new requests that violate a stated limit such as "no more than 100 requests in any 2-second interval." Writing such a facility in Scala is straightforward.

Listing 12.2 Protecting a component by using a rate limiter

```
import scala.concurrent.duration.FiniteDuration
import scala.concurrent.duration.Deadline
import scala.concurrent.Future

case object RateLimitExceeded extends RuntimeException

class RateLimiter(requests: Int, period: FiniteDuration) {
```

```
private val startTimes = {
  val onePeriodAgo = Deadline.now - period
  Array.fill(requests)(onePeriodAgo)
}
private var position = 0

private def enqueue(time: Deadline) = {
  startTimes(position) = time
  position += 1
  if (position == requests) position = 0
}
def call[T](block: => Future[T]): Future[T] = {
  val now = Deadline.now
  if ((now - startTimes(position)) < period) {
    Future.failed(RateLimitExceeded)
  } else {
    enqueue(now)
    block
  }
}
}
```

Index of the next slot to be used, keeping track of when the last job was enqueued in it to enforce the rate limit ⊲─ (points to `private var position = 0`)

Obtains the current timestamp ⊲─ (points to `val now = Deadline.now`)

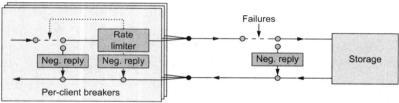

Figure 12.12   Complete circuit breaker setup between the client interface and the storage subsystem

Now you can combine both kinds of circuit breakers to obtain the full picture shown in figure 12.12. Clients are identified by their authentication credentials, so you can assign one `CircuitBreaker` for each user independent of how many network connections they use. For each client, you maintain a `RateLimiter` that protects the client interface from being flooded with requests. On the outgoing side, toward the storage component, you use one shared `CircuitBreaker` to guard against the remote subsystem's failures. The per-client code could look like the following.

Listing 12.3   Circuit breaker: limiting requests from a client

```
private val limiter = new RateLimiter(100, 2.seconds)

def persistForThisClient(job: Job): Future[StorageStatus] =
  limiter
    .call(persist(job))
    .recover {
      case RateLimitExceeded => StorageStatus.Failed
    }
```

This is assumed to not be invoked concurrently as it is for a single client.

ADVANCED USAGE

It is common practice to *gate* a client that repeatedly violates its rate limit: gating informs the client that it has made too many requests beyond the allowed rate and will be blocked temporarily. This is an incentive to the writers of client code to properly limit the service calls on their end instead of always sending at full speed—that is an efficient tactic for achieving maximum throughput. In order to do that, you only need to add another circuit breaker, as shown next.

Listing 12.4 Gating a client

```
private val limiter = new RateLimiter(100, 2.seconds)
private val breaker = CircuitBreaker(system.scheduler,
                                     10, Duration.Zero, 10.seconds)

def persistForThisClient(job: Job): Future[StorageStatus] =
  breaker
    .withCircuitBreaker(limiter.call(persist(job)))
    .recover {
      case RateLimitExceeded            => StorageStatus.Failed
      case _: CircuitBreakerOpenException => StorageStatus.Gated
    }
```

In order to trip the circuit breaker, the client will have to send 10 requests while being above the rate limit; assuming regular request spacing, this means the client needs to submit at a rate that is at least 10% higher than allowed. In this case, it will be blocked from service for the next 10 seconds, and it will be informed by way of receiving a `Gated` status reply. `Duration.Zero` in listing 12.4 has the function of turning off the timeout tracking for individual requests; this is not needed here because it will be performed by the `persist` call.

12.4.3 The pattern, revisited

You have decoupled the client interface and the storage subsystem by introducing predetermined breaking points on the path from one to the other. Thereby, you have protected the storage from being overloaded in general (the main circuit breaker) and you have protected the client interface's function from single misbehaving clients (the rate-limiting per-client circuit breakers). Being overloaded is a condition that you should strive to avoid when possible because running at 100% capacity is in most cases less efficient than leaving a little headroom. The reason is that at full capacity, more time is wasted competing for the available resources (CPU time, memory bandwidth, caches, IO channels) than it is when requests can travel through the system mostly unhindered by congestion.

The second problem we have considered here is that the client interface cannot acknowledge reception of a job description before it receives the successful reply from the storage subsystem. If this reply does not arrive within the allotted time, then the response to the client will be delayed for longer than the SLA allows—the service will violate its latency bound. This means during time periods when the storage subsystem fails to answer promptly, the client interface will have to come to its own conclusions; if it cannot ask another (nonlocal) component, then it must locally determine the appropriate response to its own clients. You have also used the circuit breaker to protect the client interface from failures of the storage subsystem, fabricating negative responses in case no others are readily available.

In addition, you have seen that the circuit breaker you installed for overload protection handles the situation where the storage subsystem does not answer successfully or in time—the reaction is independent of the underlying reason. *This makes the system more resilient compared to handling every single error case separately.* And this is what is meant by *bulkheading* failure domains to achieve compartmentalization and encapsulation.

12.4.4 *Applicability*

This pattern is applicable wherever two decoupled components communicate and where failures—foreseen or unexpected—will not travel upstream to infect and slow other components, or where overload conditions will not travel downstream to induce failure. Decoupling has a cost in that all calls pass through another tracking step, and timeouts need to be scheduled. Hence, it should not be applied at too fine a level of granularity; it is most useful between different components in a system. This applies especially to services that are reached via network connections (such as authentication providers and persistent storage), where the circuit breaker also reacts appropriately to network failures by concluding that the remote service is not currently reachable.

Another important aspect of using circuit breakers is that monitoring their state reveals interesting insight into the runtime behavior and performance of a service. When circuit breakers trip while protecting a given service, operations personnel will usually want to be alerted in order to look into the outage.

> **NOTE** A circuit breaker is a means to fail fast—it must not be used to postpone requests and send them later. The problem with such a scheme is that when the circuit breaker closes, the deferred requests will likely overload the target system. This phenomenon is called a *thundering herd*, and it can create feedback loops that lead to a system oscillating between being unavailable and being overloaded.

12.5 *Summary*

In this chapter, we have covered a lot of ground on the design and implementation of resilient systems:

- We described simple components that obey the single responsibility principle.
- You saw the application of hierarchical failure handling in practice while implementing the Error Kernel pattern.
- We noted the implications of relying on component restarts to recover from failure, in our discussion of the Let-It-Crash pattern.

- You learned how to decouple components from each other using the Circuit Breaker pattern for either side's protection.

In the next chapter, we will dive into stateful replication patterns in order to implement components that are impervious to outages at varying degrees of downtime and implementation complexity. Although these patterns are also related to fault tolerance and recovery, they warrant a chapter of their own.

Replication patterns

13

The previous chapter introduced powerful architectural and implementation patterns for breaking down a larger system into simple components that are isolated from each other while encapsulating failures. One aspect that we did not cover is how to distribute the functionality of a component such that it can withstand hardware and infrastructure outages without loss of availability. This topic is large enough by itself to be treated in a separate chapter. In particular, in this chapter you will learn about the following:

- The Active–Passive Replication pattern, for cases where explicit failover is acceptable or desirable
- Three different Multiple-Master Replication patterns that allow clients to contact any replica of their choosing
- The Active–Active Replication pattern, which specializes in zero downtime for a selected class of failures

NOTE This chapter presents some deep treatment of replication with its pitfalls and limitations. Unfortunately, for this topic, the devil is in the details, and some surprising semantics result from seemingly insignificant properties of the underlying implementation. Therefore, it may be adequate to only skim this chapter upon reading this book for the first time and come back to it when necessary or when your experience with building Reactive systems inspires a wish to deepen your knowledge of these aspects.

13.1 The Active–Passive Replication pattern

Keep multiple copies of the service running in different locations, but only accept modifications to the state in one location at any given time.

This pattern is also sometimes referred to as *failover* or *master–slave replication*. You have already seen one particular form of failover: the ability to restart a component means that after a failure, a new instance is created and takes over functionality, like passing the baton from one runner to the next. For a stateful service, the new instance accesses the same persistent storage location as the previously failed one, recovering the state before the crash and continuing from there. This works only as long as the persistent storage is intact; if that fails, then restarting is not possible—the service will forget all of its previous state and start from scratch. Imagine your web shop forgetting about all registered users—that would be a catastrophe!

We use the term *active–passive replication* to more precisely denote that in order to be able to recover even when one service instance fails completely—including loss of its persistent storage—you distribute its functionality and its full dataset across several physical locations. The need for such measures was discussed in section 2.4: replication means not putting all of your eggs in one basket.

Replicating and thereby distributing a piece of functionality requires a certain amount of coordination, in particular considering operations that change the persistent state. The goal of active–passive replication is to ensure that at any given time, only one of the replicas has the right to perform modifications. This allows individual modifications to be made without requiring consensus about them, as long as there is consensus about what the currently active party is, just as electing a mayor serves the purpose of simplifying the process of coordination within a city.

13.1.1 The problem setting

In the batch service example, the most important component used by all the other components is the storage module. Restarting this component after a failure allows it to recover from many issues, but you must take care to protect its data from being lost. This means storing the data in multiple places and allowing the other components to retrieve the data from any of them.

In order to visualize what this means, we will consider an incoming request that arrives at the client interface. Because the storage component is now spread across multiple locations, the client interface will need to know multiple addresses in order to talk to it. Assume that there is a service registry via which all components can obtain the addresses of their communication partners. When the storage component starts up, it will register all of its locations and their addresses in the registry, where the client interface can retrieve them. This allows new replicas to be added and old ones to be replaced at runtime. A static list of addresses might be sufficient in some cases, but it is in general desirable to be able to change addresses, especially in a cloud computing environment.

Which replica is the active one will change over time. There are several options for routing requests to it:

- The storage component can inform its clients via the service registry regarding which address belongs to the currently active replica. This simplifies the implementation of the client but also leads to additional lag for picking up a change of replica after a failure.

- The internal consensus mechanism for electing the active replica can be made accessible to the clients, allowing them to follow changes by listening in on the election protocol. This provides timely updates but couples the implementation of client and service by requiring them to share a larger protocol.

- All replicas can offer the service of forwarding requests to the currently active replica. This frees clients from having to track replica changes closely while avoiding downtime or close coupling. A possible downside of this approach is that requests sent via different replicas may arrive with substantially different delays, thereby making the ordering of request processing less deterministic.

The task: Your mission is to implement active–passive replication for a key–value store (represented by an in-memory map) using Akka Cluster, with the location of the active replica being managed by the Cluster Singleton feature. An important property of the implementation is that once the service replies with a confirmation, the request must have been processed and its results persisted to disk such that after a subsequent failure, the new active replica will behave correctly.

13.1.2 *Applying the pattern*

Basing this illustration on Akka Cluster allows us to focus on the replication logic and delegate the election of the active replica to the Cluster Singleton feature that is offered by this library. A *cluster singleton* is an actor that is spawned on the oldest cluster member with a given role. The Akka implementation ensures that there cannot be conflicting information about which member is the oldest within the same cluster, which means there cannot be two instances of the cluster singleton running simultaneously. This guarantee relies on the proper configuration of the cluster: during a network partition, each of the isolated parts will have to decide whether to continue operation or shut itself down; and if the rules are formulated such that two parts can continue running, then a singleton will be elected within each of these parts. Where this is not desired, a strict quorum must be employed that is larger than half the total number of nodes in the cluster—with the consequence that during a three-way split, the entire cluster may shut down. Further discussion of these topics can be found in chapter 17; for now, it is sufficient to know that the Cluster Singleton mechanism ensures that there will be only one active replica running at any time.

As a first step, you implement the actor that controls the active replica. This actor will be instantiated by the Cluster Singleton mechanism as a cluster-wide singleton, as just explained. Its role is to accept and answer requests from clients as well as to disseminate updates to all passive replicas. To keep things simple, you will implement a generic key–value store that associates JSON values and uses text strings as keys. This will save you the trouble of defining the required data types for your batch service operation— which is not central to the application of this pattern, in any case. The full source code for this example can be found at www.manning.com/books/reactive-design-patterns and in the book's GitHub repository at https://github.com/ReactiveDesignPatterns.

Before we begin, here are the protocol messages by which clients interact with the replicated storage:

```
case class Put(key: String, value: JsValue, replyTo: ActorRef)
case class PutConfirmed(key: String, value: JsValue)
case class PutRejected(key: String, value: JsValue)
case class Get(key: String, replyTo: ActorRef)
case class GetResult(key: String, value: Option[JsValue])
```

In response to a `Put` command, you expect either a confirmation or rejection reply, whereas the result of a `Get` command will always indicate the currently bound value for the given key (which may optionally be empty). A command may be rejected in case of replication failures or service overload, as you will see later. The type `JsValue` represents an arbitrary JSON value in the `play-json` library, but the choice of serialization library is not essential here.

When the singleton actor starts up, it must first contact a passive replica to obtain the current starting state. It is most efficient to ask the replica within the same actor system (that is, on the same network host), because doing so avoids serializing the entire data store and sending it over the network. In the following implementation, the address of the local replica is provided to the actor via its constructor.

Listing 13.1 Singleton taking over as the active replica

```
class Active(localReplica: ActorRef,
             replicationFactor: Int,
             maxQueueSize: Int)
    extends Actor with Stash with ActorLogging {

  private var theStore: Map[String, JsValue] = _        ⟵  Data store, held in memory for the sake of a simple example

  private var seqNr: Iterator[Int] = _                  ⟵  Sequence-number generator for Replicate requests

  log.info("taking over from local replica")
  localReplica ! TakeOver(self)                         ⟵  Asks for InitialData to be provided by the local storage replica

  def receive = {
    case InitialState(m, s) =>
      log.info("took over at sequence {}", s)
      theStore = m
      seqNr = Iterator from s
      context.become(running)
      unstashAll()
    case _ => stash()
  }

  val running: Receive = ...                            ⟵  Behavior of the running state
}
```

While the actor is waiting for the initial state message, it needs to ignore all incoming requests. Instead of dropping them or making up fake replies, you stash them within the actor, to be answered as soon as you have the necessary data. Akka directly supports this usage by mixing in the Stash trait. In the running state, the actor will use the data store and the sequence-number generator, but it will need several more data structures to organize its behavior, as follows.

Listing 13.2 Active replica disseminating replication requests

```scala
class Active(localReplica: ActorRef,
             replicationFactor: Int,
             maxQueueSize: Int)
    extends Actor with Stash with ActorLogging {

  ...

  private val MaxOutstanding = maxQueueSize / 2

  private val toReplicate = Queue.empty[Replicate]

  private var replicating = TreeMap.empty[Int, (Replicate, Int)]

  val timer = system.scheduler.schedule(
    1.second, 1.second, self, Tick)(context.dispatcher)
  override def postStop() = timer.cancel()

  val running: Receive = {
    case p @ Put(key, value, replyTo) =>
      if (toReplicate.size < MaxOutstanding) {
        toReplicate.enqueue(Replicate(seqNr.next, key, value, replyTo))
        replicate()
      } else {
        replyTo ! PutRejected(key, value)
      }

    case Get(key, replyTo) =>
      replyTo ! GetResult(key, theStore get key)

    case Tick =>
      replicating.valuesIterator foreach {
        case (replicate, count) => disseminate(replicate)
      }

    case Replicated(confirm) =>
      replicating.get(confirm) match {
        case None =>
        case Some((rep, 1)) =>
          replicating -= confirm
          theStore += rep.key -> rep.value
          rep.replyTo ! PutConfirmed(rep.key, rep.value)
        case Some((rep, n)) =>
          replicating += confirm -> (rep, n - 1)
      }
      replicate()
  }

  private def replicate(): Unit =
    if (replicating.size < MaxOutstanding && toReplicate.nonEmpty) {
      val r = toReplicate.dequeue()
      replicating += r.seq -> (r, replicationFactor)
      disseminate(r)
    }
```

Initialization as shown in listing 13.1

Queue of outstanding items to be replicated

Ordered collection of ongoing replication requests

Recurring timer to resend outstanding replication requests

Already removed

Helper method that dispatches further replication requests when appropriate

```
  private def disseminate(r: Replicate): Unit = {
    val req = r.copy(replyTo = self)
    val members = Cluster(context.system).state.members
    members.foreach(m => replicaOn(m.address) ! req)
  }

  private def replicaOn(addr: Address): ActorSelection =
    context.actorSelection(localReplica.path.toStringWithAddress(addr))
}
```

Sends a replication request to all replicas, including local

The actor keeps a queue of items to be replicated, called `toReplicate`, plus a queue of replication requests that are currently in flight. The latter—`replicating`—is implemented as an ordered map because you need direct access to its elements as replication requests complete. Whenever the actor receives a `Put` request, it checks whether there is still room in the queue of items to be replicated. If the queue is full, the client is immediately informed that the request is rejected; otherwise, a new `Replicate` object is enqueued that describes the update to be performed, and then the `replicate()` method is invoked. This method transfers updates from the `toReplicate` queue to the `replicating` queue if there is space. The purpose of this setup is to place a limit on the number of currently outstanding replication requests so that clients can be informed when the replication mechanism cannot keep up with the update load.

When an update is moved to the replicating queue, the `disseminate` function is called. Here, you implement the core piece of the algorithm: every update that is accepted by the active replica is sent to all passive replicas for persistent storage. Because you are using Akka Cluster, you can obtain a list of addresses for all replicas from the Cluster Extension, using the local replica `ActorRef` as a pattern into which each remote address is inserted in turn. The `replicate` function stores the update together with a required replication count into the `replicating` queue, indexed by the update's sequence number. The update will stay in the queue until enough confirmations have been received in the form of `Replicated` messages, as can be seen in the definition of the running behavior in listing 13.1. Only when this count is reached is the update applied to the local storage and the confirmation sent back to the original client.

Update requests as well as confirmations may be lost on the way between network nodes. Therefore, the active replica schedules a periodic reminder upon which it will resend all updates that are currently in the replicating queue. This ensures that, eventually, all updates are received by enough passive replicas. It is not necessary for all replicas to receive the updates from the active one, as you will see when we look at the implementation of a passive replica. The reason for this design choice is that burdening the active replica with all the concerns of successful replication will make its implementation more complex and increase the latency for responding to requests.

Before we focus on the passive replica implementation, you need to enable it to persist data on disk and read the data back. For the purpose of this example, you use the following simple file storage. It should be obvious that this is not suitable for production systems; we will discuss persistence patterns in chapter 17.

Listing 13.3   Implementing persistence by writing a JSON file to the local disk

```scala
import play.api.libs.json.{ JsValue, Json }
import java.io.File
import sbt.IO

object Persistence {
  case class Database(seq: Int, kv: Map[String, JsValue])
  object Database { implicit val format = Json.format[Database] }

  def persist(name: String, seq: Int, kv: Map[String, JsValue]): Unit = {
    val bytes = Json.stringify(Json.toJson(Database(seq, kv)))
    val current = new File(s"./theDataBase-$name.json")
    val next = new File(s"./theDataBase-$name.json.new")
    IO.write(next, bytes)
    IO.move(next, current)
  }

  def readPersisted(name: String): Database = {
    val file = new File(s"theDataBase-$name.json")
    if (file.exists()) Json.parse(IO.read(file)).as[Database]
    else Database(0, Map.empty)
  }
}
```

Extremely simple model of a versioned key–value store → (`case class Database(seq: Int, kv: Map[String, JsValue])`)

Uses the Play framework's JSON serialization → (`object Database { implicit val format = Json.format[Database] }` and `IO.write(next, bytes)`)

First writes to a separate file to avoid leaving behind incomplete data during a crash...

...and then renames it in place of the current file to atomically replace the old version with the new one. → (`IO.move(next, current)`)

The following listing assumes an import of the `Persistence` object so that you can use the `persist` and `readPersisted` methods where needed.

Listing 13.4   Passive replicas tracking whether they are up to date

```scala
class Passive(askAroundCount: Int,
              askAroundInterval: FiniteDuration,
              maxLag: Int) extends Actor with ActorLogging {
  private val applied = Queue.empty[Replicate]

  val selfAddress = Cluster(context.system).selfAddress
  val name = selfAddress.toString.replaceAll("[:/]", "_")

  def receive = readPersisted(name) match {
    case Database(s, kv) =>
      log.info("started at sequence {}", s)
      upToDate(kv, s + 1)
  }

  def upToDate(theStore: Map[String, JsValue],
               expectedSeq: Int): Receive = {

    case TakeOver(active) =>
      log.info("active replica starting at sequence {}", expectedSeq)
      active ! InitialState(theStore, expectedSeq)
```

Constructs a name identifying this replica for data storage → (`val name = selfAddress.toString.replaceAll("[:/]", "_")`)

```
    case Replicate(s, _, _, replyTo) if s - expectedSeq < 0 =>
      replyTo ! Replicated(s)

    case r: Replicate if r.seq == expectedSeq =>
      val nextStore = theStore + (r.key -> r.value)
      persist(name, expectedSeq, nextStore)
      r.replyTo ! Replicated(r.seq)
      applied.enqueue(r)
      context.become(upToDate(nextStore, expectedSeq + 1))

    case r: Replicate =>
      if (r.seq - expectedSeq > maxLag)
        fallBehind(expectedSeq, TreeMap(r.seq -> r))
      else
        missingSomeUpdates(theStore, expectedSeq, Set.empty,
                           TreeMap(r.seq -> r))
  }

  // ...
}
```

Implementation of fallBehind and missingSomeUpdates elided for now

The passive replica serves two purposes: it ensures the persistent storage of all incoming updates, and it maintains the current state of the full database so the active replica can be initialized when required. When the passive replica starts up, it first reads the persistent state of the database into memory, including the sequence number of the latest applied update. As long as all updates are received in the correct order, only the third case of the up-to-date behavior will be invoked, applying the updates to the local store, persisting it, confirming successful replication, and changing behavior to expect the update with the following sequence number. Updates that are retransmitted by the active replica will have a sequence number that is less than the expected one and therefore will only be confirmed because they have already been applied. A `TakeOver` request from a newly initializing active replica can in this state be answered immediately.

But what happens when messages are lost? In addition to ordinary message loss, this could also be due to a replica being restarted: between the last successful persistence before the restart and the initialization afterward, any number of additional updates may have been sent by the active replica that were never delivered to this instance because it was inactive. Such losses can only be detected upon receiving a subsequent update. The size of the gap in updates can be determined by comparing the expected sequence number with the one contained in the update; if it is too large—as determined by the `maxLag` parameter—you consider this replica as having fallen behind; otherwise, it is merely missing some updates. The difference between these two lies in how you recover from the situation, as shown next.

Listing 13.5 Passive replica requesting a full update when it falls too far behind

```
class Passive(askAroundCount: Int,
              askAroundInterval: FiniteDuration,
              maxLag: Int) extends Actor with ActorLogging {
  private val applied = Queue.empty[Replicate]
```

```scala
private var awaitingInitialState = Option.empty[ActorRef]

// ...                                         ⟵── Initialization elided

private var tickTask = Option.empty[Cancellable]
def scheduleTick() = {
  tickTask foreach (_.cancel())
  tickTask = Some(context.system.scheduler.scheduleOnce(
    askAroundInterval, self, DoConsolidate)(context.dispatcher))
}

def caughtUp(theStore: Map[String, JsValue], expectedSeq: Int) {
  awaitingInitialState foreach (_ ! InitialState(theStore, expectedSeq))
  awaitingInitialState = None
  context.become(upToDate(theStore, expectedSeq))
}

def upToDate(theStore: Map[String, JsValue],
             expectedSeq: Int): Receive = {
  // ...                                       ⟵── Cases shown previously elided
  case GetFull(replyTo) =>
    log.info("sending full info to {}", replyTo)
    replyTo ! InitialState(theStore, expectedSeq)
}

def fallBehind(expectedSeq: Int, _waiting: TreeMap[Int, Replicate]) {
  askAroundFullState()
  scheduleTick()
  var waiting = _waiting
  context.become {
    case Replicate(s, _, _, replyTo) if s < expectedSeq =>
      replyTo ! Replicated(s)

    case r: Replicate =>
      waiting += (r.seq -> r)

    case TakeOver(active) =>
      log.info("delaying active replica take-over until upToDate")
      awaitingInitialState = Some(active)

    case InitialState(m, s) if s > expectedSeq =>
      log.info("received newer state at sequence {} (was at {})",
               s, expectedSeq)
      persist(name, s, m)
      waiting.to(s).valuesIterator foreach (r =>
                                      r.replyTo ! Replicated(r.seq))
      val nextWaiting = waiting.from(expectedSeq)
      consolidate(m, s + 1, Set.empty, nextWaiting)

    case DoConsolidate =>
      askAroundFullState()
      scheduleTick()
  }
}

private val random = new Random

private def getMembers(n: Int): Seq[Address] = {
  val members = Cluster(context.system).state.members
  random.shuffle(members.map(_.address).toSeq).take(n)
```

```
  }
  private def askAroundFullState(): Unit = {
    log.info("asking for full data")
    getMembers(1).foreach(addr => replicaOn(addr) ! GetFull(self))
  }
  private def replicaOn(addr: Address): ActorSelection =
    context.actorSelection(self.path.toStringWithAddress(addr))
}
```

When falling behind, you first ask a randomly selected replica for a full dump of the database and schedule a timer. Then you change behavior into a waiting state in which new updates are accumulated for later application, very old updates are immediately confirmed, and requests to take over are deferred. This state can only be left once an initial-state message has been received; at this point, you persist this newer state of the database, confirm all accumulated updates whose sequence number is smaller than the now-expected one, and try to apply all remaining updates by calling the consolidate function that is shown next.

Listing 13.6 Consolidation: applying updates that were held previously

```
private val matches = (p: (Int, Int)) => p._1 == p._2

private def consolidate(theStore: Map[String, JsValue],
                        expectedSeq: Int,
                        askedFor: Set[Int],
                        waiting: TreeMap[Int, Replicate]): Unit = {
  val prefix =
    waiting.keysIterator
      .zip(Iterator from expectedSeq)        ◁─┐ Calculates the length of the
      .takeWhile(matches)                        directly applicable queue prefix
      .size

  val nextStore =
    waiting.valuesIterator
      .take(prefix)
      .foldLeft(theStore) { (store, replicate) =>
        persist(name, replicate.seq, theStore)
        replicate.replyTo ! Replicated(replicate.seq)
        applied.enqueue(replicate)
        store + (replicate.key -> replicate.value)
      }
  val nextWaiting = waiting.drop(prefix)
  val nextExpectedSeq = expectedSeq + prefix
                                                    ◁─┐ Caps the size of
  applied.drop(Math.max(0, applied.size - maxLag))       the applied buffer

                                                    ◁─┐ Checks whether you
  if (nextWaiting.nonEmpty) {                            fell behind too much
    if (nextWaiting.lastKey - nextExpectedSeq > maxLag)
      fallBehind(nextExpectedSeq, nextWaiting)
    else
      missingSomeUpdates(nextStore, nextExpectedSeq, askedFor,
                          nextWaiting)
  } else caughtUp(nextStore, nextExpectedSeq)
}
```

The waiting parameter contains the accumulated updates ordered by their sequence number. You then take and apply as many sequential updates as you have. Because the updates are stored in an ordered map, you can do this by matching sequence numbers in the map against a simple integer sequence until there is a mismatch (gap) in the sequence. The length of that matching prefix is the number of updates to persist, confirm, and drop from the waiting list. If the list is now empty—which means all accumulated updates had consecutive sequence numbers—you conclude that you have caught up with the active replica and switch back into up-to-date mode. Otherwise, you again determine whether the knowledge gap that remains is too large or whether remaining holes can be filled individually. The latter is done by the behavior that is shown next.

> **Listing 13.7 Determining whether holes in updates can be filled individually**

```scala
class Passive(askAroundCount: Int,
              askAroundInterval: FiniteDuration,
              maxLag: Int) extends Actor with ActorLogging {
  private val applied = Queue.empty[Replicate]
  private var awaitingInitialState = Option.empty[ActorRef]

  // ...                                     <—— Initialization elided

  def upToDate(theStore: Map[String, JsValue],
               expectedSeq: Int): Receive = {
    ... // cases shown previously elided
    case GetSingle(s, replyTo) =>
      log.info("GetSingle from {}", replyTo)
      if (applied.nonEmpty &&
          applied.head.seq <= s && applied.last.seq >= s) {
        replyTo ! applied.find(_.seq == s).get
      } else if (s < expectedSeq) {
        replyTo ! InitialState(theStore, expectedSeq)
      }
  }

  def missingSomeUpdates(theStore: Map[String, JsValue],
                         expectedSeq: Int,
                         prevOutstanding: Set[Int],
                         waiting: TreeMap[Int, Replicate]): Unit = {
    val askFor =
      (expectedSeq to waiting.lastKey).iterator
        .filterNot(seq =>
          waiting.contains(seq) || prevOutstanding.contains(seq))
        .toList
    askFor foreach askAround
    if (prevOutstanding.isEmpty) scheduleTick()
    val outstanding = prevOutstanding ++ askFor

    context.become {
      case Replicate(s, _, _, replyTo) if s < expectedSeq =>
        replyTo ! Replicated(s)

      case r: Replicate =>
        consolidate(theStore, expectedSeq, outstanding - r.seq,
                    waiting + (r.seq -> r))
```

```
      case TakeOver(active) =>
        log.info("delaying active replica take-over until upToDate")
        awaitingInitialState = Some(active)

      case GetSingle(s, replyTo) =>
        if (applied.nonEmpty &&
            applied.head.seq <= s && applied.last.seq >= s) {
          replyTo ! applied.find(_.seq == s).get
        } else if (s < expectedSeq) {
          replyTo ! InitialState(theStore, expectedSeq)
        }

      case GetFull(replyTo) =>
        log.info("sending full info to {}", replyTo)
        replyTo ! InitialState(theStore, expectedSeq)

      case DoConsolidate =>
        outstanding foreach askAround
        scheduleTick()
    }
  }

  // ...                              <─── Other helpers elided

  private def askAround(seq: Int): Unit = {
    log.info("asking around for sequence number {}", seq)
    getMembers(askAroundCount).foreach(addr => replicaOn(addr) ! GetSingle(se
    q, self))
  }
}
```

Here, you finally use the queue of applied updates that you previously maintained. When you conclude that you are missing some updates, you enter this state knowing the next expected consecutive sequence number and a collection of future updates that cannot yet be applied. You use this knowledge to first create a list of sequence numbers that you are missing—you have to ask the other replicas in order to obtain the corresponding updates. Again, you schedule a timer to ask, in case some updates are not received; to avoid asking for the same update repeatedly, you must maintain a list of outstanding sequence numbers that you already asked for. Asking is done by sending a GetSingle request to a configurable number of passive replicas. In this state, you install a behavior that will confirm known updates, defer initialization requests from an active replica, reply to requests for a full database dump, and, whenever possible, answer requests for specific updates from other replicas that are in the same situation. When a replication request is received, it may be either a new one from the active replica or one that you asked for. In any case, you merge this update into the waiting list and use the consolidate function to process all applicable updates and possibly switch back to up-to-date mode.

This concludes the implementation of both the active and passive replicas. In order to use them, you need to start a passive replica on every cluster node in addition to starting the Cluster Singleton manager. Client requests can be sent to the active replica by using the Cluster Singleton Proxy helper, an actor that keeps track of the current singleton location by listening to the cluster-membership change events. The full source code, including a runnable demo application, can be found at www.manning.com/books/reactive-design-patterns or https://github.com/ReactiveDesignPatterns.

13.1.3 *The pattern, revisited*

The implementation of this pattern consists of four parts:

- A cluster membership service that allows discovery and enumeration of all replica locations
- A Cluster Singleton mechanism that ensures that only one active replica is running at all times
- The active replica that accepts requests from clients, broadcasts updates to all passive replicas, and answers them after successful replication
- A number of passive replicas that persist state updates and help each other recover from message loss

For the first two, this example uses the facilities provided by Akka Cluster, because the implementation of a full cluster solution is complex and not usually done from scratch. Many other implementations can be used for this purpose; the only important qualities are listed here. The implementation of both types of replica is more likely to be customized and tailored to a specific purpose. We demonstrated the pattern with a use case that exhibits the minimal set of operations representative of a wide range of applications: the Get request stands for operations that do not modify the replicated state and that can therefore be executed immediately on the active replica, whereas the Put request characterizes operations whose effects must be replicated such that they are retained across failures.

The performance of this replication scheme is very good as long as no failures occur, because the active replica does not need to perform coordination tasks; all read requests can be served without requiring further communication, and write requests only need to be confirmed by a large enough subset of all replicas. This allows write performance to be balanced with reliability, in that a larger replication factor reduces the probability of data loss and a smaller replication factor reduces the impact of slow responses from some replicas—by requiring N responses, you are satisfied by the N currently fastest replicas.

During failures, you will see two different modes of performance degradation. If a network node hosting a passive replica fails, then there will be increased network traffic after its restart in order to catch up with the latest state. If the network host running the active replica fails, there will be a period during which no active replica will be running: it takes a while for the cluster to determine that the node has failed and to disseminate the knowledge that a new singleton needs to be instantiated. These coordination tasks need to be performed carefully in order to be reasonably certain that the old singleton cannot interfere with future operations even if its node later becomes reachable again after a network partition. For typical cloud deployments, this process takes on the order of seconds; it is limited by fluctuations in network transmission latency and reliability.

While discussing failure modes, we must also consider edge cases that can lead to incorrect behavior. Imagine that the active replica fails after sending out an update, and the next elected active replica does not receive this message. In order to notice that some information was lost, the new active replica would need to receive an update with a higher sequence number—but with the presented algorithm, that will never happen. Therefore, when it accepts the first update after the failover, the new active replica will unknowingly reuse a sequence number that some other replicas have seen for a different update. This can be avoided by requiring all known replicas to confirm the highest-known sequence number after a failover, which of course adds to the downtime.

Another problem is to determine when to erase and when to retain the persistent storage after a restart. The safest option is to delete and repopulate the database in order to not introduce conflicting updates after a network partition that separated the active replica from the surviving part of the cluster. On the other hand, this will lead to a significant increase in network usage that is unnecessary in most cases, and it would be fatal if the entire cluster were shut down and restarted. This problem can be solved by maintaining an epoch counter that is increased for every failover so a replica can detect that it has outdated information after a restart—for this, the active replica will include its epoch and its starting sequence number in the replication protocol messages.

Depending on the use case, you must make a trade-off among reliable operation, performance, and implementation complexity. Note that it is impossible to implement a solution that works perfectly for all imaginable failure scenarios.

13.1.4 Applicability

Because active–passive replication requires consensus regarding the active replica, this scheme may lead to periods of unavailability during widespread outages or network partitions. This is unavoidable because the inability to establish a quorum with the currently reachable cluster members may mean there is a quorum among those that are unreachable—but electing two active replicas at the same time must be avoided in order to retain consistency for clients. Therefore, active–passive replication is not suitable where perfect availability is required.

13.2 Multiple-Master Replication patterns

Keep multiple copies of a service running in different locations, accept modifications everywhere, and disseminate all modifications among them.

With active–passive replication, the basic mode of operation is to have a relatively stable active replica that processes read and write requests without further coordination, keeping the nominal case as simple and efficient as possible, while requiring special action during failover. This means clients have to send their requests to the currently active replica, with uncertainty resulting in case of failure. Because the selection of the active replica is done until further notice instead of per request, the client will not know what happened in case of a failure: has the request been disseminated or not?

Allowing requests to be accepted at all replicas means the client can participate in the replication and thereby obtain more precise feedback about the execution of its requests. The collocation of the client and the replica does not necessarily mean both are running in the process; placing them in the same failure domain makes their communication more reliable and their shared failure model simpler, even if this just means running both on the same computer or even in the same computing center. The further distributed a system becomes, the more prominent are the problems inherent to distribution, exacerbated by increased communication latency and reduced transmission reliability.

There are several strategies for accepting requests at multiple active replicas, which differ mainly in how they handle requests that arrive during a network partition. In this section, we will look at three classes of strategies:

- The most consistent results are achieved by establishing *consensus* about the application of each single update at the cost of not processing requests while dealing with failures.
- Availability can be increased by accepting potentially conflicting updates during a partition and *resolving the conflicts afterward*, potentially discarding updates that were accepted at either side.
- Perfect availability without data losses can be achieved by restricting the data model such that concurrent updates are *conflict-free* by definition.

13.2.1 *Consensus-based replication*

Given a group of people, we have a basic understanding of what *consensus* means: within the group, all members agree on a proposal and acknowledge that this agreement is unanimous. From personal experience, we know that reaching consensus is a process that can take quite a bit of time and effort for coordination, especially if the matter starts out as being contentious—in other words, if initially there are multiple competing proposals, and the group must decide which single one to support.

In computer science, the term *consensus*[1] means roughly the same thing, but of course the definition is more precise: given a cluster of N nodes and a set of proposals P_1 to P_m every nonfailing node will eventually decide on a single proposal P_x without the possibility to revoke that decision. All nonfailing nodes will decide on the same P_x. In the example of a key–value store, this means one node proposes to update a key's value, and, after the consensus protocol is finished, there will be a consistent cluster-wide decision about whether the update was performed—or in which order, relative to other updates. During this process, some cluster nodes may fail; and if the number of failing nodes is less than the failure-tolerance threshold of the algorithm, then consensus can

---

[1] See, for example, https://en.wikipedia.org/wiki/Consensus_(computer_science) for an overview.

be reached. Otherwise, consensus is impossible; this is equivalent to requiring a quorum for Senate decisions in order to prevent an absent majority from reverting the decision in the next meeting.[2]

A distributed key–value store can be built by using the consensus algorithm to agree on a replicated log. Any incoming updates are put into numbered rows of a virtual ledger; and, because all nodes eventually agree about which update is in which row, all nodes can apply the updates to their own local storage in the same order, resulting in the same state once everything is said and done. Another way to look at this is that every node runs its own copy of a replicated state machine; based on the consensus algorithm, all individual state machines make the same transitions in the same order, as long as not too many of them fail along the way.

APPLYING THE PATTERN

There are several consensus algorithms and even more implementations to choose from. In this section, we use an existing example from the CKite project,[3] in which a key–value store is written as simply as the following listing.

> **Listing 13.8   Using CKite to implement a key–value store**

```
class KVStore extends StateMachine {

  private var map = Map[String, String]()
  private var lastIndex: Long = 0

  def applyWrite = {
    case (index, Put(key: String, value: String)) => {
      map.put(key, value);
      lastIndex = index
      value
    }
  }

  def applyRead = {
    case Get(key) => map.get(key)
  }

  def getLastAppliedIndex: Long = lastIndex

  def restoreSnapshot(byteBuffer: ByteBuffer) =
    map =
      Serializer.deserialize[Map[String, String]](byteBuffer.array())

  def takeSnapshot(): ByteBuffer =
    ByteBuffer.wrap(Serializer.serialize(map))
}
```

---

[2]   Incidentally, a similar analogy is used in the original description of the PAXOS consensus algorithms by Leslie Lamport in "The Part-Time Parliament," *ACM Transactions on Computer Systems* 16, no. 2 (May 1998): 133-169, http://research.microsoft.com/en-us/um/people/lamport/pubs/lamport-paxos.pdf.

[3]   See https://github.com/pablosmedina/ckite for the implementation of the library and http://mng.bz/dLYZ for the full sample source code.

This class describes only the handling of Get and Put requests once they have been agreed on by the consensus algorithm, which is why this implementation is completely free from this concern. Applying a Put request means updating the Map that stores the key–value bindings and returning the written value, whereas applying a Get request will only return the currently bound value (or None if there is none).

Because applying all writes since the beginning of time can be a time-consuming process, there is also support for storing a snapshot of the current state, noting the last applied request's index in the log file. This is done by the takeSnapshot() function, which is called by the CKite library at configurable intervals. Its inverse—the restoreSnapshot() function—turns the serialized snapshot back into a Map, in case the KVStore is restarted after a failure or maintenance downtime.

CKite uses the Raft consensus protocol (https://raft.github.io). In order to use the KVStore class, you need to instantiate it as a replicated state machine, as follows.

Listing 13.9 Instantiating KVStore as a replicated state machine

```
object KVStoreBootstrap extends App {
  val ckite =
    CKiteBuilder()
      .stateMachine(new KVStore())
      .rpc(FinagleThriftRpc)
      .build
  ckite.start()
  HttpServer(ckite).start()
}
```

The HttpServer class starts an HttpService in which HTTP requests are mapped into requests to the key–value store, supporting consistent reads (which are applied via the distributed log), local reads that just return the currently applied updates at the local node (which may be missing updates that are currently in flight), and writes (as discussed). The API for this library is straightforward in this regard:

```
val consistentRead    = ckite.read(Get(key))
val possiblyStaleRead = ckite.readLocal(Get(key))
val write             = ckite.write(Put(key, value))
```

THE PATTERN, REVISITED

Writing your own consensus algorithm is almost never a good idea. There are so many pitfalls and edge cases to be considered that using one of the sound, proven ones is a very good default. Due to the nature of separating a replicated log from the state machine that processes the log entries, it is easy to get started with existing solutions, as demonstrated by the minimal amount of code necessary to implement the KVStore example. The only parts that need to be written are the generation of the requests to be replicated and the state machine that processes them at all replica locations.

The advantage of consensus-based replication is that it is guaranteed to result in all replicas agreeing on the sequence of events and thereby on the state of the replicated data. It is therefore straightforward to reason about the correctness of the distributed program, in the sense that it will not get into an inconsistent state.

The price for this peace of mind is that in order to avoid mistakes, the algorithm must be conservative: it cannot boldly make progress in the face of arbitrary failures like network partitions and node crashes. Requiring a majority of the nodes to agree on an update before progressing to the next one not only takes time but also can fail altogether during network partitions, such as a three-way split where none of the parts represents a majority.

13.2.2 *Replication with conflict detection and resolution*

If you want to change your replication scheme such that it can continue to operate during a transient network partition, then you will have to make some compromises. Obviously, it is impossible to reach consensus without communication, so if all cluster nodes are to make progress in accepting and processing requests at all times, conflicting actions may be performed.

Consider the example of the storage component within your batch service that stores the execution status of some computing job. When the job is submitted, it is recorded as "new"; then it becomes "scheduled," "executing," and finally "finished" (ignoring failures and retries for the sake of simplicity here). But another possibility is that the client that submitted the job decides to cancel its execution because the computation is no longer needed, perhaps because parameters have changed and a new job has been submitted. The client will attempt to change the job status to "canceled," with further possible consequences, depending on the current job status—it may be taken out of the scheduled queue, or it may need to be aborted if it is currently executing.

Assuming that you want to make the storage component as highly available as possible, you may let it accept job-status updates even during a network partition that separates the storage cluster into two halves and renders it unable to successfully apply a consensus protocol until communication is restored. If the client interface sends the write of the "canceled" status to one half while the execution service starts running the job and therefore sets the "executing" status on the other half, then the two parts of the storage component have accepted conflicting information. When the network partition is repaired and communication is possible again, the replication protocol will need to figure out that this has occurred and react accordingly.

APPLYING THE PATTERN

The most prominent tool for detecting whether cluster nodes have performed conflicting updates is called a *version vector*.[4] With this, each replica can keep track of who updated the job status since the last successful replication, by incrementing a counter:

---

[4] In particular, you do not need a vector clock: see Carlos Baquero, "Version Vectors Are Not Vector Clocks," HASlab, July 8, 2011, https://haslab.wordpress.com/2011/07/08/version-vectors-are-not-vector-clocks for a discussion (in short: you only need to track whether updates were performed by a replica, not how many were performed). See also Nuno Preguiça et al., "Dotted Version Vectors," November 2010, http://arxiv.org/abs/1011.5808 for a description.

- The status starts out as "scheduled" with an empty version vector on both nodes A and B.
- When the client interface updates the status on node A, the replica will register it as "canceled" with a version vector of <A:1> (all nodes that are not mentioned are assumed to have version zero).
- When the executor updates the status on node B, it will be registered as "executing" with the version vector <B:1>.
- When replicas A and B compare notes after the partition has been repaired, the status will be both "canceled" and "executing," with version vectors <A:1> and <B:1>; and because neither fully includes the other, a conflict will be detected.

The conflict will then have to be resolved one way or another. A SQL database will decide based on a fixed or configurable policy: for example, storing a timestamp together with each value and picking the latest update. In this case, there is nothing to code, because the conflict resolution happens within the database; the user code can be written just like in the nonreplicated case.

Another possibility is implemented by the Riak database (http://mdocs.basho .com/riak/latest/theory/concepts/Replication), which presents both values to any client that subsequently reads the key affected by the conflict, requiring the client to figure out how to proceed and bring the data store back into a consistent state by issuing an explicit write request with the merged value; this is called *read repair*. An example of how this is done is part of the Riak documentation.[5]

In the batch service example, you could employ domain-specific knowledge within your implementation of the storage component: after a partition was repaired, all replicas would exchange version information for all intermediately changed keys. When this conflict was noticed, it would be clear that the client wished to abort the now-executing job—the repair procedure would automatically change the job status to "canceled" (with a version vector of <A:1,B:1> to document that this included both updates) and ask the executor to terminate the execution of this job. One possibility for implementing this scheme would be to use a data store like Riak and perform read repair at the application level together with the separately stored knowledge about which keys were written to during the partition.

THE PATTERN, REVISITED

We have introduced conflict detection and resolution at the level of a key–value store or database where the concern of state replication is encapsulated by an existing solution in the form of a relational database management system or other data store. In this case, the pattern consists of recording all actions as changes to the stored data such that the storage product can detect and handle conflicts that arise from accepting updates during network partitions or other times of partial system unavailability.

When using server-side conflict resolution (as is done by popular SQL database products), the application code is freed from this concern at the cost of potentially

---

[5] See http://docs.basho.com/riak/latest/dev/using/conflict-resolution/.

losing updates during the repair process—choosing the most recent update means discarding all others. Client-side conflict resolution allows tailored reactions that may benefit from domain-specific knowledge; but, on the other hand, it makes application code more complex to write, because all read accesses to a data store managed in this fashion must be able to deal with receiving multiple equally valid answers to a single query.

13.2.3 *Conflict-free replicated data types*

In the previous section, you achieved perfect availability of the batch service's storage component—where *perfect* means "it works as long as one replica is reachable"—at the cost of either losing updates or having to care about manual conflict resolution. You can improve on this even further, but unfortunately at another cost: it is not possible to avoid conflicts while maintaining perfect availability without restricting the data types that can be expressed.

As an example, consider a counter that should be replicated. Conflict freedom would be achieved by making sure an increment registered at any replica would eventually be visible (effective) at all replicas independent of other concurrent increments. Clearly it is not enough to replicate the counter value: if an increment of 3 is accepted by node A, whereas an increment of 5 is accepted at node B, then the value after replication will either signal a conflict or miss one of the updates, as discussed in the previous section. Therefore, you split the counter into individual per-node subcounters, where each node only ever modifies its own subcounter. Reading the counter then means summing up all the per-node subcounters.[6] In this fashion, both increments of 3 and 5 will be effective, because the per-node values cannot see conflicting updates. And after the replication is complete, the total sum will have been incremented by 8.

With this example, it becomes clear that it is possible to create a data structure that fulfills the goal, but the necessary steps in the implementation of this replicated counter are tailored to this particular use case and cannot be used in general—in particular, it relies upon the fact that summing all subcounters correctly expresses the overall counter behavior. This is possible for a wide range of data types, including sets and maps, but it fails wherever global invariants cannot be translated to local ones. For a set, it is easy to avoid duplicates because duplicate checking can be done on each insertion, but constructing a counter whose value must stay within a given range requires coordination again.

The data types we are talking about here are called *conflict-free replicated data types* (CRDTs)[7] and are currently being introduced in a number of distributed systems

---

[6] An implementation in the context of Akka Distributed Data can be studied at http://mng.bz/rf2V. This type of counter can only grow, hence its name: GCounter.

[7] See M. Shapiro et al., "A Comprehensive Study of Convergent and Commutative Replicated Data Types," 2011, https://hal.inria.fr/inria-00555588 for an overview; and C. Baquero, "Specification of Convergent Abstract Data Types for Autonomous Mobile Computing," 1997, http://haslab.uminho.pt/cbm/publications/specification-convergent-abstract-data-types-autonomous-mobile-computing for early ground work.

libraries and data stores. In order to define such a data type, you need to formulate a rule about how to merge two of its values into a new resulting value. Instead of detecting and handling conflicts, such a data type knows how to merge concurrent updates so that no conflict occurs.

The most important properties of the merge function are that it is symmetric and monotonic: it must not matter whether you merge value1 with value2 or value2 with value1; and after having merged two values into a third one, future merges must not ever go back to a previous state (example: if v1 and v2 were merged to v2, then any merge of v2 with another value must not ever result in v1—you can picture this as the values following some order and merging only ever goes forward in this order, never backward).

APPLYING THE PATTERN

Coming back to the example of updating the status of a batch job, we will now demonstrate how a CRDT works. First, you define all possible status values and their merge order, as shown in figure 13.1—such a graphical representation is the easiest way to get started when designing a CRDT with a small number of values. When merging two statuses, there are three cases:

- If both statuses are the same, then obviously you just pick that status.
- If one of them is reachable from the other by walking in the direction of the arrows, then you pick the one toward which the arrows are pointing; as an example, merging "new" and "executing" will result in "executing."
- If that is not the case, then you need to find a new status that is reachable from both by walking in the direction of the arrows, but you want to find the closest such status (otherwise, "finished" would always be a solution, but not a useful one). There is only one example in this graph, which is merging "executing" and "canceled," in which case you choose "aborted"—choosing "finished" would technically be possible and consistent, but that choice would lose information (you want to retain both pieces of knowledge that are represented by "executing" and "canceled").

The next step is to cast this logic into code. This example prepares the use of the resulting status representation with the Akka Distributed Data module that takes care

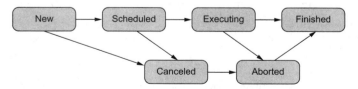

Figure 13.1   Batch job status values as CRDTs with their merge ordering indicated by state progression arrows: walking in the direction of the arrows goes from predecessor to successor in the merge order.

of the replication and merging of CRDT values. All that is needed is the `merge` function, which is the only abstract method on the `ReplicatedData` interface.

> **Listing 13.10   Code representation of the graph in figure 13.1**

```
final case class Status(val name: String)(_pred: => Set[Status],
                                           _succ: => Set[Status])
    extends ReplicatedData {

  type T = Status
  def merge(that: Status): Status = mergeStatus(this, that)    ◁──┐  Merges another
                                                                   │  status with this
  lazy val predecessors = _pred        Arrows into and             │  status
  lazy val successors = _succ          out of this status
}

val New: Status =
            Status("new")(Set.empty, Set(Scheduled, Canceled))
val Scheduled: Status =
            Status("scheduled")(Set(New), Set(Executing, Canceled))
val Executing: Status =
            Status("executing")(Set(Scheduled), Set(Aborted, Finished))
val Finished: Status =
            Status("finished")(Set(Executing, Aborted), Set.empty)
val Canceled: Status =
            Status("canceled")(Set(New, Scheduled), Set(Aborted))
val Aborted: Status =
            Status("aborted")(Set(Canceled, Executing), Set(Finished))
```

This is a trivial transcription of the graph from figure 13.1, where each node in the status graph is represented by a Scala object with two sets of nodes describing the incoming and outgoing arrows, respectively: an arrow always goes from predecessor to successor (for example, `Scheduled` is a successor of `New`, and `New` is a predecessor of `Scheduled`). We could have chosen a more compact representation where each arrow is encoded only once: for example, if we had provided only the successor information, then after construction of all statuses, a second pass would have filled in the predecessor sets automatically. Here, we opted to be more explicit and save the code for the post-processing step. Now it is time to look at the merge logic in the following listing.

> **Listing 13.11   Merging two statuses to produce a third, merged status**

```
def mergeStatus(left: Status, right: Status): Status = {
  /*
   * Keep the left Status in hand and determine whether it is a
   * predecessor of the candidate, moving on to the candidate's
   * successor if not successful. The list of exclusions is used to
   * avoid performing already determined unsuccessful comparisons
   * again.
   */
  def innerLoop(candidate: Status, exclude: Set[Status]): Status =
    if (isSuccessor(candidate, left, exclude)) {
      candidate
```

```
      } else {
        val nextExclude = exclude + candidate
        val branches =
          candidate.successors.map(succ => innerLoop(succ, nextExclude))
        branches.reduce((l, r) =>
          if (isSuccessor(l, r, nextExclude)) r else l)
    }
  def isSuccessor(candidate: Status, fixed: Status,
                  exclude: Set[Status]): Boolean =
    if (candidate == fixed) true
    else {
      val toSearch = candidate.predecessors -- exclude
      toSearch.exists(pred => isSuccessor(pred, fixed, exclude))
    }

  innerLoop(right, Set.empty)
}
```

In this algorithm, you merge two statuses, one called `left` and one called `right`. You keep the `left` value constant during the entire process and consider `right` a candidate that you may need to move in the direction of the arrows. As an illustration, consider merging `New` and `Canceled`:

- If `New` is taken as the `left` argument, then you will enter the inner loop with `Canceled` as the candidate, and the first conditional will call `isSuccessor`, with the first two arguments being `Canceled` and `New`. These are not equal, so the `else` branch of `isSuccessor` will search all predecessors of `Canceled` (`New` and `Scheduled`) to determine whether one of them is a successor of `New`; this now satisfies the condition of candidate `==` `fixed`, so `isSuccessor` returns `true` and the candidate in `innerLoop` (`Canceled`) will be returned as the merge result.

- If `New` is taken as the `right` argument, then the first `isSuccessor` call will yield `false`. You enter the other branch in which both successors of the candidate `New` will be examined; trying `Scheduled` will be equally fruitless, escalating to `Executing` and `Canceled` as its successors. Abbreviating the story a little, you will eventually find that the merge result for the `Executing` candidate will be `Aborted`, whereas for `Canceled` it is `Canceled` itself. These branches are then reduced into a single value by pairwise comparison and picking the predecessor, which is `Canceled` in the case of trying `Scheduled` just now. Returning to the outermost loop invocation, you thus twice get the same result of `Canceled` for the two branches, which is also the end result.

This procedure is somewhat complicated by the fact that you have allowed the two statuses of `Executing` and `Canceled` to be unrelated to each other, necessitating the ability to find a common descendant. We will come back to why this is needed in the example, but first we will look at how this CRDT is used by a hypothetical (and vastly oversimplified) client interface. In order to instantiate the CRDT, you need to define a key that identifies it across the cluster:

```
object StorageComponent extends Key[ORMap[Status]]("StorageComponent")
```

You need to associate a `Status` with each batch job, and the most fitting predefined CRDT for this purpose is an *observed-remove map* (ORMap). The name stems from the fact that only keys whose presence has previously been observed can be removed from the map. Removal is a difficult operation because you have seen that CRDTs need a monotonic, forward-moving `merge` function—removing a key at one node and replicating the new map would mean only that the other nodes would add it right back during merges, because that is the mechanism by which the key is spread across the cluster initially.[8]

One thing to note here is that CRDTs can be composed as shown earlier: the ORMap uses `Strings` as keys (this is fixed by the Akka Distributed Data implementation) and some other CRDTs as values. Instead of using the custom `Status` type, you could use an *observed-remove set* (ORSet) of PNCounters if you needed sets of counters to begin with, just to name one possibility. This makes it possible to create container data types with well-behaved replication semantics that are reusable in different contexts. Within the client interface—represented as a vastly oversimplified actor in the following listing—you can use the status map by referencing the `StorageComponent` key.

Listing 13.12   Using Akka Distributed Data to disseminate state changes

```
class ClientInterface
extends Actor with ActorLogging {
  val replicator = DistributedData(context.system).replicator
  implicit val cluster = Cluster(context.system)

  def receive = {
    case Submit(job) =>
      log.info("submitting job {}", job)
      replicator !
        Replicator.Update(StorageComponent, ORMap.empty[Status],
                          Replicator.WriteMajority(5.seconds))
                         (map => map + (job -> New))

    case Cancel(job) =>
      log.info("cancelling job {}", job)
      replicator !
        Replicator.Update(StorageComponent, ORMap.empty[Status],
                          Replicator.WriteMajority(5.seconds))
                         (map => map + (job -> Canceled))

    case r: Replicator.UpdateResponse[_] =>
      log.info("received update result: {}", r)
```

---

[8] For details of how this is implemented, see Annette Bieniusa et al., "An Optimized Conflict-Free Replicated Set," October 2012, https://hal.inria.fr/hal-00738680.

```
    case PrintStatus =>
      replicator ! Replicator.Get(StorageComponent,
                             Replicator.ReadMajority(5.seconds))

    case g: Replicator.GetSuccess[_] =>
      log.info("overall status: {}", g.get(StorageComponent))
  }
}
```

The Replicator is the actor provided by the Akka Distributed Data module that is responsible for running the replication protocol between cluster nodes. Most generic CRDTs like ORMap need to identify the originator of a given update, and for that the Cluster extension is implicitly used—here it is needed by both function literals that modify the map during the handing of Submit and Cancel requests.

With the Update command, you include the StorageComponent key, the initial value (if the CRDT was not referenced before), and a replication-factor setting. This setting determines the point at which the confirmation of a successful update will be sent back to the ClientInterface actor: you choose to wait until the majority of cluster nodes have been notified, but you could just as well demand that all nodes have been updated, or you could be satisfied once the local node has the new value and starts to disseminate it. The latter is the least reliable but is perfectly available (assuming that a local failure implies that the ClientInterface is affected as well); waiting for all nodes is most reliable for retaining the stored data but can easily fail at storage. Using the majority is a good compromise that works well in many situations—just as for legislative purposes.

The modifications performed by the client interface do not care about the previous job status. They create a New entry or overwrite an existing one with Canceled. The executor component demonstrates more interesting usage, as shown next.

Listing 13.13 Introducing a request identifier for the job

```
class Executor extends Actor with ActorLogging {
  val replicator = DistributedData(context.system).replicator
  implicit val cluster = Cluster(context.system)

  var lastState = Map.empty[String, Status]

  replicator ! Replicator.Subscribe(StorageComponent, self)

  def receive = {
    case Execute(job) =>
      log.info("executing job {}", job)
      replicator !
        Replicator.Update(StorageComponent, ORMap.empty[Status],
                          Replicator.WriteMajority(5.seconds),
                          Some(job))
                         { map =>
                           require(map.get(job) == Some(New))
                           map + (job -> Executing)
                         }
```

```
    case Finish(job) =>
      log.info("job {} finished", job)
      replicator !
        Replicator.Update(StorageComponent, ORMap.empty[Status],
                          Replicator.WriteMajority(5.seconds))
                        (map => map + (job -> Finished))

    case Replicator.UpdateSuccess(StorageComponent, Some(job)) =>
      log.info("starting job {}", job)

    case r: Replicator.UpdateResponse[_] =>
      log.info("received update result: {}", r)

    case ch: Replicator.Changed[_] =>
      val current = ch.get(StorageComponent).entries
      for {
        (job, status) <- current.iterator
        if (status == Aborted)
        if (lastState.get(job) != Some(Aborted))
      } log.info("aborting job {}", job)
      lastState = current

  }
}
```

When it is time to execute a batch job, the update request for the CRDT includes a request identifier (`Some(job)`) that has so far been left out: this value will be included in the success or failure message that the replicator sends back. The provided `update` function now checks a precondition: that the currently known status of the given batch job is still `New`. Otherwise, the update will be aborted with an exception. Only upon receiving the `UpdateSuccess` message with this job name will the actual execution begin; otherwise, a `ModifyFailure` will be logged (which is a subtype of `Update-Response`).

Finally, the executor should abort batch jobs that were canceled after being started. This is implemented by subscribing to change events from the replicator for the `StorageComponent` CRDT. Whenever there is a change, the replicator will take note of it; and as soon as the (configurable) notification interval elapses, a `Replicator.Changed` message will be sent with the current state of the CRDT. The executor keeps track of the previously received state and can therefore determine which jobs have newly become `Aborted`. In this example, you log this; in a real implementation, the `Worker` instance(s) for this job would be asked to terminate. The full example, including the necessary cluster setup, can be found in the source code archives for this chapter.

THE PATTERN, REVISITED

Conflict-free replication allows perfect availability but requires the problem to be cast in terms of special data types (CRDTs). The first step is to determine which semantics are needed. In this case, you needed a tailor-made data type, but a number of generically useful ones are readily available. Once the data type has been defined, a replication mechanism must be used or developed that will disseminate all state changes and invoke the merge function wherever necessary. This could be a library, as in the example shown in listing 13.12, or an off-the-shelf data store based on CRDTs.

Although it is easy to get started like this, note that this solution cannot offer strong consistency: updates can occur truly concurrently across the entire system, making the value history of a given key nonlinearizable (which means different clients can see conflicting value histories that are eventually reconciled). This may present a challenge in environments that are most familiar with and used to transactional behavior of a central authority—the centrality of this approach is precisely the limitation in terms of resilience and elasticity that conflict-free replication overcomes, at the cost of offering at most eventual consistency.

13.3 *The Active–Active Replication pattern*

Keep multiple copies of a service running in different locations, and perform all modifications at all of them.

In the previous patterns, you achieved resilience for the storage subsystem of the example batch job processing facility by replicating it across different locations (data centers, availability zones, and so on). You saw that you can achieve strong consistency only when implementing a failover mechanism; both CRDT-based replication and conflict detection avoid this at the cost of not guaranteeing full consistency. One property of failover is that it takes some time: first, you need to detect that there is trouble, and then, you must establish consensus about how to fix it—for example, by switching to another replica. Both activities require communication and therefore cannot be completed instantaneously. Where this is not tolerable, you need a different strategy, but because there is no magic bullet, you must expect different restrictions.

Instead of failing over as a consequence of detecting problems, you can assume that failures occur and therefore hedge your bets: rather than contacting only one replica, always perform the desired operation on all of them. If a replica does not respond correctly, then you conclude that it has failed and refrain from contacting it again. A new replica will be added based on monitoring and supervision.

In computer science, the first description of active–active replication was offered by Leslie Lamport,[9] who proposed that distributed state machines can be synchronized by using the fact that time passes in a sufficiently similar fashion for all of them. His description yields a more generic framework for replication than is presented in this section. The definition of active–active replication used here[10] is inspired by the space industry, where, for example, measurements are performed using multiple sensors at all times and hardware-based voting mechanisms select the prevalent observation among them, discarding minority deviations by presuming them to be the result of failures. As an example, the main bus voltage of a satellite may be monitored by a regulator

---

[9] Leslie Lamport, "Using Time Instead of Timeout for Fault-Tolerant Distributed Systems," *ACM Transactions on Programming Languages and Systems* 6, no. 2 (April 1984): 254-280.

[10] Note that database vendors sometimes use *active–active replication* to mean conflict detection and resolution as described in the previous section.

that decides whether to drain the batteries or charge them with excess power coming from the solar panels; making the wrong decision in this regard will ultimately destroy the satellite, and therefore three such regulators are taken together and their signals are fed into a majority voting circuit to obtain the final decision.

The drawback of this scheme is that you must assume that the inputs to all replicas are the same, so that the responses will also be the same; all replicas internally go through the same state changes together. In contrast to the concrete bus voltage that is measured in the satellite example—the one source of truth—having multiple clients contact three replicas of a stateful service means there must be a central point that ensures that requests are delivered to all replicas in the same order. This will either be a single choke point (concerning both failures and throughput) or require costly coordination again. But instead of theorizing, we will look at a concrete example.

13.3.1 The problem setting

Again, you will apply this replication scheme to the key–value store that represents the storage component of the batch job service. The two involved subcomponents—a coordinator and a replica—are represented as vastly simplified Actors, concentrating on the basic working principle. The idea behind the pattern is that all replicas go through the same state changes in lockstep without coordinating their actions and while running fully asynchronously. Because coordination is necessary nevertheless, you need to control the requests that are sent to the replicas by introducing a middle-man that also acts as bookkeeper and supervisor.

13.3.2 Applying the pattern

The starting point for implementing this solution is the replicas, which, due to the lack of coordination, can be kept simple.

Listing 13.14 Starting active–active replication with an uncoordinated implementation

```scala
private case class SeqCommand(seq: Int, cmd: Command,
                             replyTo: ActorRef)
private case class SeqResult(seq: Int, res: Result,
                             replica: ActorRef, replyTo: ActorRef)

private case class SendInitialData(toReplica: ActorRef)
private case class InitialData(map: Map[String, JsValue])

class Replica extends Actor with Stash {
  var map = Map.empty[String, JsValue]

  def receive = {
    case InitialData(m) =>
      map = m
      context.become(initialized)
      unstashAll()
    case _ => stash()
  }
```

```
def initialized: Receive = {
  case SeqCommand(seq, cmd, replyTo) =>
    // ...
    cmd match {
      case Put(key, value, r) =>
        map += key -> value
        replyTo ! SeqResult(seq, PutConfirmed(key, value), self, r)
      case Get(key, r) =>
        replyTo ! SeqResult(seq, GetResult(key, map get key), self, r)
    }
  case SendInitialData(toReplica) => toReplica ! InitialData(map)
  }
}
```

> **Tracking of sequence numbers and resends is elided here.**

First, you define sequenced command and result wrappers for the communication between the coordinator and the replicas as well as initialization messages to be sent between replicas. The replica starts out in a mode where it waits for a message containing the initial state to begin from—you must be able to bring new replicas online in the running system. Once the initialization data have been received, the replica switches to its initialized behavior and replays all previously stashed commands. In addition to Put and Get requests, it also understands a command to send the current contents of the key–value store to another replica in order to initialize that replica.

As noted, in the code, we have left out all sequence-number tracking and resend logic (the same is true in the coordinator actor discussed in listing 13.15) in order to concentrate on the essence of this pattern. Because we already solved reliable delivery of updates for active–passive replication, we consider this part of the problem solved; please refer back to section 13.1. In contrast to having the replicas exchange missing updates among each other, you, in this case, establish the resend protocol only between the coordinator and each replica individually.

Assuming that all replicas perform their duties if they are fed the same requests in the same order, you now need to fulfill that condition: it is the responsibility of the coordinator to broadcast the commands, handle and aggregate the replies, and manage possible failures and inconsistencies. In order to nicely formulate this, you need to create an appropriate data type that represents the coordinator's knowledge about the processing status of a single client request, as follows.

Listing 13.15 Encapsulating knowledge about the status of a single client request

```
private sealed trait ReplyState {
  def deadline: Deadline
  def missing: Set[ActorRef]
  def add(res: SeqResult): ReplyState
  def isFinished: Boolean = missing.isEmpty
}

private case class Unknown(deadline: Deadline, replies: Set[SeqResult],
                          missing: Set[ActorRef], quorum: Int)
         extends ReplyState {
  override def add(res: SeqResult): ReplyState = {
```

```
    val nextReplies = replies + res
    val nextMissing = missing - res.replica
    if (nextReplies.size >= quorum) {
      val answer =
        replies.toSeq
          .groupBy(_.res)
          .collectFirst { case (k, s) if s.size >= quorum => s.head }
      if (answer.isDefined) {
        val right = answer.get
        val wrong =
          replies.collect {
            case SeqResult(_, res, replica, _) if res != right =>
              replica
          }
        Known(deadline, right, wrong, nextMissing)
      } else if (nextMissing.isEmpty) {
        Known.fromUnknown(deadline, nextReplies)
      } else Unknown(deadline, nextReplies, nextMissing, quorum)
    } else Unknown(deadline, nextReplies, nextMissing, quorum)
  }
}

private case class Known(deadline: Deadline, reply: SeqResult,
                         wrong: Set[ActorRef], missing: Set[ActorRef])
        extends ReplyState {
  override def add(res: SeqResult): ReplyState = {
    val nextWrong =
      if (res.res == reply.res) wrong else wrong + res.replica
    Known(deadline, reply, nextWrong, missing - res.replica)
  }
}
private object Known {
    def fromUnknown(deadline: Deadline,
                    replies: Set[SeqResult]): Known = {
    val counts = replies.groupBy(_.res)
    val biggest = counts.iterator.map(_._2.size).max
    val winners = counts.collectFirst {
      case (res, win) if win.size == biggest => win
    }.get
    val losers = (replies -- winners).map(_.replica)
    Known(deadline, winners.head, losers, Set.empty)
  }
}
```

Did not reach consensus on this one: use a simple majority

ReplyState tracks when the time limit for a client response expires; whether the reply value is already known; which replica's response deviated from the prevalent one; and which replica's response is still outstanding. When a new request is made, you begin with an Unknown reply state containing an empty set of replies and a set of missing replica ActorRefs that contains all current replicas. As responses from replicas are received, your knowledge grows, as represented by the add() function: the response is added to the set of replies, and as soon as the required quorum of replicas has responded with a consistent answer, ReplyState switches to Known (taking note of the replica `ActorRefs` from which the wrong answer was received). If, after receiving the last expected response, no answer has reached a quorum, one of the answers must be selected in order to make progress; in this case, you use a simple majority as implemented in the `fromUnknown` function. Within the `Known` state, you still keep track of arriving responses so that corrupted replicas can be detected. Before we dive into this aspect, the following listing shows the overall structure of the `Coordinator`.

Listing 13.16   Managing replicas as child actors

```
class Coordinator(N: Int) extends Actor {
  private var replicas = (1 to N).map(_ => newReplica()).toSet
  private val seqNr = Iterator from 0
  private var replies = TreeMap.empty[Int, ReplyState]
  private var nextReply = 0

  override def supervisorStrategy = SupervisorStrategy.stoppingStrategy

  private def newReplica(): ActorRef =
    context.watch(context.actorOf(Replica.props))

  context.setReceiveTimeout(1.second)                    ◁──┐ Schedules timeout messages
                                                            │ for quiescent periods
  def receive = ({
    case cmd: Command =>
      val c = SeqCommand(seqNr.next, cmd, self)
      replicas foreach (_ ! c)
      replies += c.seq -> Unknown(5 seconds fromNow, Set.empty,
                                  replicas, (replicas.size + 1) / 2)

    case res: SeqResult if replies.contains(res.seq) &&
                           replicas.contains(res.replica) =>
      val prevState = replies(res.seq)
      val nextState = prevState.add(res)
      replies += res.seq -> nextState

    case Terminated(ref) =>
      replaceReplica(ref, terminate = false)

    case ReceiveTimeout =>
  }: Receive) andThen { _ =>
    doTimeouts()
    sendReplies()
    evictFinished()          ┌── Definitions of doTimeouts,
  }                          │   sendReplies, and
  // ...                  ◁──┘   evictFinished withheld
}
```

In this simplified code, `Coordinator` directly creates the replicas as child actors; a real implementation would typically request the infrastructure to provision and start replica nodes that would then register themselves with `Coordinator` once `Replica` is running on them. `Coordinator` also registers for lifecycle monitoring of all replicas using `context.watch()`, in order to be able to react to permanent failures that are detected by the infrastructure—in the case of Akka, this service is implicitly provided

by the `Cluster` module. Another thing to
note is that, in this example, `Coordinator`
is the parent actor of the replicas and
therefore also their supervisor. Because
failures escalated to `Coordinator` usually
imply that messages have been lost, and
this simplified example assumes reliable
delivery, you install a supervisor strategy
that will terminate any failing child actor;
this will eventually lead to the reception
of a `Terminated` message, upon which a
new replica will replace the previously terminated one.

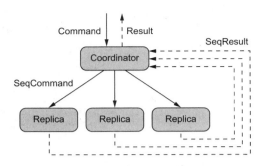

**Figure 13.2   Flow of messages in the Active–
Active Replication pattern**

The flow of messages through the coordinator is depicted in figure 13.2. Whereas
the external client sends commands and expects returned results, looping the requests
through the replicas requires some additional information; hence, the messages are
wrapped as `SeqCommand` and `SeqResult`, respectively. The name signifies that these are
properly sequenced, although, as discussed, we omit the implementation of reliable
delivery that would normally be based on the contained sequence numbers. The only
sequencing aspect modeled is that the external client sees the results in the same order
in which their corresponding commands were delivered; this is the reason for the
`nextReply` variable that is used by the following implementation of `sendReplies()`.

Listing 13.17   Sending replies in sequence

```
@tailrec private def sendReplies(): Unit =
  replies.get(nextReply) match {
    case Some(k @ Known(_, reply, _, _)) =>
      reply.replyTo ! reply.res
      nextReply += 1
      sendReplies()
    case _ =>
  }
```

If the next reply to be sent has a
"known" value, then you send it back
to the client and move on to the next
one. This method is called after every
handled message in order to flush
replies to the clients whenever they
are ready. The overall flow of replies
through the coordinator's response-
tracking queue (implemented by a
`TreeMap` indexed by command
sequence) is shown in figure 13.3.

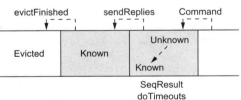

**Figure 13.3   The movement of replies through the
status tracking within the coordinator: new entries
are generated whenever a command is received, and
they move from "unknown" to "known" status either
by receiving `SeqResult` messages or due to timeout.
Consecutive "known" results are sent back to the
external client, and replies where no more replica
responses are expected are evicted from the queue.**

You have seen the handling of SeqResult messages already in the coordinator's behavior definition, leaving the following doTimeouts() function as the other possibility through which an "unknown" reply status can be transformed into a "known" reply.

Listing 13.18 Upon timeout, forcing "missing" replies to "known" replies

```
private def doTimeouts(): Unit = {
  val now = Deadline.now
  val expired = replies.iterator.takeWhile(_._2.deadline <= now)
  for ((seq, state) <- expired) {
    state match {
      case Unknown(deadline, received, _, _) =>
        val forced = Known.fromUnknown(deadline, received)
        replies += seq -> forced
      case Known(deadline, reply, wrong, missing) =>
        replies += seq -> Known(deadline, reply, wrong, Set.empty)
    }
  }
}
```

Because sequence numbers are allocated in strictly ascending order and all commands have the same timeout, replies will also time out in the same order. Therefore, you can obtain all currently expired replies by computing the prefix of the replies queue for which the expiry deadline lies in the past. You turn each of these entries into a "known" one for which no more responses are expected—even wrong replies that come in late are discarded. Notice the corrupted replicas during one of the subsequent requests. If no result has been determined yet for a command, you again use the fromUnknown function to select a result with simple majority, noting which replicas responded with a different answer (which is wrong by definition). The last remaining step is similar to a debriefing: for every command that you responded to, you must check for deviating responses and replace their originating replicas immediately.

Listing 13.19 Terminating and replacing replicas that did not finish

```
@tailrec private def evictFinished(): Unit =
  replies.headOption match {
    case Some((seq, k @ Known(_, _, wrong, _))) if k.isFinished =>
      wrong foreach (replaceReplica(_, terminate = true))
      replies -= seq
      evictFinished()
    case _ =>
  }

private def replaceReplica(r: ActorRef, terminate: Boolean): Unit =
  if (replicas contains r) {
    replicas -= r
    if (terminate) r ! PoisonPill
    val replica = newReplica()
    replicas.head ! SendInitialData(replica)
    replicas += replica
  }
```

The `evictFinished` function checks whether the reply status of the oldest queued command is complete (no more responses are expected). If so, it initiates the replacement of all faulty replicas and removes the status from the queue, repeating this process until the queue is empty or an unfinished reply status is encountered. Replacing a replica would normally mean asking the infrastructure to terminate the corresponding machine and provision a new one, but in this simplified example you just terminate the child actor and create a new one.

In order to get the new replica up to speed, you need to provide it with the current replicated state. One simple possibility is to ask one of the remaining replicas to transfer its current state to the new replica. Because this message will be delivered after all currently outstanding commands and before any subsequent commands, this state will be exactly the one needed by the new replica to be included in the replica set for new commands right away—the stashing and replay of these commands within the `Replica` actor has exactly the correct semantics. In a real implementation, there would need to be a timeout-and-resend mechanism for this initialization, to cover cases where the replica that is supposed to transfer its state fails before it can complete the transmission. It is important to note that the faulty replica is excluded from being used as the source of the initialization data, just as the new replica is.

13.3.3 *The pattern, revisited*

The Active–Active Replication pattern emerged from a conversation with some software architects working at a financial institution. It solves a specific problem: how can you keep a service running in fault-tolerant fashion with fully replicated state while not suffering from costly consensus overhead and avoiding any downtime during failure—not even allowing a handful of milliseconds for failure detection and failover?

The solution consists of two parts: the replicas execute commands and generate results without regard to each other, and the coordinator ensures that all replicas receive the same sequence of commands. Faulty replicas are detected by comparing the responses received to each individual command and flagging deviations. In the example implementation, this was the only criterion; a variation might be to also replace replicas that are consistently failing to meet their deadlines.

A side effect of this pattern is that external responses can be generated as soon as there is agreement about what that response will be, which means requiring only three out of five replicas would shorten the usually long tail of the latency distribution. Assuming that slow responses are not correlated between the replicas (that is, they are not caused by the specific properties of the command or otherwise related), then the probability of more than two replicas exceeding their 99th percentile latency is only 0.001%, which naïvely means the individual 99th percentile is the cluster's 99.999th percentile.[11]

---

[11] This is of course too optimistic, because outliers in the latency distribution are usually caused by something that might well be correlated between machines. For example, garbage collection pauses for JVMs that were started at the same time, and executing the same program with the same inputs will tend to occur roughly at the same time as well.

13.3.4 *The relation to virtual synchrony*

This pattern is similar in some aspects to the *virtual synchrony*[12] work done by Ken Birman et al. in the 1980s. The goal of both is to allow replicated distributed processes to run as if synchronized and to make the same state transitions in the same order. Although our example restricts and simplifies the solution by requiring a central entry point—the coordinator—the virtual synchrony model postulates no such choke point. As we discussed in section 13.2, this would normally require a consensus protocol to be used to ensure that transitions occur only once all replicas have acknowledged that they will make the transition. Unfortunately, this approach is doomed to fail, as proven by Fischer, Lynch, and Paterson in what is usually referred to as the *FLP*[13] result. The practical probability for this kind of failure is vanishingly small, but it is enough to question the endeavor of trying to provide perfect ordering guarantees in a distributed system.

Virtual synchrony avoids this limitation by noticing that, in most cases, the ordering of processing two requests from different sources is not important: if the effects of two requests A and B are commutative, then it does not matter whether they are applied in the order A, B or B, A, because the state of the replica will be identical in the end. This is similar to how CRDTs achieve perfect availability without conflicts: impossibility laws do not matter if the available data types and operations are restricted in a way that conflicts cannot arise.

Taking a step back and considering daily life, we usually think in terms of cause and effect: I (Roland) observe that my wife's coffee mug is empty, fill it with coffee, and tell her about it, expecting that when she looks at the mug, she will be pleased because it is now full. By waiting to tell her until after my refill, I make sure the laws of physics—in particular, causality—will ensure the desired outcome (barring catastrophes). This kind of thinking is so ingrained that we like to think about everything in this fashion, including distributed systems. When using a transactional database, causality is ensured by the serializability of all transactions: they happen as if one were executed after the other, every transaction seeing the complete results of all previously executed transactions. Although this works great as a programming abstraction, it is stronger than needed; causality does not imply that things happen in one universal order. In fact, the laws of special relativity clearly describe which events can be causally related and which cannot—events that happen at remote locations are truly concurrent if you cannot fly from one to the other even at the speed of light.

This fact may serve to motivate the finding that causal consistency is the best you can implement in a distributed system.[14] Virtual synchrony achieves greater resilience

---

[12] https://en.wikipedia.org/wiki/Virtual_synchrony. See Ken Birman, "A History of the Virtual Synchrony Replication Model," https://www.cs.cornell.edu/ken/history.pdf for an introduction and historical discussion.

[13] Michael Fischer, Nancy Lynch, and Michael Paterson, "Impossibility of Distributed Consensus with One Faulty Process," *ACM*, April 1985, http://dl.acm.org/citation.cfm?id=214121.

[14] Wyatt Lloyd et al., "Don't Settle for Eventual: Scalable Causal Consistency for Wide-Area Storage with COPS," SOSP '11, ACM 2011, http://dl.acm.org/citation.cfm?id=2043593.

and less coordination overhead than consensus-based replication by allowing messages that are not causally related to be delivered to the replicas in random order. In this way, it can achieve performance similar to the active–active replication described in this section, at the cost of carefully translating the desired program such that it relies only on causal ordering. If the program cannot be written in this fashion because, for example, some effects are not commutative, then at least for these operations the coordination cost of establishing consensus must be paid. In this sense, the coordinator represents a trade-off that introduces a single choke point in exchange for being able to run arbitrary algorithms in a replicated fashion without the need for adaptation.

13.4 Summary

In this chapter, we discussed various replication patterns that allow you to distribute systems in space so as to not put all of your eggs in one basket. When it comes to replication, you are presented with a choice: do you favor consistency, reliability, or availability? The answer depends on the requirements of the use case at hand and is rarely black and white—there is a continuous range between these extremes, and most patterns are tunable. The following list can be used for orientation:

- *Active–passive replication* is relatively simple to use, based on an existing cluster-singleton implementation. It is fast during normal operation, suffers downtime during fail-overs, and offers good consistency due to having a single active replica.

- *Consensus-based replication* enables greater resilience by allowing updates to be accepted by any replica. But in return for offering perfect consistency, it suffers from high coordination overhead and, consequently, low throughput. Preferring consistency entails unavailability during severe failures.

- *Replication based on conflict detection and resolution* allows the system to stay available during severe failure conditions, but this can lead to data losses or require manual conflict resolution.

- *Conflict-free replicated data types* are formulated such that conflicts cannot arise by construction. Therefore, this scheme can achieve perfect availability even during severe failures; the data types are restricted, requiring special adaptation of the program code as well as designing it for an eventual consistency model.

- *Active–active replication* addresses the concern of avoiding downtime during failures while maintaining a generic programming model. The cost is that all requests must be sent through a single choke point in order to guarantee consistent behavior of all replicas—alternatively, the program can be recast in terms of causal consistency to achieve high performance and high availability by employing virtual synchrony.

This summary is of course grossly simplified. Please refer back to the individual sections for a more complete discussion of the limitations of each approach.

Resource-management patterns

One concern that most systems share is that you need to manage or represent resources: file storage space, computation power, access to databases or web APIs, physical devices like printers and card readers, and many more. A component that you create may provide such a resource to the rest of the system on its own, or you may need to incorporate external resources. In this chapter, we will discuss patterns for dealing with resources in Reactive applications. In particular, we will look at the following:

- The Resource Encapsulation pattern
- The Resource Loan pattern
- The Complex Command pattern
- The Resource Pool pattern
- Patterns for managed blocking

In the previous two chapters, we introduced the example of the batch job service, a system that allows clients to submit computation jobs in order to have them executed by a fleet of elastically provisioned worker nodes. We focused on the hierarchical decomposition and failure handling of such a system. Now we will take a closer look at the provisioning and management of the worker nodes, which are the primary resources managed by the batch job service.

14.1 The Resource Encapsulation pattern

A resource and its lifecycle are responsibilities that must be owned by one component.

From the Simple Component pattern, you know that every component does only one thing, but does it in full; in other words, each component is fully responsible for the functionality it provides to the rest of the system. If we regard that functionality as a resource that is used by other components—inside or outside the system—then it is clear that *resource, responsibility,* and *component* exactly coincide. These three terms all denote the same boundary: in this view, resource encapsulation and the single responsibility principle are the same. The same reasoning can be applied when considering other resources, in particular those used to provide a component's function. These are not implemented but merely are managed or represented: the essence of the Resource Encapsulation pattern is that you must identify that component into whose responsibility each resource falls, and place it there. The resource becomes part of that component's responsibility. Sometimes this will lead you to identify the management of an external resource as a notable responsibility that needs to be broken out into its own simple component.

This pattern is closely related to the principles of hierarchical decomposition (chapter 6) and delimited consistency (chapter 8). You may wish to refresh your memory on these topics before diving in.

14.1.1 The problem setting

Recall the architecture of the batch job service: the client interface offers the overall functionality to external clients and represents them internally; the job-scheduling component decides which of the submitted jobs to execute in which order; the execution component takes care of running the scheduled jobs; and beneath all these, the storage component allows the rest of the system to keep track of job-status changes. Within the execution component, you have identified two responsibilities: interaction with the data center infrastructure, and the individual worker nodes that are provisioned by that infrastructure.

The task: Each worker node is a resource that must be managed by the execution component. You take over ownership and thereby responsibility by receiving worker nodes from the infrastructure. The infrastructure itself is another resource that you represent within the system. Your mission is to implement the provisioning of a worker node in the context of the execution component supervisor.

14.1.2 Applying the pattern

You will apply this pattern by considering the process the execution component will use to manage the lifecycle of a worker node. After we introduce the main management processes, you will see which pieces belong together and where they should best be placed.

When the need arises to add a node to the computation cluster, the infrastructure will need to be informed. There are many different ways to implement this: for example, by using a resource-negotiation framework like Mesos, by directly interacting with a cloud provider like Amazon EC2 or Google Compute Engine, or by using a custom mechanism accessible by a network protocol (such as an HTTP API). Although all these need to send requests across the network, they often present their client interface in the form of a library that can conveniently be used from your programming language of choice. When the execution component starts up, it will need to initialize interaction with the infrastructure provider, typically by reading access keys and network addresses from its deployment configuration.

An extremely simplified example of how a new worker node could be created is shown in the following listing using the Amazon Web Services (AWS) API for EC2[1] with the Java language binding.

Listing 14.1 Amazon EC2 instance used as a worker node

```
public Instance startInstance(AWSCredentials credentials) {
  AmazonEC2Client amazonEC2Client = new AmazonEC2Client(credentials);

  RunInstancesRequest runInstancesRequest =
    new RunInstancesRequest()
      .withImageId("my-image-id-for-a-worker")          Asks for the creation of
      .withInstanceType("m1.small")                     exactly one new node
      .withMinCount(1)
      .withMaxCount(1);

  RunInstancesResult runInstancesResult =
    amazonEC2Client.runInstances(runInstancesRequest);
  Reservation reservation = runInstancesResult.getReservation();
  List<Instance> instances = reservation.getInstances();

  return instances.get(0);            There will be exactly one instance in this list. Otherwise,
}                                     runInstances() would have thrown an exception.
```

Having the instance descriptor, you can obtain the private network address of this new worker node and start interacting with it. What that interaction looks like depends on the intercomponent communication fabric you are using, which could be as simple as an HTTP API.[2] Before we go there, we need to consider the possibility that AWS may become unreachable or fail for some reason. The client library signals this by throwing an `AmazonClientException` that you will need to handle, possibly by retrying the operation, switching into a degraded mode, or escalating the failure. As discussed in section 12.4, you should also monitor the reliability of the cloud infrastructure using a circuit breaker to avoid making a large number of pointless requests within a short time. All this is made easier by lifting the functionality into a Future so that you can describe these aspects in an event-driven fashion, as shown next.

---

[1] See "Amazon Elastic Compute Cloud Documentation" at http://aws.amazon.com/documentation/ec2.
[2] We expect the development of higher-level service definition frameworks in the near future that will abstract over the precise communication mechanism and offer a consistent code representation of service interaction in a fully location-transparent fashion.

Listing 14.2 Lifting the EC2 node into a Future to simplify failure recovery

```
import scala.PartialFunction;
import scala.concurrent.ExecutionContext;
import scala.concurrent.Future;                        Using Scala's Future and
import akka.dispatch.Futures;                          Akka's CircuitBreaker
import akka.japi.pf.PFBuilder;
import akka.pattern.CircuitBreaker;

private ExecutionContext exeCtx;
private CircuitBreaker circuitBreaker;

public Future<Instance> startInstanceAsync(AWSCredentials credentials) {
  Future<Instance> f = circuitBreaker.callWithCircuitBreaker(() ->
    Futures.future(() -> startInstance(credentials), exeCtx));

  PartialFunction<Throwable, Future<Instance>> recovery =     Defines the
    new PFBuilder<Throwable, Future<Instance>>()              recovery strategy
      .match(AmazonClientException.class,
             ex -> ex.isRetryable(),                     Some AWS calls can
             ex -> startInstanceAsync(credentials))      safely be retried.
      .build();

  return f.recoverWith(recovery, exeCtx);         The circuit breaker will take care of
}                                                 recurring failures, and any unmatched
                                                  exceptions will not be recovered.
            Decorates the Future with recovery
```

In this fashion, you wrap up the task of instantiating a new worker node such that all failures are registered—tripping the circuit breaker when necessary—and failures that are expected to routinely be fixed by trying again lead to retries. The assumption here is that such failures are complete (no partial success has already changed the system state) and transient. Refinements of this scheme may implement a backoff strategy that schedules retries for progressively delayed points in time instead of trying again immediately. It is easy to see that this would be incorporated by using a scheduler call (for example, using akka.pattern.after[3]), wrapping startInstanceAsync() in the recovery strategy—of course, you do not block a thread from the ExecutionContext's thread pool by using Thread.sleep().

The attentive reader will have noticed that the code listings use the synchronous version of AmazonEC2Client even though there is an asynchronous version as well: AmazonEC2AsyncClient provides a runInstancesAsync() method that accepts a completion callback as its second parameter (the returned java.util.concurrent .Future is not useful for event-driven programming, as discussed in chapter 3). You can use the callback to supply the value for a Promise and thereby obtain a Scala Future in an event-driven fashion.

---

[3] See http://doc.akka.io/japi/akka/current/akka/pattern/Patterns.html for the Java documentation.

Listing 14.3 Bridging client methods to execute an Amazon async client

```
public Future<RunInstancesResult> runInstancesAsync(
                                  RunInstancesRequest request,
                                  AmazonEC2Async client) {
  Promise<RunInstancesResult> promise = Futures.promise();
  client.runInstancesAsync(request,
    new AsyncHandler<RunInstancesRequest, RunInstancesResult>() {
      @Override
      public void onSuccess(RunInstancesRequest request,
                            RunInstancesResult result) {
        promise.success(result);
      }

      @Override
      public void onError(Exception exception) {
        promise.failure(exception);
      }
    });
  return promise.future();
}
```

Unfortunately, the AWS library implements the asynchronous version in terms of the same blocking HTTP network library that also powers the synchronous version (based on the Apache HTTP client library)—it just runs the code on a separate thread pool. You could configure that thread pool to be the same ExecutionContext you use to run your Scala Futures by supplying it as a constructor argument when instantiating AmazonEC2AsyncClient. That would not be a net win, however, because instead of just wrapping the synchronous call in a Future, you would have to bridge all client methods in the fashion shown in listing 14.3—an overhead of 15–20 lines per API method. The execution mechanics would be the same, but adapting the different asynchronous API styles would involve significant extra programming effort (and, hence, more opportunity for errors). We will take a deeper look at situations like this in section 14.5 when we discuss patterns for managed blocking.

Now that you have started the worker node, you need to also manage the rest of its lifecycle: the execution component needs to keep track of which workers are available, monitor their health by performing regular status checks, and shut them down when they are no longer needed. Performing health checks typically means making service calls that query performance indicators that the service is monitoring internally. The fact that a response is received signals general availability, and the measured quantities can be factored into future decisions about whether to scale the number of worker nodes up or down. The measured quantities can also be indicative of specific problems, such as unusually high memory consumption, that require dedicated reactions (for example, an operator alert or automatic reboot after a diagnostic memory dump).

This brings you to the final step of a worker node's lifecycle: the execution component needs to instruct the infrastructure to shut down a node. Completing the AWS example, this would be done as follows.

> ### Listing 14.4 Terminating the EC2 instances

```
public Future<TerminateInstancesResult> terminateInstancesAsync(
                    AmazonEC2Client client, Instance... instances) {
  List<String> ids = Arrays.stream(instances)
                            .map(i -> i.getInstanceId())
                            .collect(Collectors.toList());
  TerminateInstancesRequest request = new TerminateInstancesRequest(ids);

  Future<TerminateInstancesResult> f =
    circuitBreaker.callWithCircuitBreaker(
      () -> Futures.future(() -> client.terminateInstances(request),
                      executionContext)
    );

  PartialFunction<Throwable, Future<TerminateInstancesResult>> recovery =
    new PFBuilder<Throwable, Future<TerminateInstancesResult>>()
      .match(AmazonClientException.class,
             ex -> ex.isRetryable(),
             ex -> terminateInstancesAsync(client, instances))
      .build();
  return f.recoverWith(recovery, executionContext);
}
```

Of course, you will want to use the same circuit breaker and ExecutionContext as for the runInstancesAsync() implementation in listing 14.4, because it is the same infrastructure service that you are addressing—it is not reasonable to assume that creating and terminating machine instances are independent operations such that one keeps working while the other is systematically unavailable (as in failing to respond, not denying invalid input). Therefore, you place the responsibility for communicating with the infrastructure service in its own execution subcomponent (called the resource pool interface in section 12.3). Although AmazonEC2Client offers a rich and detailed API (we glossed over the creation of security groups, configuration of availability zones and key pairs, and so on), the resource pool need only offer high-level operations like creating and terminating worker nodes. You present only a tailored view of the externally provided capabilities to the components in your system, and you do so via a single component dedicated to this purpose.

This has another important benefit: you not only have encapsulated the responsibility for dealing with the vicissitudes of the external service's availability, but you can also switch to a completely different infrastructure service provider by replacing this one internal representation. The execution component does not need to know whether the worker nodes are running on Amazon's Elastic Compute Cloud or Google's Compute Engine (or whatever computing infrastructure is in vogue at the time you are reading this), as long as it can communicate with the services the worker nodes provide.

Another aspect of this placement of responsibility is that this is the natural—and only—location where you can implement service-call quota management: if the infrastructure API imposed limits on how frequently you could make requests, then you would keep track of the requests that passed through this access path. This would allow you to delay requests in order to avoid a temporary excess that could lead to punitively degraded service—to our knowledge this is not true for AWS, but for other web APIs, such limitations and enforcement are common. Instead of running into a quota on the external service, you would degrade the internally represented service such that the external service was not burdened with too many requests.

To recapitulate, we have considered the management actions that the execution component needs to perform in order to provision and retire worker nodes, and you have placed the responsibility for representing the infrastructure provider that performs these functions in a dedicated resource pool interface subcomponent. Although the mechanism for conveying the requests and responses between the execution component and its worker nodes will change depending on which service frameworks are available over time, the remaining aspect that we need to discuss in the context of the Resource Encapsulation pattern is how to model knowledge about and management of the worker nodes within the execution component.

Each worker node will gather its own performance metrics and react to the failures it can address, but ultimately the execution component is responsible for the currently running workers: it has taken this responsibility by asking the resource pool to provision the workers. Some classes of failures—such as fatal resource exhaustion in terms of CPU cycles or memory—cannot be dealt with from within, and the supervising component needs to keep track of its subordinates and dispose of those that have failed terminally or are otherwise inaccessible. Another way to look at this is that a worker node provides its own service to the rest of the system and is also coupled to a resource that must be managed in addition to the service that the resource powers. This is true in all cases where the supervising component assumes this kind of responsibility by effecting the creation of or by asking for the transfer of ownership of such a resource. As a demonstration of managing a worker node's underlying resource, the following listing sketches an actor that takes this responsibility.

Listing 14.5   Execution component communicating with an actor as if it were a worker node

```
class WorkerNode extends AbstractActor {
  private final Cancellable checkTimer;

  public WorkerNode(InetAddress address, FiniteDuration checkInterval) {
    checkTimer = getContext().system().scheduler()
                    .schedule(checkInterval, checkInterval,
                             self(), DoHealthCheck.instance,
                             getContext().dispatcher(), self());

    List<WorkerNodeMessage> msgs = new ArrayList<>();
    receive(ReceiveBuilder
            .match(WorkerNodeMessage.class, msgs::add)
            .match(DoHealthCheck.class, dhc -> { ... })      <---- Performs a check
            .match(Shutdown.class, s -> {
                msgs.stream().forEach(msg -> {
                  WorkerCommandFailed failMsg =
```

```
                             new WorkerCommandFailed("shutting down", msg.id());
                         msg.replyTo().tell(failMsg, self()));
                     })
                 .match(WorkerNodeReady.class, wnr -> {
                     getContext().become(initialized());
                 })
             .build());
     }

     private PartialFunction<Object, BoxedUnit> initialized() {
         /* ... */
     }

     @Override
     public void postStop() {
         checkTimer.cancel();
     }
}
```

Asks the resource pool to shut down this instance → `})`

Start forwarding messages to the worker → `getContext().become(initialized());`

Forwards commands, and deals with responses from worker node → `/* ... */`

In the spirit of delimited consistency, as discussed in chapter 8, you bundle all aspects of interaction with the worker node in this representation so that the forwarding of messages to and from the worker node can take into account the worker's lifecycle changes and current health status. With this encapsulation, the execution component creates a WorkerNode actor for every worker node it asks the resource pool to create; then, it only needs to communicate with that actor as it if were the worker node itself. This proxy hides the periodic health check processing as well as the fact that after the instance has been created, it will take a certain amount of time for the worker's services to start up and signal their readiness to accept commands.

When implementing the WorkerNode class, you need to ask the resource pool to shut down the represented instance. In a full-fledged implementation, you might want to add more features that need to interact with the resource pool: for example, monitoring the instances via the cloud infrastructure provider's facilities (in listing 14.5, that would be Amazon CloudWatch). This is another reason to place the responsibility for all such interactions in a dedicated subcomponent: otherwise, you would duplicate this code in several places and thereby lose the ability to monitor the availability of the cloud infrastructure service consistently in a single location. Note that this is meant in a logical sense and not necessarily in a physical one: the resource pool interface could well be replicated for fault tolerance, in which case you would not care about synchronizing the state it maintains because losing the circuit breaker's status in the course of a component crash would not have a large or lasting negative effect.

14.1.3 *The pattern, revisited*

We have examined the interactions between the execution component and the infrastructure service that provisions the worker nodes, and you have placed all aspects of this interaction in a dedicated resource pool interface subcomponent. It is this component's responsibility to represent the resource pool to the rest of the system, allowing consistent treatment of the infrastructure provider's availability and limitations.

This encapsulation is also in accordance with the principle of abstracting over the concrete implementation of a potentially exchangeable resource; in this case, you simplify the adaptation to a different cloud infrastructure provider.

The second aspect we have illuminated is that worker nodes are based on dynamically provisioned resources that need to be owned by their supervising component. Therefore, you have placed the responsibility of monitoring the worker node and communicating with it in a WorkerNode subcomponent of the execution component, sketched as an actor for illustration. Although communication with the services provided by a worker node is taken care of by the service fabric or framework, there is a remaining responsibility that cannot be satisfied from within the worker node because it is about the management of the node's underlying resources.

The Resource Encapsulation pattern is used in two cases: to represent an external resource and to manage a supervised resource—both in terms of its lifecycle and its function, in accordance with the Simple Component pattern and the principle of delimited consistency. One aspect we glossed over is the precise relation of the WorkerNode subcomponents to their execution component parent: should a WorkerNode supervisor be its own component, or should it be bundled with the execution component? Both approaches are certainly possible: the code modularity offered by object-oriented programming can express the necessary encapsulation of concerns just as well as deploying a WorkerNode service instance on the hardware resources that the execution component is using. Spinning up a separate node would again require you to establish a supervision scheme and therefore not solve the problem.[4] The way the decision is made will depend on the case at hand. Influential factors are as follows:

- Complexity of the resource-management task
- Runtime overhead of service separation for the chosen service framework
- Development effort of adding another asynchronous messaging boundary

In many cases, it will be preferable to run the management subcomponents within their parent's context (that is, to encapsulate this aspect in a separate class or function library). When using an actor-based framework, it is typically a good middle ground to separate resource management into its own actor, making it look and behave like a separate component while sharing most of the runtime context and avoiding large runtime overhead.

14.1.4 Applicability

The Resource Encapsulation pattern is an architectural pattern that mainly informs the design of the component hierarchy and the placement of implementation details in code modules—either reinforcing the previously established hierarchical decomposition or

---

[4] Note that this depends on the service framework used, though, in that automatic resource cleanup in combination with health monitoring may already be provided—meaning this pattern is incorporated at the framework level.

leading to its refinement. The concrete expression in code depends on the nature of the resource that is being managed or represented. The pattern is applicable wherever resources are integrated into a system, in particular when these resources have a lifecycle that needs to be managed or represented.

In some cases, the nature of resources used by the system is not immediately visible: in this section's example, a beginner's mistake might be to leave the worker node instances to their own devices after creation, having them shut themselves down when no longer needed. This works well most of the time, but failure cases with lingering but defunct instances will manifest in the form of surprisingly large infrastructure costs, at which point it will become obvious that reliable lifecycle management is required.

14.2 The Resource Loan pattern

Give a client exclusive transient access to a scarce resource without transferring ownership.

A variant of the Resource Loan pattern is widely used in non-Reactive systems, the most prominent example being that of a database connection pool. Database access is represented by a connection object via which arbitrary operations can be performed. The creation of connections is expensive, and their number is limited; therefore, a connection is not owned by client code but is taken from a pool before performing an operation and put back afterward. The connection pool is responsible for managing the lifecycle of its connections, and client code obtains temporary permission to use them. Failures in this scenario are communicated to the client, but their effect on the connection in question is handled by the pool—the pool owns and supervises the connections.

In a Reactive system, you strive to minimize contention as well as the need for coordination: hence, the classic database connection pool usually only features as an internal implementation detail of a component whose data storage is realized by means of a relational database. But you will frequently encounter the use of scarce resources in your systems, and the same philosophy that drives the connection pool abstraction is useful in Reactive system design as well.

14.2.1 The problem setting

Toward the end of the discussion of the Resource Encapsulation pattern, we touched on the possibility of separating the ownership and the use of a resource: not being responsible for supervision aspects frees the user from having to perform monitoring tasks or recovery actions. In the example of the execution component of the batch job service, it may seem extraneous that the `WorkerNode` subcomponent needs to watch over the physical instance provisioned via the resource pool interface. Would it not be nicer if the resource pool were not merely a messaging façade for talking to a cloud provider but also took responsibility for the lifecycle management of the instances it provisions?

The task: Your mission is to change the relationship between the resource pool interface component and the execution component such that the resource pool will retain ownership of the worker nodes it provides, and the execution supervisor can concentrate on managing the batch jobs.

14.2.2 Applying the pattern

Before we look at this in more detail, we need to establish some terminology. The word *loan* is often used in a financial context: a *lender* gives a certain sum to a *borrower*, who is expected to pay it back later, usually with interest. More generally, this term applies to any asset that can be transferred, with the important notions that ownership of the asset remains with the lender throughout the process and the transfer is temporary and will eventually be reversed. Renting an apartment falls in this category: the landlord lets you live in their property and expects you to vacate it when the lease ends; meanwhile, the landlord stays responsible for the general upkeep of the building and everything that was rented with it. This example also illustrates the exclusivity of the arrangement, given that an apartment can only be rented to one tenant at a time. Therefore, the resource (the apartment, in this case) is also scarce: it cannot be copied or inhabited by multiple tenants independently at the same time. This resource comes at a per-instance cost.

To answer the question of having the resource pool take responsibility for the life-cycle of the instances it provisions, we will consider the worker nodes provisioned by the resource pool interface to be like apartments that the execution component wants to use. It will place a worker in each apartment; the worker will then process batch jobs. A worker node is a potential home for a batch-job process. In this scenario, apartments are provided by the cloud infrastructure, but this is the most basic, empty apartment you can think of—there is nothing interesting in it until someone moves in. The worker node components in the structure of the batch job service correspond to people who need a apartment to live in. Once a worker has moved into an apartment, the execution component can send work items to their address and receive replies from them—business-level information can flow. The missing piece is a kind of concierge who looks after the apartments rented for workers and checks regularly with the property and with the worker to see that everything is in order. This allows the execution component (the work provider) to concentrate entirely on conversations about the work that is to be done; monitoring of the workforce is done by the concierge. The concierge is responsible for ending the lease when a worker moves out, solving the problem of possibly leaking resources.

Switching back from the anthropomorphic metaphor to computer programming, when the execution component asks the resource pool interface for a new worker node, the resource pool uses the cloud infrastructure to provision a new machine instance: for example, using the AWS EC2 API, as shown in the previous pattern discussion. But instead of just returning the instance identifier and network address to the execution component, the resource pool now assumes responsibility for the worker node: it needs to begin monitoring the service by performing regular health checks.

The execution component only receives the network address at which the new worker node service is being provided, and it assumes that the resource pool keeps this node in good working condition—or terminates it and provides a new one.

In order to do that, the resource pool must know about the kind of service that is being provided by the worker node: it must be able to ask for the relevant set of performance metrics, and it must understand their meaning to assess a worker node's fitness. The resource pool interface thus assumes more responsibility than before, and is also more tightly coupled to the function of the resources it provides. Instead of a more-or-less generic representation of the cloud infrastructure API, the pool becomes more specific, tailored to the needs of the batch job service; in return, you achieve a better separation of concerns between the lender and the borrower. The relationship in the previous pattern was that of a manufacturer (the author of `WorkerNode`) and a buyer (who instantiates a WorkerNode), and the latter's obligation to perform maintenance led to a coupling that you can, in this case, avoid. In source code, this means you will have `WorkerNode` representations in the execution component as well as in the resource pool interface component, but these take care of different aspects that were previously mixed within one class.

Listing 14.6 Separating management of the resource from management of tasks

```
class WorkerNodeForExecution extends AbstractActor {        ◁─┐ Representation used
                                                               │ in the execution
  public WorkerNodeForExecution(InetAddress address) {         │ component
    List<WorkerNodeMessage> msgs = new ArrayList<>();
    receive(ReceiveBuilder
            .match(WorkerNodeMessage.class, msgs::add)
            .match(Shutdown.class, s -> {
                msgs.stream().forEach(msg -> {
                  WorkerCommandFailed failMsg =
                    new WorkerCommandFailed("shutting down", msg.id());
                  msg.replyTo().tell(failMsg, self()));     ◁─┐ Asks the resource
                })                                             │ pool to shut down
            .match(WorkerNodeReady.class, wnr -> {             │ this instance
                getContext().become(initialized());
            })
            .build());
  }

  private PartialFunction<Object, BoxedUnit> initialized() {
    /* ... */                        ◁──────┐ Forwards commands, and deals
  }                                          │ with responses from worker node
}

class WorkerNodeForResourcePool extends AbstractActor {   ◁─┐ Representation used
  private final Cancellable checkTimer;                      │ in the resource pool
                                                             │ interface
  public WorkerNodeForResourcePool(InetAddress address,
                                   FiniteDuration checkInterval) {
    checkTimer = getContext().system().scheduler()
                    .schedule(checkInterval, checkInterval,
                          self(), DoHealthCheck.instance,
                          getContext().dispatcher(), self());
```

Start forwarding messages to the worker

```
            receive(ReceiveBuilder
                .match(DoHealthCheck.class, dhc -> { /* ... */ })
                .match(Shutdown.class, s -> { /* ... */ })
                .build());
    }

    @Override
    public void postStop() {
      checkTimer.cancel();
    }
}
```

Performs a check (annotation pointing to the `.match(DoHealthCheck...)` line)

Cleans up this resource (annotation pointing to the `.match(Shutdown...)` line)

14.2.3 *The pattern, revisited*

While applying this pattern, you segregate the responsibilities of resource maintenance and use: the execution component asks for the service of a new worker node
and gets that back in response without the additional burden that comes with a transfer of ownership. The resource that is loaned in this fashion is still exclusively available
to the borrower; the execution component can keep usage statistics, knowing the only
jobs that will be processed by the worker node are those the execution component
sent. There is no competition for this resource among different borrowers for the
duration of the loan.

The price of this simplification of the borrower is that the lender must take over
the responsibilities the borrower has shed, requiring the lender to know more about
the resource it is loaning. One important point is that this additional knowledge
should be kept minimal; otherwise, you violate the Simple Component pattern and
entangle the functionalities of lender and borrower more than necessary. This is particularly relevant when different kinds of borrowers enter the picture: the purpose of
separating the lender, borrower, and loaned resource is to keep their responsibilities
segregated and as loosely coupled as is practical. The lender should not know more
about the capabilities of the resource than it needs to perform the necessary health
checks; the concrete use of the resource by the borrower is irrelevant for this purpose.

As a counterexample, suppose that instead of loaning the resource, the resource
pool interface completely encapsulated and hid the worker nodes, forcing the execution component to go through it for every request the execution component wanted
to make. We will discuss this angle in detail later in this chapter, as the Resource Pool
pattern. This would entail enabling the resource pool interface to speak the language
of a worker node in addition to its own. By loaning the resource, the borrower may
use it in any way necessary, but unbeknownst to the lender, who is freed from the burden of having to understand this interaction. Consider the following possible conversation for a job execution:

1 Execution sends job description to Worker Node.
2 Worker Node acknowledges receipt and starts sending regular execution metrics.
3 Execution may ask for intermediate results on behalf of end user (for example,
   for a live log file viewer).

4 Worker Node replies with intermediate results when asked.

5 Worker Node signals job completion when done.

6 Execution acknowledges receipt and relieves Worker Node from this job.

The individual messages that are exchanged are small building blocks from which this interchange is built. The purpose of the Resource Loan pattern is to allow the lender to be largely unaware of this protocol, which is only shared by the borrower and the resource, as shown in figure 14.1.

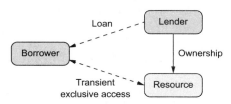

Figure 14.1 **The relationship between lender, borrower, and resource in the Resource Loan pattern. The goal is to facilitate efficient exchange between borrower and resource while placing the burden of ownership with the lender.**

14.2.4 Applicability

This pattern is applicable wherever a resource needs to be used by a component whose genuine responsibility does not *a priori* include the monitoring and lifecycle management of that resource. If the aspects of provisioning, monitoring, and disposal can be factored out into their own component, then the resource user is effectively freed from the details of these concerns: it is not forced to take on these incidental responsibilities.

When deciding this question, it is important to require the resulting resource manager component to be nontrivial. Factoring out the management of a trivial resource only leads to additional runtime and design overhead; every component that is split out should be considered to have a basic cost that needs to be offset by the benefits of the achieved decoupling and isolation.

14.2.5 Implementation considerations

In the example, the execution component is in full control of the worker nodes, and the questions of how long to use them and when to shut them down are decided at its sole discretion. This will need to change if you assume that the underlying computing resource is scarce and may need to be vacated in response to external events (for example, when the per-minute runtime cost rises above a certain threshold). The execution component will in this case only formulate the desired number of worker nodes, and the decision about how many are provisioned will be made by the resource pool interface. We can also envision worker nodes being reallocated to different execution components for separate compute clusters.

This scenario requires that the resource lender retain the power to forcefully take back resources when needed. If it handed the borrower a direct reference to the loaned resource, the borrower could hold on to that reference and keep using it after the loan was withdrawn. The solution is to hand out a proxy instead of the resource. This is easily possible in a setting where service references are location transparent, because the borrower does not care or know about the precise routing of requests to the resource. The proxy must be able to forward requests and responses between the borrower and the resource, and it also must obey a deactivation command from the lender, after which it rejects all requests from the borrower. In this fashion, the lender can cut the resource loose from the borrower as required and decommission or reallocate the resource without interference from unruly borrowers.

Another consideration is that a resource that has been loaned to another service instance should be returned when the borrower terminates. Otherwise, the lender may not notice that the resource is no longer being used—it may stay around, healthy and fully functional, for a long time. Failing to recognize this situation amounts to a resource leak.

14.2.6 Variant: using the Resource Loan pattern for partial exposure

The mechanics for handing out a subcomponent to an external client can also be used to expose part of a component's functionality or data. Imagine a component that holds a large, multidimensional array of floating-point numbers resulting from the analysis of a huge amount of data. Clients may be interested in particular slices of the array but are not allowed to make changes. Using the Resource Loan pattern, the component can offer a protocol for obtaining a handle to a particularly shaped slice of the data for read-only access. The client invokes methods on this handle to obtain particular values, wrapped in a Future. This allows the implementation to decide how many of the referenced values to ship to the client immediately and how to retrieve the rest when the client eventually asks for them—imagine a slice big enough to cause considerable network usage if it were transferred up front.

By using the Resource Loan pattern, the component that manages the multidimensional array knows exactly how many read-only handles are currently active, and it can invalidate them when needed. For example, only a limited number of snapshots can be kept in memory—with clients having handles to them—and when further changes need to be made, the oldest snapshot will be retired to free up its space.

14.3 The Complex Command pattern

Send compound instructions to the resource to avoid excessive network usage.

You have encapsulated the resources your system uses in components that manage, represent, and directly implement their functionality. This allows you to confine responsibility not only for code-modularity reasons (chapter 6) but also for vertical and horizontal scalability (chapters 4 and 5) and principled failure handling (chapter 7). The price of all these advantages is that you introduce a boundary between the resource and the rest of the system that can only be crossed by asynchronous messaging. The Resource Loan pattern may help to move a resource as close as possible to its users, but this barrier will remain, leading to increased latency and, usually, decreased communication bandwidth. The core of the Complex Command pattern lies in sending the behavior to the resource in order to save time and network bandwidth in case of loquacious interchanges between resource and users; the user of the resource is only interested in the comparatively small result.

This pattern has been used for this purpose for a long time. We will approach it by way of a common example. Consider a large dataset, so large that it cannot possibly fit into the working memory of a single machine. The data will be stored on a cluster of machines, each having only a small fraction of the data—this is known as *big data*. This dataset is a resource that will be used by other parts of the system. Other components that interact with these data will send queries that have to be dispatched to the right cluster nodes according to where the data are located. If the data store only allowed the retrieval of individual data elements and left it to the clients to analyze them, then any summarizing operation would involve the transfer of a huge amount of data; the resulting increase in network usage and the correspondingly high response latency would be exacerbated by more-complex analyses requiring frequent back and forth between the client and the data source. Therefore, big data systems work by having the user send the computation job to the cluster instead of having the computation interrogate the cluster from the outside.

Another way to think of this pattern is to picture the client and the resource (the large dataset) as two nations that are about to negotiate a contract. To facilitate an efficient exchange, an ambassador (the batch job) is sent from one nation to the other. Negotiations may take many days, but in the end the ambassador comes home with the result.

14.3.1 *The problem setting*

We can generalize this problem as follows: a client wants to extract a result from a resource, a value that is relatively small compared to the quantity of data that need to be moved in the course of the loquacious exchange required to obtain that value. The computation process is more intimately coupled with the data than with the client component that initiates it; the client is not genuinely interested in how the data are processed, as long as it gets the result. The resource, on the other hand, only holds the data and does not know the process by which the client's requested result can be extracted. Therefore, the process description needs to be sent from the client to the resource; the client needs to be provided with this description by the programmer, who presumably knows both the need and the structure of the data.

This is precisely what a batch job service is all about. You need to amend your mental picture slightly: the graphical overview has not changed from section 12.2, but we repeat it in figure 14.2 as a refresher. The worker nodes are no longer stateless services that can be provisioned and decommissioned dynamically; instead, there is a fixed set of worker nodes in the big data cluster, and each persistently holds the partition of data it has been entrusted with. The execution component will take care of sending jobs to the correct worker nodes according to the data the jobs need, which

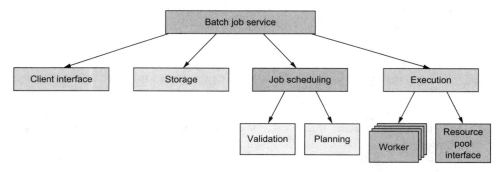

Figure 14.2   The component hierarchy of the batch job service as derived in section 12.2

in turn will have an influence on how scheduling decisions are made. These consequences—although interesting—are highly dependent on the particular example chosen. More illuminating in terms of the generic pattern is the question of what constitutes a batch job and how it is executed by a worker node. You will see in this section that there is more than one answer.

14.3.2 Applying the pattern

We will start by considering the essential pieces that need to be conveyed. In order to route the job to the correct nodes, you need to know which data will be needed; the dataset descriptor will thus need to be part of the batch job definition. The Scheduler component will have to inspect this information and factor it into its decisions, which is to say it only needs to read and understand this part. The execution component, on the other hand, must split the job into pieces according to the partitioning of the data: in addition to reading and understanding the dataset descriptor, it will need to be able to create copies of the overall batch job that act on subsets of the data, to be executed by the individual worker nodes.

Another approach would be to always send the full job description and have the worker node ignore all parts of the dataset that it does not have, but this would be problematic if the distribution of data changed or data partitions were replicated for fault tolerance: without making the data selection consistently at one location, it would be difficult or impossible to guarantee that, in the end, every requested data element was processed exactly once. Sending the narrowed-down selection to the worker nodes gives them unambiguous instructions and allows them to signal that some of the requested data are no longer available at their location.

This leads you to the conclusion that a batch job must be a data structure that can be constructed not only by the client but also by the batch service's components. The first part of the data that it contains is a dataset descriptor that several batch service components will need to understand and possibly split up.

The second piece of information that must be conveyed is the processing logic that acts on the selected data. For this purpose, the batch job must describe how this logic consumes the elements of the dataset and how the resulting value is produced in the process. The last piece is then a recipe for combining the partial results from the individual worker nodes into the overall result that is shipped back to the external client.

USING THE PLATFORM'S SERIALIZATION CAPABILITIES

Neglecting all incidental information such as client authentication, authorization, quota, priority management, and so on, the essential structure of a batch job is captured in the following class definitions: the batch job has a selector to identify data to process, some processing logic to create partial results, and merge logic to combine the partial results.

Listing 14.7   The essence of a batch job

```java
public interface ProcessingLogic {
  public PartialResult process(Stream<DataElement> input);
}

public interface MergeLogic {
  public Result merge(Collection<PartialResult> partialResults);
}

public class BatchJob {
  public final String dataSelector;
  public final ProcessingLogic processingLogic;
  public final MergeLogic mergeLogic;

  public BatchJob(String dataSelector,
                  ProcessingLogic processingLogic,
                  MergeLogic mergeLogic) {
    this.dataSelector = dataSelector;
    this.processingLogic = processingLogic;
    this.mergeLogic = mergeLogic;
  }

  public BatchJob withDataSelector(String selector) {
    return new BatchJob(selector, processingLogic, mergeLogic);
  }
}
```

The data selector is assumed to have a `String`-based syntax for the sake of simplicity—describing datasets is not the primary focus of this pattern—and a copy constructor is provided by way of the `withDataSelector()` method so that the execution component can derive jobs that act on subsets of the data.

The more interesting piece that we will now examine in greater detail is the logic that is conveyed, represented here as two interfaces for which the client will need to provide implementations. `ProcessingLogic` describes how to compute a partial result from a dataset that is represented as a stream[5] of elements: you potentially are dealing with big data that do not fit into memory all at once, so passing the full `Collection<DataElement>` into the processing logic could easily lead to fatal working-

---

[5] See https://docs.oracle.com/javase/8/docs/api/java/util/stream/Stream.html.

memory exhaustion (an `OutOfMemoryError` in Java). `MergeLogic` then takes the partial results and combines them into the overall result that the client wants; here, you expect the involved amount of data to be relatively small—even thousands of partial results should not take up a large amount of memory, because you are working under the assumption that the result value is much smaller than the analyzed dataset.

In order to send a `BatchJob` message from the client to the batch job service, you need to serialize this Java object. In listing 14.7, you could add `extends Serializable` in a few places and add some `serialVersionUID` values, with the result that the Java Runtime Environment (JRE) would be able to turn a `BatchJob` object into a sequence of bytes that could be transferred. On the other end—within the batch job service—you would need to reverse that process, but here you hit a snag: the JRE can only deserialize classes whose definition it already knows about. The serialized representation contains only the class names of the objects that are referenced and the serialized form of the primitive values they contain (integers, characters, arrays); the bytecode that describes the behavior of the objects is missing.

In order to transfer that, you will have to add the corresponding vocabulary to the protocol between the batch service and its clients. They will have to upload the JAR[6] files in conjunction with the job so that the necessary class definitions can be made known wherever a `BatchJob` message needs to be interpreted. This can be a tedious and brittle undertaking where any forgotten class or wrong library version leads to fatal JVM errors that make it impossible to run the job. Also, note that this approach ties both clients and service together in their choice of runtime environment: in listing 14.7, both parties need to use compatible versions of the Java Runtime in order to successfully transfer and run the bytecode as well as the serialized objects. Using the batch job service from a client written in JavaScript, Ruby, Haskell, and so on would not be possible.

USING ANOTHER LANGUAGE AS A BEHAVIOR TRANSFER FORMAT

Another way to look at this is that the batch job service defines a language choice that is implicit to its client interface protocol. Batch jobs must be formulated such that the service can understand and execute them. You can turn this around to exercise greater freedom in this regard: if the service—still written in Java—were to accept the processing logic in another language, preferably one that is widely used and optimized for being shipped and run in a variety of environments; then, you could sidestep the tight code coupling you faced when transferring Java classes directly. There are several options in this regard, including JavaScript, due to its ubiquity and ease of interpretation; and Python, due to its popularity for data analytics purposes. The Java 8 Runtime includes a JavaScript engine that you can readily use to demonstrate this approach.

---

[6] Java archive: basically, compressed files containing the machine-readable class definitions of a library, organized in class files.

Listing 14.8 Executing processing logic by invoking the Nashorn JavaScript engine

```
public class PartSuccess implements PartialResult {
  public final int value;
  public PartSuccess(int value) { this.value = value; }
}

public class PartFailure implements PartialResult {
  public final Throwable failure;
  public PartFailure(Throwable failure) { this.failure = failure; }
}

public class BatchJobJS {
  public final String dataSelector;
  public final String processingLogic;
  public final String mergeLogic;

  public BatchJobJS(String dataSelector,
                    String processingLogic,
                    String mergeLogic) {
    this.dataSelector = dataSelector;
    this.processingLogic = processingLogic;        ◁─── JavaScript
    this.mergeLogic = mergeLogic;
  }

  public BatchJobJS withDataSelector(String selector) {
    return new BatchJobJS(selector, processingLogic, mergeLogic);
  }
}

public class WorkerJS {

  public PartialResult runJob(BatchJobJS job) {
    ScriptEngine engine = new ScriptEngineManager()
                                .getEngineByName("nashorn");
    Invocable invocable = (Invocable) engine;                Evaluates
    try {                                                    the JavaScript
      engine.eval(job.processingLogic);              ◁─
      final Stream<DataElement> input = provideData(job.dataSelector);
      PartialResult result =
        (PartialResult) invocable.invokeFunction("process", input);
      return result;
    } catch (Exception e) {
      return new PartFailure(e);
    }
  }

  private Stream<DataElement> provideData(String selector) {
    /* ... */                         ◁──┐ Fetches data from persistent
  }                                       │ storage in streaming fashion
}
```

Invokes the JavaScript function

The processing logic is passed as a trivially serializable `String` containing a JavaScript text that defines a `process()` function when it is evaluated. This function is then invoked with the stream of data elements and expects a `Result` back. A simple example of a processing logic script could look like this:

```
var PartSuccess = Java.type(
    'com.reactivedesignpatterns.chapter13.ComplexCommand.PartSuccess');

var process = function(input) {
  var value = input.count();          ⟵ Java 8 stream
  return new PartSuccess(value);
}
```

This code is available in the source code archives at www.manning.com/books/reactive-design-patterns and on GitHub if you want to play around with embedding JavaScript parts in your Java applications.

One concern you will likely encounter with this technique is that the submitted logic may be implemented using other libraries that simplify the job. Consider, for example, the DataElement that contains an image to be analyzed. Assuming that the analysis job is written by someone who likes the hypothetical image-manipulation library Gimp JS, the job script will need this library to be present when the job is executed. This could be achieved by providing this library in the execution environment as part of the batch service's contract, or the library's code could be included with the job script. The former approach saves resources, and the latter gives you more freedom in terms of which version of which library to use.

To recapitulate, we have explored two ways of transferring behavior—the processing logic—from client to batch service, one tied to the Java language and Runtime and one in terms of a different language. The latter is used as a behavior-exchange format that may be foreign to both parties but has the advantage of being easily transferable and interpretable. What we have not considered so far are the security implications of letting clients submit arbitrary processing instructions to your big data cluster—although they are meant to only analyze heaps of data, they are capable of calling any public method in the JRE, including file system access, and so on.

In order to secure your cluster, you could implement filters that inspect the submitted code (hairy to get right in terms of not rejecting too many legitimate jobs); you could restrict the script interpreter (hairy in terms of not rejecting all malicious jobs); or you could use a behavior-exchange format that can only express those operations that you want to expose to clients. Only the last option can deliver in terms of security and safety, but the price is high because most readily available languages are intended for general purpose use and are therefore too powerful.

USING A DOMAIN-SPECIFIC LANGUAGE

> **NOTE** This section describes techniques that are very powerful but require deeper knowledge and greater skill than is available to beginners. If you do not fully understand how the presented solutions work, you can still keep their features in mind as an inspiration for what is possible.

Pursuing the first two options mentioned at the end of the previous section is specific to the example chosen and leads you to acquire an intimate knowledge of JavaScript. The third option is of more general value. To go down this path, you need to devise a *domain-specific language* (DSL). As Debasish Ghosh discusses in *DSLs in Action* (Manning, 2011), there are two basic forms of such languages:

- *Internal DSL*—Embedded and expressed in the syntax of a host language
- *External DSL*—Stands on its own

Designing an external DSL involves creating its grammar, implementing a corresponding parser in the language from which the DSL will be used, and, typically, also creating some tooling to validate or otherwise automatically process documents in this language. The advantage of an external DSL is that it is not encumbered by the syntactic rules of a host language: it can be designed with complete freedom. Imagine a big data language that describes the stepwise treatment of the input, as follows.

Listing 14.9 External DSL using different syntax than the host language

```
FOREACH Car (_, _, year, price)        ◁──┐  Gives names to the
SELECT year ? 1950 && year < 1960         │  data records' fields
MEDIAN OF price                           │  as needed
REMEMBER AS p

FOREACH Car (make, model, _, price)    ◁───  In the second iteration
SELECT price > p
DISTINCT VALUES OF (make, model)
RETURN AS RESULT
```

Evaluating this script would iterate over the dataset twice: first to find the median price for cars from the 1950s and then to collect all pairs of make and model that cost more than the median. The code shown would be the serialized form of the program; by restricting the allowed commands, you can exercise tight control over what client code can do. The worker node parses such scripts into a syntax tree and either interprets it directly or compiles it into an executable program for the platform it is running on—in the Java example, this would typically mean emitting bytecode that corresponds to the process described in the DSL. The latter is needed only when the DSL includes constructs like loops, conditionals, and recursions that lead to a high volume of interpreted expressions; in this example, interpretation of the given statements would consume a negligibly small amount of CPU cycles compared to the actual computation being carried out over a large dataset.[7]

If complete freedom of expression is not of primary importance, an internal DSL may be a better fit—constructing and maintaining a parser and interpreter for a custom language adds considerable development effort and organizational overhead, not to mention that designing a language that is reasonably self-consistent is a talent not every engineer is gifted with. As an example of an internal stream-processing DSL, consider the Akka Streams library: the user first creates a Graph—an immutable, reusable blueprint for the intended processing topology—and then materializes that to be executed, typically by way of a group of Actors. You can separate these two steps so

---

[7] The only part that would need to be interpreted for each data element is the formula used to select cars by year. Everything else lends itself to being offered as a prepackaged compound operation.

that the `Graph` is created at the client, serialized, submitted to the batch service, and finally deserialized and executed on the worker node. Defining a `Graph` corresponding to the external DSL in listing 14.9 could look like this.

Listing 14.10   Internal DSL

```
RunnableGraph<Future<Long>> p =
  Source.<DataElement>empty()                              ◁————————  Represents the
    .filter(new InRange("year", 1950, 1960))                          real data source
    .toMat(Sink.fold(0L, new Median<Long>("price")),
          Keep.<BoxedUnit, Long>right());

Source.<DataElement>empty()
  .map(new Inject<Long>(p, "p"))                    ⌉  Restricted vocabulary
  .filter(new Filter("price > p"))          ◁———— ⌟  for simple expressions
  .to(Sink.fold(Collections.emptySet(),
              new DistinctValues<Pair<String, String>>("make", "model")));
```

Normally, the `map`, `filter`, and `fold` operations will accept any function literal (lambda expression) that you provide, and syntactically that would be valid here as well. Using arbitrary code would bring you back to the problem of having to transfer the user's bytecode to the batch service, though, which is why this example provides a restricted vocabulary that is guaranteed to be known by the batch service's worker nodes. The operations you offer can be compound ones like the median calculation here: you place this element in a data sink that folds the incoming elements with the provided function, starting at the initial value (`0L`). Behind the scenes, the `Graph` layout is recorded with the objects you provide so that you can inspect the `Graph` in order to serialize it—when you encounter the `Median` object in the position of a folding function, you know you can transfer this behavior to the worker node. The only information you serialize in addition to the operation name is the field name for which the median is to be calculated. You can see a sketch of the necessary class definitions in the source archives.

The same principle applies to the filtering steps, where you may have prepackaged operations like `InRange` that are configured with a field name, a minimal, and a maximal permissible value. You can also combine this approach with an external DSL, as shown in the case of the generic `Filter` operation in listing 14.10; implementing a parser and an interpreter for simple mathematical expressions is not as complex as for a full-featured language and is general enough to be reusable across projects.

The approach shown here works best if the Akka Streams library is present on both ends, which saves you the effort of creating the basic `Graph` DSL infrastructure and the stream-processing engine. You just have to provide the specific operations to be supported. If more flexibility is needed, then the serialization format chosen for these `Graph`s[8] can serve as an external DSL for client implementations that are not based on the JVM or want to use a different code representation for the processing logic.

---

[8] Akka Streams does not offer serialization of `Graph`s at the time of writing (version 1.0).

14.3.3 *The pattern, revisited*

We started from the premise of sending the behavior to the resource in order to save time and network bandwidth in the case of loquacious interchanges between the two. The resource user is only interested in a comparatively small result. Exploring the possibilities, we found several solutions to this problem:

- If the user and the resource are programmed for the same execution environment, you can write the behavior directly in the same language as the user code and send it to the resource. Depending on the choice of execution environment, this can incur considerable incidental complexity—in the case of Java classes, you would, for example, need to identify all required bytecode, transfer it, and load it at the receiving end. Note that the choice will be hard to revert later, because the implied behavior-exchange format is coupled tightly to the runtime environment.
- To overcome the limitations of directly using the host language, you can choose a different language as your behavior-transfer format, picking one that is optimized for being transferred to remote systems and executed there. We looked at JavaScript as an ubiquitous example of this kind that has also been supported directly by the JRE since version 8.
- If security is a concern, then both previous solutions suffer from being too expressive and giving the user too much power. The resource would execute foreign behaviors that can do absolutely anything on its behalf. The best way to secure this process is to restrict what users can express by creating a DSL. This can be external, with full freedom in its design but correspondingly high cost; internal, reusing a host language; or even another internal DSL, as shown with the Akka Streams library.

In the example, a second piece of information needs to be conveyed from the user to the resource: the dataset the batch job will process. This is not a general characteristic of this pattern; the behavior that is sent to the resource may well have the power to select the target of its operations. Such routing information is typically relevant only within the implementation of the resource; in the case of a DSL-based behavior description, it is usually possible to extract the needed selectors from the serialized behavior.

14.3.4 *Applicability*

The Complex Command pattern provides decoupling of user and resource: the resource can be implemented to support only primitive operations, whereas the user can still send complex command sequences to avoid sending large results and requests over the network in the course of a single process. The price is the definition and implementation of a behavior transfer language. This has a high cost in terms of development effort, independent of whether you use the host language and make it fit for network transfer, choose a different language, or create a DSL—particular care is needed to secure the solution against malicious users where required.

The applicability of this pattern is therefore limited by the balance between the value of the achieved decoupling and network bandwidth reduction in the context of the project requirements at hand. If the cost outweighs the benefits, then you need to pick one:

- Provide only primitive operations to make the resource implementation independent of its usage, at the cost of more network round trips.
- Implement compound operations that are needed by the clients within the protocol of the resource, to obviate the need for a flexible behavior-transport mechanism.

The first option values code modularity over network usage, and the second does the reverse.

14.4 The Resource Pool pattern

Hide an elastic pool of resources behind their owner.

So far, we have discussed the modeling and operation of a single resource as well as its interaction with its clients. The astute reader will have noticed that something is missing from the full picture: the core principles of Reactive system design demand replication. Recalling the discussion from chapter 2, you know that resilience cannot be achieved without distributing the solution across all failure axes—software, hardware, human—and you know that elasticity requires the ability to distribute the processing load across a number of resources that are dynamically adjusted to the incoming demand.

In chapter 13, you learned about different ways to replicate a component. The effort put into this mechanism depends greatly on how much the component's state needs to be synchronized between replicas. This pattern focuses on the management and external presentation of the replicas. In keeping with the reasoning presented in chapters 4 and 5, it relies heavily on asynchronous message passing and location transparency to achieve scalability.

14.4.1 The problem setting

The example that readily offers itself is the batch job service you have been building and enhancing in the previous chapters. Although the overall system implements a more complicated resource pool, with sophisticated scheduling of complex commands (batch jobs), the execution component offers a simple, pure example of a resource pool: after the Scheduler component has decided the order in which upcoming jobs will be run, the execution component picks them up and assigns them to worker nodes as they become available—either by finishing their previous work or by being provisioned in response to rising demand.

Instead of investigating the details of how the relationship between the Scheduler component, the execution component, and the worker nodes is represented in code, we will focus on the messaging patterns that arise between these components: in particular, lifecycle events for worker nodes and the execution component. This will illuminate their relationship in a fashion that is more easily applied to other use cases.

14.4.2 Applying the pattern

The part of the batch job service that we are looking at is the logic in the execution component that distributes incoming batch jobs to available worker nodes. The jobs have previously been pulled from the schedule that is published by the Scheduler component. The basic process assumed so far is shown in figure 14.3, using the conventions for diagramming Reactive systems that are established in appendix A.

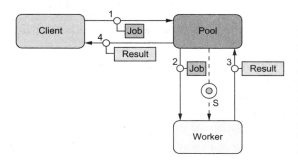

Figure 14.3 The client represents the source of the batch jobs, which is the part of the execution component that has pulled the jobs from the published schedule. The pool is the subcomponent that creates, owns, and supervises the worker nodes. Ignoring the fact that multiple workers may collaborate on one job, the basic flow sends the job to the worker and conveys the result back to the client.

Using this messaging topology, the pool stays in control of all aspects of the workers' lifecycle: it sends the jobs, gets back the results, creates and terminates workers—the pool always knows the current status of a worker node. Creating a new worker typically happens in response to work being available; the process is depicted in figure 14.4.

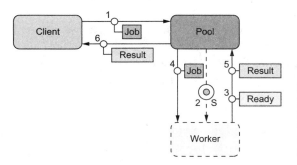

Figure 14.4 Compared to the previous process, you insert steps 2 and 3 to create the worker (using the infrastructure service as discussed for the Resource Encapsulation pattern) and await its readiness.

Although this message flow represents the working principle, it should not be taken too literally: the job that triggers the creation of the new worker node may be handed to a different worker than the one being created, especially if it takes a long time to provision the worker node. The new worker then gets the next job dispatched after it signals readiness to the pool; in this sense, readiness is the same as sending back a result for the implied job of being started up.

During periods of reduced processing load, the pool will notice that worker nodes are idle. Because the pool knows how much work it distributes and which fraction of nodes are idle, it is also in a good position to decide when to shut down a node. The corresponding message flow diagram is shown in figure 14.5.

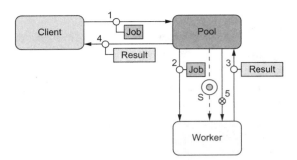

Figure 14.5   **After the worker has finished processing a job, the pool sends the termination signal and refrains from sending further jobs to that worker. There can be a sizable delay between messages 4 and 5 to implement an idle timeout.**

The final aspect of the worker's lifecycle is how to handle failures. The pool should monitor all worker nodes by performing periodic health checks[9] and possibly also asking for progress updates. When a worker fails while processing a job, the pool either sends this failure back to the execution component to be recorded and relayed to the external client or retries the job by giving it to another worker. The recovery process for the failed worker depends on the requirements of the use case. The preferable approach is described in the Let-It-Crash pattern: decommission the worker and all of its resources, and provision a fresh one. When a worker fails while idle, only the recovery process needs to be performed.

The message flows you have seen so far all assume that the worker node receives a job in a single message and replies with a result that again fits in a single message. This covers a broad range of services but nowhere near all of them, notable exceptions being streaming services that provide a response that is *a priori* not bounded, and services where the purpose is the transmission at a given rate so the external client can process the data as they arrive without having to buffer them. Another exception discussed with the Resource Loan pattern is that the external client may reserve a worker and engage in an ongoing conversation with it to perform a complex task.

Accommodating these usage patterns requires a slight reinterpretation of the basic message flow, as shown in figure 14.6. Variants of this flow send all messages between worker and external client (step 5) via the intermediary that represents the client for the pool, or do not signal completion from the worker and instead have the external client convey this signal via the same route taken by the job description. The former allows tighter control over which protocols are permitted between external client and worker, whereas the latter gives the pool more detailed information about when workers are finishing their jobs.

The important notion is that you retain the same processes for the creation and termination of worker nodes by keeping the same basic message-flow structure between pool and worker. The pool initiates the work, and the worker eventually replies with a completion notification.

---

[9] This functionality may be included in the services framework that is being used.

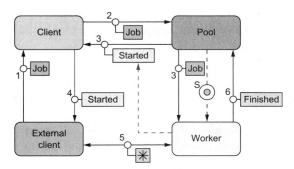

Figure 14.6 In response to the job-request message, the pool will allocate a worker node and inform that node about the work to be done. Concurrently, a message containing the worker's identity is sent to the external client. The order of these two messages is not important, which is why they share sequence number 3 in the figure. The external client can engage directly with the worker until the job is finished; the worker then signals to the pool and thereby becomes eligible for further work.

14.4.3 The pattern, revisited

To recapitulate, we have illuminated the relationship between a resource pool and the individual resources it owns by sketching their primary message flows. A resource pool is free to allocate resources or dynamically adjust their number because it is in full control of the resources, their lifecycle, and their use. How the resources are used depends on the pattern applied by external clients:

- The basic model is that a request is sent to the pool and a resource is allocated for the duration of this request only.
- To transfer a large volume of data or messages in the course of processing a single request, the resource can be loaned to the external client for direct exclusive access. All aspects of the Resource Loan pattern apply, including the possibility to employ proxies to enforce usage limitations.
- If the purpose of a loquacious exchange is only the extraction of a relatively small result value, the Complex Command pattern can be used to avoid the overhead of loaning the resource to the external client.

Another consideration is that the basic message flow we discussed involves a full round trip between resource and pool to signal the completion of a request and obtain the next one. This is the most precise, predictable model, and it makes sense where the time to process a request is much larger than the network round-trip time. Under different circumstances, it will be beneficial to use a buffering strategy, where the pool keeps multiple requests in flight toward a single resource and the resource processes them one by one. The results that the resource sends back allow the pool to keep track of how many requests are currently outstanding and limit that number.

A drawback of the queuing solution is that sending a request to a resource that is not currently free means processing may be deferred unpredictably. An SLA violation for one request then has a negative impact on some of the following requests as well. Queueing also means that, in case of a failure, multiple requests may need to be dispatched to be retried (if appropriate).

In the introduction to this pattern, we cited elasticity as well as resilience as motivations for replicating a resource; so far we have only considered the former. The latter is more troublesome due to the ownership and supervision relationship between the pool and its resources: if the pool fails, then the resources are orphaned. There are two ways to deal with this: you can replicate the pool, including its resources—running complete setups in different data centers, for example; or you can replicate only the pool manager and transfer ownership of resources in order to realize a failover between them. Ownership transfer can only be initiated by the current owner if it is still functioning; otherwise, each resource must monitor the pool it belongs to[10] and offer itself to a new owner upon receiving a failure notification for its parent.[11] To replicate the pool manager, any of the replication schemes discussed in the previous chapter can be used, chosen according to the requirements of the use case at hand.

14.4.4 *Implementation considerations*

This pattern may be implemented by the services framework: deployment of a resource includes replication factors or performance metrics for dynamic scaling, and looking up that resource results in a resource pool proxy that is interposed between client and resource implicitly. This works without central coordination of the pool proxies generated at the lookup site if the resource either is stateless (just offers computation functions) or uses multiple-master replication. In these cases, there can be one proxy per dependent service instance, removing any single point of failure. A potential difficulty with this is that it assumes the resources handle incoming requests from multiple sources. This can be challenging in the context of applying the Resource Loan pattern or the Complex Command pattern, because requests may be delayed in a less controlled fashion than if a central authority distributes them.

14.5 *Patterns for managed blocking*

Blocking a resource requires consideration and ownership.

In the example code for how the execution component in the batch job service provisions new worker nodes, you have already encountered the situation that an API you are using is designed to block its calling thread. In the case of the AWS API, there are ways around that, but this is not always the case. Many libraries or frameworks that you may want to or have to use do not offer the option of event-driven interaction. Java Database Connectivity (JDBC)[12] is a well-known example that comes to mind. In order to use these APIs in a Reactive system component, you need to take special care to properly manage the resources that are implicitly seized, most notably the threads required for their execution.

---

[10] This should typically be implemented by the services framework in a generic fashion.

[11] Readers fluent in Akka will notice that reparenting is not supported for Actors, but we are talking about a pool of resource components in general and not Actors that encapsulate resources. The service abstraction we are referring to here is a higher-level construct than the Actor model.

[12] Java Database Connectivity (http://docs.oracle.com/javase/8/docs/technotes/guides/jdbc), part of the Java platform, is a generic access layer for relational databases by which applications are decoupled from the specific database implementation that is used. It is a standard mechanism to provide data sources through dependency injection in application containers, usually driven by external deployment configuration files.

14.5.1 The problem setting

Consider a component that manages knowledge in a fashion that translates well into a relational database model—this may be a booking ledger, user and group management, the classic pet shop, and so on. In the batch service example, this may occur in the authentication and authorization service that the Client Interface component uses to decide whether a given request is legitimate. You could write this component from scratch, modeling every domain object as a persistent actor, or you can reuse the enormous power that is conveniently available through off-the-shelf database management systems. In the absence of good reasons to the contrary, it is preferable to reuse existing working solutions, so you will use a JDBC driver in your implementation based on Java and Akka actors.

The problem you are facing is that executing a database query may take an arbitrary amount of time: the database may be overloaded or failing, the query may not be fully optimized due to a lack of indices, or it might be a very complex query over a large dataset to begin with. If you execute a slow query in an Actor that runs on a shared thread pool, that thread will effectively be unavailable to the pool—and thereby to all other actors—until the result set has been communicated back. Other actors on the same thread pool may have scheduled timers that may be processed only with a large delay unless enough other threads are available. The bigger the thread pool, the more such blocking actions it can tolerate at the same time; but threads are a finite resource on the JVM, and that translates into a limited tolerance for such blockers.

14.5.2 Applying the pattern

The source of the problem is that a shared resource—the thread pool—is being used in a fashion that is violating the cooperative contract of the group of users. Actors are expected to process messages quickly and then give other actors a chance to run: this is the basis for their efficient thread-sharing mechanism. Making a resource unavailable to others by seizing it means the Actor that blocks the thread claims exclusive ownership, at least for the duration of the database query in this example. You have seen for the Resource Loan pattern that the owner can grant exclusive access to another component, but that must always happen explicitly: you must ask the owner for permission.

A thread pool usually does not have a mechanism for signaling that a given thread is being blocked exclusively for the currently running task.[13] If you cannot ask the owner of a shared thread for permission, the logical conclusion is that you need to own a thread on which you can run the database query. This can be done by creating a private thread pool that is managed by the actor: now you can submit the blocking JDBC calls as tasks to this pool.

---

[13] An exception is the `ForkJoinPool`, which can be informed using `ForkJoinPool.managedBlock()` (see https://docs.oracle.com/javase/8/docs/api/java/util/concurrent/ForkJoinPool.ManagedBlocker.html). But in this case, management of the additionally created threads is also limited.

Listing 14.11 Maintaining a private ExecutorService

```java
public enum AccessRights {
  READ_JOB_STATUS, SUBMIT_JOB;
  public static final AccessRights[] EMPTY = new AccessRights[] {};
}

public class CheckAccess {
  public final String username;
  public final String credentials;
  public final AccessRights[] rights;
  public final ActorRef replyTo;

  public CheckAccess(String username, String credentials,
                     AccessRights[] rights, ActorRef replyTo) {
    this.username = username;
    this.credentials = credentials;
    this.rights = rights;
    this.replyTo = replyTo;
  }
}

public class CheckAccessResult {
  public final String username;
  public final String credentials;
  public final AccessRights[] rights;

  public CheckAccessResult(CheckAccess ca, AccessRights[] rights) {
    this.username = ca.username;
    this.credentials = ca.credentials;
    this.rights = rights;
  }
}

public class AccessService extends AbstractActor {
  private ExecutorService pool;

  public AccessService(DataSource db, int poolSize, int queueSize) {
    pool = new ThreadPoolExecutor(0, poolSize, 60, SECONDS,
                                  new LinkedBlockingDeque<>(queueSize));

    final ActorRef self = self();
    receive(ReceiveBuilder
      .match(CheckAccess.class, ca -> {
          try {
            pool.execute(() -> checkAccess(db, ca, self));
          } catch (RejectedExecutionException e) {
            ca.replyTo.tell(new CheckAccessResult(ca, AccessRights.EMPTY),
                            self);
          }
        })
      .build());
  }

  @Override
  public void postStop() {
    pool.shutdownNow();
  }
```

```
private static void checkAccess(DataSource db, CheckAccess ca, ActorRef self) {
   try (Connection conn = db.getConnection()) {
      final Statement stmt = conn.createStatement();
      final ResultSet result = stmt.executeQuery("<get access rights>");
      final List<AccessRights> rights = new LinkedList<>();
      while (result.next()) {
         rights.add(AccessRights.valueOf(result.getString(0)));
      }
      final AccessRights[] ar = rights.toArray(AccessRights.EMPTY);
      ca.replyTo.tell(new CheckAccessResult(ca, ar), self);
   } catch (Exception e) {
      ca.replyTo.tell(new CheckAccessResult(ca, AccessRights.EMPTY), self);
   }
}                        ◁──┐
}                            │ The Connection is implicitly closed
}                            │ here as part of the try statement.
```

One peculiarity of JDBC connections is that in order to fully utilize the computation power of a database server, you typically need to create multiple connections so the server can work on several queries in parallel. For this reason, you create a thread pool of the desired `poolSize`—one thread per database connection—and submit tasks to it as they come in without keeping track of the number of running queries. When the incoming load increases, there will be a point at which all threads in the pool are constantly active; because the number of threads equals the number of database connections, all of those will be active as well. At this point, new requests will start queuing up. In this example, you do not manage this queue explicitly in the actor but instead configure the thread pool with a queue of limited capacity. Tasks that cannot be executed right away because all threads are busy will be held in this queue until threads finish their current work and ask for more. If a task is submitted while the queue is full, its execution will be rejected; you use this mechanism to implement the bounded queuing behavior that is necessary to fulfill the responsiveness of Reactive components, as discussed in chapter 2.

Because the required bounded queue is already implemented by the thread pool, you are free in this example to send the response back to the client directly from the database query task: no interaction with the `AccessService` is needed on the way back. If you need to keep this actor in the loop, you will send the database result to the actor and have it send the final response to the original client. A reason for doing this might be that you need to explicitly manage the internal request queue—for prioritization, ability to cancel, or some such—or that the database result is only one of several inputs that are needed to compose the final response. Having the queries as well as responses go through the actor in general allow it to comprehensively manage all aspects of this process: the only way to manage a unit effectively is to have exactly one person responsible and keep that person fully informed.

14.5.3 *The pattern, revisited*

In the example, you have performed multiple steps:

1   You noticed that the use case required a resource that was not immediately obvious. Resources are often represented by objects in the programming language that are explicitly passed around or configured, but there are implicit resources that are always assumed and rarely considered explicitly—like threads or working memory—because they are usually shared such that the system works well in most scenarios, by convention. Whenever you run into one of the corner cases, you will need to make these resources explicit in your system design.

2   Having recognized the resources that you need to perform a certain function, you modeled them explicitly: in the example, these are the thread pool and the database connection pool. The thread pool is configured with a given number of threads and a maximal submission queue length in order to place an upper bound on the amount of auxiliary resources that are used by it. The same goes for the database connection pool, whose configuration we left out of the example code.

3   In keeping with resource encapsulation, you placed the management of these resources in one component, represented by an actor. The lifecycle of the resources is contained within the lifecycle of the actor. The thread pool is created when starting and shut down when stopping. The database connections are managed individually on a per-request basis, taking care to obtain them such that they are released independently of how the processing ends. This is inspired by Let-It-Crash thinking in that shutting down the thread pool will release all associated resources, including the currently used database connections.

4   The last step implements the Simple Component pattern, in that the responsibility of the component you are developing is to provide authorization information for users based on their credentials. Toward this end, you need resources and the logic that uses them, all bundled up in one component that does only its job but does it in full.

Although many APIs are widely employed that make implicit use of hidden resources like the calling thread, you will see this pattern used to manage the blocking of threads: hence, the name. The term *managed blocking* first became known to us when it was used in the ForkJoinPool developed for Java 7, although it was mentioned in the .NET ecosystem several years earlier. ForkJoinPool is not intended as a generic executor but rather as a targeted tool to help the parallelization of tasks that operate on large collections of data, splitting up work among the available CPUs and joining the partial results together. Managed blocking support is needed to keep the CPUs busy while certain threads are stalled, waiting for I/O (from network or disk). Therefore, entering a managed-blocking section will, roughly speaking, spawn a new worker thread that continues the number crunching while the current thread becomes temporarily inactive.

You can generalize this pattern such that it is more widely applicable by considering any kind of resource that needs to be blocked as well as allowing for tailored management strategies of the blocked resource. An example could be the explicit management of a segregated memory region that is split off from the main application heap in order to both place an upper bound on its size and explicitly control the access to this resource—using normal heap memory is unconstrained for all components in the same process and means one misbehaving party can hamper the function of all of them. Another angle is that managed blocking is similar to the Resource Loan pattern in the case of resources that are already encapsulated as Reactive components.

14.5.4 Applicability

The first step of this pattern—investigating the use of hidden resources in ways that violate their sharing contract—should always be applied. Failure to recognize such a case will lead to scalability issues or application failures through resource exhaustion (such as `OutOfMemoryError`), as we have frequently encountered in consulting engagements.

On the other hand, it is important not to get carried away and claim exclusive ownership of resources at a too fine-grained level or in cases that could live with having only shared access. This is particularly visible in the case of thread pools: the actor model is successful in utilizing the machine's resources due to sharing the core pieces—CPUs and memory—in an event-driven activation scheme. Giving one thread to each actor would seem to give each of them exclusive access to a computing resource; but not only does this incur orders of magnitude more overhead per actor, but it also leads to significant contention on the underlying CPUs, with all threads fighting for their chance to run.

Recognizing the use of resources is as important as learning to qualify the cases in which exclusion is needed and where sharing is appropriate—and under which rules. Unfortunately, there is no simple rule to decide this.

14.6 Summary

This chapter was devoted entirely to the modeling and management of resources. Just as that term is generic, the patterns described also apply flexibly in a wide range of cases:

- Each resource should be owned by one component that is fully responsible for its lifecycle. Ownership is exclusive—there can be only one owner—but resources may be used by a wide variety of clients inside or outside the Reactive system you are building, sometimes needing more direct access than is possible by always having the owner as an intermediary.
- The Resource Loan pattern helps by bringing the resource as close to its client as possible. It allows the distance to be reduced to only one asynchronous message-passing boundary for the purpose of transient exclusive access, in order to perform a complex operation.

- The Complex Command pattern turns this around by packaging the client's part of a loquacious exchange such that it can be sent to the resource, like sending an ambassador to a foreign country.

- The Resource Pool pattern tackles the concern of implementing elasticity and resilience by hiding the individually owned resources behind their manager. The resulting increase in distance between clients and resources can be mitigated by combining this pattern with the previous two.

- We considered resource use in the implementation of components, especially those that use libraries and frameworks that implicitly utilize resources that are otherwise shared in Reactive systems, and looked at an example of managing the blocking of threads in an otherwise event-driven system.

Message flow patterns

15

In this chapter, we will explore some of the most basic patterns of communication that occur between Reactive components: specifically, we will talk about how messages flow between them. We discussed the theoretical background in chapter 10, noting that the design of communication paths within a system is crucial to its success—the same holds for real-world organizations as well as Reactive applications.

Most of the patterns we will encounter are extremely generic, starting with the Request–Response pattern. They can be applied in a variety of cases and come in many forms. The examples are therefore less specific than in other chapters, but we will use the front-end façade of a larger service as a problem setting. You can think of this as a more detailed look at the client interface component of the batch job service, our running example. The particular patterns we will cover are as follows:

- The Request–Response pattern
- The Self-Contained Message pattern
- The Ask pattern
- The Forward Flow pattern
- The Aggregator pattern
- The Saga pattern
- The Business Handshake pattern

15.1 The Request–Response pattern

Include a return address in the message to receive a response.

This is the most basic interaction pattern we know; it is the foundational building block for all natural communication, deeply ingrained in human training. A parent will say something to their infant child, who will initially gesture or make some sounds in response; later, the child will articulate words and sentences.

Request–response is the way you learn how to speak, and it underlies all sophisticated forms of communication that you develop later. Although the response can be non-verbal (in particular, facial expressions, but also the deliberate absence thereof), in most cases you require a response before successfully concluding a conversation. The response can be a piece of information that you asked for or an acknowledgment of receipt for a command that was given.

In all these cases, there is one commonality that you need to make explicit when translating this basic means of communication into a programming pattern: the process begins with two participants A and B, where A knows how to address B; when receiving requests, B will need to learn or deduce how to address A in order to send back a response. Captured in a diagram, this looks like figure 15.1.

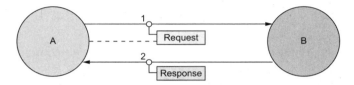

Figure 15.1 Process A sends a message to process B, including its own address (as symbolized by the dashed line), so that in step 2, the response can be conveyed in the opposite direction.

In real life, the inclusion of the sender address is implicit: when someone starts talking to you, you turn your head in the direction of the sound to identify its source, which provides all the information you need in order to respond. This scheme has intuitively been built into numerous commonly used computer protocols, a selection of which we will explore in this section.

15.1.1 The problem setting

Consider two components A and B, where A knows the address of B but not vice versa. This is the prototypical initial condition of a client–server setup, where the client is required to take the first step—the server cannot know which clients require its services at any given time. In the running example, you might be looking at the client interface component of the batch job service: in particular, the relationship between an external client and an entry point into the service. The client submits a request to initiate an action (such as starting a batch job), query for information (like a list of all currently running jobs), or both. The service will carry out the desired action or retrieve the requested information and then reply.

The task: Your mission is to implement a request–response exchange between two processes over a User Datagram Protocol (UDP)[1] network (or any other datagram-oriented transport mechanism of your choosing).

---

[1] Whereas TCP transports streams of bytes (also called *octets*) across the network, leaving the encoding of messages to the layers above it, UDP transports delimited datagrams of up to a maximum size of about 64 KB; see also https://en.wikipedia.org/wiki/User_Datagram_Protocol.

15.1.2 Applying the pattern

We will start with process B (called `Server`), which will receive a request and send back a response. The procedure is defined by the operating system and therefore follows roughly the same path in most programming languages: a socket needs to be opened and bound to a UDP port; then, a datagram needs to be received from this socket; and finally, a datagram needs to be sent via this socket. This basic process is shown in Java in the following listing.

Listing 15.1 Server responding to the address that originated the request

```java
public class Server {
  static public final int SERVER_PORT = 8888;

  static public void main(String[] args) throws IOException {

    try (final DatagramSocket socket =                         Binds a socket for
            new DatagramSocket(SERVER_PORT)) {                  receiving packets

      final byte[] buffer = new byte[1500];
      final DatagramPacket packet1 =
          new DatagramPacket(buffer, buffer.length);
      socket.receive(packet1);                    ⟵── Receives one packet

      final SocketAddress sender = packet1.getSocketAddress();  ⟵
      System.out.println("server: received " +                      Extracts
                    new String(packet1.getData()));                 the return
      System.out.println("server: sender was " + sender);           address

      final byte[] response = "got it!".getBytes();
      final DatagramPacket packet2 =
          new DatagramPacket(response, response.length, sender);
      socket.send(packet2);                      ⟵── Sends a response
    }
  }
}
```

If you run this program, nothing will happen—the process will patiently wait at the `socket.receive()` call for a UDP packet to arrive. In order to send this packet, you need to write the mirror image of this process, `Client` (process A), which will first send a packet and then receive one.

Listing 15.2 Client sending a request and then blocking until the server responds

```java
public class Client {
  static public void main(String[] args) throws IOException {
    try (final DatagramSocket socket = new DatagramSocket()) {  ⟵   Gets a local
                                                                     socket with a
      final byte[] request = "hello".getBytes();                     random port
      final SocketAddress serverAddress =
          new InetSocketAddress("localhost", Server.SERVER_PORT);
      final DatagramPacket packet1 =
          new DatagramPacket(request, request.length, serverAddress);
      socket.send(packet1);                   ⟵┐  Sends a message
                                                 │  to the server
```

```
        final byte[] buffer = new byte[1500];
        final DatagramPacket packet2 =
            new DatagramPacket(buffer, buffer.length);
        socket.receive(packet2);                    ⟵── Waits to receive one packet

        final SocketAddress sender = packet2.getSocketAddress();
        System.out.println("client: received " +
                            new String(packet2.getData()));
        System.out.println("client: sender was " + sender);
    }
  }
}
```

Running this process sets the exchange in motion. You will see that the server receives a packet:

```
server: received hello
server: sender was /127.0.0.1:55589
```

And the client receives a packet as well:

```
client: received got it!
client: sender was /127.0.0.1:8888
```

Why does this work? The crucial piece to this message exchange is that a UDP packet traveling over a network carries not only the IP address and port of its intended receiver, but also the IP address and port of the socket it was sent from. This "return address" is extracted in the server's code using the getSocketAddress() method of DatagramPacket. After logging the information to the console, you inject it into the second packet in order to describe its intended destination—you copy the return address from the received request letter onto the envelope of the response letter.

The other crucial precondition for success is that the client knows beforehand how to reach the server. Although this is intuitive and barely feels worthy of mention, it is essential. In summary:

- The client sends the request in a UDP datagram to the server using an already-known destination address.
- The server sends the response in a UDP datagram to the client using the address information contained in the previously received request datagram.

15.1.3 *Common instances of the pattern*

The Request–Response pattern may be built into a protocol. The client sends a request, and it is assumed that a response will be returned to the same client. The pattern then can be used to provide the illusion of synchronous behavior: a function makes a call and returns the result to the caller. Believing the illusion is at your peril, because there is no guarantee that the response will ever arrive. Alternatively, the pattern may be implemented using two explicit asynchronous messages.

HTTP

The most commonly—in fact, ubiquitously—used implementation of the request-response pattern is HTTP, which has the pattern built in. This protocol builds on a stream transport layer that conveys requests as streams of bytes from client to server and responses in the opposite direction; this transport layer is almost exclusively provided in the form of TCP over IPv4 or IPv6 at the time of writing, with the option of adding encryption by sandwiching Transport Layer Security (TLS)[2] between HTTP and TCP.

An HTTP connection is established from the client to the server, and these roles also determine the roles within the conversation: the client sends requests and the server sends responses, exactly one for each request. This model is popular because it fits the majority of use cases: the client wants the server to do something. In the example problem setting, you might formulate the following request:

```
GET /request?msg=hello HTTP/1.1
Host: client-interface.our.application.domain
Accept: application/json
```

The server might then respond with a message like this (the uninteresting part is replaced with an ellipsis):

```
HTTP/1.1 200 OK
...
Content-Type: application/json
Content-Length: 22

{"response":"got it!"}
```

There is a wealth of literature about how to structure the contents of these requests and responses, with representational state transfer (REST)[3] resource representation being a popular pattern, but we are currently more interested in how HTTP implements the Request–Response pattern. While applying the pattern to a simple UDP exchange, you have seen that the client's address needs to be conveyed to the server in order to allow the response to be communicated. This is easy because UDP already caters to this need: the sending port's address is included in the network packet by which the datagram travels over the network. TCP also includes the sender as well as the receiver address in all network packets that make up a connection. This allows it to transport bytes not only from client to server but also in the opposite direction, and that is exactly how the HTTP response is sent back to the HTTP client.

ACTORS

In the Actor model, the only defined means of communication is by way of sending single messages: no connections, responses, or similar are defined. Using the Akka

---

[2] The successor to the Secure Socket Layer (SSL) that was the first widely used encryption layer on top of TCP until its deprecation in 2015 (see https://tools.ietf.org/html/rfc7568).

[3] See also https://en.wikipedia.org/wiki/Representational_state_transfer.

implementation of this model, you might solve the task posed initially in the following fashion.

Listing 15.3 Untyped Akka Actors modeling request–response

```
object RequestResponseActors {

  case class Request(msg: String)
  case class Response(msg: String)

  class Responder extends Actor {
    def receive = {
      case Request(msg) =>
        println(s"got request: $msg")
        sender() ! Response("got it!")
    }
  }

  class Requester(responder: ActorRef) extends Actor {
    responder ! Request("hello")

    def receive = {
      case Response(msg) =>
        println(s"got response: $msg")
        context.system.terminate()
    }
  }
  def main(args: Array[String]): Unit = {
    val sys = ActorSystem("ReqRes")
    val responder = sys.actorOf(Props[Responder], "responder")
    val requester = sys.actorOf(Props(new Requester(responder)), "requester")
  }

}
```

You first define the message types for the request and the response, and you formulate a Responder actor that, given a request, replies with a response, printing a message to the console so you can see that something happens. Then you define a second actor—Requester—that is instantiated with the ActorRef of a responder. This requester actor first sends a request and then reacts to the reception of a response by printing a message to the console and shutting down the entire process. The main program starts up first a responder and then an associated requester. When you run this program, you will see the expected output:

```
got request: hello
got response: got it!
```

This formulation of the Request–Response pattern is enabled by an Akka-specific feature: when sending the request message, the requester's own ActorRef is implicitly picked up by the ! (tell) operator, and the Request message is placed in an Akka-internal envelope that also carries this sender ActorRef. This is how the sender() method can access the return address within the Responder actor to send back the response. The envelopes used behind the scenes are an implementation detail that has been introduced specifically because request–response is such a widely used communication pattern.

Looking at the Akka Typed module—which was introduced about six years after the initial untyped Actor implementation—you can see that the `sender()` feature is no longer present. The reasons behind this change are manifold, and a full discussion is out of scope for this book, but the main reason can be summarized by saying that it was proven infeasible to maintain this feature while also providing fully type-checked Actor messaging.

Without the `sender()` feature, the return address needs to be explicitly included in the message that is sent. As an illustration, the following listing describes the same Actor program as listing 15.3, but with fully typed Actors and `ActorRefs`.

Listing 15.4 Including the response explicitly in the request message

```
object RequestResponseTypedActors {

  case class Request(msg: String, replyTo: ActorRef[Response])
  case class Response(msg: String)

  val responder: Behavior[Request] =
    Static {
      case Request(msg, replyTo) =>
        println(s"got request: $msg")
        replyTo ! Response("got it!")
    }

  def requester(responder: ActorRef[Request]): Behavior[Response] =
    SelfAware { self =>
      responder ! Request("hello", self)
      Total {
        case Response(msg) =>
          println(s"got response: $msg")
          Stopped
      }
    }

  def main(args: Array[String]): Unit = {
    ActorSystem("ReqResTyped", Props(ContextAware[Unit] { ctx =>
      val res = ctx.spawn(Props(responder), "responder")
      val req = ctx.watch(ctx.spawn(Props(requester(res)), "requester"))
      Full {
        case Sig(ctx, Terminated(`req`)) => Stopped
      }
    }))
  }
}
```

You start again with the definition of the two message types, this time including the return address as the `replyTo` field in the request. Also note that you do not need to include a return address in the `Response` message type, because the client already knows how to contact the server if it needs to do so again—unconditionally capturing a return address is a waste of effort.

The Responder actor is described by way of its behavior, which is to react to the receipt of requests by logging them and sending a response; this is a static actor that does not change its behavior. The Requester actor needs to be instantiated with the ActorRef of a responder—now precisely typed, in contrast to the untyped actor example, where any message was permissible—and the first thing it does after being started is send a request. The return address must be extracted from the context in which the behavior is executed, and that is done using the SelfAware behavior decorator. In good object-oriented tradition,[4] you call the actor's ActorRef self and use it when constructing the Request to be sent to the responder. Afterward, the requester begins a behavior in which it reacts to the reception of a Response message by logging it and terminating itself.

The main program consists only of creating an ActorSystem whose guardianActor creates first a responder and then an associated requester. The latter's lifecycle is monitored using the watch command; when termination is signaled, the entire system shuts down.

AMQP

In the previous examples, the Request–Response pattern is supported at least to some degree directly within the communication mechanism. Advanced Message Queueing Protocol (AMQP)[5] can serve as an example of a message transport that does not natively support this pattern: messages are conveyed by being placed in queues, and neither the sender nor the recipient has an address of their own. The recipient is just the one that pulls messages out of a given queue. This means in order to send back a response, the original sender also needs to have a queue on which it can receive messages. Once that is established, you can apply the Request–Response pattern by including the address of this queue in the request message. The response will then be delivered to this queue, from which the requester can retrieve it.

Examples of how to perform such a request–response exchange are part of the RabbitMQ tutorials;[6] we show the JavaScript version here due to its conciseness. It begins again with the responder, which reacts to requests by logging them and sending back a response.

> **Listing 15.5   Request–response based on a one-way messaging protocol**

```
var amqp = require('amqplib/callback_api');

amqp.connect('amqp://localhost', function(err, conn) {
  conn.createChannel(function(err, ch) {
    var q = 'rpc_queue';
```

---

[4] Referring to the Smalltalk language created by Alan Kay et al., father of object orientation.
[5] See also https://www.amqp.org.
[6] In particular, rpc_server.js and rpc_client.js in the directory http://mng.bz/m8Oh.

```
        ch.assertQueue(q, {durable: false});
        ch.prefetch(1);
        ch.consume(q, function reply(msg) {
          console.log("got request: %s", msg.content.toString());
          ch.sendToQueue(msg.properties.replyTo,
            new Buffer('got it!'),
            {correlationId: msg.properties.correlationId});

          ch.ack(msg);
        });
      });
    });
```

The responder first establishes a connection with the local AMQP message broker, and then it creates a channel named rpc_queue and installs a message handler that will send back responses. One new aspect in comparison to the previous implementations is that the queues used for communication may not be used exclusively by a single requester and responder. Therefore, each request comes with a correlation ID that is carried over to the associated response. You can see how this is used by looking at the requester's implementation, shown next.

Listing 15.6 Listening for a response with the same correlation ID as the original request

```
var uuid = require('node-uuid');

amqp.connect('amqp://localhost', function(err, conn) {
  conn.createChannel(function(err, ch) {
    ch.assertQueue('responses', {}, function(err, q) {
      var corr = uuid.v1();

      ch.consume(q.queue, function(msg) {
        if (msg.properties.correlationId == corr) {
          console.log('got response: %s', msg.content.toString());
          setTimeout(function() { conn.close(); process.exit(0) }, 500);
        }
      }, {noAck: true});

      ch.sendToQueue('rpc_queue',
        new Buffer('hello'),
        { correlationId: corr, replyTo: q.queue });
    });
  });
});
```

The requester uses a queue named responses from which it expects to receive the reply. It installs a message handler that first verifies the correlation ID and, if it matches, logs the response and terminates. Once the handler is in place, the request is sent to rpc_queue.

15.1.4 *The pattern, revisited*

The Request–Response pattern is deeply ingrained in human nature, and it is also natively supported by many popular network protocols and higher-level message-transport mechanisms. Therefore, it is easy to miss the two important properties that make it work:

- The requester sends the request to the responder using an already-known destination address.
- The responder sends the response to the requester using the address information contained in the corresponding request.

The basis on which this pattern is founded is that addressing information can be conveyed in a location-transparent fashion: the requester's address is still valid and usable after being transported to the responder. You will think about this most often when you are trying to figure out why a particular response was not delivered to the requester.

Another consideration that will frequently come up when using this pattern is that between long-lived participants, requests and responses need to be matched up reliably: the requester must be able to correlate a received response with the corresponding request. Although this is in some cases implicit by virtue of using a dedicated communication channel (such as HTTP), it is crucial when both participants are addressable on their own, as seen in the AMQP example in listings 15.5 and 15.6. Including a unique identifier like a universally unique identifier (UUID)[7] achieves this and also allows the request to be resent without risking a duplication of its effects: the recipient can use the UUID to determine whether it has already performed the requested action if it keeps track of these identifiers.

15.1.5 *Applicability*

This pattern is applied ubiquitously, and rightfully so—for most requests you formulate, a response is needed in order to conclude that the request has been received or acted on. There are a few things to keep in mind, though:

- As in real life, computers need to be able to give up on waiting for a response after some time; otherwise, a communication error can bring the application to a halt. Thus, you need to consider a timeout duration appropriate for each such exchange.
- When the target component is unavailable—overloaded, failed, or otherwise— you should back off and give it some time to recover. Fortunately, request-response is precisely what `CircuitBreakers` need in order to fulfill their function; see chapter 12.
- When receiving the response, you need to remember the context of the corresponding request so that you can resume and complete the overall process that called for the request–response cycle. We will discuss this aspect further in the following patterns.

---

[7] See also RFC 4122 (https://tools.ietf.org/html/rfc4122).

15.2 The Self-Contained Message pattern

Each message will contain all information needed to process a request as well as to understand its response.

We touched on this at the end of the previous section: when sending a request, you need to remember what you want to do with the response that will eventually come back. In other words, you need to manage the state of the larger operation that this exchange is a part of while the request and response travel between components. This state management can be done entirely by the requester—storing contextual information—or it can be pushed out of it by having the entire context travel with the request and response across the network. In practice, this responsibility is usually shared, leaving part of the state in the requester and having part of it travel with the message. The point of this pattern is that you should strive to include sufficient information in the message so the state that is relevant to the current request is fully represented—removing and relocating relevant information should be considered a premature optimization until proven otherwise.

15.2.1 The problem setting

Imagine a service that acts as an email gateway, providing other components of the system with the functionality of sending email notifications to customers. A protocol is defined for transporting email across computer networks: the Simple Mail Transfer Protocol (SMTP).[8] This is one of the oldest protocols used on the internet, built on top of TCP and designed to be human readable. An example session for sending an email from Alice to Bob might look like this (with C being the client and S being the server):

```
S: 220 mailhost.example.com ESMTP Postfix
C: HELO alice-workstation.example.com
S: 250 Hello alice-workstation.example.com
C: MAIL FROM:<alice@example.com>
S: 250 Ok
C: RCPT TO:<bob@example.com>
S: 250 Ok
C: DATA
S: 354 End data with <CR><LF>.<CR><LF>
C: From: "Alice" <alice@example.com>
C: To: "Bob" <bob@example.com>
C: Date: Fri, 23 October 2015 10:34:12 +0200
C: Subject: lunch
C:
C: Hi Bob,
C:
C: sorry, I cannot make it, something else came up.
C:
C: Regards, Alice
C: .
```

---

[8] See also https://en.wikipedia.org/wiki/Simple_Mail_Transfer_Protocol.

```
S: 250 Ok, queued as 4567876345
C: QUIT
S: 221 Bye
```

In the course of this session, 13 messages are exchanged between client and server, with both sides tracking the progressing state of the session.

The task: Your mission is to sketch the data types and protocol sequence for transmitting an email to the email gateway service such that the client receives an acceptance confirmation from the service and the session state between client and service is minimized.

15.2.2 *Applying the pattern*

You need to transmit information both ways between client and server, and the minimal protocol shape for such an interaction is the Request–Response pattern discussed previously. The information you need to send to the service is as follows:

- Sender email address
- Recipient(s) email address(es)
- Email body
- Correlation ID so the client can recognize a subsequent confirmation

The service will then reply with, at the very least, a status code and the correlation ID. The following listing sketches the request and response data types using the Scala language, due to its convenient case class feature.

Listing 15.7 Encapsulated information needed for multiple SMTP exchanges

```
case class SendEmail(sender: String, recipients: List[String],
                    body: String, correlationID: UUID,
                    replyTo: ActorRef[SendEmailResult])

case class SendEmailResult(correlationID: UUID, status: StatusCode,
                          explanation: Option[String])
```

The inclusion of the email addresses of sender and recipients would probably be represented using a more specific class than a plain String that ensures a valid address syntax, but we leave out such details in order to concentrate on the data exchange.

Does this protocol fulfill the requirements? The client transmits all information the service needs in a single message: the sequence of protocol steps performed by SMTP is collapsed into a single request–response cycle. This enables the email gateway service to begin the further processing of the email immediately after having received the single request message. This means the gateway does not need to maintain any session state pertaining to this exchange beyond the processing of this single message; it only needs to send the response, and the session is completed. Depending on the reliability guarantees the gateway provides, the response may have to be deferred until the intention of sending an email has been recorded in persistent storage—or even until after the email has been relayed to the target mail system—in which case, the return address and correlation ID must be retained until finished. But this extension of the session lifetime is not dictated by the protocol; it is inherent in those stronger guarantees. From the client's perspective, this approach also achieves all that is needed: sending the email takes just one message, and the client then retains the correlation ID in order to continue its own processing as soon as the email has been sent.

If this simple approach fulfills all of your requirements, a question presents itself: why is the SMTP exchange so much more complex? Back in the 1970s, it took a very long time to send data across a network connection; the protocol therefore performs the exchange in many small steps, allowing the server to reject an email as early as needed (for example, after the sender or recipient address has been transmitted—the latter is done in case the target address does not exist). Today, sending a few kilobytes of text between continents is not a concern, but you still may want to avoid sending a very large email body—possibly including large file attachments—in a single request message. The reason might be so you could handle rejection without sending a potentially large number of useless bytes, but it is also important to consider resource usage in terms of how much bandwidth is taken up during the process. Receiving a large message at its own pace is the recipient's prerogative, and the line-based exclusive TCP connection handling used for SMTP allows this to be done naturally.

You do not need to change the shape of the protocol beyond request–response, though, in order to give the recipient some control over whether and how to consume the email body. The only feature required is that the bulk data transfer happens out of band: for example, if the framework supports sending parts of the message as on-demand streams.

Listing 15.8   Separating the body so it can be delivered on demand

```
case class SendEmail(sender: String, recipients: List[String],
                     correlationID: UUID, replyTo: ActorRef[SendEmailResult])
                    (body: Source[String]) extends StreamedRequest {
  override def payload = body
}
```

This sketch hints at a hypothetical microservice framework that would handle the streaming of the designated message parts transparently, serializing only the data elements in the first argument list (up to `replyTo`) eagerly in the request message and transferring the payload data on demand. Another way to achieve this is to include in the message the location (for example, by way of a URL such as http://example .com/emails/12) where the email body can be obtained; then, the gateway service can contact that location on its own if and when it needs to.

Listing 15.9   Enabling the body to be pulled by the recipient

```
case class SendEmail(sender: String, recipients: List[String],
                     bodyLocation: URL, correlationID: UUID,
                     replyTo: ActorRef[SendEmailResult])
```

15.2.3 *The pattern, revisited*

In the previous section, you collapsed a 13-step protocol session into 2 steps: sending one message in either direction is the minimum you can do while still allowing the client to ascertain that the email has in fact been relayed to the gateway service. As a variation, we considered how you can split out one part—the transmission of the email body—into a separate subprotocol that is transparently handled by the used framework or into a secondary conversation between the service and another endpoint. The variation does not complicate the client-service conversation in principle.

The advantages of this change are manifold. We started with the postulated desire of minimizing the session state that needs to be maintained between client and service throughout the conversation. This is an important aspect in that the service can now become stateless in this sense: it can react to the request with a response while not retaining any more information about the client, and the conversation does not need to continue. If the service wants to recognize subsequently re-sent requests, it only needs to store the UUID; it does not need to track the individual clients.

A possibly even greater advantage is that removing the need to store conversational state makes it possible to distribute the processing of the requests in space or time: a SendMail message can be enqueued, serialized to disk, replayed, and routed to one of many email gateway service instances; it can even be automatically retried by the framework if the correspondence with its SendEmailResult is suitably represented, and so on. Shortening the conversation to its minimum affords you a lot of freedom in how you handle and possibly transform the message.

This goes hand in hand with easier recovery procedures. Because the request contains everything needed to process it, it also is fully sufficient to reprocess it after a failure. In contrast, a lengthy, stateful conversation would have to be reestablished—and, in most cases, begun by the client—which calls for specific recovery procedures to be in place among all participants.

15.2.4 *Applicability*

This pattern is universally applicable in the sense of striving to keep the conversation protocols as simple as feasible. You may not always be able to reduce the interaction to a single request–response pair, but when that is possible, it greatly increases your freedom in handling the protocol. Where multiple steps are necessary to achieve the desired goal, it still is preferable to keep the messages that are exchanged as complete and self-contained as can be afforded, because relying on implicitly shared session state complicates the implementation of all communication partners and makes their communication more brittle.

The main reason for not applying this pattern is that the amount of state is larger than can reasonably be transmitted.

15.3 The Ask pattern

Delegate the handling of a response to a dedicated ephemeral component.

This pattern can be arrived at by two trains of thought:

- In a purely message-driven system such as the Actor model, it frequently occurs that after performing a request–response cycle with another Actor, the current business process needs to continue with further steps. Toward this end, the Actor could keep a map of correlation IDs and associated continuation information (such as the details of the ongoing business transaction started by an earlier received message), or it could spawn an ephemeral child Actor, give its address as the return address for the response, and thereby delegate the continuation of the process. The latter is the approach described in Gul Agha's thesis:[9] it is the Actor way of thinking. Because this pattern occurs frequently, it may receive special support from libraries or frameworks.

- Traditional RPC systems are exclusively based on the premise of request-response calls, pretending the same semantics as a local procedure call. Their synchronous presentation results in distributed systems coupled in undesirable ways, as discussed throughout the first part of this book. In order to decouple caller and callee, the locally returned type is changed from a strict result value to a Future—a container for a result value that may arrive later. The continuation of the caller's business process then needs to be lifted into the Future as well, using transformation combinators to perform the successive steps. This Future is an ephemeral component whose purpose is the reception of the eventual response and the initiation of follow-up actions, exactly like the child Actor in the previous bullet point.

15.3.1 The problem setting

Recall the previous section's example: a client exchanges a request–response pair with an email gateway service in order to send an email. This happens in the course of another business transaction: perhaps an account-verification process during which the account holder is sent a link via which the process will continue. After the email has been sent on its way, you may want to update the website, saying that the user should check their in-box and offering a link to send the email again in case it was lost.

The task: Your mission is to implement an Actor that, upon receiving a StartVerificationProcess command, contacts the email gateway service (represented by an ActorRef) to send the verification link. After receiving the response, the Actor should respond to the command received previously with a VerificationProcessStarted or VerificationProcessFailed message, depending on the outcome of the email request.

---

[9] Gul Agha, "ACTORS: A Model of Concurrent Computation in Distributed Systems," 1985, https://dspace.mit.edu/handle/1721.1/6952.

15.3.2   *Applying the pattern*

The following listing sets the stage by defining the message types you will need in addition to the `SendEmail` protocol defined in the previous section.

Listing 15.10   Simple protocol to request starting the verification process

```
case class StartVerificationProcess(userEmail: String,
                        replyTo: ActorRef[VerificationProcessResponse])

sealed trait VerificationProcessResponse
case class VerificationProcessStarted(userEmail: String)
            extends VerificationProcessResponse
case class VerificationProcessFailed(userEmail: String)
            extends VerificationProcessResponse
```

The Actor can then be written in Akka Typed, as shown next.

Listing 15.11   An anonymous child actor forwards results

```
def withChildActor(emailGateway: ActorRef[SendEmail]):
      Behavior[StartVerificationProcess] =
  ContextAware { ctx: ActorContext[StartVerificationProcess] =>
    val log = Logging(ctx.system.eventStream, "VerificationProcessManager")

    Static {
      case StartVerificationProcess(userEmail, replyTo) =>
        val corrID = UUID.randomUUID()
        val childRef = ctx.spawnAnonymous(Props(FullTotal[SendEmailResult] {
          case Sig(ctx, PreStart) =>
            ctx.setReceiveTimeout(5.seconds)
            Same

          case Sig(_, ReceiveTimeout) =>
            log.warning("verification process initiation timed out for {}",
                    userEmail)
            replyTo ! VerificationProcessFailed(userEmail)
            Stopped

          case Msg(_, SendEmailResult(`corrID`, StatusCode.OK, _)) =>
            log.debug("successfully started the verification process for {}",
                    userEmail)
            replyTo ! VerificationProcessStarted(userEmail)
            Stopped

          case Msg(_, SendEmailResult(`corrID`, StatusCode.Failed, expl)) =>
            log.info("failed to start the verification process for {}: {}",
                    userEmail, expl)
            replyTo ! VerificationProcessFailed(userEmail)
            Stopped

          case Msg(_, SendEmailResult(wrongID, _, _)) =>
            log.error("received wrong SendEmailResult for corrID {}", corrID)
            Same
        }))
```

```
        val request = SendEmail("verification@example.com", List(userEmail),
                        constructBody(userEmail, corrID), corrID,
                        childActor)
        emailGateway ! request
    }
}
```

Given the `ActorRef` representing the email gateway service, you construct a behavior that will keep serving `StartVerificationProcess` messages; hence, it uses the `Static` behavior constructor. You extract the enclosing `ActorContext` (the type ascription is given merely for clarity) because you will need to use it to create child Actors as well as to emit logging information. For every command you receive, you create a new UUID that serves as an identifier for the email sent subsequently. Then you create an anonymous[10] Actor whose `ActorRef` is used as the return address for the `SendEmail` request you finally send to the email gateway service.

The created child Actor uses the `FullTotal` behavior constructor because it will need to receive a system notification: the receive-timeout feature is used to abort the process if the email gateway does not respond within the allotted time. If a response is received before this timeout expires, you distinguish three cases:

- A successful result with the correct correlation ID leads to a successful response to the original request.
- A failure result with the correct correlation ID is translated to a failure response.
- A response with a nonmatching correlation ID is logged and ignored.[11]

In all cases leading to a response sent to the original client, the child Actor terminates itself after the response has been sent—the purpose of this ephemeral component is fulfilled, and there is nothing left to be done.

This pattern is so widely applicable that Akka provides special support for it: when expecting a request–response conversation, the response message can be captured in a Future where it is then further processed. The example can be reformulated as follows.

Listing 15.12 Future produced by the Ask pattern and mapped

```
def withAskPattern(emailGateway: ActorRef[SendEmail]):
    Behavior[StartVerificationProcess] =
ContextAware { ctx =>
  val log = Logging(ctx.system.eventStream, "VerificationProcessManager")
  implicit val timeout = Timeout(5.seconds)
  import ctx.executionContext
```

---

[10] That is, unnamed—the library will compute a unique name for it.

[11] Receiving the nonmatching response will reset the receive timeout, though. We do not correct for this potential lengthening of the response timeout in this case in order to not complicate the example too much; it could well be argued that a wrongly dispatched response should be a rare occurrence, if it happens at all.

```
Static {
  case StartVerificationProcess(userEmail, replyTo) =>
    val corrID = UUID.randomUUID()                          The ask operator
    val response: Future[SendEmailResult] =                 produces a Future.
      emailGateway ? (SendEmail("",
                      List(userEmail), constructBody(userEmail, corrID),
                      corrID, _))
    response.map {
      case SendEmailResult(`corrID`, StatusCode.OK, _) =>
        log.debug("successfully started the verification process for {}",
                  userEmail)
        VerificationProcessStarted(userEmail)

      case SendEmailResult(`corrID`, StatusCode.Failed, explanation) =>
        log.info("failed to start the verification process for {}: {}",
                 userEmail, explanation)
        VerificationProcessFailed(userEmail)

      case SendEmailResult(wrongID, _, _) =>
        log.error("received wrong SendEmailResult for corrID {}", corrID)
        VerificationProcessFailed(userEmail)
    }.recover {
      case _: AskTimeoutException =>
        log.warning("verification process initiation timed out for {}",
                    userEmail)
        VerificationProcessFailed(userEmail)
    }.foreach(result => replyTo ! result)
  }
}
```

The Future is then mapped based on the result.

The execution of Future transformations requires the designation of an execution context: you use the actor's dispatcher to perform these tasks. The handling of the response timeout is an inherent feature of the AskPattern support implemented in Akka; it is configured via the implicitly declared timeout value. Use of the pattern implementation proceeds via the ? operator that is made available by importing akka.typed.AskPattern._. This operator takes as its argument not the message but a function that injects the internally created PromiseActorRef into the message. Under the hood, a lightweight, ephemeral actor is created, just as in the previous implementation, but this actor's sole purpose is to place any received message into the Future that the ? operator returns.

It comes as no surprise that you need to handle all the same cases when interpreting the contents of the Future, although the timeout surfaces not as a ReceiveTimeout signal but as a failed Future. One difference is that a Future can only be completed exactly once; therefore, the reception of a response with the wrong correlation ID can no longer be ignored. The asker will have to abort the process instead.

15.3.3 *The pattern, revisited*

Implementing this process without the Ask pattern might have looked like the following.

Listing 15.13 Implementing the Ask pattern without using built-in support

```
def withoutAskPattern(emailGateway: ActorRef[SendEmail]):
    Behavior[StartVerificationProcess] =
  ContextAware[MyCommands] { ctx =>
    val log = Logging(ctx.system.eventStream, "VerificationProcessManager")
    var statusMap = Map.empty[UUID,
                             (String, ActorRef[VerificationProcessResponse])]
    val adapter = ctx.spawnAdapter((s: SendEmailResult) =>
                      MyEmailResult(s.correlationID, s.status, s.explanation))

    Static {
      case StartVerificationProcess(userEmail, replyTo) =>
        val corrID = UUID.randomUUID()
        val request = SendEmail("verification@example.com", List(userEmail),
                        constructBody(userEmail, corrID), corrID, adapter)
        emailGateway ! request
        statusMap += corrID -> (userEmail, replyTo)
        ctx.schedule(5.seconds, ctx.self, MyEmailResult(corrID,
                    StatusCode.Failed, "timeout"))

      case MyEmailResult(corrID, status, expl) =>
        statusMap.get(corrID) match {
          case None =>
            log.error("received result for unknown corrID {}", corrID)

          case Some((userEmail, replyTo)) =>
            status match {
              case StatusCode.OK =>
                log.debug("successfully started verification process for {}",
                        userEmail)
                replyTo ! VerificationProcessStarted(userEmail)

              case StatusCode.Failed =>
                log.info("failed to start verification process for {}: {}",
                        userEmail, expl)
                replyTo ! VerificationProcessFailed(userEmail)
            }
            statusMap -= corrID
        }
    }
  }.narrow[StartVerificationProcess]
```

In comparison to the solutions given in listing 15.12, this has several disadvantages:

- The Actor needs to incorporate the foreign protocol of the email gateway (in particular, the SendEmailResult message type) into its own repertoire of messages. Toward this end, Akka Typed provides the facility of spawning an adapter ActorRef that turns SendEmailResult messages into MyEmailResult objects; such an adapter is used in listing 15.13 as the return address for the SendEmail request.

- The Actor needs to explicitly maintain the sum of the status information for all currently open transactions. You implement this in listing 15.13 by maintaining a mapping from correlation IDs to the eventually needed parameters—the user's email and the original requester's `ActorRef`, in this case. Maintaining this mapping requires more discipline than with the Ask pattern in that you need to take care to properly remove stale state when transactions end; this cleanup is conveniently bundled with the ephemeral actor's lifecycle when using the Ask pattern.

- Handling timeouts requires notification of this Actor while retaining enough identifying information. In this example, it needs to track the correlation ID of each transaction. In the example case, this can be trivially mapped to a failed `SendEmailResult`, but in general this may necessitate the addition of yet another message type to the Actor's internal protocol.

- The Actor needs to respond to more messages than it would otherwise need, opening up the possibility of wrong messages being sent to this exposed service more easily and with greater reach than would be the case if handling these other types of messages were delegated to ephemeral endpoints as with the Ask pattern.

In listing 15.13, the sketched verification-management service confers with only one other service, and handling the associated status information amounts to roughly the same number of lines as when using the Ask pattern. If you imagine a service that needs to communicate with several other services as well, it becomes clear that consistent management of all associated state will pile up—it will become intertwined in nontrivial ways and be more difficult to evolve and maintain. Using the Ask pattern, on the other hand, allows you to separate out the subconversations that occur while processing a larger business transaction; it helps you to decouple the handling of session state by segregating it for each conversation and delegating it to a subcomponent.

15.3.4 Applicability

The Ask pattern is applicable wherever a request–response cycle needs to be performed before continuing with the further processing of an enclosing business transaction. This holds only for non-ephemeral components, though: if the enclosing transaction is already handled by a dedicated ephemeral component, then usually no complexity overhead is incurred by keeping the state management for the request-response cycle within that component.

One consequence of using the Ask pattern is that the parent component is not automatically aware of the progress of the subconversation; it must be informed explicitly if it needs to stay in the loop. This can be relevant if the number of concurrently outstanding requests needs to be limited, whether in order to protect the target service from being overwhelmed with a sudden onslaught of requests or in order to not overwhelm local computing and network resources with too many concurrent conversations. Using the Ask pattern indiscriminately can easily be equivalent to employing an unbounded queue, with all the negative effects on response latency that are discussed in section 2.1.3, plus ample opportunity to exhaust all available memory.

15.4   The Forward Flow pattern

Let the information and the messages flow directly toward their destination where possible.

This pattern sounds intuitive, maybe even trivial: why would you deliberately send messages via detours when that is not required? The answer is that this rarely occurs consciously; it is the result of applying a convenient, well-known pattern overeagerly. The pattern in question is your good friend the Request–Response pattern, with or without the Ask pattern's sugar coating. Overusing this pattern leads to unnecessary consumption of network bandwidth and increased response latency; thinking about forward flow lets you recognize these cases and improve your service quality.

15.4.1   The problem setting

Imagine a message router that dispatches incoming file streaming requests to a pool of service instances that host these files. They could be video files that are sent to clients for streaming display on users' screens.

   The task: Your mission is to sketch the sequence of messages sent among client, router, and file server such that the router does not become a bottleneck in the streaming video dissemination process.

15.4.2   Applying the pattern

Starting from naïve request–response communication, you might foresee that the client sends to the router, the router embodies the client from the perspective of the file server, and thus responses flow via the router back to the client. This is shown in figure 15.2.

   In this scheme, the router must be able to forward all the streams coming from the file servers back to all the clients, meaning its network interface's bandwidth will place an upper limit on how many bytes per second can be streamed by the entire system. Network links are becoming faster and faster, but if this streaming service is intended to serve customers on the internet, then it will reach its limit fairly soon. Therefore, you must think a bit more about the meaning of *request* and *response* in this scenario: the client sends a request, and the logical destination is the file server, not the router. The response is a video stream whose source is the file server and whose destination is the client. Although you need the router as an intermediary for the request—balancing the load across a pool of replicated file servers hosting the particular video file

Figure 15.2   Flow of messages when nesting the Ask pattern: all responses travel via the intermediate router component.

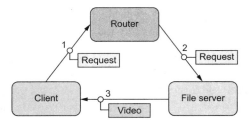

Figure 15.3   Flow of messages when applying forward flow: although the request needs to pass through the router for load balancing, the (large) response does not need to take the same route. It can travel back directly from file server to client.

that is requested—you do not need to involve it in handling the response. The resulting message-flow diagram is shown in figure 15.3.

Here, the requests flow toward their destination via the shortest possible path, and the responses also do not waste any time on their way back. Because the file servers communicate directly with the clients, you are free to scale up the available computing and network resources without limit.

15.4.3 *The pattern, revisited*

We have analyzed the initial draft of applying the Request–Response pattern individually for each step along a request's path and found that responses profit from not taking the same path; instead, they may take a more direct route. By cutting out the middleman, you gain the freedom to scale the available response bandwidth without being limited by what a single router can provide.

The same applies to a file-upload service in reverse: the uploaded data streams go directly to the file servers, but the response may be routed via another service to update the file catalog or otherwise perform accounting tasks. Sending the voluminous data streams via the accounting system would require that the system be scaled such that it can handle the resulting load, but this is a purely incidental concern because the accounting system is not interested in the data bytes.

Another aspect is that removing intermediate hops from a message's path reduces the time it takes for the message to reach its final destination. Every time it is enqueued and dispatched again, there is a latency cost.

15.4.4 *Applicability*

Using forward flow to optimize the overall resource consumption or response-latency time requires participating services to allow for these shortcuts. Either they need to know about each other—as demonstrated by the router that is intimately aware of the file server pool—or the message protocol needs to include the possibility to specify the target route a message will take so that the middleman can remain ignorant of its location within the message flow. Applying this pattern hence involves an assessment of how big the gains in service quality are in relation to the additional complexity or coupling the pattern introduces. In the example of the video-streaming service, it is evident that the performance requirements of the system dictate this approach; but in other cases, it may not be as clear. As with all optimizations, the application must be predicated on having measured the performance of the simpler alternative solution and found the results to be inadequate.

15.5 *The Aggregator pattern*

Create an ephemeral component if multiple service responses are needed to compute a service call's result.

We have introduced the Ask pattern for the case of requiring a request–response cycle before a service call can be answered. There are cases, though, where a larger number of these cycles need to be completed, and none of the requests depend on the responses of the others—in other words, the request–response cycles can be made in parallel. Disregarding this opportunity for parallelism means prolonging the time until the overall response can be sent back to the client, thus leaving an opportunity for latency reduction unused.

15.5.1 *The problem setting*

Imagine a personalized front page for a news site. In order to render the page, you need multiple inputs:

- Theme the user has configured to be used for styling the site
- News items to be displayed as per the user's topic selection
- Top news items that are displayed to all users

Each of these inputs is provided by a different service by way of a request–response protocol.

The task: Your mission is to formulate an Actor that, upon receiving a GetFrontPage request, creates an ephemeral component that retrieves the three inputs in parallel and, when ready, sends their composition back to the original requester.

15.5.2 *Applying the pattern*

Using the Ask pattern, you can decompose the task into two steps: first, you initiate three ask operations, one for each of the needed inputs; and then, you combine their result using Future combinators. In other words, you use a Future's facilities as the ephemeral component that oversees this entire process. The full code is available with the book's downloads; we omit the message definitions here because they are trivial and intuitive. The code looks like the following listing.

Listing 15.14 Using a for-comprehension to aggregate the result of three Future expressions

```
def futureFrontPage(themes: ActorRef[GetTheme],
                    personalNews: ActorRef[GetPersonalNews],
                    topNews: ActorRef[GetTopNews]): Behavior[GetFrontPage] =
  ContextAware { ctx =>
    import ctx.executionContext
    implicit val timeout = Timeout(1.second)
```

```
Static {
    case GetFrontPage(user, replyTo) =>
      val cssFuture =
        (themes ? (GetTheme(user,
                        _: ActorRef[ThemeResult])))
          .map(_.css)
          .recover {
            case _: AskTimeoutException => "default.css"
          }
      val personalNewsFuture =
        (personalNews ? (GetPersonalNews(user,
                        _: ActorRef[PersonalNewsResult])))
          .map(_.news)
          .recover {
            case _: AskTimeoutException => Nil
          }
      val topNewsFuture =
        (topNews ? (GetTopNews(_: ActorRef[TopNewsResult])))
          .map(_.news)
          .recover {
            case _: AskTimeoutException => Nil
          }
      for {
        css <- cssFuture
        personalNews <- personalNewsFuture
        topNews <- topNewsFuture
      } {
        val topSet = topNews.toSet
        val allNews = topNews ::: personalNews.filterNot(topSet.contains)
        replyTo ! FrontPageResult(user, css, allNews)
      }
    }
  }
}
```

Creates a Future for each section

Uses a combinator to produce a single result

This code defines an actor that, for each `GetFrontPage` request, creates three Futures, each based on the Ask pattern with a value transformation for extracting the desired piece of information and a recovery step that defines the replacement value to be used in case of a timeout. We present here only the aspects that are directly relevant; in a complete program, you would of course take care to install circuit breakers as appropriate and also ensure that you limit the total number of outstanding ask requests in order to prevent unbounded resource usage. As the second step, the actor uses a for-comprehension to tie together the three individual Futures in order to compute the full result that is finally sent back to the return address provided with the initial request.

Another way to implement the same process would be to create an ephemeral child Actor instead of using Future combinators, as shown next.

Listing 15.15 Using a child Actor in place of Future combinators

```
private def pf(p: PartialFunction[AnyRef, Unit]): p.type = p

def frontPage(themes: ActorRef[GetTheme],
              personalNews: ActorRef[GetPersonalNews],
```

Helper to avoid type ascription

```
              topNews: ActorRef[GetTopNews]): Behavior[GetFrontPage] =
      ContextAware { ctx =>
        Static {
          case GetFrontPage(user, replyTo) =>
            val childRef = ctx.spawnAnonymous(Props {
              val builder = new FrontPageResultBuilder(user)
              Partial[AnyRef](
                pf {
                  case ThemeResult(css)         => builder.addCSS(css)
                  case PersonalNewsResult(news) => builder.addPersonalNews(news)
                  case TopNewsResult(news)      => builder.addTopNews(news)
                  case ReceiveTimeout           => builder.timeout()
                } andThen { _ =>
                  if (builder.isComplete) {
                    replyTo ! builder.result
                    Stopped
                  } else Same
                })
            })
            themes ! GetTheme(user, childRef)
            personalNews ! GetPersonalNews(user, childRef)
            topNews ! GetTopNews(childRef)
            ctx.schedule(1.second, childRef, ReceiveTimeout)
        }
      }
```

> **Spawns an ephemeral child Actor**

> **Direct responses to the child Actor**

> **Ensures that the child times out if it does not receive a complete set of responses**

The structure of the ephemeral child Actor consists of two aspects: first, any new piece of information is incorporated into the current set of knowledge as managed by a mutable builder (shown in listing 15.15), and then the builder is queried as to whether the answer is now complete, in which case the process is completed by sending the result back to the original requester. The process is set in motion by sending the three requests to their respective providers while giving the child Actor's reference as the return address.

Listing 15.16 Using a builder to express the domain more directly

```
class FrontPageResultBuilder(user: String) {
  private var css: Option[String] = None
  private var personalNews: Option[List[String]] = None
  private var topNews: Option[List[String]] = None

  def addCSS(css: String): Unit = this.css = Option(css)
  def addPersonalNews(news: List[String]): Unit =
      this.personalNews = Option(news)
  def addTopNews(news: List[String]): Unit = this.topNews = Option(news)

  def timeout(): Unit = {
    if (css.isEmpty) css = Some("default.css")
    if (personalNews.isEmpty) personalNews = Some(Nil)
    if (topNews.isEmpty) topNews = Some(Nil)
  }

  def isComplete: Boolean =
    css.isDefined && personalNews.isDefined && topNews.isDefined
```

```
def result: FrontPageResult = {
  val topSet = topNews.get.toSet
  val allNews = topNews.get ::: personalNews.get.filterNot(topSet.contains)
  FrontPageResult(user, css.get, allNews)
}
}
```

This builder adds more lines of code to the weight of the program than the Future-based solution requires, but it also lets you express the domain of your problem natively and unencumbered: the Ask pattern and its underlying Future API place the focus on the eventual availability or failure of each single value, making it more difficult to formulate actions or reactions that affect multiple aspects at once. An example appears in listing 15.16's timeout handling: the Actor-based approach allows the more natural formulation of an overall timeout that is handled in one place only, whereas AskTimeoutException's recovery logic must be repeated for each of the three individual Futures.

Another use case that illustrates this point is a mechanism that can override the front page's contents and style in case of special events. In the Actor-based implementation, this could be done by sending a request to a fourth service; for a given reply, you could override fields of the builder as appropriate, completing the result right away. This can be implemented by adding a single line to the message-reception cases. In the Future-based approach, you would need to formulate these as two competing operations, because adding a fourth input to the current scheme would require you to wait for the irrelevant responses to the other three requests in case of an override. The resulting code becomes less readable, as shown in the following listing.

> **Listing 15.17   Adding a fourth service, making the code less readable**

```
val cssFuture = ...
val personalNewsFuture = ...
val topNewsFuture = ...
val overrideFuture =
  (overrides ? (GetOverride(_: ActorRef[OverrideResult])))
    .recover {
      case _: AskTimeoutException => NoOverride
    }

for {
  css <- cssFuture
  personalNews <- personalNewsFuture
  topNews <- topNewsFuture
  ovr <- overrideFuture
} ovr match {                              Sends the normal result
  case NoOverride =>                       only when NoOverrides
    val topSet = topNews.toSet             were returned
    val allNews = topNews ::: personalNews.filterNot(topSet.contains)
    replyTo ! FrontPageResult(user, css, allNews)  <─┘
  case other =>         <─┐
}                        Nothing to do here
```

```
for {
  ovr <- overrideFuture
} ovr match {
  case NoOverride =>
  case Override(css, news) =>
    replyTo ! FrontPageResult(user, css, news)
}
```

Sends the override result only when Override was returned

Although this is not a major change in terms of lines added, it makes it more difficult to reason about the behavior of this code. In particular, an important hidden constraint is only expressed in the annotations: the execution is bifurcated, and only the careful treatment of OverrideResult ensures that the overall result is deterministic.

15.5.3 *The pattern, revisited*

You extended the Ask pattern to include more than one request–response pair in the calculation of an overall result. While doing so, you found Future combinators to express this in a straightforward way as long as all individual results can be treated independently—as soon as the aggregation process involves decisions that affect the aggregation logic, it becomes preferable to create an explicit ephemeral component that bundles this process. The reason is that Futures are limited in that they do not have a name or an identity that can be spoken to after their creation; their input value is fixed as soon as the combinator that produces them has been invoked. This is their greatest strength, but it can also be a weakness.

In contrast, the ephemeral component that the Aggregator pattern gives rise to—modeled as an Actor in listing 15.15—can easily express any process of arriving at the aggregation result, independent of which inputs are needed and which scope they affect. This is an advantage particularly in cases where the aggregation process conditionally chooses different computations to be applied based on some of the inputs it collects.

15.5.4 *Applicability*

The Aggregator pattern is applicable wherever a combination of multiple Ask pattern results is desired and where straightforward Future combinators cannot adequately or concisely express the aggregation process. Whenever you find yourself using multiple layers of Futures or using nondeterministic "racy" combinators like Future .firstCompletedOf(), you should sketch out the equivalent process with Actors (or other named, addressable components) and see whether the logic can be simplified. One concern that frequently drives this is the need for complex, layered handling of timeouts or other partial failures.

15.6   *The Saga pattern*

Divide long-lived, distributed transactions into quick local ones with compensating actions for recovery.

In other words: Create an ephemeral component to manage the execution of a sequence of actions distributed across multiple components.

The term *saga* was coined by Hector Garcia-Molina.[12] His paper describes a scheme for breaking up long-lived business transactions in order to shorten the time period during which databases need to hold locks—these locks are needed to ensure atomicity and consistency of the transaction, the downside of which is that other transactions touching the same data cannot proceed concurrently.

In a distributed system, you need to break up transactions involving multiple participants for other reasons: obtaining a shared lock is an expensive operation that can even be impossible in the face of certain failures like network partitions. As we discussed in chapter 8, the key to scalability and loose coupling is to consider each component an island of *delimited consistency*. But how do you model business transactions that require inputs from multiple components while also effecting modifications to multiple components? It turns out the research topic of sagas provides an effective, robust solution for many use cases.

NOTE   This section gives only a brief overview; a full book could be written on this topic alone. A very similar concept is the *process manager* in the CQRS literature[13]—the main difference is that a *saga* focuses on transactional aspects (atomicity and consistency), whereas a *process manager* is primarily seen as factoring out the description of a particular process from the components that participate in it.

15.6.1   *The problem setting*

The prototypical example of a business transaction that affects more than one consistent entity (or *aggregate* in domain-driven design [DDD] terms) is a money transfer from one bank account to another. Questions of this kind arise immediately when scaling out the application state managed previously by a single RDBMS instance onto a distributed cluster of machines, whether for elasticity or resilience reasons. The code of the nondistributed system would tie the update to both accounts in a single transaction, relying on the RDBMS to uphold the guarantees of atomicity, consistency, isolation, and durability. In the distributed system, there is no such mechanism, requiring the use of the Saga pattern.

The task: Your mission is to sketch the conversation between an ephemeral saga component and the two bank account components in order to perform a money

---

[12] Hector Garcia-Molina, "Sagas," *ACM*, 1987 (http://dl.acm.org/citation.cfm?id=38742).

[13] See "CQRS Journey" (July 2012) on MSDN, reference 6: "A Saga on Sagas," https://msdn.microsoft.com/en-us/library/jj591569.aspx.

transfer, considering that individual steps can fail permanently (for example, because the source account does not have sufficient funds or the destination account is closed after the process begins). Unreliable communication will be considered in the following pattern. You may then also implement the saga component in code: for example, as a persistent actor.

15.6.2 Applying the pattern

When designing a communication protocol between multiple parties, one natural analogy is to envision a conversation among a group of people. Here, you want to describe how Sam—the saga—confers with Alice and Bob to transfer part of Alice's budget to Bob. The analogy works best if the essential properties of the process are represented: in this case, handing over the money in cash would not be possible, because that kind of fully synchronous process is not how distributed systems work. Therefore, you will reallocate $10,000 of budget between them.

Before we consider various failure scenarios, we will sketch the nominal successful case, which might go like the following:

Sam: "Alice, please reduce your budget by $10,000 if possible."
Alice: "OK. I've done so."
Sam: "Bob, please increase your budget by $10,000."
Bob: "Thanks, Sam; it's done."
Sam: "Thanks everyone; transfer finished!"

There is no need for Alice and Bob to talk to each other, because Sam coordinates the transfer. Given this scenario, we might as well have let both subconversations occur in parallel to each other. Now we will consider some failure modes—for example, if Alice does not have sufficient budget:

Sam: "Alice, please reduce your budget by $10,000 if possible."
Alice: "Sorry, Sam, my budget is too low already."
Sam: "Listen up, everyone—this transfer is aborted!"

This case is simple. The first step of the process fails in a nontransient fashion, so no harm is done and an abort is immediately possible. A more complicated case occurs if Bob is unable to receive the increased budget amount:

Sam: "Alice, please reduce your budget by $10,000 if possible."
Alice: "OK. I've done so."
Sam: "Bob, please increase your budget by $10,000."
Bob: "Sorry, Sam, my project was just canceled—I no longer have a budget."
Sam: "Alice, please increase your budget by $10,000.""
Alice: "Thanks, Sam; it's done."
Sam: "Listen up, everyone—this transfer is aborted!"

In this case, the second step that Sam wants to perform cannot be carried out. At this point, Alice has already reduced her budget, so logically Sam holds $10,000 in his hands—but he has no budget to manage for himself. The solution for this dilemma is that Sam gives the $10,000 back to Alice. This is called a *compensating transaction*. Using this trick, we can also make the entire transfer opportunistically parallel and still remain correct:

Sam: "Alice, please reduce your budget by $10,000 if possible. Bob, please increase your budget by $10,000."

Bob: "Thanks, Sam. It's done.""

Alice: "Sorry, Sam, my budget is too low already."

Sam: "Bob, please reduce your budget by $10,000."

Bob: "OK. I've done so."

Sam: "Listen up, everyone—this transfer is aborted!"

Of course, we have assumed here that the compensating transactions always succeed; but what if that is not the case? What if in the last example Bob had already—and surprisingly quickly—spent the $10,000 while Sam was waiting for Alice to respond? In this case, the system would be in an inconsistent state that Sam could not fix without external help. The moral of this gedankenexperiment is that computers and algorithms cannot be held responsible for dealing with all possible corner cases, especially when it comes to distributed systems where the convenient simplifications of a fully sequential local execution cannot be applied. In such cases, inconsistencies must be recognized as possible system states and signaled upward: for example, to be decided by the humans who operate the system. For further reading on this topic, please see Pat Helland's "Memories, Guesses, and Apologies."[14]

15.6.3   *The pattern, revisited*

Given two accounts—symbolized by Alice and Bob—we have introduced another process: a saga whose role was played by Sam in order to orchestrate the transfer of budget from one account to the other. Getting Alice and Bob to agree directly on this transfer would be a costly process during which both would be unavailable for other requests, because those could invalidate the current state of the consensus-building conversation; this would be the analogous solution using a distributed transaction in the ACID sense (a transaction like the ones we are used to from relational database management systems [RDBMSs]). Instead, we have placed the responsibility for leaving the system in a consistent state with the new external process that runs this process.

You have seen that in order to do this, you have to not only describe the individual transactions that are done on each account but also provide compensating transactions that come into play if the saga needs to be aborted. This is the same as performing a transaction rollback on a RDBMS; but because you are no longer dealing with a

---

[14] MSDN blog, 2007, http://blogs.msdn.com/b/pathelland/archive/2007/05/15/memories-guesses-and-apologies.aspx.

single realm of consistency, the system can no longer automatically deduce what constitutes a rollback. Hector Garcia-Molina notes that writing the compensating transactions is not a black art, though; it is usually of the same difficulty as encoding the transactions.

One property of compensating transactions that we have glossed over so far requires a bit of formalism: where transaction T_1 takes the component from state S_0 to state S_1, the compensating transaction C_1 takes it from S_1 back to S_0. We are applying these transactions within the consistency boundaries of several different components—Alice and Bob, in the earlier example—and within one of these components an execution of a sequence of transactions $T_1..T_n$ would take that component from state S_0 to S_n. Because transactions do not, in general, commute with each other, taking the system back from state S_n to S_0 would require the application of the compensating transactions $C_n..C_1$: the compensating transactions would be applied in reverse order, and this order matters. We have played with the thought of parallelizing parts of the two subconversations (Sam-Alice and Sam-Bob), but you must always be careful to maintain a deterministic and thus reversible order for all transactions that are performed with Alice and Bob individually. For an in-depth discussion of compensation semantics, please refer to Garcia-Molina's "Sagas" paper.

At the beginning of this pattern's description, we mentioned the term *process manager* from CQRS terminology. This term refers to another property of the pattern we have described: in order to carry out the budget transfer, neither Alice nor Bob needed to know how it worked; they only needed to be able to manage their own budget and respond to requests to reduce or increase it. This is an important benefit in that it allows the description of complex business processes to be decoupled from the implementation of the affected components both at runtime and during development. The process manager is the single place that holds all knowledge about this business process: if changes are required, they are made only to this software module.

In Reactive systems, the need to factor out this process into its own ephemeral component arises from both sides: we need to model workflows that affect multiple components while maintaining eventual consistency, and we need to factor out cross-component activities such that we do not strongly couple the development or execution of these components. The "Sagas" paper was not written with distributed systems in mind, but it does offer a solution to both these problems. It also predates the CQRS terminology by nearly two decades; and because we like the concise and metaphorical name of the proposed abstraction, we call this pattern the Saga pattern.

Coming back to the example, Sam has one quality we have not yet discussed: when you model a process this way, you expect that the transfer will eventually be finished or aborted, no matter what happens. You do not expect Sam to be distracted and forget about the whole thing. Not only would that be pushing the analogy too far, but it is also a property that you do not wish your computer systems to have—you want them to be reliable. In computer terms, the state the saga manages must be *persistent*. If the machine that runs the saga fails, you need the ability to restart the process elsewhere and have it resume its operations. Only then can you be sure the process will eventually complete, assuming that you keep providing computing resources.

The Aggregator pattern describes a simple form of a workflow—the retrieval of information from multiple sources and its subsequent conversion into an overall result—whereas the Saga pattern allows arbitrary processes to be formulated. The Aggregator pattern is a simple, special case, whereas the Saga pattern describes service composition in general.

15.6.4 Applicability

The astute reader will have grown increasingly impatient, waiting for the discussion of the elephant in the room: if this pattern is presented as a solution in place of distributed transactions, then how do we reconcile this with the fact that sagas are not isolated from each other? Going back to the example, you could easily imagine another process that tallies all allocated budgets across the company by interrogating all project leads, including Alice and Bob: if this tally process asks during the transfer such that Alice has already reduced her budget but Bob has not yet increased his, the tally will come up $10,000 short because the money is "in flight." Running the tallying process during a quiescent period when no transfers are ongoing would lead to the correct result, but otherwise there would always be a risk of errors.

In some systems this is not acceptable. These systems cannot tolerate being distributed in the sense of splitting them into multiple autonomous, decoupled components. Sagas cannot be used to fix this problem in general.

The Saga pattern is applicable wherever a business process needs to be modeled that involves multiple independent components: in other words, wherever a business transaction spans multiple regions of delimited consistency. In these cases, the pattern offers *atomicity* (the ability to roll back by applying compensating transactions) and *eventual consistency* (in the sense that application-level consistency is restored by issuing *apologies*; see Pat Helland's aforementioned blog article), but it does not offer isolation.

15.7 The Business Handshake pattern (a.k.a. Reliable Delivery pattern)

Include identifying and/or sequencing information in the message, and keep retrying until confirmation is received.

While discussing the previous pattern, we made the implicit assumption that communication between the saga and the affected components is reliable. We pictured a group of people standing in the same office and discussing the process without external disturbances. This is a useful way to begin, because it allows you to focus on the essential parts of a conversation; but we know that life does not always work like that—in particular in distributed systems, where messages can be lost or delayed due to unforeseeable, inexorable subsystem failures.

Fortunately, we can treat the two concerns on separate levels: imagining that the conversation occurs in a busy, noisy office does not invalidate the basic structure of the business process we are modeling. All that is needed is to deliver every message more carefully, transmitting it again if it is overshadowed by some other event. This second level is what the Business Handshake pattern is all about.

15.7.1 *The problem setting*

In the previous example, we assumed that Sam—the saga—conveyed the message "Please reduce your budget by $10,000 if possible" to Alice, who replied with either an affirmative or a negative response. In a setting where communication becomes unreliable, it may happen that either the message to Alice or the response is not heard—in technical terms, it is lost. If this happens, the process will be stuck, because without further provisions, Sam will wait indefinitely to hear back from Alice. In real life, impatience and social conventions would solve this conflict, but computers are dumb and cannot figure this out without help.

The task: Your mission is to describe the process of conveying the request and response in a reliable fashion, considering that every single message could be lost undetectably. You should write this down from the perspectives of both Sam and Alice, using your message-driven communication tool kit of choice, but without exploiting the potential reliable-delivery guarantees of such a tool kit.

15.7.2 *Applying the pattern*

As a general working principle, we will again begin from a real-world example. Imagine Sam and Alice sitting at their desks, several meters apart, in a noisy office—so noisy that both need to shout to have a chance of hearing what the other is saying. Sam shouts, "Please reduce your budget if possible!" and then listens intently for Alice's response. If none is forthcoming, Alice may not have heard, so Sam shouts again until a reaction comes back from Alice. Alice, on the other hand, sits there working on other things until she hears Sam shouting; she has no clue how often Sam may have shouted previously. Having heard the request, Alice brings up the budget spreadsheet, takes out $10,000 for Sam, and then shouts that she has done so. From Alice's perspective, everything is finished—but Sam may not have heard her reply, in which case he'll shout again. In fact, he has to keep shouting until Alice responds again so he has another chance to hear the response. When Alice hears Sam make the same request again, she will naturally shout back, "Hey, I already did that!" After some time, Sam will finally hear her, and the exchange will be complete.

Implementing this using Actors looks like the following listing (the full source code can be found with the book's downloads).

Listing 15.18 Implementing the exchange using Actors

```
case class ChangeBudget(amount: BigDecimal, replyTo: ActorRef)
case object ChangeBudgetDone
case class CannotChangeBudget(reason: String)

class Sam(alice: ActorRef, bob: ActorRef, amount: BigDecimal) extends Actor {
  def receive = talkToAlice()
```

```
  def talkToAlice(): Receive = {
    alice ! ChangeBudget(-amount, self)
    context.setReceiveTimeout(1.second)

    {
      case ChangeBudgetDone           => context.become(talkToBob())
      case CannotChangeBudget(reason) => context.stop(self)
      case ReceiveTimeout             => alice ! ChangeBudget(-amount, self)
    }
  }

  def talkToBob(): Receive = ...         ◁─── Analog to the previous code
}
class Alice extends Actor {
  var budget: BigDecimal = 10
                                                You need to keep track of
  var alreadyDone: Set[ActorRef] = Set.empty ◁─ what has already been done.
                                                Here each "Sam" issues only
                                                one request (being a Saga).
  def receive = {
    case ChangeBudget(amount, replyTo) if alreadyDone(replyTo) =>
      replyTo ! ChangeBudgetDone

    case ChangeBudget(amount, replyTo) if amount + budget > 0 =>
      budget += amount
      alreadyDone += replyTo
      context.watch(replyTo)
      replyTo ! ChangeBudgetDone

    case ChangeBudget(_, replyTo) =>
      replyTo ! CannotChangeBudget("insufficient budget")

    case Terminated(saga) =>
      alreadyDone -= saga
  }
}
```

First, note that Sam includes identifying information with the ChangeBudget command in the form of his own ActorRef—this is a token that is guaranteed to be unique, and it identifies exactly one budget change for Alice because Sam is a short-lived saga. Second, note how Sam keeps resending the same command using the Receive-Timeout mechanism until the reply from Alice has been received. If the budget reduction fails, the saga terminates; otherwise, it continues by talking with Bob in the same fashion it did with Alice.

On the receiving end, you see that Alice validates the incoming command: if you have already seen a command with the same return address, then there is nothing to be done apart from confirming that it has already been done, whereas in the case of insufficient funds, you must send a negative response. But if the command is new and valid, you execute its effect—changing the budget—and reply to the requester that you have done so. In addition, you must keep track of what you have done. Here, you store the return address in a set so that you can later recognize it in case of a retransmitted command. This set would grow indefinitely over time unless you clean it up; for this, you use the DeathWatch mechanism. When the saga ends, its Actor is terminated, and you can remove the reference from the set because there cannot be any more retransmissions with this return address.

What we have sketched so far is the volatile in-memory version of performing the business handshake. If the execution must be reliable across machine failures and restarts, you have to make Sam and Alice persistent. The following listing shows how this changes Sam.

Listing 15.19 Adding persistence to the budget messages

Due to an implementation restriction, "deliver" does not work from here.

Therefore, you start the process from the preStart lifecycle hook.

```scala
case class AliceConfirmedChange(deliveryId: Long)
case class AliceDeniedChange(deliveryId: Long)

class PersistentSam(alice: ActorPath, bob: ActorPath, amount: BigDecimal,
                    override val persistenceId: String)
    extends PersistentActor with AtLeastOnceDelivery {
  def receiveCommand = Actor.emptyBehavior

  override def preStart(): Unit = context.become(talkToAlice())

  def talkToAlice() = {

    var deliveryId: Long = 0
    deliver(alice)(id => { deliveryId = id
                           ChangeBudget(-amount, self, persistenceId) })

    {
      case ChangeBudgetDone =>
        persist(AliceConfirmedChange(deliveryId)) { ev =>
          confirmDelivery(ev.deliveryId)
          context.become(talkToBob())
        }
      case CannotChangeBudget(reason) =>
        persist(AliceDeniedChange(deliveryId)) { ev =>
          confirmDelivery(ev.deliveryId)
          context.stop(self)
        }
    }
  }

  def talkToBob() = ...

  def receiveRecover = {
    case AliceConfirmedChange(deliveryId) =>
      confirmDelivery(deliveryId)
      context.become(talkToBob())
    case AliceDeniedChange(deliveryId) =>
      confirmDelivery(deliveryId)
      context.stop(self)
  }
}
```

Instead of letting the delivery ID travel with the message, you keep it here because there can be only this one message on its way.

◁—— Analog to the previous code

This Actor is very similar to the Sam actor presented in listing 15.18, but instead of sending to Alice and Bob via their `ActorRef`, you now can only use their `ActorPath`—the difference is that the latter stays valid across machine restarts whereas the former does not. `PersistentSam` also needs to store its state changes by emitting events to its persistent journal, identified by the `persistenceId`. The `AtLeastOnceDelivery` mixin provides the `deliver()` and `confirmDelivery()` methods that implement the persistent version of the retransmission scheme previously based on the `Receive-Timeout` mechanism: delivery is retried periodically until the confirmation is registered. During recovery, all previously persisted events from the journal are replayed, and the persistent actor goes through the same state transitions and delivers and confirms the same messages it previously did. Thus, after recovery it will have reached the same state as before the (forceful) restart.

One noteworthy detail is that the state progression toward talking to Bob is effected only after having successfully persisted Alice's confirmation, as shown in listing 15.20. If the machine crashes after that message is delivered but before it is written to persistent storage, the effect is as if the message were lost on the way—which is exactly the right semantics, because the confirmation must reach Sam's memory and not only his ears.

Listing 15.20   The persistent version of Alice

```
case class BudgetChanged(amount: BigDecimal, persistenceId: String)
case object CleanupDoneList
case class ChangeDone(persistenceId: String)

class PersistentAlice extends PersistentActor with ActorLogging {
  def persistenceId: String = "Alice"

  implicit val mat = ActorMaterializer()
  import context.dispatcher

  var alreadyDone: Set[String] = Set.empty
  var budget: BigDecimal = 10

  val cleanupTimer =
    context.system.scheduler.schedule(1.hour, 1.hour, self, CleanupDoneList)

  def receiveCommand = {
    case ChangeBudget(amount, replyTo, id) if alreadyDone(id) =>
      replyTo ! ChangeBudgetDone

    case ChangeBudget(amount, replyTo, id) if amount + budget > 0 =>
      persist(BudgetChanged(amount, id)) { ev =>
        budget += ev.amount
        alreadyDone += ev.persistenceId
        replyTo ! ChangeBudgetDone
      }

    case ChangeBudget(_, replyTo, _) =>
      replyTo ! CannotChangeBudget("insufficient budget")

    case CleanupDoneList =>
      val journal = PersistenceQuery(context.system)
```

```
          .readJournalFor[LeveldbReadJournal](LeveldbReadJournal.Identifier)
      for (persistenceId <- alreadyDone) {
        val stream = journal
              .currentEventsByPersistenceId(persistenceId)
              .map(_.event)
              .collect {
                case AliceConfirmedChange(_) => ChangeDone(persistenceId)
              }
        stream.runWith(Sink.head).pipeTo(self)
      }

    case ChangeDone(id) =>
      persist(ChangeDone(id)) { ev =>
        alreadyDone -= ev.persistenceId
      }
  }

  def receiveRecover = {
    case BudgetChanged(amount, id) =>
      budget += amount
      alreadyDone += id
    case ChangeDone(id) =>
      alreadyDone -= id
  }

  override def postStop(): Unit = cleanupTimer.cancel()
}
```

The main difference between the persistent and the transient versions of Alice lies in how you recognize commands that have already been executed. Here, you again use the uniqueness of the requesting saga's name: in this case, you use the persistenceId that is included in the message for this purpose. Triggering the cleanup of the set of known identities by using DeathWatch is not the correct answer here, because sagas can be restarted after a crash: reception of the Terminated notification does not signal the completion of the saga but rather that its current actor ceased to exist—which might be caused by a machine failure or network outage. Instead, you use the events that the saga persists. Once per hour, Alice asks the journal for all currently stored events for all sagas it knows: every saga that has persisted an AliceConfirmedChange event clearly will not retransmit that command, so you can safely remember that this saga's change is finished and remove its identity from the stored set.

This example uses a specific event that Alice knows Sam persists. This may be too close a coupling between the code modules of the saga and the account entity; instead it may be preferable to emit a known, well-documented event at the end of the saga's lifecycle so that all affected components can hook their cleanup actions to that event. This minimizes the shared knowledge that the teams developing either module must have, and it simplifies writing tests that mock out the saga from the affected component's viewpoint.

15.7.3 *The pattern, revisited*

The reliable execution of transactions across components and thereby across consistency boundaries requires four things:

- The requester must keep resending the request until a matching response is received.
- The requester must include identifying information with the request.
- The recipient must use the identifying information to prevent multiple executions of the same request.
- The recipient must always respond, even for retransmitted requests.

We call this the Business Handshake pattern because it is crucial that the response implies successful processing of the request. This is what enables the pattern to ensure exactly-once execution of the desired effects. It would not be enough to merely confirm the delivery of the request to the recipient; this would not allow the conclusion that the recipient also performed the requested work. The distinction is naturally clear in cases where a response carries desired information as part of the business process, but the same applies to requests that just result in a state change for the recipient and where the requester does not need any resulting values in order to continue. For this reason, reliable communication cannot be delegated to a transport mechanism or middleware software product—you must foresee the necessary confirmations on the business level in order to achieve reliable processing.

The example uses a saga as the source of the requests. This makes it necessary to track the individual identities of commands (by using the uniqueness of the saga's identity), which presents a burden in that cleaning up the memory of what has been done can be nontrivial. If the sender and recipient of reliable communication are both long-lived, and the exchange spans a large number of messages, it is more efficient to use sequence numbers, instead. With this simplification, a single counter is sufficient within the sender and recipient to track the number of the next message (in the sender) and the youngest message's number that has successfully been received (in the recipient). The recipient then expects the sequence number to increase monotonically and contiguously, enabling the recipient to detect missing messages and thereby maintain the correct order of processing even when messages are retransmitted out of order.

15.7.4 *Applicability*

The Business Handshake pattern is applicable wherever requests must be conveyed and processed reliably. In situations where commands must not be lost even across machine failures, you need to use the persistent form of the pattern; if losses due to unforeseen failures can be tolerated, you can use the nonpersistent form. It is important to note that persistent storage is a costly operation that significantly reduces the throughput between two components.

One noteworthy aspect is that this pattern can be applied between two components that are communicating via intermediaries: if handling of requests and/or responses along the path between the business handshake partners is idempotent, then the intermediaries can forgo the use of expensive persistence mechanisms and instead rely on at-least-once delivery that the exchange between the handshake partners gives them.

15.8 Summary

In this chapter, you learned the elementary building blocks for modeling information flows in Reactive systems:

- We familiarized you with the superficially trivial pattern of request and response, taking note of the benefits of complete and self-contained messages.
- We presented the Ask pattern as a shrink-wrapped request–response pair, in contrast with the performance advantages of forward message flow.
- For more-complex relations between components, we explored the Aggregator and Saga patterns. The latter provides a way to distribute systems that would otherwise be difficult to separate due to transaction boundaries.
- We added reliability to peer-to-peer communications using the Business Handshake pattern.

Many other specialized patterns are relevant to building message-driven applications. For further reading, we recommend Vaughn Vernon's *Reactive Messaging Patterns with the Actor Model* (Addison-Wesley, 2015) and *Enterprise Integration Patterns* by Gregor Hohpe and Bobby Woolf (Addison-Wesley, 2003).

Flow control patterns

16

In the previous chapters, you learned how to decompose systems into smaller pieces and how these pieces communicate to solve greater tasks. One aspect we have left out so far is that in addition to who interacts with whom, you must also consider the timeliness of communication. In order for your system to be resilient to varying loads, you need mechanisms that prevent components from failing uncontrollably due to overwhelming request rates. This chapter therefore introduces four basic patterns:

- The Pull pattern propagates back pressure from consumers to producers.
- The Managed Queue pattern makes back pressure measurable and actionable.
- The Drop pattern protects components under severe overload conditions.
- The Throttling pattern helps you avoid overload conditions where possible.

There are many variations on these patterns and a lot of applicable theory to be studied (in particular, control theory and queueing theory), but a treatment of these fields of research is outside the scope of this book. We hope you will be inspired by the basics presented in this chapter and refer to the scientific literature for in-depth coverage.

16.1 The Pull pattern

Have the consumer ask the producer for batches of data.

One challenge in Reactive systems is how to balance the relationship between producers and consumers of messages—be they requests that need processing or facts on their way to persistent storage. The difficulty lies in the dynamic nature of the problems that may arise from incorrect implementations: only under realistic input load can you observe whether a fast producer might overwhelm a resource-constrained consumer. Often, your load test environments are based on business forecasts that may be exceeded in real usage.

The formulation of the Pull pattern presented here is the result of Roland's involvement in the Reactive Streams initiative,[1] where the resulting behavior is also characterized as *dynamic push–pull*, an aspect that we will discuss later.

16.1.1 The problem setting

As an illustration of a case that clearly needs flow control, suppose you want to compute the alternating harmonic series:

$1 - 1/2 + 1/3 - 1/4$ ... *(converges toward the natural logarithm of 2)*

Generating the input for the terms that are to be computed is as simple as emitting the series of all natural numbers, but the more costly operation is to invert each of these with high precision and then sum them with the correct signs. For the sake of simplicity, you will keep the number generation and summation within one manager actor and distribute the sign-correct inversion across a number of worker actors. These worker actors are child actors of the manager: the number generator controls the entire process and terminates when the desired precision has been reached.

The task: Your mission is to implement both the manager and the worker actors such that each worker signals demand for work in batches of 10 whenever the number of outstanding work items is less than 5.

16.1.2 Applying the pattern

We will first consider the worker actor, because in this pattern it is the active party. The worker starts the process by asking for the first batch of inputs, and when it has processed enough of them, it keeps the process going by asking for more. Multiple workers can ask the manager for inputs independently, a fact that you will use to scale out the processing across multiple CPU cores. A worker has to manage two concerns: keeping track of how much work it has already asked for and how much it has received so far, and performing the actual computation, as illustrated in the following listing.

> **Listing 16.1 Processing expensive calculations in a worker that pulls inputs**

```
class Worker(manager: ActorRef) extends Actor {
  val mc = new MathContext(1000, RoundingMode.HALF_EVEN)   ◁─┐ Sets up precision
  val plus = BigDecimal(1, mc)                                │ and bases for
  val minus = BigDecimal(-1, mc)                             │ inversion

  var requested = 0                                  ◁─┐ Keeps track of the
  def request(): Unit =                                │ difference between
    if (requested < 5) {                               │ requested and
      manager ! WorkRequest(self, 10)                  │ performed work
      requested += 10
    }
}
```

---

[1] See www.reactive-streams.org (version 1.0.0, published April 30, 2015).

```
request()                    ◁─── Kicks off the processing

def receive = {
  case Job(id, data, replyTo) =>
    requested -= 1
    request()
    val sign = if ((data & 1) == 1) plus else minus
    val result = sign / data               ◁┐
    replyTo ! JobResult(id, result)         │  Performs the expensive
  }                                         │  calculation after having
}                                           │  asked for more work
```

The numbers used here are obviously tunable to the problem and resources at hand. It is important to note that you do not implement a stop–wait scheme in which the worker pulls, then waits for the data, then computes, then replies, and then pulls again. Instead, the worker is more proactive in requesting an entire batch of inputs in one go and then renews the request when the number of outstanding work items becomes low again. In this way, the worker's mailbox never grows beyond 14 items (requesting 10 when 4 are outstanding, and then miraculously not receiving any CPU time until those arrive—this is the worst-case scenario). It also ensures that if the worker outperforms the manager, there will always be outstanding demand signaled such that the manager can send new work immediately.

The manager shown in listing 16.2 needs to implement the other side of the Pull pattern, sending a number of work items according to each request it gets from one of the workers. The important part is that both need to agree on the notion of how much work is outstanding—requests for work must eventually be satisfied, lest the system get stuck with the worker waiting for work and the manager waiting for demand. In this example, the implementation can trivially ensure this property by always satisfying every work request immediately and in full.

Listing 16.2   Supplying a worker with tasks as it asks for them

```
class Manager extends Actor {                           Defines a stream of
  val workStream: Iterator[Job] =                       1,000,000 jobs
    Iterator from 1 map (x => Job(x, x, self)) take 1000000  ◁┘

  val aggregator = (x: BigDecimal, y: BigDecimal) => x + y
  val mc = new MathContext(1000, RoundingMode.HALF_EVEN)
  var approximation = BigDecimal(0, mc)                  Keeps track of jobs
                                                         that were sent but
  var outstandingWork = 0                      ◁──────┘  not completed

  (1 to 8) foreach (_ => context.actorOf(Props(new Worker(self))))

  def receive = {
    case WorkRequest(worker, items) =>
      workStream.take(items).foreach { job =>
        worker ! job
        outstandingWork += 1
      }
    case JobResult(id, result) =>
      approximation = aggregator(approximation, result)
```

Aggregation logic → points to the `val aggregator` / `val mc` / `var approximation` lines

Starts eight worker actors → points to the `(1 to 8) foreach` line

```
      outstandingWork -= 1
      if (outstandingWork == 0 && workStream.isEmpty) {
        println("final result: " + approximation)
        context.system.terminate()
      }
    }
  }
}
```

The manager only starts the workers. From then on, it is passively driven by their requests for work and their computation results. Once the stream of work items has been processed completely, the manager terminates the application after printing the final approximation result to the console.

16.1.3 *The pattern, revisited*

We have illustrated the case of an arbitrarily fast producer and slow consumers by distributing a computation over a group of worker actors. Were you to implement the manager such that it distributed all work items at once, you would find a few problems:

- Given enough work items (or larger ones than in this simple example), the system would run out of memory early in the process, because the work items would accumulate in the workers' mailboxes.
- An even distribution decided up front would result in uneven execution, with some actors finishing their share later than others. CPU utilization would be lower than desired during that time period.
- If a worker failed, all of its allocated work items would be lost—the manager would need to send them again to some other worker. With the current scheme, the amount of memory to store the currently outstanding computation jobs is strictly limited, whereas with up-front distribution, it might exceed available resource limits.

You avoid these issues by giving the workers control over how much work they are willing to buffer in their mailbox, while at the same time giving the manager control over how much work it is willing to hand out for concurrent execution.

One very important aspect in this scheme is that work is requested in batches and proactively. Not only does this save on messaging cost by bundling multiple requests into a single message, but it also allows the system to adapt to the relative speed of producer and consumer:

- When the producer is faster than the consumer, the producer will eventually run out of demand. The system runs in "pull" mode, with the consumer pulling work items from the producer with each request it makes.
- When the producer is slower than the consumer, the consumer will always have demand outstanding. The system runs in "push" mode, where the producer never needs to wait for a work request from the consumer.
- Under changing load characteristics (by way of deployment changes or variable usage patterns), the mechanism automatically switches between the previous

two modes without any further need for coordination—it behaves as a *dynamic push–pull* system.

The other notable aspect of this pattern is that it enables the composition of flow-control relationships across a chain of related components. Via the presence or absence of demand for work, the consumer tells the producer about its momentary processing capacity. In situations where the producer is merely an intermediary, it can employ the Pull pattern to retrieve the work items from their source. This implements a nonblocking, asynchronous channel over which back pressure can be transmitted along a data-processing chain. For this reason, this scheme has been adopted by the Reactive Streams standard.

16.1.4   Applicability

This pattern is well suited for scenarios where an elastic worker pool processes incoming requests that are self-contained and do not depend on local state that is maintained on each worker node. If requests need to be processed by a specific node in order to be treated correctly, the Pull pattern may still be used, but then it needs to be established between the manager and each worker individually: sending a request to the wrong worker just because it has processing capacity available would not lead to the correct result.

16.2   *The Managed Queue pattern*

Manage an explicit input queue, and react to its fill level.

One of the conclusions drawn from analyzing the Pull pattern is that it can be used to mediate back pressure across multiple processing steps in a chain of components. Transmitting back pressure means halting the entire pipeline when a consumer is momentarily overwhelmed, which may, for example, be caused by unfair scheduling or other execution artifacts, leading to avoidable inefficiencies in the system.

This kind of friction can lead to "stuttering" behavior in a processing engine, where short bursts of messages alternate with periods of inactivity during which back pressure signals travel through the system. These bursts can be smoothed out by employing buffers that allow the data to keep flowing even during short back pressure situations. These buffers are queues that temporarily hold messages while remembering their ordering. We call them *managed queues* because their use extends beyond this direct benefit: queues can be used to monitor and steer the performance of a messaging system. Buffering and managed queues are even more important at the boundaries of a system that employs back pressure: if data or requests are ingested from a source that cannot be slowed down, you need to mediate between the bounded internal capacity and the potentially unbounded influx.

16.2.1   The problem setting

In the example of the Pull pattern, you implemented a manager that had the formula for creating all required work items. Now, you will consider the manager to be just a mediator, with the source of the work items outside of its control: the manager will receive work requests while maintaining the Pull pattern with its workers. In order to smooth out the behavior in the case of momentary lack of requests from the workers, you will install a buffer within the manager.

The task: Your mission is to adapt the worker and manager actors from the Pull pattern example such that the numbers to be inverted are generated externally. The manager will keep a buffer of no more than 1,000 work items, responding with a rejection message to work items that are received while the buffer is full.

16.2.2 Applying the pattern

The main part you need to change is the manager actor. Instead of generating work items on demand, it now needs to hold two queues: one for work items while all workers are busy and one for workers' requests when no work items are available. An example is shown next.

Listing 16.3 **Managing a work queue to react to overload**

```
class Manager extends Actor {
  var workQueue = Queue.empty[Job]
  var requestQueue = Queue.empty[WorkRequest]

  (1 to 8) foreach (_ => context.actorOf(Props(new Worker(self))))

  def receive = {
    case job @ Job(id, _, replyTo) =>
      if (requestQueue.isEmpty) {
        if (workQueue.size < 1000) workQueue :+= job
        else replyTo ! JobRejected(id)
      } else {
        val WorkRequest(worker, items) = requestQueue.head
        worker ! job
        if (items > 1) worker ! DummyWork(items - 1)
        requestQueue = requestQueue.drop(1)
      }
    case wr @ WorkRequest(worker, items) =>
      if (workQueue.isEmpty) {
        requestQueue :+= wr
      } else {
        workQueue.iterator.take(items).foreach(job => worker ! job)
        val sent = Math.min(workQueue.size, items)
        if (sent < items) worker ! DummyWork(items - sent)
        workQueue = workQueue.drop(items)
      }
  }
}
```

> If there are no requests, the work queue will grow, leading to rejection when full.

> Work requests that cannot be satisfied immediately are queued for later.

Because you would like to use workers in round-robin fashion in this example, a case arises that requires an adaptation of the protocol between manager and worker: when satisfying a queued work request from a received job, you need to follow up the Job message with a DummyWork message that tells the worker that the remaining requested work items will not be sent. This leads to the worker sending a new request very soon and simplifies the manager's state management. You do so because the interesting point lies not with the management of the requestQueue but with the workQueue: this queue holds the current knowledge of the manager with respect to its workers' load situation. This queue will grow while the external producer outpaces the pool of workers, and it will shrink while workers catch up with the external requests. The fill level of this queue can thus be used as a signal to steer the worker pool's size, or it can be used to determine whether this part of the system is over-loaded—you implement the latter in this example.

The worker actor does not need to change much, compared to the Pull pattern; it only needs to handle the DummyWork message type:

```
class Worker(manager: ActorRef) extends Actor {
  ...

  def receive = {
    ...
    case DummyWork(count) =>
      requested -= count
      request()
  }
}
```

16.2.3   *The pattern, revisited*

You have used the Pull pattern between the manager and its workers and made the back pressure visible by observing the fill level of a queue that is filled with external requests and emptied based on the workers' demands. This measurement of the difference between requested and performed work can be used in many ways:

- We have demonstrated the simplest form, which is to use the queue as a smoothing buffer and reject additional requests while the queue is full. This implements service responsiveness while placing an upper bound on the size of the work queue.
- You could spin up a new worker once a given high–water mark was reached, adapting the worker pool elastically to the current service usage. Spinning down extraneous workers could be done by observing the size of the requestQueue as well.
- Rather than observe the momentary fill level of the queue, you could instead monitor its rate of change, taking sustained growth as a signal to enlarge the pool and sustained decrease as a signal to shrink it again.

This list is not exhaustive. There is an entire field of research called *control theory*[2] around the issue of how to steer process characteristics based on continuous measurements and reference values.

---

[2] See, for example, https://en.wikipedia.org/wiki/Control_theory.

16.2.4 *Applicability*

Using managed queues instead of using implicit queues as discussed in section 2.1.3 is always desirable, but it does not need to be done at every step in a processing chain. Within domains that mediate back pressure (for example, by using the Pull pattern), buffers often have the primary function of smoothing out bursts. Observable or intelligent queues are used predominantly at the boundaries of such a system, where the system interacts with other parts that do not participate in the back pressure mechanism. Note that back pressure represents a form of coupling, and as such its scope must be justified by the requirements of the subsystem it is applied to.

Applying intelligent queues is fun and invites forays into advanced control-theory concepts, feedback loops, self-tuning systems, and so on. Although this can be a stimulating learning experience, it also makes the system more complex and presents a barrier for newcomers to understand why and how it works. Another consideration is that the theoretical equations that describe the system's behavior become ever more complex the more numerous the active elements are within it, so going overboard with this pattern will defeat its purpose and likely lead to more erratic system behavior and suboptimal throughput and latency characteristics. Typical symptoms of having too much "intelligence" built into the system are oscillations in the decisions of the regulatory elements, which lead to potentially fatal oscillations in the system's behavior—scaling up and down too quickly and too frequently and sometimes hitting hard resource limits or failing completely.

16.3 *The Drop pattern*

Dropping requests is preferable to failing uncontrollably.

Imagine a system that is exposed to uncontrollable user input (for example, a site on the internet). Any deployment will be finite in both its processing capability and its buffering capacity, and if user input exceeds the former for long enough, the latter will be used up and something will need to fail. If this is not foreseen explicitly, then an automatic out-of-memory killer will make a decision that is likely to be less satisfactory than a planned load-shedding mechanism—and shedding load means dropping requests.

This is more of a philosophy than an implementation pattern. Network protocols, operating systems, programming platforms, and libraries will all drop packets, messages, or requests when overloaded; they do so in order to protect the system so that it can recover when load decreases. In the same spirit, authors of Reactive systems need to be comfortable with the notion of sometimes deliberately losing messages.

16.3.1 *The problem setting*

We will revisit the example from the Managed Queue pattern, where the source of requests is situated outside of your control. When work items are sent to the manager faster than workers can process them, the queue will grow, and eventually `JobRejected` messages will be sent back. But even this can only happen at a certain maximum rate; when jobs are sent at a higher rate, the manager's mailbox will begin to grow, and it will do so until the system runs out of memory.

The task: Your mission is to adapt the manager actor such that it accepts all work items into its queue up to a queue size of 1,000 and drops work items without sending back a response when the incoming rate exceeds the workers' capacity by more than a factor of 8.

16.3.2 *Applying the pattern*

The modification you are seeking to make will require two levels of rejection: past a queue size of 1,000, you will send back rejections; but you still need to keep track of the incoming rate in order to stop sending rejections when the incoming rate is more than 8 times the worker pool's capacity. But how can you do that?

If you keep the scheme from the Managed Queue pattern of not enqueueing work when the queue size has reached 1,000, then you will need to introduce another data structure that maintains the rate information: you will need to track `WorkRequest` messages in order to know how fast workers can process their work items, and you will need to track rejections to measure the excess rate of incoming work items. The data structure will need current timestamps for every piece of information that is fed into it, and it will need to know the current time when asking for a decision about whether to drop an item. All this is possible to implement, but doing so has a cost both at development time and at runtime—looking at the clock does not come free, plus the data structure will consume space and require CPU time to remain up to date.

Looking back at the manager actor, you see a data structure whose usage you can change slightly to provide the required information: the queue can always tell you about its length, and you can make it so the queue length reflects the excess rate. The key to this trick is that for a slowly changing incoming rate, the queue fill level will stabilize if there is a point at which ingress and egress are balanced: when workers pull items out at the same rate items enter the queue, both will even out. To make this work, you must decouple the incoming work-item rate from the enqueueing rate—you assume the worker pool's capacity to be constant, so the enqueueing rate is all you can work with.

The solution to this riddle to keep enqueueing in general, but for every item, you roll the dice to decide whether it gets in. The probability of being enqueued must decrease with growing queue size, as shown in figure 16.1: a longer queue results in fewer items getting in. The ratio between the two is the probability for the dice roll, and at the same time it matches the ratio of excess rate to worker-pool rate.

It is instructive to conduct a thought experiment to understand how and why this works.

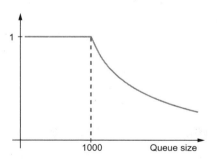

Figure 16.1   The probability of enqueueing incoming work items into the managed queue decreases once the nominal size has been reached.

Assume that the system starts with an empty queue and a rate mismatch of a factor of 10. The queue will quickly become full (reach 1,000 elements), at which point rejections will be generated. But the queue will continue to grow—only more slowly, due to the probabilistic enqueueing. Once the queue size is so big that the enqueueing probability drops to 10%, the enqueueing rate will match the dequeueing rate, and the size of the queue will remain stable until either the external work-item rate or the worker-pool capacity changes.

In terms of code, not much is needed to implement this scheme, as you can see here:

```
val queueThreshold = 1000
val dropThreshold = 1384
def random = ThreadLocalRandom.current

def shallEnqueue(atSize: Int) =
  (atSize < queueThreshold) || {
    val dropFactor = (atSize - queueThreshold) >> 6
    random.nextInt(dropFactor + 2) == 0
  }
```

You use this logic to handle incoming `Job` messages:

```
case job @ Job(id, _, replyTo) =>
  if (requestQueue.isEmpty) {
    val atSize = workQueue.size
    if (shallEnqueue(atSize)) workQueue :+= job
    else if (atSize < dropThreshold) replyTo ! JobRejected(id)
  } else ...
```

This means you will enqueue a certain fraction of incoming jobs even when the queue size is greater than 1,000, and the probability of enqueueing a given job decreases with growing queue size. At size 1,000, `dropFactor` is 0, and the probability of picking a zero from `nextInt(2)` is 50%. At size 1,064, `dropFactor` is 1, and the probability decreases to 33%—and so on, until at the drop threshold of 1,384, the probability is 1/8. `dropThreshold` is therefore chosen such that the desired cutoff point for rejection messages is implemented.

16.3.3 *The pattern, revisited*

The example includes two modes of overload reactions: either you send back an incomplete response (degraded functionality), or you do not reply at all. You implement the metric for selecting one of these modes based on the work-item queue the manager maintains. For this, you need to allow the queue to grow past its logical capacity bound, where the excess is regulated to be proportional to the rate mismatch between producers and consumers of work items—by choosing a different formula for `dropFactor`, you could make this relation quadratic, exponential, or whatever is required.

The important piece here is that providing degraded functionality only works up to a given point, and the service should foresee a mechanism that kicks in once this point is reached. Providing no functionality at all—*dropping* requests—is cheaper than providing degraded functionality, and under severe overload conditions this is all the service can do to retain control over its resources.

One notable side effect of the chosen implementation technique is that during an intense burst, you now enqueue a certain fraction of work items, whereas the strictly bounded queue as implemented in the Managed Queue pattern example would reject the entire burst (assuming that the burst occurs faster than consumption by the workers).

EXTENSION TO IMPLICIT QUEUES

We have so far only regarded the behavior of the explicit queue maintained by the manager actor. This actor, however, has only finite computing resources at its disposal, and even the calculations for deciding whether to drop a message have a certain cost. If the incoming rate is higher than the manager actor can decide about, its mailbox will grow: over time, it will eat up the JVM heap and lead to fatal termination through an OutOfMemoryError. This can only be avoided by limiting the implicit queues—the manager's mailbox, in this case—in addition to the explicit queues.

Because you are dealing with an aspect that is implicitly handled by the framework (Akka, in this example), you do not need to write much code to implement this. You only need to instruct Akka to install a bounded mailbox for the manager actor:

```
val managerProps = Props(new Manager).withMailbox("bounded-mailbox")
```

When this description is used to create the manager actor, Akka will look in its configuration for a section describing the bounded mailbox. The following settings configure a mailbox that is bounded to 1,000 messages:

```
bounded-mailbox {
  mailbox-type = "akka.dispatch.BoundedMailbox"
  mailbox-capacity = 1000
  mailbox-push-timeout-time = 0s
}
```

This has an important drawback: this mailbox drops not only Job messages from external sources but also WorkRequest messages from the worker actors. In order to make those cope with such losses, you must implement a resending mechanism (which would be needed in any case, if the workers were deployed remotely), but this will not fix a more severe issue. For example, if the external rate is 10 times as high as what can be processed, then only 1 in 10 work requests will make it back, leading to workers idling because they cannot tell the manager about their demand as quickly as they need to.

This demonstrates that dropping at a lower level will always be less precise than dropping at the level that has all the necessary information, but it is the nature of overload situations that this knowledge can be too costly to maintain. The bounded

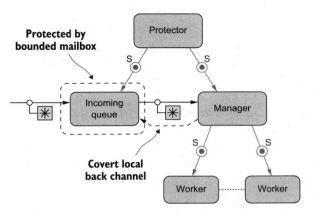

Protected by bounded mailbox

Incoming queue

Protector

Manager

Covert local back channel

Worker .... Worker

Figure 16.2 Placing an actor with a bounded mailbox in front of the manager actor requires that the manager uses a non-message-based back channel to signal that it has received a given message. In this fashion, the incoming queue can remain strictly bounded.

mailbox in Akka is well suited for actors that do not need to communicate with other actors in the course of handling their main input, but it has weaknesses for manager-like scenarios.

To protect the manager actor with a bounded mailbox, you have to keep that mailbox separate from the one used to communicate with worker actors. Because every actor can have only one mailbox, this means installing another actor, as shown in figure 16.2.

The `IncomingQueue` actor will be configured to use the bounded mailbox, which protects it from extremely fast producers. Under high load, this actor will constantly be running, pulling work items out of its mailbox and sending them on to the manager actor. If this happens without feedback, the manager can still experience unbounded growth of its own mailbox, but you cannot use actor messages to implement the feedback mechanism. In this case, it is appropriate to consider the deployment to be local—only in this case is it practically possible to run into the envisioned overload scenario—and therefore the manager can communicate with the incoming queue also using shared memory. A simple design is shown in the following listing:

```
private case class WorkEnvelope(job: Job) {
  @volatile var consumed = false
}

private class IncomingQueue(manager: ActorRef) extends Actor {
  var workQueue = Queue.empty[WorkEnvelope]
  def receive = {
    case job: Job =>
      workQueue = workQueue.dropWhile(_.consumed)
      if (workQueue.size < 1000) {
        val envelope = WorkEnvelope(job)
        workQueue :+= envelope
        manager ! envelope
      }
  }
}
```

The only thing the manager has to do is set the `consumed` flag to `true` upon receipt of a `WorkEnvelope`. Further improvements that are omitted for the sake of simplicity include cleaning out the incoming queue periodically, in case there are long pauses in the incoming request stream during which work items would be unduly retained in memory. The full code for this example can be found with the book's downloads in the file DropPatternWithProtection.scala.

Although this extension seems specific to Akka, it is generic. In any OS and service platform, there will be implicit queues that transport requests from the network to local processes as well as within these processes—these could be message queues, thread pool task queues, threads that are queued for execution, and so on. Some of these queues are configurable, but changing their configuration will have indiscriminate effects on all kinds of messages passing through them; we noted earlier that the necessary knowledge exists at a higher level, but that higher level may need protection from lower levels that can only make coarse-grained decisions. The workarounds differ; the Akka example given in this section is tailored to this particular case, but the need to apply such custom solutions will arise wherever you push a platform to its limits.

16.3.4 Applicability

During system overload, some kind of failure is bound to happen. Determining what kind it will be is a business decision: should the system protect itself by foregoing responsiveness, or should it come to a crawling but uncontrolled halt when resources are exhausted? The intuitive answer is the former, whereas typical engineering practice implements the latter—not deliberately, but due to neglect resulting from other aspects of the application design having higher priority. This pattern is always applicable, if only in the sense that not shedding load by dropping requests should be a well-understood and deliberate decision.

16.4   The Throttling pattern

Throttle your own output rate according to contracts with other services.

We have discussed how each component can mediate, measure, and react to back pressure in order to avoid uncontrollable overload situations. With these means at your disposal, it is not just fair but obligatory that you respect the ingestion limits of other components. In situations where you outpace consumers of your outputs, you can slow to match their rate, and you can even ensure that you do not violate a prearranged rate agreement.

In section 12.4.2, you saw that a circuit breaker can be designed such that it rejects requests that would otherwise lead to a request rate that is too high. With the Pull pattern, you can turn this around and not generate requests more quickly than they are allowed to be sent.

16.4.1 *The problem setting*

Borrowing from the Pull pattern example, suppose you have a source of work items from which you can request work. We will demonstrate the Throttling pattern by combining this source with the worker-pool implementation from the Managed Queue pattern example. The goal is to transfer work items at a rate the pool can handle so that, under normal conditions, no jobs are rejected by the managed queue.

The task: Your mission is to implement a `CalculatorClient` actor that pulls work from the work source and forwards it to the worker-pool manager such that the average rate of forwarded messages does not exceed a configurable limit. Bonus points are awarded for allowing short bursts of configurable size in order to increase efficiency.

16.4.2 *Applying the pattern*

A commonly used rate-limiting algorithm is called *token bucket*.[3] It is usually employed to reject or delay network traffic that exceeds a certain bandwidth allocation. The mechanism is simple:

- A bucket of fixed size is continually filled with tokens at a given rate. Tokens in excess of the bucket size are discarded.
- When a network packet arrives, a number of tokens corresponding to the packet's size should be removed from the bucket. If this is possible, then the packet travels on; if not, then the packet is not allowed through.

Depending on the size of the bucket, a burst of packets might be admitted after a period of inactivity; but when the bucket is empty, packets will either be dropped or delayed until enough tokens are available.

You will have to adapt this algorithm slightly in order to use it for your purposes. First, each work item carries the same weight in this example, so you require just one token per message. Second, messages do not just arrive at the actor: you must request them from the work source. Because you do not wish to drop or delay messages—where the latter would imply buffering that you want to avoid where possible—you must not request more work items from the source than you can permit through based on the current fill level of the token bucket. In the worst case, you must assume that all work items arrive before the bucket gains another token. Using the `Worker` actor from listing 16.1 (the Pull pattern example) as a basis, you arrive at the following implementation.

> **Listing 16.4 Pulling work according to a specified rate using a token bucket**

```
class CalculatorClient(workSource: ActorRef, calculator: ActorRef,
                       ratePerSecond: Long, bucketSize: Int,
                       batchSize: Int) extends Actor {
  /*
   * first part: the token bucket implementation
```

---

[3] See, for example, https://en.wikipedia.org/wiki/Token_bucket.

```
  */
def now() = System.nanoTime()
val nanoSecondsBetweenTokens = 1000000000L / ratePerSecond

var tokenBucket = bucketSize
var lastTokenTime = now()

def refillBucket(time: Long): Unit = {
  val accrued = (time -
    lastTokenTime) * ratePerSecond / 1000000000L
  if (tokenBucket + accrued >= bucketSize) {
    tokenBucket = bucketSize
    lastTokenTime = time
  } else {
    tokenBucket += accrued.toInt
    lastTokenTime += accrued * nanoSecondsBetweenTokens
  }
}
def consumeToken(time: Long): Unit = {
  // always refill first since we do it upon activity and not scheduled
  refillBucket(time)
  tokenBucket -= 1
}

/*
 * second part: managing the pull pattern's demand
 */
var requested = 0
def request(time: Long): Unit =
  if (tokenBucket - requested >= batchSize) {
    sendRequest(time, batchSize)
  } else if (requested == 0) {
    if (tokenBucket > 0) {
      sendRequest(time, tokenBucket)
    } else {
      val timeForNextToken =
          lastTokenTime + nanoSecondsBetweenTokens - time
      context.system.scheduler.scheduleOnce(timeForNextToken.nanos,
          workSource, WorkRequest(self, 1))(context.dispatcher)
      requested = 1
    }
  }
def sendRequest(time: Long, items: Int): Unit = {
  workSource ! WorkRequest(self, items)
  requested += items
}

request(lastTokenTime)

/*
 * third part: using the above for rate-regulated message forwarding
 */
def receive = {
  case job: Job =>
    val time = now()
    consumeToken(time)
    requested -= 1
```

- **Calculates new tokens since last time, rounding down** (annotation pointing to `val accrued = (time - lastTokenTime) * ratePerSecond / 1000000000L`)
- **Caps the token bucket at its maximum size** (annotation pointing to `if (tokenBucket + accrued >= bucketSize) {`)
- **Only advances the time to the last integer token, to pick up a fractional part next time** (annotation pointing to `lastTokenTime += accrued * nanoSecondsBetweenTokens`)
- **Kicks off the process** (annotation pointing to `request(lastTokenTime)`)

```
        request(time)
        calculator ! job
    }
}
```

The code for the actor is organized into three parts: the first manages the token bucket, the second derives the work requests to be sent from the currently outstanding work items and the bucket fill level, and the third forwards received work items while keeping the token bucket updated and requesting more work when appropriate. There are some subtleties in writing such code, pertaining to time granularity caused by the execution of the actor at discrete times that you cannot control precisely:

- The scheduler typically does not have nanosecond-level resolution, so you must foresee that the scheduled WorkRequest is delivered later than intended.
- The actor may run more frequently than the token bucket's refill rate, which requires you to deal with fractional tokens. You avoid this by not advancing the last update time when you encounter such cases.
- Because you do not wish to involve the imprecise scheduler more than necessary, you run the token-bucket algorithm triggered by work-item activity. Hence, you must always bring the token bucket up to date before performing other operations.

With these considerations, you arrive at an efficient and precise implementation that will ensure that the average forwarded message rate will be at most ratePerSecond (slower if the source cannot deliver quickly enough), with momentary bursts that are limited to the bucket size and with best-effort request batching for pulling items out of the source.

The full source code for this example is available with the book's downloads. Notice that the example application does not begin the process by creating a CalculatorClient actor: instead, it first performs 100,000 calculations on the worker pool using Akka Streams. Akka Streams uses the Pull pattern internally and implements strict back pressure based on it, ensuring with the chosen combinators that no more than 1,000 calculations are outstanding at any given time. This means the worker pool will not reject a single request while exercising all code paths sufficiently to trigger the JVM just-in-time compilation; afterward, a rate of 50,000 per second will not be a problem on today's portable hardware. Without this warm-up, you would see rejections caused by the worker pool being too slow as well as measurable interruptions caused by just-in-time compilation.

16.4.3 The pattern, revisited

You have used a rate-tracking mechanism—the token bucket—to steer the demand that you used for the Pull pattern. The resulting work-item rate then is bounded by the token bucket's configuration, allowing you to ensure that you do not send more work to another component than was agreed on beforehand. Although a managed queue lets a service protect itself to a degree (see also the discussion of the Drop pattern and its limitations), the Throttling pattern implements service collaboration where the user also protects the service by promising to not exceed a given rate. This can be used restrictively to make rejections unlikely under nominal conditions, or it can be used more liberally to avoid having to call on the Drop pattern. But neither the Managed Queue pattern nor the Drop pattern is replaced by the Throttling pattern; it is important to consider overload protection from both the consumer and producer sides.

16.5 *Summary*

In this chapter, we considered that communication happens at a certain rate. You learned about different ways in which this rate can be regulated and acted on:

- The Pull pattern matches the rates of producer and consumer such that the slower party sets the pace. It works without explicitly measuring time or rates.
- The Managed Queue pattern decouples the incoming and outgoing rates with a configurable leeway—the queue size—and makes the rate difference between producer and consumer measurable and actionable.
- The Drop pattern provides an escalation for the Managed Queue pattern when the rate mismatch is too big to be handled by degrading the service functionality.
- The Throttling pattern regulates a message stream's speed according to configured rate and burstiness parameters; it is the only presented pattern that explicitly deals with time.

State management and persistence patterns

The previous chapter introduced the concepts of message rate, load, and time; previously, we had only considered the timeless relationship between different components. This chapter adds another orthogonal dimension to complete the picture: it is the purpose of almost all components to maintain state, and we have not yet discussed how this should be done. The patterns presented are closely related to each other and form a cohesive unit:

- The Domain Object pattern decouples business logic from communication machinery.
- The Sharding pattern allows you to store any number of domain objects on an elastic cluster.
- The Event-Sourcing pattern unifies change notifications and persistence by declaring the event log to be the sole source of truth.
- The Event Stream pattern uses this source of truth to derive and disseminate information.

This chapter can only serve as a basic introduction to these patterns. We hope it inspires you to delve into the rich literature and online resources on domain-driven design, event sourcing, and command-query responsibility separation (see the footnotes throughout the chapter for pointers).

17.1   *The Domain Object pattern*

Separate the business domain logic from communication and state management.

In chapter 6, we discussed the principle of *divide and conquer*, and in section 12.1, you learned how to apply this in the form of the Simple Component pattern. The resulting components have a clearly defined responsibility: they do one thing and do it in full. Often, this involves maintaining state that persists between invocations of these components. Although it may be intuitive to identify a component with its state—for example, by saying that a shopping cart in its entirety is implemented by an actor—this has notable downsides:

- The business logic becomes entangled with the communication protocols and with execution concerns.
- The only available mode of testing this component is through asynchronous integration tests—the implemented business behavior is accessible only via the externally defined protocols.

The Domain Object pattern describes how to maintain a clear boundary and separation between the different concerns of business logic, state management, and communication. This pattern is intuitively understandable without additional knowledge, but we highly recommended that you study domain-driven design,[1] because it provides more in-depth techniques for defining the *ubiquitous language* used within each *bounded context*. Bounded contexts typically correspond to components in your hierarchical system decomposition, and the ubiquitous language is the natural language in which domain experts describe the business function of the component.

17.1.1   *The problem setting*

In this chapter, we will use the example of implementing a shopping cart component. Although there may be a variety of facets to be covered in a real-world implementation, it is sufficient for the demonstration of the important aspects of these patterns to be able to associate an owner, add and remove items, and query the list of items in the shopping cart.

The task: Your mission is to implement a domain model for the shopping cart that contains only the business information and offers synchronous methods for performing business operations. Then, you will implement an actor that encapsulates a domain model instance and exposes the business operations as part of its communication protocol.

---

[1] See, for example, Eric Evans, *Domain-Driven Design* (Addison-Wesley, 2003); or Vaughn Vernon, *Implementing Domain-Driven Design* (Addison-Wesley, 2013).

17.1.2 Applying the pattern

You will begin by defining how the shopping cart will be referenced and how it will reference its contained items and its owner:

```
case class ItemRef(id: URI)
case class CustomerRef(id: URI)
case class ShoppingCartRef(id: URI)
```

You use URIs to identify each of these objects and wrap them in named classes so that you can distinguish their purpose with their static type to avoid programming errors. With these preparations, a minimalistic shopping cart looks like the following listing.

Listing 17.1 A minimalistic shopping cart definition

```
case class ShoppingCart(items: Map[ItemRef, Int],
                        owner: Option[CustomerRef]) {
  def setOwner(customer: CustomerRef): ShoppingCart = {
    require(owner.isEmpty, "owner cannot be overwritten")
    copy(owner = Some(customer))
  }

  def addItem(item: ItemRef, count: Int): ShoppingCart = {
    require(count > 0,
      s"count must be positive (trying to add $item with count $count)")
    val currentCount = items.get(item).getOrElse(0)
    copy(items = items.updated(item, currentCount + count))
  }

  def removeItem(item: ItemRef, count: Int): ShoppingCart = {
    require(count > 0,
      s"count must be positive (trying to remove $item with count $count)")
    val currentCount = items.get(item).getOrElse(0)
    val newCount = currentCount - count
    if (newCount <= 0) copy(items = items - item)
    else copy(items = items.updated(item, newCount))
  }
}

object ShoppingCart {
  val empty = ShoppingCart(Map.empty, None)
}
```

A shopping cart starts out empty, with no owner; through its class methods, it can obtain an owner and be filled with items. You can completely unit-test this class with synchronous and deterministic test cases, which should make you happy. It is also straightforward to discuss this class with the person in charge of the website's commercial function, even if that person is not a programming expert. In fact, this class should be written not by a distributed systems expert but by a software engineer who is fluent in business rules and processes.

Next, you will define the interface between this domain class and the message-driven execution engine that will manage and run it. This includes commands and their resulting events as well as queries and their results, as shown in the next listing.

Listing 17.2   Messages for communication with a shopping cart object

```
trait ShoppingCartMessage {
  def shoppingCart: ShoppingCartRef
}

sealed trait Command extends ShoppingCartMessage
case class SetOwner(shoppingCart: ShoppingCartRef, owner: CustomerRef)
                                                     extends Command
case class AddItem(shoppingCart: ShoppingCartRef, item: ItemRef, count: Int)
                                                     extends Command
case class RemoveItem(shoppingCart: ShoppingCartRef, item: ItemRef, count: Int)
                                                     extends Command

sealed trait Query extends ShoppingCartMessage
case class GetItems(shoppingCart: ShoppingCartRef) extends Query

sealed trait Event extends ShoppingCartMessage
case class OwnerChanged(shoppingCart: ShoppingCartRef, owner: CustomerRef)
                                                     extends Event
case class ItemAdded(shoppingCart: ShoppingCartRef, item: ItemRef, count: Int)
                                                     extends Event
case class ItemRemoved(shoppingCart: ShoppingCartRef, item: ItemRef, count: Int)
                                                     extends Event

sealed trait Result extends ShoppingCartMessage
case class GetItemsResult(shoppingCart: ShoppingCartRef, items: Map[ItemRef, Int])
    4                                                extends Result
```

A *command* is a message that expresses the *intent to make a modification*; if successful, it results in an *event*, which is an *immutable fact about the past*. A *query*, on the other hand, is a message that expresses the desire to *obtain information* and that may be answered by a *result* that describes an aspect of the domain object at the point in time when the query was processed. With these business-level definitions, you are ready to declare an actor and its communication protocol, which allows clients to perform commands and queries, as in the following listing.

Listing 17.3   A shopping cart manager actor

```
case class ManagerCommand(cmd: Command, id: Long, replyTo: ActorRef)
case class ManagerEvent(id: Long, event: Event)
case class ManagerQuery(cmd: Query, id: Long, replyTo: ActorRef)
case class ManagerResult(id: Long, result: Result)
case class ManagerRejection(id: Long, reason: String)

class Manager(var shoppingCart: ShoppingCart) extends Actor {
  /*
   * this is the usual constructor, the above allows priming with
   * previously persisted state.
   */
  def this() = this(ShoppingCart.empty)

  def receive = {
    case ManagerCommand(cmd, id, replyTo) =>
      try {
```

```
    val event = cmd match {
      case SetOwner(cart, owner) =>
        shoppingCart = shoppingCart.setOwner(owner)
        OwnerChanged(cart, owner)
      case AddItem(cart, item, count) =>
        shoppingCart = shoppingCart.addItem(item, count)
        ItemAdded(cart, item, count)
      case RemoveItem(cart, item, count) =>
        shoppingCart = shoppingCart.removeItem(item, count)
        ItemRemoved(cart, item, count)
    }
    replyTo ! ManagerEvent(id, event)
  } catch {
    case ex: IllegalArgumentException =>
      replyTo ! ManagerRejection(id, ex.getMessage)
  }
case ManagerQuery(cmd, id, replyTo) =>
  try {
    val result = cmd match {
      case GetItems(cart) =>
        GetItemsResult(cart, shoppingCart.items)
    }
    replyTo ! ManagerResult(id, result)
  } catch {
    case ex: IllegalArgumentException =>
      replyTo ! ManagerRejection(id, ex.getMessage)
  }
  }
}
```

The pattern here is regular: for every command, you determine the appropriate event and send it back as a response. The same goes for queries and results. Validation errors will be raised by the ShoppingCart domain object as IllegalArgumentExceptions and turned into ManagerRejection messages. This is a case where catching exceptions within an actor is appropriate: this actor manages the domain object and handles a specific part of failures emanating from it.

The state management you implement here is that the actor maintains a reference to the current snapshot of the shopping cart's state. In addition to keeping it in memory, you could also write it to a database upon every change or dump it to a file; the plethora of ways to do this are not shown here because they are not necessary for demonstrating the point that the actor controls this aspect as well as the external communication. The full source code is available with this book's downloads, including an example conversation between a client and this manager actor.

17.1.3 *The pattern, revisited*

You have disentangled the domain logic from the state management and communication aspects by starting out from the domain expert's view. First, you defined what a shopping cart contains and which operations it offers, and you codified this as a class. Then, you defined message representations for all commands and queries as well as their corresponding events and results. Only as the last step did you create a message-driven component that serves as a shell for the domain object and mediates between the messages and the methods offered by the domain object.

One noteworthy, deliberate aspect is a clear separation of domain object, commands, events, queries, and results on the one hand and the actor's protocol on the other. The former reference only domain concepts, whereas the latter references what is needed for communication (the `ActorRef` type, in this Akka-based example, as well as message IDs that could be used for deduplication). Having to include message-related types in source files that define domain objects is a signal that the concerns have not been separated cleanly.

17.2 The Sharding pattern

Scale out the management of a large number of domain objects by grouping them into shards based on unique and stable object properties.

The Domain Object pattern gives you the ability to wrap the domain's state in small components that can, in principle, be distributed easily across a cluster of network nodes in order to provide the resources for representing even very large domains that cannot be held in memory by a single machine. The difficulty then becomes how to address the individual domain objects without having to maintain a directory that lists every object's location—such a directory could easily reach a size that is impractical to hold in memory.

The Sharding pattern places an upper bound on the size of the directory by grouping the domain objects into a configurable number of shards—the domain is fractured algorithmically into pieces of manageable size. The term *algorithmically* means the association between objects and shards is determined by a fixed formula that can be evaluated whenever an object needs to be located.

17.2.1 The problem setting

Coming back to this chapter's running example, suppose you need to store a huge number of shopping carts—imagine writing the back end for a huge retail website on the internet, with millions of customers creating billions of shopping carts every day. Rather than manually creating the manager actors, you need to employ a sharding strategy that can effectively and efficiently distribute this dataset over an elastic cluster of machines.

The task: Your mission is to change the minimalistic Domain Actor pattern example in the book's downloads such that the manager actors are created on a cluster of nodes according to a sharding algorithm based on 256 shards.

17.2.2 Applying the pattern

Because you are already using Akka, you can concentrate on the essence of the problem by using the `akka-cluster-sharding` module, which implements low-level sharding mechanics. An overview of how these mechanics work is given in figure 17.1.

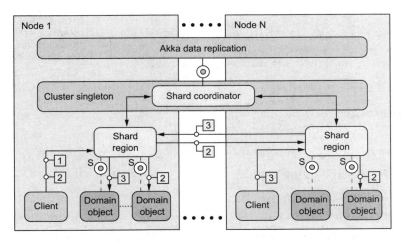

Figure 17.1 Sharding requires that a `ShardRegion` is started on all participating nodes and registers itself with the `ShardCoordinator`. When a message is to be sent from a client to one of the managed domain objects—called an entity here—it will be sent via the local `ShardRegion`, which will consult the coordinator cluster singleton as to where the shard that contains the domain object should be located. The shard will be created on demand if it does not yet exist. The shard is maintained by an actor situated between the region and the entities (not shown here for the sake of simplicity). The allocation of shards to regions is replicated in memory among all nodes using the Data Replication module (see section 13.2.3 on CRDTs).

The only remaining pieces needed to enlist the sharding module's support are as follows:

- A recipe for how to create entities when they are first referenced
- A formula that extracts the unique entity ID from a command or query
- A formula that extracts the shard number from a command or query

The first will be a `Props` object, and the latter two will be functions. The shard extraction guides the message to the correct shard region, and the shard actor then uses the entity ID to find the correct domain object manager among its child actors. You group these two functions together with an identifier for the shopping cart sharding system, as follows.

Listing 17.4 Defining sharding algorithms for a shopping cart

```
object ShardSupport {
  val extractEntityId: ShardRegion.ExtractEntityId = {
    case mc @ ManagerCommand(cmd, _, _) =>
      cmd.shoppingCart.id.toString -> mc
    case mc @ ManagerQuery(query, _, _) =>
      query.shoppingCart.id.toString -> mc
  }
```

Identifies entities by the shopping cart ID; commands that do not match are dropped

```
val extractShardId: ShardRegion.ExtractShardId = {       ◁───┐   Shard entities
  case ManagerCommand(cmd, _, _) =>                               according to the
    toHex(cmd.shoppingCart.id.hashCode & 255)                    smallest 8 bits of the
  case ManagerQuery(query, _, _) =>                               ID's hash code
    toHex(query.shoppingCart.id.hashCode & 255)
}
private def toHex(b: Int) =
  new java.lang.StringBuilder(2)
    .append(hexDigits(b >> 4))
    .append(hexDigits(b & 15))
    .toString
private val hexDigits = "0123456789ABCDEF"

val RegionName = "ShoppingCart"
}
```

With this preparation, you can start the cluster nodes and try it, as shown next.

Listing 17.5   Starting up a cluster to host the shards

```
val sys1 = ActorSystem("ShardingExample", node1Config.withFallback(clusterConfig))
val seed = Cluster(sys1).selfAddress

def startNode(sys: ActorSystem): Unit = {
  Cluster(sys).join(seed)
  ClusterSharding(sys).start(
    typeName = ShardSupport.RegionName,
    entityProps = Props(new Manager),
    settings = ClusterShardingSettings(sys1),
    extractEntityId = ShardSupport.extractEntityId,
    extractShardId = ShardSupport.extractShardId)
}

startNode(sys1)

val sys2 = ActorSystem("ShardingExample", clusterConfig)
startNode(sys2)
```

From this point on, you can talk to the sharded shopping carts via the shard region, which acts as a local mediator that sends commands to the correct node:

```
val shardRegion = ClusterSharding(sys1).shardRegion(ShardSupport.RegionName)
```

For the other configuration settings that are necessary to enable clustering and sharding, please refer to the full source code available with the book's downloads.

17.2.3   *The pattern, revisited*

You have used Akka's Cluster Sharding support to partition shopping carts across an elastic cluster—the underlying mechanics allocate shards to network nodes in a fashion that maintains an approximately balanced placement of shards, even when cluster nodes are added or removed. In order to use this module, you had to provide a recipe for creating a domain object manager actor and two functions: one for extracting the target shard ID from a command or query message and one for extracting the domain object's unique ID, which is used to locate it within its shard.

Implementing the basic mechanics of clustering and sharding is a complex endeavor that is best left to supporting frameworks or tool kits. Akka is not the only one supporting this pattern natively: another example on the .NET platform is Microsoft's Orleans framework.[2]

17.2.4 Important caveat

One important restriction of this scheme in Akka is that in the case of elastic shard reallocations, the existing actors will be terminated on their old home node and re-created at their new home node. If the actor only keeps its state in memory (as demonstrated in the examples so far), then its state is lost after such a transition—which usually is not desired.

Orleans avoids this caveat by automatically making all Grains (the Orleans concept corresponding to Actors) persistent by default, taking snapshots of their state after every processed message. A better solution is to consider persistence explicitly, as we will do in the following section; Orleans also allows this behavior to be customized in the same fashion.

17.3 The Event-Sourcing pattern

Perform state changes only by applying events. Make them durable by storing the events in a log.

Looking at the Domain Object pattern example, you can see that all state changes the manager actor performs are coupled to an event that is sent back to the client that requested this change. Because these events contain the full history of how the state of the domain object evolved, you may as well use it for the purpose of making the state changes persistent—this, in turn, makes the state of the domain object persistent. This pattern was described in 2005 by Martin Fowler[3] and picked up by Microsoft Research,[4] and it has shaped the design of the Akka Persistence module.[5]

17.3.1 The problem setting

You want your domain objects to retain their state across system failures as well as cluster shard–rebalancing events, and toward this end you must make them persistent. As noted earlier, you could do this by always updating a database row or a file, but these solutions involve more coordination than is needed. The state changes for different domain objects are managed by different shell components and are naturally serialized—when you persist these changes, you could conceptually write to one separate database per object, because there are no consistency constraints to be upheld between them.

---

[2] See http://dotnet.github.io/orleans and http://research.microsoft.com/en-us/projects/orleans.

[3] See http://martinfowler.com/eaaDev/EventSourcing.html.

[4] See https://msdn.microsoft.com/en-us/library/dn589792.aspx and https://msdn.microsoft.com/en-us/library/jj591559.aspx.

[5] See http://doc.akka.io/docs/akka/2.4.1/scala/persistence.html.

Instead of transforming the state-changing events into updates of a single storage location, you can turn things around and make the events themselves the source of truth for your persistent domain objects—hence, the name *event-sourcing*. The source of truth needs to be persistent, and because events are generated in strictly sequential order, you merely need an append-only log data structure to fulfill this requirement.

The task: Your mission is to transform the manager actor from the Domain Object pattern into a `PersistentActor` whose state is restored upon restart.

17.3.2 Applying the pattern

You saw the `PersistentActor` trait in action in section 15.7.2 when you implemented at-least-once delivery to attempt to keep this promise even across system failures. With the preparations from the previous sections, it is straightforward to recognize the events you need to make persistent and how to apply them. First, you need to lift the association between events and domain-object methods from the manager actor into the business domain—this is where they belong, because both the object and the events are part of the same business domain. Therefore, the domain object should know how the relevant domain events affect its state, as shown in the following listing.

Listing 17.6   Adding the domain events to the business logic

```
case class ShoppingCart(items: Map[ItemRef, Int], owner: Option[CustomerRef])
    {
  ...

  def applyEvent(event: Event): ShoppingCart = event match {
    case OwnerChanged(_, owner)     => setOwner(owner)
    case ItemAdded(_, item, count)  => addItem(item, count)
    case ItemRemoved(_, item, count) => removeItem(item, count)
  }
}
```

With this in place, you can formulate the persistent object manager actor in terms of commands, events, queries, results, and one in-memory snapshot of the current domain object state. This ensemble is shown in the next listing.

Listing 17.7   Persisting an event-sourced domain object

```
class PersistentObjectManager extends PersistentActor {
  override def persistenceId = context.self.path.name      ◁┐  The actor's name
                                                            │   will match the
  var shoppingCart = ShoppingCart.empty                    │   extracted entity ID:
                                                            │   the shopping cart ID.
  def receiveCommand = {
    case ManagerCommand(cmd, id, replyTo) =>
      try {
        val event = cmd match {
          case SetOwner(cart, owner)        => OwnerChanged(cart, owner)
          case AddItem(cart, item, count)   => ItemAdded(cart, item, count)
          case RemoveItem(cart, item, count) => ItemRemoved(cart, item, count)
        }
```

```
      // perform the update here to treat validation errors immediately
      shoppingCart = shoppingCart.applyEvent(event)
      persist(event) { _ =>
        replyTo ! ManagerEvent(id, event)
      }
    } catch {
      case ex: IllegalArgumentException =>
        replyTo ! ManagerRejection(id, ex.getMessage)
    }
  case ManagerQuery(cmd, id, replyTo) =>
    try {
      val result = cmd match {
        case GetItems(cart) => GetItemsResult(cart, shoppingCart.items)
      }
      replyTo ! ManagerResult(id, result)
    } catch {
      case ex: IllegalArgumentException =>
        replyTo ! ManagerRejection(id, ex.getMessage)
    }
  }
}
def receiveRecover = {
  case e: Event => shoppingCart = shoppingCart.applyEvent(e)
}
}
```

Instead of invoking business operations directly on the ShoppingCart object, you perform a mapping from commands to events and ask the shopping cart to apply the events to itself. In case of validation errors, this will still result in an IllegalArgument-Exception that you turn into a rejection message; otherwise, you first persist the event before replying to the client that you have performed the change—this scheme interoperates smoothly with the Reliable Delivery pattern presented in section 15.7.

The biggest change is that instead of defining a single receive behavior, you declare the live behavior as receiveCommand and add a receiveRecover behavior as well. This second behavior is not invoked for actor messages: it only receives the persisted events as they are read from the event log (also called a *journal*) right after the actor is created and before it processes its first message. The only thing you need to do here is apply the events to the shopping cart snapshot to get it up to date. The full source code is available in the book's downloads, together with an example application that demonstrates the persistent nature of this actor.

17.3.3 *The pattern, revisited*

You have taken the events the domain object manager sent in its replies to clients and repurposed them as representations of the state changes the domain object goes through. In the case we discussed, every command corresponds to exactly one event; but sometimes, in addition to confirmation events being sent back to clients, internal state changes occur as well—these will have to be lifted into events and persisted like the others.

It is important to note that the events that describe state changes of domain objects are part of the business domain as well: they have business meaning outside the technical context of the program code. With this in mind, it may be appropriate to choose a smaller granularity for the events than would be the case by following the derivation from the Domain Object pattern followed here—this path is more useful as a learning guide and should not be taken to be a definition. Please refer to the event-sourcing literature for an in-depth treatment of how to design and evolve events.

17.3.4 Applicability

This pattern is applicable where the durability of an object's state history is practical and potentially interesting (you will hear more about this last part in the following section). A shopping cart may see some fluctuation before checkout, payment, and delivery, but the total number of events within it should not exceed hundreds—these correspond to manual user actions, after all. The state of a token bucket filter within a network router, on the other hand, changes constantly, goes back and forth through the same states, and may, most important, see trillions of changes within relatively short periods of time; it is therefore not likely to be practically persistable, let alone by using event sourcing.

For domain objects that may accumulate state over a longer time period, and where the event reply during recovery may eventually take longer than is affordable, there is a workaround, but it should be used with care. From time to time, the domain object's snapshot state may be persisted together with the event sequence number it is based on; then, recovery can start from this snapshot instead of having to go back to the beginning of time. The problem with this approach is that changes to the domain logic (bug fixes) can easily invalidate the snapshots, which fact must be recognized and considered. The underlying issue is that although the events have meaning in the business domain, the snapshot does not—it is just a projection of the implementation details of the domain object logic.

Event sourcing generally is not applicable in cases where it would be desirable to delete events from the log. Not only is the entire concept built on the notion of representing *immutable* facts, but this desire usually arises when the persisted state does not have meaning in the business domain—for example, when using a `PersistentActor` as a durable message queue. There are much more performant solutions to this problem that are also easier to use: see, for example, Kafka (http://kafka.apache.org) and other distributed queues.

17.4 *The Event Stream pattern*

Publish the events emitted by a component so that the rest of the system can derive knowledge from them.

The events that a component stores in its log represent the sum of all the knowledge it has ever possessed. This is a treasure trove for the rest of the system to delve into: although the shopping cart system is only interested in maintaining the current state of customer activity, other concerns are tangential to it, such as tracking the popularity of various products. This secondary concern does not need to be updated in a guaranteed fashion in real time; it does not matter if it lags behind the most current information by a few seconds (individual humans usually would not be able to notice even a delay of hours in this information). Therefore, it would be an unnecessary burden to have the shopping cart component provide this summary information, and it would also violate the Simple Component pattern by introducing a second responsibility.

The first dedicated event log that specializes in supporting use cases like this is Greg Young's Event Store.[6] Akka offers the Persistence Query module[7] as a generic implementation framework for this pattern.

17.4.1 The problem setting

You have previously implemented a `PersistentObjectManager` actor that uses event sourcing to persist its state. The events are written by Akka Persistence into the configured event log (also called a *journal*). Now you want to use this information to feed another component, whose function will be to keep track of the popularity of different items put into shopping carts. You want to keep this information updated and make it available to the rest of the system via a query protocol.

The task: Your mission is to implement an actor that uses a persistence query to obtain and analyze the `AddItem` events of all shopping carts, keeping up-to-date status information available for other components to query. You will need to add tagging for the events as they are sent to the journal, to enable the query.

17.4.2 Applying the pattern

By default, the events persisted by Akka Persistence journals are only categorized in terms of their `persistenceId` for later playback during recovery. All other queries may need further preparation, because keeping additional information has an extra cost—for example, database table indexes or duplication into secondary logs. Therefore, you must add the categorization along other axes in the form of an event adapter, as shown next.

Listing 17.8 Tagging events while writing to the journal

```scala
class ShoppingCartTagging(system: ExtendedActorSystem)
    extends WriteEventAdapter {
  def manifest(event: Any): String = "" // no additional manifest needed

  def toJournal(event: Any): Any =
    event match {
      case s: ShoppingCartMessage => Tagged(event, Set("shoppingCart"))
      case other                  => other
    }
}
```

---

[6] See https://geteventstore.com and Greg's presentation at React 2014 in London: https://www.youtube.com/watch?v=DWhQggR13u8.

[7] See http://doc.akka.io/docs/akka/2.4.1/scala/persistence-query.html.

The tags are simple strings, and every event can have zero or more of them. You use this facility to mark all ShoppingCartMessage types—this will be useful for further experiments that look into correlations between addition and removal of the same item relating to the same shopping cart, an exercise that will be left for you. With this preparation, you can write the popularity-tracking actor.

Listing 17.9   An actor listening to the event stream

```
object TopProductListener {
  private class IntHolder(var value: Int)
}

class TopProductListener extends Actor with ActorLogging {
  import TopProductListener._
  implicit val materializer = ActorMaterializer()

  val readJournal =
    PersistenceQuery(context.system)
      .readJournalFor[LeveldbReadJournal](LeveldbReadJournal.Identifier)

  readJournal.eventsByTag("shoppingCart", 0)
    .collect { case EventEnvelope(_, _, _, add: ItemAdded) => add }
    .groupedWithin(100000, 1.second)
    .addAttributes(Attributes.asyncBoundary)
    .runForeach { seq: Seq[ItemAdded] =>
      val histogram = seq.foldLeft(Map.empty[ItemRef, IntHolder]) {
        (map, event) =>
          map.get(event.item) match {
            case Some(holder) => { holder.value += event.count; map }
            case None => map.updated(event.item, new IntHolder(event.count))
          }
      }
      self ! TopProducts(0, histogram.map(p => (p._1, p._2.value)))      ◁──┐
    }                                                                         │
                                                        **Transforms into a truly**
  var topProducts = Map.empty[ItemRef, Int]             **immutable map before**
                                                        **sending to the actor**
  def receive = {
    case GetTopProducts(id, replyTo) =>
      replyTo ! TopProducts(id, topProducts)
    case TopProducts(_, products) =>
      topProducts = products
      log.info("new {}", products)
  }
}
```

First, you obtain a read-journal interface for the journal implementation you are using in this example—the LevelDb journal is simple to use for small trials that are purely local, but it does not support clustering or replication and is unsuitable for production use. You then construct a source of events using the eventsByTag query, selecting all previously tagged events starting at the journal's beginning (marked by the zero argument). The resulting Akka Stream is then transformed to select only the ItemAdded events and group them in intervals spanning at most 1 second or 100,000 events, whichever occurs first. Then, you mark the grouped source you have constructed up to this point as having an asynchronous boundary around it—you want to inform Akka Streams that it should run these steps in an actor that is separate from what follows, because you do not want the analysis process to influence the time-based grouping. The last step is to create a histogram that assigns the addition frequency to each type of item. To avoid creating a lot of garbage objects in the process, you use an immutable map to hold mutable counters that are then updated in the foldLeft operation.

The resulting histograms are then sent to the actor wrapped in a TopProducts message at least once per second. The actor will store this information and allow others to retrieve it with a GetTopProducts inquiry. The book's downloads include the full source, including a shopping cart simulator that creates enough activity to see this in action.

17.4.3 *The pattern, revisited*

You have added a common categorization for all shopping cart events to the persistence-journal configuration and used this from another actor that consumes the events to derive a secondary view from the data. This secondary view does not hold the same information; it removes the individual, fine-grained structure and introduces a time-based analysis into it—you have transformed one representation of information into a related but decoupled second representation of information.

In the example code above, the derived information is computed live, initially catching up from the beginning of the journal; but there are other approaches: you could make TopProductListener persistent, storing up to the offset at which the journal has already been analyzed and restarting at that point. You could also persist the computation results, aggregating the product-popularity history for yet another step of analysis by another component.

Another use case for this pattern is to use the events emitted by the authoritative source—the shopping cart's business logic—to maintain another representation: for example, in a relational database, allowing extensive, flexible querying capabilities. This could also be described in other terms: the normal form of the data is kept in the place that accepts updates, whereas the information is asynchronously distributed to other places that hold the same data in denormalized form, optimized for retrieval and not updates. This explains why the Event Stream pattern is central to the idea of CQRS.

Event streams may also transport information across different components and thereby into foreign bounded contexts where a different business domain defines the ubiquitous language. In this case, the events need to be translated from one language to the other by a component at the boundary. This component will usually live within the bounded context that consumes the stream, in order to free the source of data from having to know all of its consumers.

17.4.4 *Applicability*

An important property of event streams is that they do not represent the current state of an object of the system: they only consist of immutable facts about the past that have already been committed to persistent storage. The components that emit these events may have progressed to newer states that will only be reflected later in the event stream. The delay between event emission and stream dissemination is a matter of journal-implementation quality, but the fact that there is a significant delay is inherent to this architecture and cannot be avoided.

This implies that all operations that must interact with the authoritative, current data must be done on the original domain objects and cannot be decoupled by the Event Stream pattern. For a more in-depth discussion, please refer back to chapter 8 on delimited consistency.

For all cases where time delay and consistency restrictions are not an issue, it is preferable to rely on this pattern instead of tightly coupling the source of changes with its consumers. The Event Stream pattern provides the reliable dissemination of information across the entire system, allowing all consumers to choose their desired reliability by maintaining read offsets and persisting their state where needed. The biggest benefit is that this places the source of truth firmly in a single place—the journal—and removes doubt as to the location from which different pieces of information may be derived.

17.5   *Summary*

With this chapter, we conclude the third and final part of this book. The patterns in the chapter provide guidance about how to structure the state management in Reactive systems and should be used in unison:

- The Domain Object pattern decouples the business domain representation from message-driven execution and allows domain experts to describe, specify, and test logic without having to care about distributed system concerns or asynchrony.
- The Sharding pattern allows the efficient storage of an arbitrary number of domain objects, given a cluster with sufficient resources.
- The Event-Sourcing pattern turns the destructive update of persistent state into a nondestructive accumulation of information by recognizing that the full history of an object's state is represented by the change events it emits.
- The Event Stream pattern uses these persisted change events to implement reliable and scalable dissemination of information throughout the entire system without burdening the originating domain objects with this task. The emitted events can be distributed by the supporting infrastructure and consumed by any number of interested clients to derive new information from their combination or to maintain denormalized views onto the data that are optimized for queries.

appendix A
Diagramming Reactive systems

The central aspect of designing Reactive systems is considering the message flows that occur within them. This appendix establishes a graphical notation that is used to depict message flows throughout the book.

In table A.1, a number (like 1 or 2) always represents an ordering constraint: if a component does something in response to an incoming event with number N, then the number on the outgoing event(s) must be greater than N. These usually are not single natural numbers but a variant of vector clocks.

Table A.1 Message-flow diagram components

Description	Diagram representation
Primordial component—A component that was created before the depicted message flow starts.	Name
Transient component—A component that is created (and usually also destroyed) after the depicted message flow starts.	Name
Primordial creation—A parent–child relationship. The component on the left initiates the creation of the component on the right.	

Table A.1   Message-flow diagram components *(continued)*

Description	Diagram representation
Creation with supervision—A parent–child relationship with supervision. In addition to the above, the child component's failures are handled by the parent.	
Creation during the flow—A parent–child relationship that begins with the creation of the child during the processing flow of the diagram (may be combined with supervision, as well, by adding the S).	
Termination command—A termination command to a component, usually sent by its parent.	
Message—A message sent from the component on the left to the component on the right. There are several variants of this where only the central piece is depicted in the following rows, but the arrows are implied for all of them.	
Message description—A message dispatch that is annotated with a description of the message's contents. This variant is available for all kinds of message depictions shown in the following rows.	Description
Reference inclusion—A message that includes the address of a component. The sender of this message must be in possession of this address when this message is sent.	
Causality tracking number—A message with its causality tracking number.	
Recurring message—A recurring message send that begins at the indicated number.	
Scheduled message—A message that is entered into the scheduler at number 1 and scheduled to be sent at number 2. The second number must always be greater than the first.	
Termination notification—A message generated by the system to inform a component that another component has terminated (or is declared as such, in the case of a network partition).	
Sequence of messages—A sequence of multiple messages sent one after the other, summarized with the same number.	
Failure notification—A failure message sent from a component to its supervisor.	

appendix B
An illustrated example

This appendix demonstrates a hands-on approach to Reactive system design, illustrating the tenets of the Manifesto through concrete examples. We encounter these while solving issues that come up when building applications that are scalable to a global user base. Globally distributed interaction is also at the heart of the example problem we will tackle here: you will build an app with which users can share their location in real time and in which they can watch others move on a map. An extension to this core function is that users can exchange text messages with other users in their vicinity.

To be more precise, the location of each individual is used for two purposes:

- Each user can share their location with a set of other users who can track it on a map.
- Each user can share their location in anonymized form so that aggregated data can be displayed to all users (such as, "37 users per hour moving westward on highway 50 through Dodge City, Kansas").

B.1   Geographic partitioning

How do you construct such an application? One thing is clear: most of the information processing will be local, as in pertaining to some specific place on Earth. Therefore, you need to divide the Earth into regions, starting perhaps with one region per continent (plus some for the oceans). The granularity of countries within each continent varies greatly, so for simplicity you will continue by cutting each continent along lines of latitude and longitude. The result is 16 tiles, 4 by 4, as shown in figure B.1.

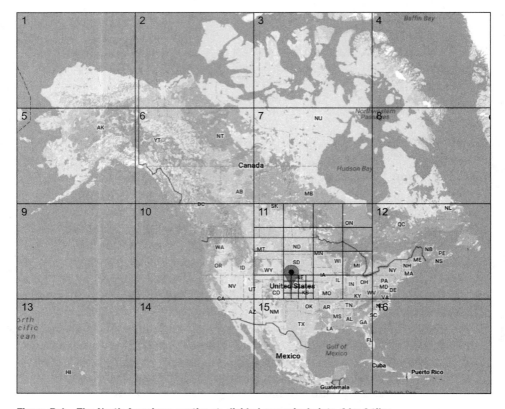

Figure B.1   The North American continent, divided recursively into 4-by-4 tiles

Continue this process recursively, as shown in the figure, quadrupling the resolution in longitude and latitude at each step until it is fine enough—say, less than one mile in either direction.[1] Now you have a way to associate every possible location on Earth with a map region. For example, consider Dodge City, Kansas:

- It is in North America ...
- ... in tile number 11 (at level 1)
- ... within that in subtile number 14 (at level 2)
- ... within that in subtile number 9 (at level 3)
- ... and so on

When someone shares their location, the lowest-level map tile containing that location must be informed that there is a user positioned within it. Other users looking at the same map tile can register for (anonymized) updates about what happens in that

---

[1]   There are more-refined ways to partition a map, but this is a sufficiently simple approach that allows you to concentrate on the essence of the program. For further study, please refer to information about R-trees or other literature.

little map area. The influx of position updates for each of these lowest-level map tiles is given by how many users are logged in to the application in that geographic area, and the outflux conversely is given by how many users are watching that precise map tile. Therefore, no matter how many users may eventually be using this application, you can regulate the amount of information processing per map tile by choosing the granularity—which means choosing the number of levels in your partitioning.

The first important point about implementing a Reactive application is thus to identify the minimal unit of processing that can operate independently. You can execute the bookkeeping functions of where people are moving within a map tile separately from the bookkeeping of all other map tiles, possibly on different computers or even in different data centers—each catering to one continent, for example. You can adapt the processing capacity of the overall system to the load by growing or shrinking the number of these processing units: merging two or more into one is not a problem, because they were independent to begin with, so the only limit is given by how fine you can make this split. The result is a system that can be scaled up and down elastically and can thereby react to varying load.

But we are getting ahead of ourselves, because the current design is not yet complete. Users will always—knowingly or not—push applications to their limits, and in this case a simple exploit will ruin your calculations: zoom out on the map tile you are watching, and your interest will cover a large number of map tiles, resulting in a correspondingly large rate of position updates being requested and sent. This will overwhelm the curious user's client with too much data; and if too many users do this, your expectations about the outflux of data from a map tile will be exceeded. Both of these factors cause more communication bandwidth to be used than you planned for, and the consequence will be system overload and failure.

B.2   *Planning the flow of information*

In a Reactive application, each part—each independent unit of processing—reacts to the information it receives. Therefore, it is very important to consider which information flows where and how large each of these flows is. The principle data flows for the example application are shown in figure B.2.

In the example application, you could define that each user sends one position update every 5 seconds while the app is running on their mobile device—phone, tablet, or watch. You can ascertain that by writing the client app yourself or by enforcing this limit in the API that the application offers to the author of client apps. Each position update will amount to roughly 100 bytes, give or take (10 bytes each for timestamp, latitude, and longitude; 40 bytes for lower-level protocol overhead, such as TCP/IPv4; plus additional space for encryption, authentication, and integrity data). Factoring in some overhead for congestion avoidance and message scheduling between multiple clients, you will assume that each client's position-update stream costs roughly 50 bytes per second on average.

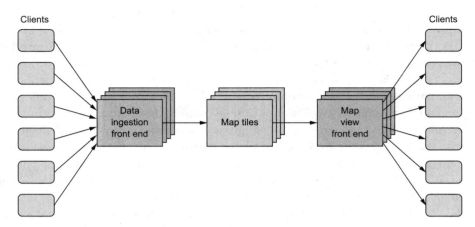

Figure B.2   Data are flowing from the clients that submit their position updates through a front end that handles the client connections into the map tiles and on to those clients that are watching the map.

B.2.1   Step 1: Accepting the data

The position updates need to be sent via the internet to a publicly addressable and accessible endpoint; we call this the *front-end node*. The current lingua franca for such purposes is HTTP, in which case you need to offer a web service that clients contact in order to transmit their data; the choice of protocol may vary in the future, but the fact remains that you need to plan the capacity of this data-ingestion endpoint according to the number of users you expect. The functionality in terms of the processing the endpoint provides is merely to validate incoming data according to protocol definitions, authenticate clients, and verify the integrity of their submitted data. The endpoint does not care about the details of the position; for those purposes, it will forward the sanitized data to the map tile it belongs to.

Common networks today operate at 100–1,000 Mbps. This example conservatively assumes an available bandwidth of 50 Mbps, half of which you will allocate to the reception of position updates; you can therefore arrive at a capacity of 500,000 clients that can be handled by one front-end node. For the sake of simplicity, also assume that this node's computing resources are sufficient to handle the validation of the corresponding rate of data packets that need to validated, authenticated, and verified—otherwise, you would reduce the nominal capacity per node accordingly.

Given these numbers, it is clear that one node will probably suffice for the initial deployment from a data-rate perspective; you will want to have two in any case, for fault tolerance. Serving the entire world's population of 7.5 billion people would hypothetically require 14,000 active network nodes for data ingestion, preferably distributed among data centers spread across the planet and with a healthy percentage of spares for redundancy. The important point is that each of these nodes operates fully independently of all the others: no communication or coordination is necessary between them in order to unwrap, check, and route position updates, which enables you to do this simple back-of-an-envelope estimation of what you need to grow this part of the system to a given scale.

B.2.2 *Step 2: Getting the data to their geographical home*

The function of the front-end node is to accept and sanitize the incoming data and then send it on to the map tile it belongs to. The rough estimate of the data rates likely applies to the sanitized data as well; you will trade data integrity and authentication data for client IDs and associated data. Those were implicit to the client's network connection with the front-end node, but now they need to be explicitly incorporated in the data packet on the network connection between the front-end node and each map tile for which it receives updates.

Hosting a map tile on a single network node translates to the ability to handle 500,000 clients within that map area. Therefore, the tiles need to be small enough that this limit is never violated. If all map tiles are the same size—that is, if the same level of partitioning is used throughout the entire map—then some tiles will be much more frequented than others. Densely populated areas like Manhattan, San Francisco, and Tokyo will be close to the limit, whereas most of the tiles covering the Pacific Ocean will rarely have anyone move on them. You can account for this asymmetry by collocating a number of low-rate map tiles on the same processing node while keeping high-rate tiles on their own nodes.

Recall that it is crucial for the front-end nodes to be able to perform their work independently of each other, in order to be able to adjust the system capacity by adding or removing nodes; you will see another reason for this when we discuss how to react to failures within the system. But how can you achieve consensus about which map tile is hosted by which internal network node? The answer is that you make the routing process simple and deterministic by having a map tile–allocation service disseminate a data structure that describes the placement of all tiles. This data structure can be optimized and compressed by using the hierarchical structure of the map partitioning. Another consideration is that once this application has grown beyond a single data center, you can route clients to the correct data center that hosts the geographic region in which they are currently located, at which point each front-end node only needs to know the location of tiles for which its data center is responsible.

An interesting question at this point is how you react to changes in your application deployment: when a node dies or is manually replaced, or when map tiles are reshuffled to adapt to changed user habits, how is this communicated to the front-end nodes? And what happens to updates that are sent to the "wrong" node? The straightforward answer is that during such a change, there will be a time window during which position updates pertaining to certain map tiles will be lost. As long as you can reasonably expect this outage to be temporary and on the order of a few seconds long, then chances are, nobody will notice; one or two missing location updates will not have a major effect on the aggregated statistics of a map tile (or can be compensated for), and not seeing a friend's position move on a map for a few seconds once in a blue moon is unlikely to be of consequence.

B.2.3   Step 3: Relocating the data for efficient querying

You have now ensured that the influx of each map tile will not exceed a certain threshold that is given by the capabilities of the processing hardware. The issue that sparked this foray into data-rate planning was that the outflux is not limited, because clients can zoom out and thereby request and consume more data than they produce and submit.

When you visualize the map that will show the movement of all the anonymized users within its area, what do you expect to see when you zoom out? You certainly cannot follow each individual and track their course once there are more than a handful of them in the region you are looking at. And when you zoom out to view all of Europe, the best you can hope for is aggregate information about population density or average velocity—you will not be able to discern individual positions.

In the same way you designed the information flow for data ingestion, you can look at data extraction. Looking at a map of Europe is an easy case, because it does not require much data: the large-scale averages and aggregate numbers do not change quickly. The largest data demand will be given by users who are being tracked individually while being closely zoomed in. Assume that you allow up to 30 users to be shown individually before switching to an aggregated view, and further assume that you can limit the data consumption of the aggregate view to be equivalent to those 30 tracked points. One update will have to contain a timestamp and up to 30 tuples of identifier, latitude, and longitude. These can presumably be compressed because they are in a small map region, perhaps amounting to 15 bytes for each 3-tuple. Including some overall status information, you arrive at roughly 500 bytes for a single update, which means about 100 bytes per second on average for 1 update every 5 seconds.

Calculating again with an available network bandwidth of 50 Mbps, where half is allocated to client-facing traffic, this yields a capacity of serving 200,000 map views from a single front-end node (subtracting 20% overhead).[2] These front-end nodes are also answering requests from clients, but they are of a different kind than the nodes responsible for data ingestion. When a user logs in to the app, their mobile device will begin sending position updates to the ingestion nodes; and every time the user changes the map view on their device, a request will be sent to the front-end nodes, registering for the updates to be displayed on the screen. This naturally decouples the two activities and allows a user to view a far-away map region without additional headaches for implementers.

---

[2] Sending from one host to a multitude of others requires less overhead than having a multitude of clients send to a single host. See also the TCP incast problem (www.pdl.cmu.edu/Incast).

At this point, the big question is, where do these map-view front-end nodes get their data? You have so far only provided the position updates to the lowest-level map tiles, and requesting their updates in order to calculate aggregate values will not work: serving 200,000 views could mean having to listen to the updates of millions of map tiles, corresponding to hundreds of terabytes per second.

There is only one solution to this dilemma: you must filter and preprocess the data at their source. Each lowest-level map tile knows the precise location and movement of all users within its geographic region, and it is easy to calculate their number, average movement speed and direction, center of gravity, and other interesting quantities. These summary data are then sent every 5 seconds to the map tile one level up that contains this tile.

As a concrete example, consider that the lowest level is seven partition steps below the North American continent. The center of Dodge City, Kansas, on level 7 calculates the summary information and sends it to the encompassing level-6 map tile, which also receives such summaries from the 15 other level-7 neighbors it contains. The good thing about aggregate quantities such as user count, center of gravity, and so on is that they can be merged with one another to aggregate at higher and higher granularity (summing up the users, calculating the weighted center of gravity of the individual centers, and so on). The level-6 map tile performs this aggregation every 5 seconds and sends its summary up to its encompassing level-5 parent, and this process is repeated all the way up to the top level.

The data rate needed for this transfer is fixed to the size of the summary data packet: once every 5 seconds for each sender, and 16 times that amount for each recipient. You can assume that each data packet should fit within 100 bytes. In many cases, these data do not even need to travel across the network, because sparsely populated map areas are collocated on the same processing node, and the summary levels can be collocated with the lowest-level map tiles as well.

When a map view front-end node needs to access the summary information at level 4 to display a map spanning approximately 100 by 100 miles, it will request the summary information from the roughly 16 level-4 map tiles covering the viewport. Knowing that network bandwidth will likely be the most limiting factor for these view front-end nodes, you can optimize their use internally by redirecting external clients between them such that one front-end node handles many similar requests—for the same approximate geographic region at the same summary level. That way, a node can satisfy multiple clients from the same internal data stream. This is shown in figure B.3.

The one piece that still needs consideration is how to handle the fully zoomed-in case: when a user points their map at Big Ben to see all the tourists milling about in the center of London, care must be taken to not send all the data from that highly frequented map tile to the front-end node, because that could potentially take up all the available bandwidth by itself. We said earlier that a map should display only summary information as soon as the number of individual data points exceeds 30. In this case,

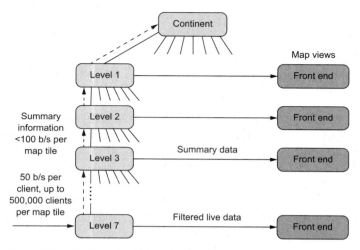

Figure B.3   The flow of data from data ingestion on the left to the map views on the right, with summary data traveling upward in the hierarchical map tile structure

the calculation of this summary must happen on the network node that hosts the Big Ben map tile: the request from the front-end node will contain the coordinates of the desired viewport, and the map tile can determine whether to calculate aggregate information or send the updates of up to 30 individual user positions, depending on how many people are moving within the map area in question.

One aspect of this flow diagram deserves mention: it takes a little while for each new piece of information to make its way up to the top. In this example, which has 7 levels, it takes on average about 18 seconds (7 times an average delay of 2.5 seconds). This should not be a problem, though, because the summary information changes much more slowly, the higher up you get in the hierarchy.

B.2.4   *Taking stock*

What have you achieved so far? You have designed the flow of information through an application as shown in figure B.4. You have avoided the introduction of a single bottleneck through which the data must pass: all parts of the design can be scaled individually. The front ends for data ingestion and map views can be adapted to user activity, and the map data are modeled as a hierarchy of map tiles whose granularity can be chosen by picking the number of partition steps. The processing of the data passing through the map tiles can be deployed onto a number of network nodes as needed, in terms of processing and network resources. In the simplest scenario, everything can run on a single computer—but at the same time, the design supports deployment in a dozen data centers and on thousands of nodes.

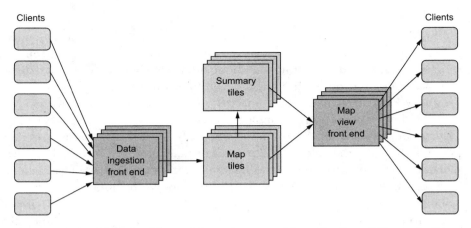

Figure B.4   The flows of position updates and summary information through the application, from position updates generated on the left through the map tile hierarchy toward the map views on the right

B.3   *What if something fails?*

Now that you have a good overview of the parts of the application and the data flows within it, you should consider how failures will affect it. This is not a black art—on the contrary. You can follow a simple procedure: consider every node in your processing network and every data flow link, one by one, and determine what happens if it fails. In order to do this, you need a failure model. A good starting point for a network-based system is the following:

- Network links can drop arbitrary bursts of messages (which includes the case where "the link was down for three hours").
- Processing nodes can stop responding and never recover (for example, by way of a hardware failure).
- Processing nodes can intermittently fail to respond (for example, due to temporary overload).
- Processing nodes can experience arbitrary delays (for example, due to garbage collection pauses, as for the JVM).

More possibilities of what can go wrong should be considered, and you will need to assess your system requirements carefully to decide what else to include. Other choices are that network links may corrupt data packets; data packets may experience arbitrary delay; processing nodes may respond with erroneous data, or they may execute malicious code and perform arbitrary actions. You also need to consider the effect of executing multiple parts of the application on the same hardware, because this means hardware failure or resource exhaustion can affect all these parts simultaneously. The more vital the function of your application is for your organization, the more detailed the considered failure model should be. For this example case, you will stick to the simple list from the previous bullet points.

B.3.1 A client fails

Mobile devices can fail for a host of reasons ranging from their destruction, to empty batteries, to a software crash. Users are used to dealing with those (replacing the phone, charging it, or restarting the phone or an app), and they do not expect things to work while their device has failed. Therefore, you only need to concern yourself with the effects of a failure on the internal processes of your application.

First, the stream of position updates will cease. When this happens, we might want to generate a visible representation for others who were seeing this user on their map, perhaps changing the color of the marker or making it translucent. The lowest-level map tile will be responsible for tracking whether the users that move within it are alive.

Second, the map view for the client will no longer be able to send updates, network buffers will fill up, and socket writes will eventually time out. Therefore, you must protect the map view front ends from becoming clogged with defunct client registrations. This is commonly done by including a heartbeat signal in the protocol and closing the connection when the heartbeats stop coming in.

B.3.2 A client network link fails

From the perspective of the application, it does not matter why position updates cease: the failure of the mobile device or its software is indistinguishable from a failed network connection. The consequences are thus the same as discussed in the previous section.

From the perspective of the client, on the other hand, in general it is not distinguishable whether the front-end node it was connected to failed or the network link is at fault: both will look largely the same. Hence, the remedy is also the same as discussed in the next section.

B.3.3 A data-ingestion front-end node fails

The role of such a node is to sanitize and forward position updates, so a failure means the client will eventually run into trouble sending data to it. In the same way the map view monitors the health of its client using heartbeats, you can also solve this situation: the client will reconnect to a different front-end node if something goes amiss, regardless of whether the failure is temporary or fatal. This is typically realized by placing a network load balancer in front of the pool of real web service endpoint nodes, a strategy that is possible only because it does not matter exactly which node a client sends its updates through into the system: the gateways are all equally suited.

In any case, the mobile app should let the user know that there is trouble with the connection. This is much better than having the user figure it out via missing activity—that way, you can clearly distinguish between problems local to the app and problems with network communication.

The other action that must be taken upon the failure of a front-end node is to properly dispose of it (stopping the application, taking down the machine) and spin up a new instance that starts from a known good configuration. The precise kind of failure is irrelevant: the overall system returns to a fully fault-tolerant state by doing the most robust, simplest thing possible. Consequently, whatever went wrong is contained within the removed node and cannot spread to the others. The recovery must be initiated by a separate service that cannot be infected with the failure; this is called a *supervisor service*. The supervisor monitors its subordinates for proper function and, as described, takes corrective action when necessary.

B.3.4   A network link from data ingestion to map tile fails

This situation has no negative impact on the overall function of the application. Its effect is the same as if the connected clients stop sending position updates to the affected map tile. Therefore, depending on which communication protocol is used for this network link, both parties should monitor the health of their connection and release all associated resources if the connection becomes stale.

The simplicity of this problem and of its solution is due to the fact that neither side—front-end node nor map tile—depends on the other for correct function. Data flow in only one direction from one to the other, and if data stop flowing, both sides know how to deal with the situation. This is called *loose coupling*, and it is essential for achieving robust failure handling.

B.3.5   A map tile–processing node fails

Because this is the heart of the application, we will consider the different failure modes more carefully:

- *Hardware failure*—In case of a node crash, all map tiles that were hosted by this node will be failed with it. The front-end nodes will eventually notice and stop sending updates, but you need to recover from this situation. The front ends cannot be responsible for that, because it would involve coordination of who performs the necessary steps. Therefore, you install a supervisor service that monitors all map tile nodes and spins up a new instance in case of a crash. We discussed earlier that this service will then update the routing knowledge of all front-end nodes so they begin sending updates to the new destination.

- *Temporary overload*—If a map tile sees more traffic than was planned for, it will need to be moved to a separate processing node; otherwise, it will take resources from all of its collocated neighbors, and the overload will spread and turn into a node failure. This scenario must also be handled by the supervisor service, which for this purpose needs to gather usage statistics and, if necessary, rebalance the map tiles across the available nodes. If the load is increasing in all parts of the system, then this supervisor should also be able to request that new nodes be brought online so the additional load can be handled. Conversely, once load drops significantly, the supervisor should reallocate map tiles to free up and release redundant nodes.

- *Permanent overload*—It is also possible that the partitioning of your map is not adequate and a single map tile is hit consistently by too many requests. Because you cannot split or reallocate this map tile, such a failure will need to raise an alert when it is detected, and the system configuration must be adapted manually to correct the mistake.

- *Processing delays*—In some cases, the inability to process new data lasts only a few seconds (for example, while the JVM is performing a major garbage collection cycle). In such cases, no specific recovery mechanism is necessary beyond possibly dropping some updates that are outdated by the time the machine comes back to life. There is a point, of course, where such an interruption is mistaken for a node crash; you will have to configure the supervisor service to tolerate pauses up to a given duration and take corrective measures once that is exceeded.

As in the case of a front-end node failure, you need a supervisor service that keeps an eye on all the deployed processing nodes and can heal the system in case of failure by using its global view and, if necessary, disposing of faulty instances and creating fresh ones. The supervisor does not become a bottleneck in the system because you keep it outside of the main information flows of the application.

B.3.6 *A summary map tile fails*

These processing units are very similar in function to the lowest-level map tiles. They are part of the same information routing infrastructure, so you supervise them in the same fashion.

B.3.7 *A network link between map files fails*

This case is similar to front-end nodes being unable to forward position updates to map tiles—data will not arrive while the failure lasts. You need network monitoring in place so the operations crew is notified and will fix the issue; other than that, you have to throw away data as they grow stale. This last part is important to avoid the so-called *thundering herd problem* when network connectivity is restored: if all data are buffered and then sent at once, the destination will likely be overloaded as a result. Fortunately you do not need to buffer data for long periods of time in this part of the application, because all you are modeling is a live view on a map with no historic information; lost updates are a fact of life.

B.3.8 *A map view front-end node fails*

In this case, you can act in the same fashion as for the data-ingestion front-end nodes: you have clients reconnect through a load balancer as soon as they determine something is wrong, and you have a supervisor service that disposes of nodes and provisions new ones when needed. The latter actions can also occur in response to changes in load; this way, monitoring by the supervisor enables the system to elastically scale up and down.

There is one more consideration in this situation: map view updates are sent by the map tiles according to the front ends' registrations. If a front end becomes unavailable and is replaced, then map tiles need to stop sending data their way as soon as possible, because the new client registrations that replace the failed ones will soon take up their share of the planned bandwidth again. Therefore, map tiles need to pay attention to their connections with map views and drop updates when they cannot be transmitted in a timely fashion.

B.3.9 *Failure-handling summary*

As we systematically walked along all data flows and considered the consequences of node and communication failures, we encountered two main needs:

- Communication partners frequently are required to monitor the availability of their interlocutors. Where no steady stream of messages is readily available, traffic can be generated using a heartbeat mechanism.
- Processing nodes must be monitored by supervising services in order to detect failures and load problems (both over- and under-utilization) and take corrective action.

Figure B.5 shows the complete deployment structure of the example application with the added supervisors. It also notes that the service supervising the map tiles must inform both types of front-end nodes about the current mapping where each map tile is hosted.

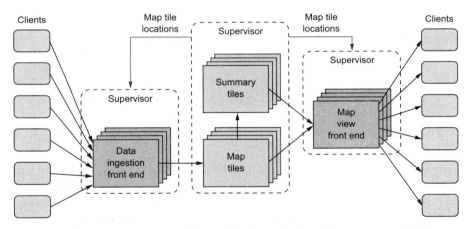

Figure B.5 Deployment structure of the application, with supervisor services and their relationship: the map tiles' supervisor informs the front-end supervisors about where position updates and map view registrations should go.

B.4 *What have you learned from this example?*

We have modeled an application that can serve any number of clients, allowing them to share their location and see how others are moving on a map. The design is such that you can easily scale its capacity from trying it on a development notebook—running all parts locally—to, hypothetically, supporting use by all humans on Earth. Doing so would require considerable resources, and their operation would require a large effort, but from the technical side, the application is prepared. You have achieved that by considering foremost the information that will be processed by the application and the main flows of data that are necessary.

The most important characteristic is that data always flow forward from their source (position updates of mobile devices) via processing stages (map tiles) toward their final destination (the map displayed on mobile devices). The processing nodes on this path of information are *loosely coupled* in that failures of one are dealt with the same way as communication outages.

You build resilience into a design by considering the major parts of the application to be isolated from each other, communicating only over networks. If multiple parts are running on the same machine, a failure of the machine—or resource exhaustion caused by one part—will make all of them fail simultaneously. It is especially important for achieving fault tolerance that the services tasked with repairing the system after failures—the supervisors—are isolated from other parts and are running on their own resources.

In this way, you have experienced all the main tenets of the Reactive Manifesto:

- The application is *responsive* due to resource planning and map partitioning.
- The application is *resilient* because you built in mechanisms to repair failed components and connect to properly functioning ones.
- The application is *elastic* because it monitors the load experienced by the different parts and can redistribute the load when it changes, a feat that is possible due to the lack of global bottlenecks and processing units that can work independently of each other.
- All of this is enabled by *message-driven* communication between the parts of the application.

B.5   *Where do you go from here?*

The attentive reader will have noticed that not all functionality has been implemented for the example application. We have detailed how to implement the second requirement of sharing anonymized position updates, but we left out the first requirement that a user should be able to share their location with a set of other users. It will be a good exercise to apply the same reasoning in this case, designing additional parts of the application that keep data in a user-centric fashion rather than the map-centric one you have built so far. Modifications of the trust relationship between users will have to be processed more reliably than position updates, but they will also be vastly less frequent.

appendix C
The Reactive Manifesto

Version 2.0, published on September 16, 2014

C.1   Main text

Organisations working in disparate domains are independently discovering patterns for building software that look the same. These systems are more robust, more resilient, more flexible and better positioned to meet modern demands.

These changes are happening because application requirements have changed dramatically in recent years. Only a few years ago a large application had tens of servers, seconds of response time, hours of offline maintenance and gigabytes of data. Today applications are deployed on everything from mobile devices to cloud-based clusters running thousands of multi-core processors. Users expect millisecond response times and 100% uptime. Data is measured in Petabytes. Today's demands are simply not met by yesterday's software architectures.

We believe that a coherent approach to systems architecture is needed, and we believe that all necessary aspects are already recognised individually: we want systems that are Responsive, Resilient, Elastic and Message Driven. We call these Reactive Systems.

Systems built as Reactive Systems are more flexible, loosely-coupled and scalable (see section C.2.15). This makes them easier to develop and amenable to change. They are significantly more tolerant of failure (see section C.2.7) and when failure does occur they meet it with elegance rather than disaster. Reactive Systems are highly responsive, giving users (see section C.2.17) effective interactive feedback.

Reactive Systems are:

- *Responsive:* The system (see section C.2.16) responds in a timely manner if at all possible. Responsiveness is the cornerstone of usability and utility, but more than that, responsiveness means that problems may be detected quickly and dealt with effectively. Responsive systems focus on providing rapid and consistent response times, establishing reliable upper bounds so they deliver a consistent quality of service. This consistent behaviour in turn simplifies error handling, builds end user confidence, and encourages further interaction.

- *Resilient:* The system stays responsive in the face of failure (see section C.2.7). This applies not only to highly-available, mission critical systems—any system that is not resilient will be unresponsive after a failure. Resilience is achieved by replication (see section C.2.13), containment, isolation (see section C.2.8) and delegation (see section C.2.5). Failures are contained within each component (see section C.2.4), isolating components from each other and thereby ensuring that parts of the system can fail and recover without compromising the system as a whole. Recovery of each component is delegated to another (external) component and high-availability is ensured by replication where necessary. The client of a component is not burdened with handling its failures.

- *Elastic:* The system stays responsive under varying workload. Reactive Systems can react to changes in the input rate by increasing or decreasing the resources (see section C.2.14) allocated to service these inputs. This implies designs that have no contention points or central bottlenecks, resulting in the ability to shard or replicate components and distribute inputs among them. Reactive Systems support predictive, as well as Reactive, scaling algorithms by providing relevant live performance measures. They achieve elasticity (see section C.2.6) in a cost-effective way on commodity hardware and software platforms.

- *Message Driven:* Reactive Systems rely on asynchronous (see section C.2.1) message-passing (see section C.2.10) to establish a boundary between components that ensures loose coupling, isolation, and location transparency (see section C.2.9). This boundary also provides the means to delegate failures (see section C.2.7) as messages. Employing explicit message-passing enables load management, elasticity, and flow control by shaping and monitoring the message queues in the system and applying back-pressure (see section C.2.2) when necessary. Location transparent messaging as a means of communication makes it possible for the management of failure to work with the same constructs and semantics across a cluster or within a single host. Non-blocking (see section C.2.11) communication allows recipients to only consume resources (see section C.2.14) while active, leading to less system overhead.

Large systems are composed of smaller ones and therefore depend on the Reactive properties of their constituents. This means that Reactive Systems apply design principles so these properties apply at all levels of scale, making them composable. The largest systems in the world rely upon architectures based on these properties and serve the needs of billions of people daily. It is time to apply these design principles consciously from the start instead of rediscovering them each time.

C.2   Glossary

C.2.1   Asynchronous

The Oxford Dictionary defines asynchronous as "not existing or occurring at the same time." In the context of this manifesto we mean that the processing of a request occurs at an arbitrary point in time, sometime after it has been transmitted from client to service. The client cannot directly observe, or synchronize with, the execution that occurs within the service. This is the antonym of synchronous processing which implies that the client only resumes its own execution once the service has processed the request.

C.2.2   Back-Pressure

When one component (see section C.2.4) is struggling to keep-up, the system (see section C.2.16) as a whole needs to respond in a sensible way. It is unacceptable for the component under stress to fail catastrophically or to drop messages in an uncontrolled fashion. Since it can't cope and it can't fail it should communicate the fact that it is under stress to upstream components and so get them to reduce the load. This back-pressure is an important feedback mechanism that allows systems to gracefully respond to load rather than collapse under it. The back-pressure may cascade all the way up to the user, at which point responsiveness may degrade, but this mechanism will ensure that the system is resilient under load, and will provide information that may allow the system itself to apply other resources to help distribute the load, see Elasticity (section C.2.6).

C.2.3   Batching

Current computers are optimized for the repeated execution of the same task: instruction caches and branch prediction increase the number of instructions that can be processed per second while keeping the clock frequency unchanged. This means that giving different tasks to the same CPU core in rapid succession will not benefit from the full performance that could otherwise be achieved: if possible we should structure the program such that its execution alternates less frequently between different tasks. This can mean processing a set of data elements in batches, or it can mean performing different processing steps on dedicated hardware threads.

The same reasoning applies to the use of external resources (see section C.2.14) that need synchronization and coordination. The I/O bandwidth offered by persistent storage devices can improve dramatically when issuing commands from a single thread (and thereby CPU core) instead of contending for bandwidth from all cores. Using a single entry point has the added advantage that operations can be reordered to better suit the optimal access patterns of the device (current storage devices perform better for linear than random access).

Additionally, batching provides the opportunity to share out the cost of expensive operations such as I/O or expensive computations. For example, packing multiple data items into the same network packet or disk block to increase efficiency and reduce utilisation.

C.2.4   Component

What we are describing is a modular software architecture, which is a very old idea, see for example Parnas (1972).[1] We are using the term "component" due to its proximity with compartment, which implies that each component is self-contained, encapsulated and isolated (see section C.2.8) from other components. This notion applies foremost to the runtime characteristics of the system, but it will typically also be reflected in the source code's module structure as well. While different components might make use of the same software modules to perform common tasks, the program code that defines the top-level behavior of each component is then a module of its own. Component boundaries are often closely aligned with Bounded Contexts[2] in the problem domain. This means that the system design tends to reflect the problem domain and so is easy to evolve, while retaining isolation. Message protocols (see section C.2.12) provide a natural mapping and communications layer between Bounded Contexts (components).

C.2.5   Delegation

Delegating a task asynchronously (see section C.2.1) to another component (see section C.2.4) means that the execution of the task will take place in the context of that other component. This delegated context could entail running in a different error handling context, on a different thread, in a different process, or on a different network node, to name a few possibilities. The purpose of delegation is to hand over the processing responsibility of a task to another component so that the delegating component can perform other processing or optionally observe the progress of the delegated task in case additional action is required such as handling failure or reporting progress.

C.2.6   Elasticity (in contrast to Scalability)

Elasticity means that the throughput of a system scales up or down automatically to meet varying demand as resource is proportionally added or removed. The system needs to be scalable (see section C.2.15) to allow it to benefit from the dynamic addition, or removal, of resources at runtime. Elasticity therefore builds upon scalability and expands on it by adding the notion of automatic resource (see section C.2.14) management.

---

[1] https://www.cs.umd.edu/class/spring2003/cmsc838p/Design/criteria.pdf
[2] http://martinfowler.com/bliki/BoundedContext.html

C.2.7 *Failure (in contrast to Error)*

A failure is an unexpected event within a service that prevents it from continuing to function normally. A failure will generally prevent responses to the current, and possibly all following, client requests. This is in contrast with an error, which is an expected and coded-for condition—for example an error discovered during input validation, that will be communicated to the client as part of the normal processing of the message. Failures are unexpected and will require intervention before the system (see section C.2.16) can resume at the same level of operation. This does not mean that failures are always fatal, rather that some capacity of the system will be reduced following a failure. Errors are an expected part of normal operations, are dealt with immediately and the system will continue to operate at the same capacity following an error.

Examples of failures are hardware malfunction, processes terminating due to fatal resource exhaustion, program defects that result in corrupted internal state.

C.2.8 *Isolation (and Containment)*

Isolation can be defined in terms of decoupling, both in time and space. Decoupling in time means that the sender and receiver can have independent life-cycles—they do not need to be present at the same time for communication to be possible. It is enabled by adding asynchronous (see section C.2.1) boundaries between the components (see section C.2.4), communicating through message-passing (see section C.2.10). Decoupling in space (defined as Location Transparency, see section C.2.9) means that the sender and receiver do not have to run in the same process, but wherever the operations division or the runtime itself decides is most efficient—which might change during an application's lifetime.

True isolation goes beyond the notion of encapsulation found in most object-oriented languages and gives us compartmentalization and containment of:

- State and behavior: it enables share-nothing designs and minimizes contention and coherence cost (as defined in the Universal Scalability Law;[3]
- Failures: it allows failures (see section C.2.7) to be captured, signalled and managed at a fine-grained level instead of letting them cascade to other components.

Strong isolation between components is built on communication over well-defined protocols (see section C.2.12) and enables loose coupling, leading to systems that are easier to understand, extend, test and evolve.

C.2.9 *Location Transparency*

Elastic (see section C.2.6) systems need to be adaptive and continuously react to changes in demand, they need to gracefully and efficiently increase and decrease scale. One key insight that simplifies this problem immensely is to realize that we are

---

[3] http://www.perfdynamics.com/Manifesto/USLscalability.html

all doing distributed computing. This is true whether we are running our systems on a single node (with multiple independent CPUs communicating over the QPI link) or on a cluster of nodes (with independent machines communicating over the network). Embracing this fact means that there is no conceptual difference between scaling vertically on multi-core or horizontally on the cluster.

If all of our components (see section C.2.4) support mobility, and local communication is just an optimization, then we do not have to define a static system topology and deployment model upfront. We can leave this decision to the operations personnel and the runtime, which can adapt and optimize the system depending on how it is used.

This decoupling in space (see the definition for Isolation, section C.2.8), enabled through asynchronous (see section C.2.1) message-passing (see section C.2.10), and decoupling of the runtime instances from their references is what we call Location Transparency. Location Transparency is often mistaken for "transparent distributed computing", while it is actually the opposite: we embrace the network and all its constraints—like partial failure, network splits, dropped messages, and its asynchronous and message-based nature—by making them first class in the programming model, instead of trying to emulate in-process method dispatch on the network (à la RPC, XA etc.). Our view of Location Transparency is in perfect agreement with *A Note On Distributed Computing*[4] by Waldo et al.

C.2.10 *Message-Driven (in contrast to Event-Driven)*

A message is an item of data that is sent to a specific destination. An event is a signal emitted by a component (see section C.2.4) upon reaching a given state. In a message-driven system addressable recipients await the arrival of messages and react to them, otherwise lying dormant. In an event-driven system notification listeners are attached to the sources of events such that they are invoked when the event is emitted. This means that an event-driven system focuses on addressable event sources while a message-driven system concentrates on addressable recipients. A message can contain an encoded event as its payload.

Resilience is more difficult to achieve in an event-driven system due to the short-lived nature of event consumption chains: when processing is set in motion and listeners are attached in order to react to and transform the result, these listeners typically handle success or failure (see section C.2.7) directly and in the sense of reporting back to the original client. Responding to the failure of a component in order to restore its proper function, on the other hand, requires a treatment of these failures that is not tied to ephemeral client requests, but that responds to the overall component health state.

---

[4] http://citeseerx.ist.psu.edu/viewdoc/summary?doi=10.1.1.41.7628

C.2.11 Non-Blocking

In concurrent programming an algorithm is considered non-blocking if threads competing for a resource do not have their execution indefinitely postponed by mutual exclusion protecting that resource. In practice this usually manifests as an API that allows access to the resource (see section C.2.14) if it is available otherwise it immediately returns informing the caller that the resource is not currently available or that the operation has been initiated and not yet completed. A non-blocking API to a resource allows the caller the option to do other work rather than be blocked waiting on the resource to become available. This may be complemented by allowing the client of the resource to register for getting notified when the resource is available or the operation has completed.

C.2.12 Protocol

A protocol defines the treatment and etiquette for the exchange or transmission of messages between components (see section C.2.4). Protocols are formulated as relations between the participants to the exchange, the accumulated state of the protocol and the allowed set of messages to be sent. This means that a protocol describes which messages a participant may send to another participant at any given point in time. Protocols can be classified by the shape of the exchange, some common classes are request-reply, repeated request-reply (as in HTTP), publish-subscribe, and stream (both push and pull).

In comparison to local programming interfaces a protocol is more generic since it can include more than two participants and it foresees a progression of the state of the message exchange; an interface only specifies one interaction at a time between the caller and the receiver.

It should be noted that a protocol as defined here just specifies which messages may be sent, but not how they are sent: encoding, decoding (i.e., codecs), and transport mechanisms are implementation details that are transparent to the components' use of the protocol.

C.2.13 Replication

Executing a component (see section C.2.4) simultaneously in different places is referred to as replication. This can mean executing on different threads or thread pools, processes, network nodes, or computing centers. Replication offers scalability (see section C.2.15), where the incoming workload is distributed across multiple instances of a component, or resilience, where the incoming workload is replicated to multiple instances which process the same requests in parallel. These approaches can be mixed, for example by ensuring that all transactions pertaining to a certain user of the component will be executed by two instances while the total number of instances varies with the incoming load, (see Elasticity, section C.2.6).

C.2.14 Resource

Everything that a component (see section C.2.4) relies upon to perform its function is a resource that must be provisioned according to the component's needs. This includes CPU allocation, main memory and persistent storage as well as network bandwidth, main memory bandwidth, CPU caches, inter-socket CPU links, reliable timer and task scheduling services, other input and output devices, external services like databases or network file systems etc. The elasticity (see section C.2.6) and resilience of all these resources must be considered, since the lack of a required resource will prevent the component from functioning when required.

C.2.15 Scalability

The ability of a system (see section C.2.16) to make use of more computing resources (see section C.2.14) in order to increase its performance is measured by the ratio of throughput gain to resource increase. A perfectly scalable system is characterized by both numbers being proportional: a twofold allocation of resources will double the throughput. Scalability is typically limited by the introduction of bottlenecks or synchronization points within the system, leading to constrained scalability, see Amdahl's Law and Gunther's Universal Scalability Model.[5]

C.2.16 System

A system provides services to its users (see section C.2.17) or clients. Systems can be large or small, in which case they comprise many or just a few component (see section C.2.4). All components of a system collaborate to provide these services. In many cases the components are in a client-server relationship within the same system (consider for example front-end components relying upon back-end components). A system shares a common resilience model, by which we mean that failure (see section C.2.7) of a component is handled within the system, delegated (see section C.2.5) from one component to the other. It is useful to view groups of components within a system as subsystems if they are isolated (see section C.28) from the rest of the system in their function, resources (see section C.2.14) or failure modes.

C.2.17 User

We use this term informally to refer to any consumer of a service, be that a human or another service.

---

[5] http://blogs.msdn.com/b/ddperf/archive/2009/04/29/parallel-scalability-isn-t-child-s-play-part-2-amdahl-s-law-vs-gunther-s-law.aspx

index

MORE TITLES FROM MANNING

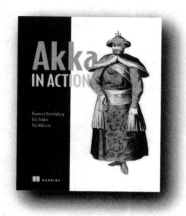

Akka in Action
by Raymond Roestenburg, Rob Bakker,
and Rob Williams

ISBN: 9781617291012
448 pages
$49.99
September 2016

Functional Programming in Scala
by Paul Chiusano and Rúnar Bjarnason

ISBN: 9781617290657
320 pages
$44.99
September 2014

Java 8 in Action
Lambdas, streams, and functional-style programming
by Raoul-Gabriel Urma, Mario Fusco,
and Alan Mycroft

ISBN: 9781617291999
424 pages
$49.99
August 2014

For ordering information go to www.manning.com